STUDY GUIDE

Harvey B. King — *University of Regina*

Avi J. Cohen — *York University*

MACROECONOMICS

CANADA IN THE GLOBAL ENVIRONMENT

SIXTH EDITION

MICHAEL PARKIN ROBIN BADE

Toronto

ISBN 0-321-41844-1

Editor-in-Chief, Business & Economics: Gary Bennett
Senior Developmental Editor: Madhu Ranadive
Production Editor: Jen Handel
Production Coordinator: Andrea Falkenberg

1 2 3 4 5 11 10 09 08 07

Printed and bound in Canada.

Contents

Acknowledgments

This sixth edition of the *Study Guide* has benefited from help and advice from Beverly Cameron, University of Manitoba; Glen Stirling, University Western Ontario; Andrew Wong, Grant MacEwan College; and from students who pointed out mistakes and ambiguities they found in using the *Study Guide*. Thanks to Joshua Borg, Ka Sin Chui, Elian Demangos, Ying Liu, Hyunseok Park, Anthony Patmanidis, Wai Pho, Amir Shuster, Joanna Warren, and Yunyun Wu for helping us in this area. Thanks also to Robin Bade and Michael Parkin for their dedication to the continuous improvement of the textbook, the *Study Guide*, and the teaching of economics.

Harvey King dedicates this edition to Morgan, for showing me how much fun life can be, to Harrison for explaining the intricacies of the undead, and to Tracy for putting up with all of us. Avi Cohen dedicates this edition to Robert Cohen, my father, whose extraordinary qualities as a teacher make him my role model.

Harvey King
Avi Cohen
March 2006

Introduction

Before You Begin ...

Our experience has taught us that what first-year economics students want most from a *Study Guide* is help in mastering course material in order to do well on examinations. We have developed this *Study Guide* to respond specifically to that demand. Using this *Study Guide* alone, however, is not enough to guarantee that you will do well in your course. In order to help you overcome the problems and difficulties that most first-year students encounter, we have some general advice on how to study, as well as some specific advice on how to best use this *Study Guide*.

Some Friendly Advice

The study of economics requires a different style of thinking from what you may encounter in other courses. Economists make extensive use of assumptions to break down complex problems into simple, analytically manageable parts. This analytical style, while not ultimately more demanding than the styles of thinking in other disciplines, feels unfamiliar to most students and requires practice. As a result, it is not as easy to do well in economics simply on the basis of your raw intelligence and high-school knowledge as it is in many other first-year courses. Many students who come to our offices are frustrated and puzzled by the fact that they are getting As and Bs in their other courses but only a C or worse in economics. They have not recognized that the study of economics is different and requires practice. In order to avoid a frustrating visit to your instructor after your first test, we suggest you do the following.

Don't rely solely on your high-school economics. If you took high-school economics, you will have seen the material on demand and supply which your instructor will lecture on in the first few weeks. Don't be lulled into feeling that the course will be easy. Your high-school knowledge of economic concepts will be very useful, but it will not be enough to guarantee high marks on exams. Your college or university instructors will demand much more detailed knowledge of concepts and ask you to apply them in new circumstances.

Keep up with the course material on a weekly basis. Read the appropriate chapter in the textbook before your instructor lectures on it. In this initial reading, don't worry about details or arguments you can't quite follow—just try to get a general understanding of the basic concepts and issues. You may be amazed at how your instructor's ability to teach improves when you come to class prepared. As soon as your instructor has finished covering a chapter, complete the corresponding *Study Guide* chapter. Avoid cramming the day before or even just the week before an exam. Because economics requires practice, cramming is an almost certain recipe for failure.

Keep a good set of lecture notes. Good lecture notes are vital for focusing your studying. Your instructor will only lecture on a subset of topics from the textbook. The topics your instructor covers in a lecture should usually be given priority when studying. Also give priority to studying the figures and graphs covered in the lecture.

Instructors do differ in their emphasis on lecture notes or the textbook, so early on in the course ask which is more important in reviewing for exams—lecture notes or the textbook. If your instructor answers that both are important, then ask the following, typically economic question: at the margin, which will be more beneficial—spending an extra hour rereading your lecture notes or an extra hour rereading the textbook? This question assumes that you have read each textbook chapter twice (once before lecture for a general understanding, and then later for a thorough understanding); that you have prepared a good set of lecture notes; and that you have worked through all of the problems in the appropriate *Study Guide* chapters. By applying this style of analysis to the problem of efficiently allocating your study time, you are already beginning to think like an economist!

Use your instructor and/or teaching assistants for help. When you have questions or problems with course material, come to the office to ask questions. Remember, you are paying for your education and instructors are there to help you learn. We are often amazed at how few students come to see us during office hours. Don't be shy. The personal contact that comes from one-on-one tutoring is professionally gratifying for us as well as (hopefully) beneficial to you.

Form a study group. A very useful way to motivate your studying and to learn economics is to discuss the course material and problems with other students. Explaining the answer to a question out loud is a very effective way of discovering how well you understand the question. When you answer a question only in your head, you often skip steps in the chain of reasoning without realizing it. When you are forced to explain your reasoning aloud, gaps and mistakes quickly appear, and you (with your fellow group members) can quickly correct your reasoning. The true/false and explain questions in the *Study Guide* and the critical thinking questions at the end of each textbook chapter are good study-group material. You might also get together after having worked the *Study Guide* problems, but before looking at the answers, and help each other solve unsolved problems.

Work old exams. One of the most effective ways of studying is to work through exams your instructor has given in previous years. Old exams give you a feel for the style of question your instructor may ask, and give you the opportunity to get used to time pressure if you force yourself to do the exam in the allotted time. Studying from old exams is not cheating, as long as you have obtained a copy of the exam legally. Some institutions post old exams online, others keep them in the library, the department or at the student union. Upper-year students who have previously taken the course are usually a good source as well. Remember, though, that old exams are a useful study aid only if you use them to understand the reasoning behind each question. If you simply memorize answers in the hopes that your instructor will repeat the identical question, you are likely to fail. From year to year, instructors routinely change the questions or change the numerical values for similar questions.

Use the MyEconLab Web site. In addition to this *Study Guide*, we believe the MyEconLab site (www.pearsoned.ca/myeconlab) is worth using for the valuable help it will provide in mastering course material and doing well on examinations. However, don't just take our word for it—ask students who have used it for their opinions. MyEconLab is an online homework and tutorial system that includes practice tests, personalized study plans, practice exercises, tutorial instruction, a powerful graphing tool, Economics in the News updates, and a virtual Office Hours feature that enables you to get help by email from Michael Parkin and Robin Bade.

Using the *Study Guide*

You should only attempt to complete a chapter in this *Guide* after you have read the corresponding textbook chapter and listened to your instructor lecture on the material. Each *Study Guide* chapter contains the following sections.

Key Concepts This first section is a one-to-two-page summary, in point form, of all key definitions, concepts, and material from the textbook chapter. The summary is organized using the same major section headings from the textbook chapter. Key terms from the textbook appear in bold. This section is designed to focus you quickly and precisely on the core material that you must master. It is an excellent study aid for the night before an exam. Think of it as crib notes that will serve as a final check of the key concepts you have studied.

Helpful Hints When you encounter difficulty in mastering concepts or techniques, you will not be alone. Many students find certain concepts difficult and often make the same kinds of mistakes. We have seen these common mistakes often enough to have learned how to help students avoid them. The hints point out these mistakes and offer tips to avoid them. The hints focus on the most important concepts, equations, and techniques for problem solving. They also review crucial graphs that appear on every instructor's exams. We hope that this section will be very useful, since instructors always ask exam questions designed to test these possible mistakes in your understanding.

This section sometimes includes extra material that your instructor may add to the course, but is not in textbook chapters. An example is the discussion in Chapter 2 of mathematics of the slope of the production possibilities frontier. Such extra material is marked with the symbol ⓔ ("e" for "extra") and may be skipped if your instructor does not cover it.

The same symbol is used throughout the *Study Guide* to identify questions and answers based on extra material.

Self-Test This should be one of the most useful sections of this *Study Guide*. The questions are designed to give you practice and to test skills and techniques you must master to do well on exams. You are encouraged to write directly in the *Guide*. There are plenty of the multiple-choice questions (25 for each chapter) you are most likely to encounter on course tests and exams. There are also other types of questions, described below, each with a specific pedagogical purpose. Questions (and answers) based on extra material covered in the Helpful Hints are marked with the "extra" symbol ⓔ so that you can easily skip them if your instructor does not assign that material.

Before we describe the three parts of the Self-Test section, here are some tips that apply to all parts:

Use a pencil. This will allow you to erase your mistakes and have neat, completed pages from which to study. Draw graphs wherever applicable. Some questions will ask explicitly for graphs; many others will not, but will require a chain of reasoning that involves shifts of curves on a graph. *Always draw the graph.* Don't try to work through the reasoning in your head—you are much more likely to make mistakes that way. Whenever you draw a graph, even in the margins of this *Guide*, label the axes. You may think that you can keep the labels in your head, but you will be confronting many different graphs with many different variables on the axes. Avoid confusion: label. As an added incentive, remember that on exams where graphs are required, instructors will deduct marks for unlabelled axes.

Do the Self-Test questions as if they were real exam questions, which means do them without looking at the answers. This is the single most important tip we can give you. Struggling for the answers to questions that you find difficult is one of the most effective ways to learn. The athletic adage "No pain, no gain" applies equally to studying. You will learn the most from right answers you had to struggle for and from your wrong answers and mistakes. Only after you have attempted all the questions should you look at the answers. When you finally do check the answers, be sure to understand where you went wrong and why the right answer is right.

If you want to impose time pressure on yourself to simulate the conditions of a real exam, allow two minutes for each true/false and multiple-choice question. The short answer problems vary considerably in their time requirements, so it is difficult to give time estimates for them. However, we believe that such time pressure is probably not a good idea for Study Guide questions. A state of relaxed concentration is best. If you want practice with time pressure, use old exams, or use the Part Wrap Up Midterm Examinations (see description on page x).

There are many questions in each chapter, and it will take you somewhere between two and five hours to answer all of them. If you get tired (or bored), don't burn yourself out by trying to work through all of the questions in one sitting. Consider breaking up your Self-Test over two (or more) study sessions.

One other tip about the Self-Test. *Before* you jump in and do the questions, be sure to read through the Key Concepts and Helpful Hints. This will save you frustration at getting wrong answers to questions. When you do get wrong answers, you will often find an explanation of the right answers in Key Concepts or Helpful Hints.

The three parts of the Self-Test section are:

True/False and Explain These questions test basic knowledge of chapter concepts and your ability to apply the concepts. Some challenge your understanding, to see if you can identify mistakes in statements using basic concepts. These questions will quickly identify gaps in your knowledge and are useful to answer out loud in a study group. There are 15 of these questions, organized using the same major section headings from the textbook. The Test Bank that your instructor will likely use to make up tests and exams also contains true/false questions like those in the Self-Test.

When answering, identify each statement as *true* or *false*. Explain your answer in one sentence. The space underneath each question should be sufficient in every case for writing your answer.

Multiple-Choice These more difficult questions test your analytical abilities by asking you to apply concepts to new situations, manipulate information, and solve numerical and graphical problems.

This is the most frequently used type of test and exam question, and the Self-Test contains 25 of them organized using the same major section headings from the textbook. Your instructor's Test Bank contains all of the *Study Guide* multiple-choice questions, numerous questions that closely parallel the *Study Guide* questions, plus many similar questions.

Before you answer, read each question and all five choices carefully. Many of the choices will be plausible and will differ only slightly. You must choose the one *best* answer. A useful strategy is to first eliminate any obviously wrong choices and then focus on the remaining alternatives. Be aware that sometimes the correct answer will be "none of the above." Don't get frustrated or think that you are dim if you can't immediately see the correct answer. These questions are designed to make you work to find the correct choice.

Short Answer Problems The best way to learn to do economics is to do problems. Problems are also a popular type of test and exam question—practise them as much as possible! Each Self-Test concludes with ten short answer, numerical, or graphical problems, often based on economic policy issues. In many chapters, this is the most challenging part of the Self-Test. It is also likely to be the most helpful for deepening your understanding of the chapter material. We have, however, designed the questions to teach as much as to test. We have purposely arranged the parts of each multipart question to lead you through the problem-solving analysis in a gradual and sequential fashion, from easier to more difficult parts.

Problems that require critical thinking are marked with the symbol ⓒⓣ, to alert you to the need for extra time and effort. This symbol gives you the same indication you would have on a test or exam from the number of marks or minutes allocated to a problem.

Answers The Self-Test is followed by a section that gives answers to all the questions. But do not look at any answer until you have attempted the question.

When you finally do look, use the answer to understand where you went wrong, and think about why the answer is right. Every true/false and multiple-choice answer includes a brief, point-form explanation to suggest where you might have gone wrong and the economic reasoning behind the answer. At the end of each answer are page references to the textbook, so you can read a more complete explanation.

Answers to critical thinking questions are marked with ⓒⓣ to indicate why you might have struggled with that question! (We purposely did not mark which true/false and multiple-choice questions were critical thinking, to stay as close as possible to a real test or exam format. In an exam, all multiple-choice questions, for example, are worth the same number of marks, and you would have no idea which questions are the more difficult ones requiring critical thinking.)

The detailed answers to the short answer problems should be especially useful in clarifying and illustrating typical chains of reasoning involved in economic analysis. Answers to critical thinking problems are marked with ⓒ. If the answers alone do not clear up your confusion, go back to the appropriate sections of the textbook and to Key Concepts and Helpful Hints in this *Study Guide*. If that still does not suffice, go to your instructor's or teaching assistants' office, or to your study-group members, for help and clarification.

Part Wrap Up Problem and Midterm Examination

Every few chapters, at the end of each of the nine Parts of the textbook, you will find a special multipart problem (and answer). These problems draw on material from all chapters in the Part, and emphasize policy and real-world questions (e.g., the impact of cigarette smuggling on tax revenues). They will help you integrate concepts from different chapters that may seem unrelated, but actually are. We often design exam questions similar to these problems.

Each Wrap Up also contains a Midterm Examination, consisting of four or more multiple-choice questions from each chapter in the textbook part. The midterm is set up like a real examination or test, with a scrambled order and a time limit for working the questions. Like the other multiple-choice questions, there are answers with point-form explanations as well as page references to the textbook so you can go find more complete explanations.

If you effectively combine the use of the textbook, the *Study Guide*, MyEconLab, and all other course resources, you will be well prepared for exams. Equally importantly, you will also have developed analytical skills and powers of reasoning that will benefit you throughout life and in whatever career you choose.

Do You Have Any Friendly Advice for Us?

We have attempted to make this *Study Guide* as clear and as useful as possible, and to avoid errors. No doubt, we have not succeeded entirely, and you are the only judges who count in evaluating our attempt. If you discover errors, or if you have other suggestions for improving the *Guide*, please write to us. In future editions, we will try to acknowledge the names of all students whose suggestions help us improve this supplement. Send your correspondence or email to either of us:

Professor Avi J. Cohen
Department of Economics
Vari Hall, York University
Toronto, Ontario M3J 1P3
avicohen@yorku.ca

Professor Harvey B. King
Department of Economics
University of Regina
Regina, Saskatchewan S4S 0A2
Harvey.King@uregina.ca

Should the Study of Economics Be Part of Your Future?

By Harvey King (University of Regina) and Robert Whaples (Wake Forest University)

Should You Take More Economics Courses?

Soon you will learn about supply and demand, utility and profit maximization, employment and unemployment. First, however, let's take a moment to look to the future.

- Should you take more classes or maybe even major in economics?
- What about graduate school in economics?

Economists generally assume that people try to make rational choices to maximize their own well-being. The purpose of this chapter is help you make that rational maximizing choice by providing low-cost information. Let us assess the benefits and see whether they outweigh the costs of studying economics.

Benefits from Studying Economics

Knowledge, Enlightenment, and Liberation

As John Maynard Keynes, a famous British economist, said, "The ideas of economists … both when they are right and when they are wrong, are more powerful than is commonly understood. Indeed the world is ruled by little else. Practical men, who believe themselves to be quite exempt from any intellectual influences, are usually the slaves of some defunct economist." Studying economics is a liberating and enlightening experience. You don't want to be the slave of a defunct economist, do you? Liberate yourself. It's better to bring your ideas out in the open, to confront and understand them, rather than to leave them buried.

Knowledge, Understanding, and Satisfaction

Many of the most important problems in the world are economic. Studying economics gives you a practical set of tools to understand and solve them. Every day, on television and in the newspapers, we hear and read about big issues such as economic growth, inflation, unemployment, health care reform, welfare reform, the environment, and the transition away from Communism. Your introduction to economics will let you watch the news or pick up a newspaper and better understand these issues. As an added bonus, economics helps you understand smaller, more immediate concerns, such as: How much Spam should I buy? Is skipping class today a good idea? Should I put my retirement funds in government bonds or in the stock market? After all, as George Bernard Shaw put it, "Economy is the art of making the most of life." Mick Jagger, who dropped out of the London School of Economics, complains that he "can't get no satisfaction." Maybe he should have studied more economics. The economic way of thinking will help you maximize your satisfaction.

Career Opportunities

All careers are not equal. While the wages in many occupations have not risen much lately, the wages of "symbolic analysts" who "solve, identify, and broker problems by manipulating symbols" are soaring.[1] These people "simplify reality into abstract images that can be rearranged, juggled, experimented with, communicated to other specialists, and then, eventually, transformed back into reality." Their wages have been rising as the globalization of the economy increases the demand for their insights and as technological developments (especially computers) have enhanced their productivity. Economists are the quintessential symbolic analysts as we manipulate ideas about abstractions such as supply and demand, cost and benefits, and equilibrium. You can think of your training in economics as an exercise regimen, a workout for your brain.

You will use many of the concepts you will learn in introductory economics during your career, but it is the practice in abstract thinking that will really pay off. In fact, most economics majors do not go on to become economists. They enter fields that use their analytical abilities, including business, management, insurance, finance, real estate, marketing, law, education, policy analysis, consulting, government, planning, and even medicine, journalism, and the arts.

A recent survey of 100 former economics majors at one university included all of these careers. If you want to verify that economics majors graduate to successful and rewarding careers, just ask your professors or watch what happens to economics majors from your school as they graduate.

Statistics from the 2001 Canadian census (the most recent available at the time of writing) show that economics majors earn a healthy salary. Table 1 shows the average yearly earnings for females who worked full-year, full-time by age and type of education, while Table 2 shows the same data for males. (Want to understand why women get paid less than men? Take some more economics!)

We can also see that economics degrees do well by examining data on entry-level wages (***Source:*** *Job Futures, Part 2: Career Outlooks for Graduates*, Human Resources and Development Canada, accessed at www.jobfutures.ca). The average starting salary for a B.A. in economics is $31,600. Although this is lower than degrees in engineering ($39,200) or computing science, it is higher than the starting salary for a B.A. in humanities

TABLE 1 AVERAGE YEARLY EARNINGS, FULL-YEAR, FULL-TIME WORKERS (FEMALE), 2000

	Age				
Highest Degree and Major Field of Study	**20–24**	**25–34**	**35–44**	**45–54**	**55–64**
High school graduation certificate	18,449	27,144	31,529	33,176	31,663
Trade certificate or diploma	19,297	25,836	29,896	31,236	30,004
College certificate or diploma	22,169	30,506	36,890	38,212	36,358
Bachelor's degree					
Educational, recreational and counselling services	23,403	35,819	45,312	49,630	44,942
Humanities and related fields	23,747	37,132	47,962	51,401	46,477
Social sciences and related fields	24,913	39,070	53,562	53,770	51,050
Economics	**27,605**	**44,266**	**57,493**	**52,086**	**57,313**
Geography	24,211	38,054	48,861	47,835	41,194
Political science	26,345	40,916	54,701	53,173	55,676
Psychology	23,724	36,282	47,095	49,385	48,534
Sociology	23,525	36,533	46,783	51,178	44,526
Commerce, management, and business administration	28,383	44,097	56,189	54,434	46,102

Source: Statistics Canada "Highest Degree, Certificate or Diploma (12), Major Field of Study (122), 2000 Employment Income (3), Work Activity in 2000 (2), Age Groups (13B) and Sex (3) for Total Population 15 Years and Over, for Canada, Provinces and Territories, 2001 Census—20% Sample Data," 2001 Census, with calculations by H. King, Catalogue no. 97F0018XCB2001043 <www12.statcan.ca/english/census01/products/standard/themes/AboutProduct.cfm?Temporal=2001&APATH=3&ALEVEL=9&THEME=52&VID=0&FL=0&RL=0&GK=NA&GC=99&IPS=97F0018XCB2001043&CATNO=97F0018XCB2001043&FREE=0&S=1>, accessed June 26, 2006.

TABLE 2 AVERAGE YEARLY EARNINGS, FULL-YEAR, FULL-TIME WORKERS (MALE), 2000

	Age				
Highest Degree and Major Field of Study	**20–24**	**25–34**	**35–44**	**45–54**	**55–64**
High school graduation certificate	14,400	30,971	40,375	44,334	40,497
Trade certificate or diploma	20,178	34,172	41,683	44,460	39,857
College certificate or diploma	16,259	35,770	47,829	51,016	46,234
Bachelor's degree					
Educational, recreational and counselling services	22,830	40,155	52,256	56,662	50,625
Humanities and related fields	25,827	42,191	55,915	64,407	69,687
Social sciences and related fields	26,659	51,863	75,689	85,429	107,034
Economics	**28,656**	**58,012**	**81,049**	**79,961**	**152,870**
Geography	23,946	45,027	62,531	66,531	55,349
Political science	26,801	51,639	68,645	73,960	78,127
Psychology	25,506	45,056	56,913	66,708	84,615
Sociology	28,557	46,833	55,340	64,905	62,609
Commerce, management, and business administration	31,595	54,926	81,890	87,062	98,484

Source: Same as for Table 1.

(English degrees earned $27,600, French degrees $29,500), or for a B.A. in the other social sciences (psychology degrees earned $28,000, sociology degrees $27,800), or for a B.Sc. in many of the sciences (physics degrees earned $31,600, biology degrees $27,400). In addition, employment rates for economics B.A.s were higher than average, and salaries grew over the first five years at a higher-than-average rate.

You might like to consider graduate school in economics—the entry-level wage for an M.A. in economics is roughly $42,100.

The Costs of Studying Economics

Since the "direct" costs of studying economics (tuition, books, supplies) aren't generally any higher or lower than the direct costs of other courses, indirect costs will be the most important of the costs to studying economics.

Forgone Knowledge

If you study economics, you can't study something else. This forgone knowledge could be very valuable.

Time and Energy

Economics is a fairly demanding major. Although economics courses do not generally take as much time as courses in English and history (in which you have to read a lot of long books) or anatomy and physiology (in which you have to spend hours in the lab and hours memorizing things), they do take a decent amount of time. In addition, some people find the material "tougher" than most subjects because memorizing is not the key. In economics (like physics), analyzing and solving are the keys.

Grades

As Table 3 shows, grades in introductory economics courses are generally lower than grades in some other majors, including other social sciences and the humanities. On the other hand, grades in economics are similar to grades in some sciences and math.

TABLE 3 AVERAGE GRADES AND GRADE DISTRIBUTION IN INTRODUCTORY COURSES AT SEVEN ONTARIO UNIVERSITIES

Department	Mean Grade*	% (A + B)	% (D + F)
Music	3.02	72.1	9.7
English	2.76	64.0	9.4
French	2.69	61.1	12.4
Philosophy	2.54	57.6	15.3
Biology	2.52	54.5	19.7
Sociology	2.51	52.8	14.2
Political Science	2.49	55.6	14.1
Psychology	2.40	48.4	20.6
Physics	2.38	46.1	28.4
Mathematics	2.19	44.4	33.9
Chemistry	2.18	42.9	30.9
Economics	2.18	41.6	30.7

*A = 4, B = 3, C = 2, D = 1, F = 0.

Source: Paul Anglin and Ronald Meng, "Evidence on Grades and Grade Inflation at Ontario's Universities," *University of Windsor Working Paper*, November 1999. Used with permission.

Caveat Emptor (Buyer Beware): Interpreting Your Grades Is Not Straightforward

High grades provide direct satisfaction to most students, but they also act as a signal about the student's ability to learn the subject material. Unfortunately, because the grade distribution is not uniform across departments, you may be confused and misled by your grades. You may think that you are exceptionally good at a subject because of a high grade, when in fact nearly everyone gets a high grade in that subject. The important point here is that you should be informed about your own school's grade distribution. Just because you got a B in economics and an A in history does not necessarily mean that your comparative advantage is in learning history rather than economics. Everyone—or virtually everyone—may receive an A in history. Earning a B or a C in economics might mean that it is the best major for you, because high grades are much harder to earn in economics. It is fun to have a high GPA in college, but maximizing GPA should not be your goal. Maximizing your overall well-being is probably your goal, and this might be obtained by trading off a tenth or so of your GPA for a more rewarding major—perhaps economics.

Potential Side Effects from Studying Economics

Studying economics has some potential side effects. We're not sure whether they are costs or benefits and will let you decide.

Changing Ideas About What Is Fair

One study compared students at the beginning and end of the semester in an introductory economics course.[2] It found that by the end of the semester, significantly more of the students thought that the functioning of the market is "fair." This was especially true for female students. The results were consistent across a range of professors who fell across the ideological spectrum.

For example, the proportion of students who regarded it as unfair to increase the price of flowers on a holiday fell almost in half. The proportion that favoured government control over flower prices, rather than market determination, fell by over 60 percent. The study argues that these responses do not reflect changes in deep values, but instead represent the discovery of previous inconsistencies and their modification in the light of new information learned during the semester.

Changing Behaviour

Many people believe that the study of economics changes students' values and behaviour. Some think that it changes them for the worse. Others disagree. In particular, it is argued that economics students become more self-interested and less likely to cooperate, perhaps because they spend so much time studying economic models, which often assume that people are self-interested. For example, one study reports experimental evidence that economics students are more likely than nonmajors to behave self-interestedly in prisoners' dilemma games and ultimatum bargaining games.[3]

This need not mean that studying economics will change you, however. Another study compares beginning freshmen and senior economics students and concludes that economics students "are already different when they begin their study of economics."[4] In other words, students signing up for economics courses are already different; studying economics doesn't change them. However, there are reasons to question both of these conclusions, because it is not clear whether these laboratory experiments using economic games reflect reality. One experiment asked students whether they would return money that had been lost. It found that economics students were more likely than others to say that they would keep the cash.

However, what people say and what they do are sometimes at odds. In a follow-up experiment, this theory was tested by dropping stamped, addressed envelopes containing $10 in cash in different campus classrooms. To return the cash, the students had only to seal the envelopes and mail them. The results were that 56 percent of the envelopes dropped in economics classes were returned, while only 31 percent of the envelopes dropped in history, psychology, and business classes were sent in.[5] Perhaps economics students are less selfish than others!

Obviously, no firm conclusions have been reached about whether or how studying economics changes students' behaviour.

Cost Versus Benefits

Suppose that you've weighed the costs and benefits of studying economics and you've decided that the benefits are greater than or equal to the costs. Obviously, then, you should continue to take economics courses. If you can't decide whether the benefits outweigh the costs, then you should probably collect more information—especially if it is good but inexpensive. In either case, read the rest of this section.

The Economics Major

The study of economics is like a tree. The introductory microeconomics and macroeconomics courses you begin with are the tree's roots. Most colleges and universities require that you master this material before you go on to any other courses. The way of thinking, the language, and the tools that you acquire in the introductory course are usually reinforced in intermediate microeconomics and macroeconomics courses before they are applied in more specialized courses that you take. The intermediate courses are the tree's trunk. Among the specialized courses that make up the branches of economics are econometrics (statistical economics), financial economics, labour economics, resource economics, international trade, industrial organization, public finance, public choice, economic history, the history of economic thought, mathematical economics, current economic issues, and urban economics. The branches of the tree vary from department to department, but these are common. It will pay to check your school calendar and discuss these courses with professors and other students.

Graduate School in Economics

Preparing for Graduate School in Economics

You can prepare for graduate school in economics by taking several math classes. This would probably include one year of calculus plus a couple of courses in probability and statistics and linear/matrix algebra. Ask your advisor about the particular courses to take at your university. In addition, the mathematical economics and econometrics courses in the economics department are essential. (*Hint:* Even if you aren't going to graduate school, these mathematical courses can be valuable to you, just as more economics courses can be valuable for nonmajors.)

If your school offers graduate level economics courses, you might want to sit in on a few to get accustomed to the flavour of graduate school.

Most graduate programs require strong grades in economics, a good score on the Graduate Record Examination (GRE) for U.S. schools, and solid letters of recommendations. It is a good idea to get to know a few professors very well and to go above and beyond what is expected so that they can write glowing letters about you.

Financing Graduate School

Unlike some other graduate and professional degree programs, you probably won't need to pile up a massive amount of debt while pursuing an M.A. or Ph.D. in economics. Most graduate programs hire their economics graduate students as teaching or research assistants. Teaching assistants begin by grading papers and running review sessions and can advance to teaching classes on their own. Research assistants generally do data collection, statistical work, and library research for professors and often jointly write papers with them. Most assistantships will pay for tuition and provide you with enough money to live on.

Where Should You Apply?

The best graduate school for you depends on a lot of things, especially your ability level, geographical location, areas of research interests, and, of course, financing. You should talk with your professors about ability level and areas of research. In addition, for U.S. schools there are informative articles that give overall departmental rankings and rankings by subfield. See especially John Tschirhart, "Ranking Economics Department in Areas of Expertise," *Journal of Economic Education*, Spring 1989, and Richard Dusansky and Clayton J. Vernon, "Rankings of U.S. Economics Departments," *Journal of Economic Perspectives*, vol. 12, no. 1 (Winter 1998), pp. 157–70.

What You Will Do in Graduate School

Most students who go on to graduate school do only an M.A. These degrees typically take one year for the non-thesis route and about two years for the thesis route. Course work will include 2–4 courses in economic theory, plus 4–6 courses in specific subfields.

Most Ph.D. programs in economics begin with a year of theory courses in macroeconomics and microeconomics. After a year you will probably take a series of tests to show that you have mastered this core theory. If you pass these tests, in the second and third year of courses you will take more specialized subjects and perhaps take lengthy examinations in a couple of subfields. After this you will be required to write a dissertation—original research that will contribute new knowledge to one of the fields of economics. These stages are intertwined with work as a teaching and/or research assistant, and the dissertation stage can be quite drawn out. In the social sciences the median time it takes for a student to complete the Ph.D. degree is about 7.5 years.[6] Be aware that a high percentage (roughly 50%) of students do not complete their doctoral degree.

What Is Graduate School Like?

Graduate school in economics comes as a surprise to many students. The material and approach are distinctly different from what you will learn as an undergraduate. The textbooks and journal articles you will read in graduate school are often very theoretical and abstract. A good source of information is sitting in on courses or reading the reflections of recent students. See especially *The Making of an Economist* by Arjo Klamer and David Colander (Boulder, CO: Westview Press, 1990).

The Committee on Graduate Education in Economics (COGEE) undertook an important review of graduate education in economics and reported its findings in the September 1991 issue of the *Journal of Economic Literature*. COGEE asked faculty members, graduate students, and recent Ph.D.s to rank the most important skills needed to be successful in the study of graduate economics. At the top of the list were analytical skills and mathematics, followed by critical judgment, the ability to apply theory, and computational skills. At the bottom of the list were creativity and the ability to communicate. If you are interested in economic issues but do not have the characteristics required by graduate economics departments, there are other economics-related fields to consider, such as graduate school in public policy. Many economics majors go to business schools to obtain an MBA and are often better prepared than students who have undergraduate degrees in business.

Economics Reading

If you decide to make studying economics part of your future, or if you're hungry for more economics, you should immediately begin reading the economic news and books by economists. Life is short. Why waste it watching TV?

The easiest way to get your daily recommended dose of economics is to keep up with current economic events. Here are a few sources to pick up at the newsstand, bookstore, or library over your summer or winter break.

The Globe and Mail *or* The National Post

Many undergraduates subscribe to *The Globe and Mail* or *The National Post* at low student rates. Join them! Not only are these well-written business newspapers, but they also have articles on domestic and international news, politics, the arts, travel, and sports, as well as lively editorial pages. Reading one of these papers is one of the best ways to tie the economics you are studying to the real world and to prepare for your career.

Magazines and Journals

The Economist, a weekly magazine published in England, is available at a student discount rate. Pick up a copy at your school library and you will be hooked by its informative, sharp writing. *Business Week* is also well worth the read.

Also recommended are *Challenge* magazine and *The Public Interest*, two quarterlies that discuss economic policy, as well as *Policy Options*, a bimonthly publication of the Institute for Research on Public Policy. Finally, there is the *Journal of Economic Perspectives*, which is published by the American Economic Association and written to be accessible to undergraduate economics students.

Books by Economists

Below is a list of suggested readings, compiled from asking other professors, and from our own readings.

Steven Levitt and Stephen Dubner, *Freakonomics: A Rogue Economist Explores the Hidden Side of Everything.*

Milton Friedman, *Capitalism and Freedom*.

Robert Heilbroner, *The Worldly Philosophers: The Lives, Times, and Ideas of the Great Economic Thinkers*.

Steve Landsburg, *The Armchair Economist: Economics and Everyday Life*.

Jared Diamond, *Guns, Germs, and Steel: The Fates of Human Societies*.

Diane Coyle, *Sex, Drugs and Economics: An Unconventional Introduction to Economics*.

Patrick Luciani, *Economics Myths: Making Sense of Canadian Policy Issues*.

Hernando deSoto, *The Mystery of Capital: Why Capitalism Triumphed in the West and Failed Everywhere Else*.

David Friedman, *Hidden Order: The Economics of Everyday Life*.

Adam Smith's *The Wealth of Nations* is a must-read for every student of economics. It was written in 1776, yet it is the most influential work of economics ever and its insights are still valuable.

Endnotes

1. This term is used by Robert Reich in *The Work of Nations*. The quote is from p. 178.

2. Robert Whaples, "Changes in Attitudes About the Fairness of Free Markets Among College Economics Students," *Journal of Economic Education*, vol. 26, no. 4 (Fall 1995).

3. Robert H. Frank, Thomas Gilovich, and Dennis T. Regan, "Does Studying Economics Inhibit Cooperation?' *Journal of Economic Perspectives*, vol. 7, no. 2 (Spring 1993), pp. 159–171.

4. John R. Carter and Michael D. Irons, "Are Economists Different, and If So, Why?" *Journal of Economic Perspectives*, vol. 5, no. 2 (Spring 1991), pp. 171–177.

5. "Economics Students Aren't Selfish, They're Just Not Entirely Honest," *Wall Street Journal*, January 18, 1995, B1.

6. See Ronald Ehrenberg, "The Flow of New Doctorates," *Journal of Economic Literature*, vol. 30, June 1992, pp. 830–875. If breaks in school attendance are included, this climbs to 10.5 years. Of course, some students attend only part time, and most have some kind of employment while completing their degrees.

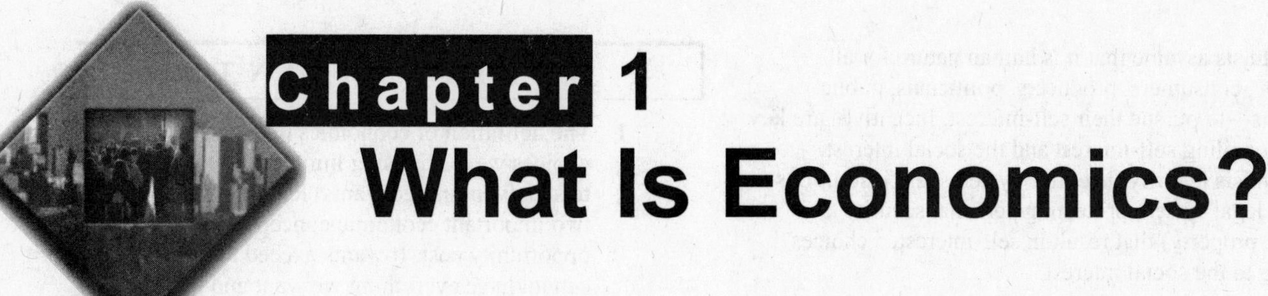

Chapter 1 What Is Economics?

KEY CONCEPTS

Definition of Economics

All economic questions arise from **scarcity**.

- Because wants exceed the resources available to satisfy them, we cannot have everything we want and must make choices.
  - Choices depend on **incentives**—rewards that encourage actions and penalties that discourage action.
- **Economics** is the social science that studies the choices people make to cope with scarcity.
  - **Microeconomics** studies choices of individuals and businesses.
  - **Macroeconomics** studies national and global economies.

Two Big Economic Questions

Two questions summarize the scope of economics:

- How do choices determine *what*, *how*, and *for whom* **goods and services** are produced, and in what quantities?
- When do choices made in the pursuit of self-interest also promote the social interest?

The **factors of production** used to produce goods and services are

- **land** (shorthand for all natural resources) which earns **rent**.
- **labour** (includes **human capital**—knowledge and skills from education, training, experience) which earns **wages**.
- **capital** (machinery) which earns **interest**.
- entrepreneurship which earns profit.

Choices made in **self-interest** are best for the person making them. Choices that are in the **social interest** are best for society as a whole.

- Markets often provide incentives so that the pursuit of our self-interest also promotes the social interest; but self-interest and social interest sometimes conflict.
- Economic principles allow us to understand when self-interest promotes the social interest, when they conflict, and policies to reduce those conflicts.

The Economic Way of Thinking

A choice is a **tradeoff**—we give up one thing to get something else—and the **opportunity cost** of any action is the highest-valued alternative forgone. Opportunity cost is the single most important concept for making choices.

Economic tradeoffs:

- "guns" versus "butter" tradeoffs (between any pair of goods).
- "what," "how," and "for whom" tradeoffs.
- the **big tradeoff**—between equality and efficiency. Government redistribution using taxes and transfers weaken incentives, so a more equally shared pie results in a smaller pie.

We make choices in small steps, or at the **margin**, and choices are influenced by incentives.

- Economic choices are made by comparing the *additional* benefit—**marginal benefit**—and *additional* cost—**marginal cost**—of a small increase in an activity. If marginal benefit exceeds marginal cost, we choose to increase the activity.
- By choosing only activities that bring greater benefits than costs, we use our scarce resources in the way that makes us as well off as possible.
- Given a change in incentives—rewards and penalties for particular actions—we can predict how choices will change by looking for changes in marginal benefit and marginal cost.

Economists assume that it is human nature for all people—consumers, producers, politicians, public servants—to pursue their self-interest. Incentives are key for reconciling self-interest and the social interest. Economists identify incentive systems and institutions (like a legal system protecting personal security and private property) that result in self-interested choices leading to the social interest.

Economics: A Social Science

Economics, as a social science, distinguishes between

- *positive* statements—statements about what *is*, that can be tested by checking them against the facts.
- *normative* statements—statements about what *ought* to be, that depend on values and cannot be tested.

Economic science attempts to understand the economic world and is concerned with positive statements. Economists try to discover positive statements that are consistent with observed facts by

- observation and measurement.
- building **economic models**—abstract, simplified representations of the real world with two components:
  - *assumptions* about what is essential versus inessential detail.
  - *predictions* that can be tested by comparison with observed facts.
- testing economic models to develop **economic theories**—generalizations for understanding economic choices and economic performance.

Useful economic models and theories isolate important economic forces and disentangle cause and effect. This requires

- ***ceteris paribus*** assumptions to hold other things equal to isolate the effects of one force at a time.
- avoiding errors of reasoning, including the
  - fallacy of composition—the false statement that what is true of the parts is true of the whole, or what is true of the whole is true of the parts.
  - *post hoc* fallacy—the false claim that event *a* caused event *b* just because event *a* occurred first.

Economists agree on a wide range of questions about how the economy works.

HELPFUL HINTS

1 The definition of economics (explaining the choices we make using limited resources to try to satisfy unlimited wants) leads us directly to two important economic concepts—choice and opportunity cost. If wants exceed resources, we cannot have everything we want and therefore must make *choices* among alternatives. In making a choice, we forgo other alternatives, and the *opportunity cost* of any choice is the highest-valued alternative forgone.

2 Marginal analysis is a fundamental tool economists use to predict people's choices. The key to understanding marginal analysis is to focus on *additional*, rather than total, benefits and costs. For example, to predict whether or not Taejong will eat a fourth Big Mac, the economist compares Taejong's *additional* benefit or satisfaction from the fourth Big Mac with its *additional* cost. The total benefits and costs of all four Big Macs are not relevant. Only if the marginal benefit exceeds the marginal cost will Taejong eat a fourth Big Mac.

3 In attempting to understand how and why something works (e.g., an airplane, a falling object, an economy), we can try to use description or theory. A description is a list of facts about something. But it does not tell us which facts are essential for understanding how an airplane works (the shape of the wings) and which facts are less important (the colour of the paint).

Scientists use theory to abstract from the complex descriptive facts of the real world and focus only on those elements essential for understanding. Those essential elements are fashioned into models—highly simplified representations of the real world.

In physics and some other natural sciences, if we want to understand the essential force (gravity) that causes objects to fall, we use theory to construct a simple model, then test it by performing a controlled experiment. We create a vacuum to eliminate less important forces like air resistance.

Economic models are also attempts to focus on the essential forces (competition, self-interest) operating in the economy, while abstracting from less important forces (whims, advertising, altruism). Unlike physicists, economists cannot easily perform controlled experiments to test their models. As a result, it is difficult to conclusively prove or disprove a theory and its models.

4 Models are like maps, which are useful precisely because they abstract from real-world detail. A map that reproduced all of the details of the real world (street lamps, fireplugs, electric wires) would be useless. A useful map offers a simplified view, which is carefully selected according to the purpose of the map. Remember that economic models are not claims that the real world is as simple as the model. Models claim to capture the simplified effect of some real force operating in the economy. Before drawing conclusions about the real economy from a model, we must be careful to consider whether, when we reinsert all of the real-world complexities the model abstracted from, the conclusions will be the same as in the model.

5 The most important purpose of studying economics is not to learn what to think about economics but rather *how* to think about economics. The "what"—the facts and descriptions of the economy—can always be found in books. The value of an economics education is the ability to think critically about economic problems and *to understand how* an economy works. This understanding of the essential forces governing how an economy works comes through the mastery of economic theory and model-building.

SELF-TEST

True/False and Explain

Definition of Economics

1 Economics explains how we use unlimited resources to satisfy limited wants.

2 Economics studies the choices people make to cope with scarcity and the institutions that influence and reconcile choices.

Two Big Economic Questions

3 In economics, the definition of "land" includes nonrenewable resources but excludes renewable resources.

4 In economics, the definition of "capital" includes financial assets like stocks and bonds.

5 Entrepreneurs bear the risks arising from the business decisions they make.

6 "How do choices determine *what*, *how* and *for whom* goods and services are produced?" is one of the big economic questions.

7 "When do choices made in the pursuit of the social interest also promote self-interest?" is one of the big economic questions.

8 Choices made in the pursuit of self-interest always promote the social interest.

The Economic Way of Thinking

9 When the opportunity cost of an activity increases, the incentive to choose that activity increases.

10 Tradeoffs and opportunity costs are the key concepts for understanding the economic way of thinking.

11 Economists assume that it is human nature for all people to act selfishly.

Economics: A Social Science

12 A positive statement is about what is, while a normative statement is about what will be.

13 Economics is not a science since it deals with the study of willful human beings and not inanimate objects in nature.

14 *Ceteris paribus* means "after this, therefore because of this."

15 Observers are correct in noting that economists disagree on most questions.

Multiple-Choice

Definition of Economics

1 The fact that human wants cannot be fully satisfied with available resources is called the problem of
- **a** opportunity cost.
- **b** scarcity.
- **c** normative economics.
- **d** what to produce.
- **e** who will consume.

2 The problem of scarcity exists
- **a** only in economies with government.
- **b** only in economies without government.
- **c** in all economies.
- **d** only when people have not optimized.
- **e** now, but will be eliminated with economic growth.

3 Scarcity differs from poverty because
- **a** resources exceed wants for the rich.
- **b** wants exceed resources even for the rich.
- **c** the rich do not have to make choices.
- **d** the poor do not have any choices.
- **e** the poor do not have any wants.

4 The branch of economics that studies the choices of individual households and firms is called
- **a** macroeconomics.
- **b** microeconomics.
- **c** positive economics.
- **d** normative economics.
- **e** home economics.

5 Microeconomics studies all of the following *except* the
- **a** decisions of individual firms.
- **b** effects of government safety regulations on the price of cars.
- **c** global economy as a whole.
- **d** prices of individual goods and services.
- **e** effects of taxes on the price of beer.

Two Big Economic Questions

6 The two big economic questions
- **a** arise from scarcity.
- **b** summarize the scope of economics.
- **c** describe choices we make.
- **d** examine incentives that influence choices.
- **e** are all of the above.

7 The first big economic question about goods and services includes all of the following *except*
- **a** *what* to produce.
- **b** *why* produce.
- **c** *how* to produce.
- **d** *what* quantities to produce.
- **e** *who* gets what is produced.

8 The trends over the past 60 years in what we produce show that ________ has expanded and ________ has shrunk.
- **a** manufacturing; services
- **b** manufacturing; agriculture
- **c** agriculture; services
- **d** agriculture; manufacturing
- **e** services; agriculture

9 All of the following are resources *except*
- **a** natural resources.
- **b** tools.
- **c** entrepreneurship.
- **d** government.
- **e** land.

10 The knowledge and skill obtained from education and training is
- **a** labour.
- **b** human capital.
- **c** physical capital.
- **d** entrepreneurship.
- **e** technological know-how.

11 Which statement about incomes earned by factors of production is *false*?
- **a** Land earns rent.
- **b** Natural resources earn rent.
- **c** Labour earns wages.
- **d** Capital earns profit.
- **e** Entrepreneurship earns profit.

12 When a drug company pursuing maximum profits charges $5,000 per dose for a new HIV drug, that is certainly a(n)
- **a** self-interested choice.
- **b** altruistic choice.
- **c** globalization choice.
- **d** factor of production choice.
- **e** choice in the social interest.

The Economic Way of Thinking

13 When the government chooses to use resources to build a dam, those resources are no longer available to build a highway. This illustrates the concept of
- **a** a market.
- **b** macroeconomics.
- **c** opportunity cost.
- **d** a "how" tradeoff.
- **e** the big tradeoff.

14 The big tradeoff is between
- **a** taxes and transfers.
- **b** equality and efficiency.
- **c** current consumption and a higher future standard of living.
- **d** guns and butter.
- **e** personal security and private property.

15 Renata has the chance to either attend an economics lecture or play tennis. If she chooses to attend the lecture, the value of playing tennis is
- **a** greater than the value of the lecture.
- **b** not comparable to the value of the lecture.
- **c** equal to the value of the lecture.
- **d** the opportunity cost of attending the lecture.
- **e** zero.

16 Which of the following sayings best describes opportunity cost?
- **a** "Make hay while the sun shines."
- **b** "Money is the root of all evil."
- **c** "Boldly go where no one has gone before."
- **d** "There's no such thing as a free lunch."
- **e** "Baseball has been very good to me."

17 Marginal benefit is the
- **a** total benefit of an activity.
- **b** additional benefit of a decrease in an activity.
- **c** additional benefit of an increase in an activity.
- **d** opportunity cost of a decrease in an activity.
- **e** opportunity cost of an increase in an activity.

18 Monika will choose to eat a seventh pizza slice if
- **a** the marginal benefit of the seventh slice is greater than its marginal cost.
- **b** the marginal benefit of the seventh slice is less than its marginal cost
- **c** the total benefit of all seven slices is greater than their total cost.
- **d** the total benefit of all seven slices is less than their total cost.
- **e** she is training to be a Sumo wrestler.

19 Economists assume that
- **a** self-interested actions are all selfish actions.
- **b** consumers and producers pursue their self-interest while politicians and public servants pursue the social interest.
- **c** incentives are key in reconciling self-interest and the social interest.
- **d** all people pursue the social interest.
- **e** human nature changes as incentives change.

Economics: A Social Science

20 A positive statement is
- **a** about what ought to be.
- **b** about what is.
- **c** always true.
- **d** capable of evaluation as true or false by observation and measurement.
- **e** **b** and **d**.

21 Which of the following is a positive statement?
- **a** Low rents will restrict the supply of housing.
- **b** High interest rates are bad for the economy.
- **c** Housing costs too much.
- **d** Owners of apartment buildings ought to be free to charge whatever rent they want.
- **e** Government should control the rents that apartment owners charge.

22 A normative statement is a statement regarding
a what is usually the case.
b the assumptions of an economic model.
c what ought to be.
d the predictions of an economic model.
e what is.

23 Which of the following statements is/are normative?
a Scientists should not make normative statements.
b Warts are caused by handling toads.
c As compact disc prices fall, people will buy more of them.
d If income increases, sales of luxury goods will fall.
e None of the above.

24 An economic model is tested by
a examining the realism of its assumptions.
b comparing its predictions with the facts.
c comparing its descriptions with the facts.
d the Testing Committee of the Canadian Economic Association.
e all of the above.

25 The Latin term *ceteris paribus* means
a "Innocent until proven guilty."
b "Fallacies are composed."
c "Compositions are fallacious."
d "The whole is not the sum of the parts."
e "If all other relevant things remain the same."

Short Answer Problems

1 What is meant by scarcity, and why does the existence of scarcity mean that we must make choices?

2 "If all people would only economize, the problem of scarcity would be solved." Agree or disagree, and explain why.

3 Ashley, Doug, and Mei-Lin are planning to travel from Halifax to Sydney. The trip takes one hour by airplane and five hours by train. The air fare is $100 and train fare is $60. They all have to take time off from work while travelling. Ashley earns $5 per hour in her job, Doug $10 per hour, and Mei-Lin $12 per hour.

Calculate the opportunity cost of air and train travel for each person. Assuming they are all economizers, how should each of them travel to Sydney?

4 Suppose the government builds and staffs a hospital in order to provide "free" medical care.
a What is the opportunity cost of the free medical care?
b Is it free from the perspective of society as a whole?

ⓒⓣ **5** Branko loves riding the bumper cars at the amusement park, but he loves the experience a little less with each successive ride. In estimating the benefit he receives from the rides, Branko would be willing to pay $10 for his first ride, $7 for his second ride, and $4 for his third ride. Rides actually cost $5 apiece for as many rides as Branko wants to take. This information is summarized in Table 1.1.

TABLE **1.1**

Ride	1st	2nd	3rd
Marginal benefit	10	7	4
Marginal cost	5	5	5

a If Branko chooses by comparing total benefit and total cost, how many rides will he take?
b If Branko chooses by comparing marginal benefit and marginal cost, how many rides will he take?
c Is Branko better off by choosing according to total or marginal benefit and cost? Explain why.

ⓒⓣ **6** Assume Branko's benefits are the same as in Short Answer Problem **5**. Starting fresh, if the price of a bumper car ride rises to $8, how many rides will Branko now take? Explain why.

7 Indicate whether each of the following statements is positive or normative. If it is normative (positive), rewrite it so that it becomes positive (normative).
a The government ought to reduce the size of the deficit in order to lower interest rates.
b Government imposition of a tax on tobacco products will reduce their consumption.

8 Consider the following paradox. If one farmer has a bumper crop, her income increases. On the basis of the experience of the individual farmer, you predict that, in general, bumper crops cause rising farm incomes. But when all farmers have bumper crops, the excess supply causes prices to fall drastically and farm income actually decreases. What error in reasoning ruined your prediction? Explain.

9 Suppose we examine a model of plant growth that predicts that, given the amount of water and sunlight, the application of fertilizer stimulates plant growth.

a How might you test the model?

b How is the test different from what an economist could do to test an economic model?

ⓒⓣ 10 Suppose your friend, who is a history major, claims that economic theories are useless because the models on which they are based are so unrealistic. He claims that since the models leave out so many descriptive details about the real world, they can't possibly be useful for understanding how the economy works. How would you defend your decision to study economic theory?

ANSWERS

True/False and Explain

1 F Limited resources and unlimited wants. (2)

2 T This is the full definition of economics—the institutional aspect is often omitted for brevity. (2)

3 F "Land" includes all natural resources, whether nonrenewable (oil) or renewable (forests). (3)

4 F "Capital" only consists of physical equipment like tools and buildings used in production. (4)

5 T Entrepreneurs earn profits in return for bearing the risks of organizing labour, land, and capital. (4)

6 T See text discussion. (3–4)

7 F When do choices made in the pursuit of self-interest also promote the social interest? (5)

8 F Markets often provide incentives so that pursuit of self-interest also promotes social interest, but self-interest and social interest sometimes conflict. (5–8).

9 F Incentive decreases because activity is now more expensive. (11)

10 T Scarcity requires choice, choice involves tradeoffs, and tradeoffs involve opportunity cost. (9–11)

11 F Economists assume people act in their self-interest, but self-interested actions are not necessarily selfish actions, if what makes you happy is to help others. (11)

12 F Normative statements are about what *ought* to be. (12)

13 F Science not defined by subject, but by method of observation, measurement, and testing of theoretical models. (12–13)

14 F *Ceteris paribus* means "other things being equal." Other quote is *post hoc ergo propter hoc*. (13–14)

15 F There is agreement on a wide range of (mostly positive) questions. (14)

Multiple-Choice

1 b Definition. (2)

2 c With infinite wants and finite resources, scarcity will never be eliminated. (2)

3 b Poverty is a low level of resources. But wants exceed resources for everyone, necessitating choice. (2)

4 b Definition. (2)

5 c Macroeconomic topic. (2)

6 e Economics explains choices created by scarcity and incentives that help reconcile self-interest and social interest. (2–5)

7 b *Why* is not part of first big question. (3–8)

8 e Services have expanded; agriculture and manufacturing have shrunk. See Text Figure 1.1. (3)

9 d Government is a social institution. (3–4)

10 b Definition. (3)

11 d Capital earns interest. (4)

ⓒⓣ 12 a Certainly in company's self-interest; may or may not be altruistic or in social interest depending on cost of producing drug. (5–8)

13 c Highway is forgone alternative. (9–11)

14 b Greater equality (using taxes and transfers) reduces efficiency by weakening incentives. **c**, **d**, are other tradeoffs, **e** nonsense. (9–11)

15 d Choosing lecture means its value > tennis. Tennis = (highest-valued) forgone alternative to lecture. (9–11)

16 d Every choice involves a cost. (10)

17 c Definition; **e** is marginal cost, **b** and **d** are nonsense. (11)

18 a Choices are made at the margin, when marginal benefit exceeds marginal cost. (11)

19 c Assume human nature given and all people pursue self-interest. When self-interested choices not in social interest, there are wrong incentives. (11)

20 e Definition. (12)

21 a While **a** may be evaluated as true or false, other statements are matters of opinion. (12)

22 c Key word for normative statements is *ought*. (12)

23 a Key word is *should*. Even statement **b** is positive. (12)

24 b Assumptions not realistic descriptions; are simplified representations of world. (12–13)

25 e Definition. **a**, **b**, and **c** are nonsense. **d** is fallacy of composition. (13)

Short Answer Problems

1 Scarcity is the universal condition that human wants always exceed the resources available to satisfy them. The fact that goods and services are scarce means that individuals cannot have all of everything they want. It is therefore necessary to choose among alternatives.

2 Disagree. If everyone economized, then we would be making the best possible use of our resources and would be achieving the greatest benefits or satisfaction possible, given the limited quantity of resources. But this does not mean that we would be satisfying all of our limitless needs. The problem of scarcity can never be "solved" as long as people have infinite needs and finite resources for satisfying those needs.

3 The main point is that the total opportunity cost of travel includes the best alternative value of travel time as well as the train or air fare. The total costs of train and air travel for Ashley, Doug, and Mei-Lin are calculated in Table 1.2.

TABLE **1.2**

Traveller	Train	Plane
Ashley		
(a) Fare	$ 60	$100
(b) Opportunity cost of travel time at $5/hr	$ 25	$ 5
Total cost	**$ 85**	**$105**
Doug		
(a) Fare	$ 60	$100
(b) Opportunity cost of travel time at $10/hr	$ 50	$ 10
Total cost	**$110**	**$110**
Mei-Lin		
(a) Fare	$ 60	$100
(b) Opportunity cost of travel time at $12/hr	$ 60	$ 12
Total cost	**$120**	**$112**

On the basis of the cost calculation in Table 1.2, Ashley should take the train, Mei-Lin should take the plane, and Doug could take either.

4 a Even though medical care may be offered without charge ("free"), there are still opportunity costs. The opportunity cost of providing such health care is the highest-valued alternative use of the resources used in the construction of the hospital, and the highest-valued alternative use of the resources (including human resources) used in the operation of the hospital.

b These resources are no longer available for other activities and therefore represent a cost to society.

ⓒ **5 a** If Branko rides as long as total benefit is greater than total cost, he will take 3 rides.

Total benefit (cost) can be calculated by adding up the marginal benefit (cost) of all rides taken. Before taking any rides, his total benefit is zero and his total cost is zero. The first ride's marginal benefit is $10, which when added to 0 yields a total benefit of $10. The first ride's marginal cost is $5, which when added to zero yields a total cost of $5. Total cost is greater than total benefit, so Branko takes the first ride. For the first and second rides together, total benefit is $17, which is greater than total cost of $10. For all 3 rides together, total benefit is $21, which is greater than total cost of $15.

b If Branko compares the marginal benefit of each ride with its marginal cost, he will only take 2 rides. He will take the first ride because its marginal benefit ($10) is greater than its marginal cost ($5). After the first ride, he will still choose to take the second ride because its marginal benefit ($7) is greater than its marginal cost ($5). But he will quit after the second ride. The third ride would add a benefit of $4, but it costs $5, so Branko would be worse off by taking the third ride.

c The marginal rule for choosing will make Branko better off. It would be a mistake to pay $5 for the third ride when it is only worth $4 to Branko. He would be better off taking that final $5 and spending it on something (the roller coaster?) that gives him a benefit worth at least $5.

You will learn much more about applying marginal analysis to choices like Branko's in Chapters 2 and 5.

6 If the price of a bumper car rises to $8, Branko now takes only 1 ride. He will take the first ride because its marginal benefit ($10) is greater than its marginal cost ($8). After the first ride, he will quit. The marginal benefit of the second ride ($7) is now less than its marginal cost ($8).

7 a The given statement is normative. The following is positive: If the government reduces the size of the deficit, interest rates will fall.

b The given statement is positive. The following is normative: The government ought to impose a tax on tobacco products.

8 The paradox is an example of the fallacy of composition—the (false) statement that what is true of the parts is true of the whole. We cannot always generalize from the parts to the whole, and the prediction that bumper crops cause rising incomes for all farmers is a false generalization from the parts to the whole.

9 a The prediction of the model can be tested by conducting the following controlled experiment and carefully observing the outcome. Select a number of plots of ground of the same size that have similar characteristics and are subject to the same amount of water and sunlight. Plant equal quantities of seeds in all the plots. In some of the plots apply no fertilizer and in some of the plots apply (perhaps varying amounts of) fertilizer. When the plants have grown, measure the growth of the plants and compare the growth of the fertilized plots and the unfertilized plots. If plant growth is greater in fertilized plots, we provisionally accept the model and the theory on which it is based. If plant growth is not greater in fertilized plots, we discard the theory (model), or modify its assumptions. Perhaps the effective use of fertilizer requires more water.

Then construct a new model that predicts that, given more water (and the same amount of sunlight), fertilized plants will grow larger than equivalently watered unfertilized plants. Test that model and continue modifying assumptions until predictions are consistent with the facts.

b Economists cannot easily perform such controlled experiments and instead must change one assumption at a time in alternative models and compare the results. Then differences in outcomes can only be tested against variations in data that occur naturally in the economy. This is a more difficult and less precise model-building and testing procedure than exists for the controlled fertilizer experiment.

10 A brief answer to your friend's challenge appears in Helpful Hint **3**. Models are like maps, which are useful precisely because they abstract from real-world detail. A useful map offers a simplified view, which is carefully selected according to the purpose of the map. No mapmaker would claim that the world is as simple as her map, and economists do not claim that the real economy is as simple as their models. What economists claim is that their models isolate the simplified effect of some real forces (like optimizing behaviour) operating in the economy, and yield predictions that can be tested against real-world data.

Another way to answer your friend would be to challenge him to identify what a more realistic model or theory would look like. You would do well to quote Milton Friedman (a Nobel Prize winner in economics) on this topic: "A theory or its 'assumptions' cannot possibly be thoroughly 'realistic' in the immediate descriptive sense. … A completely 'realistic' theory of the wheat market would have to include not only the conditions directly underlying the supply and demand for wheat but also the kind of coins or credit instruments used to make exchanges; the personal characteristics of wheat-traders such as the color of each trader's hair and eyes, … the number of members of his family, their characteristics, … the kind of soil on which the wheat was grown, … the weather prevailing during the growing season; … and so on indefinitely. Any attempt to move very far in achieving this kind of 'realism' is certain to render a theory utterly useless." From Milton Friedman, "The Methodology of Positive Economics," in *Essays in Positive Economics* (Chicago: University of Chicago Press, 1953), p. 32.

Chapter 1 Appendix: Graphs in Economics

KEY CONCEPTS

Graphing Data

Graphs represent quantity as a distance. On a two-dimensional graph,

- ♦ horizontal line is *x-axis*.
- ♦ vertical line is *y-axis*.
- ♦ intersection (0) is the *origin*.

Main types of economic graphs:

- ♦ **Time-series graph**—shows relationship between time (measured on *x*-axis) and other variable(s) (measured on *y*-axis). Reveals variable's level, direction of change, speed of change, and **trend** (general tendency to rise or fall).
- ♦ **Cross-section graph**—shows level of a variable across different groups at a point in time.
- ♦ **Scatter diagram**—shows relationship between two variables, one measured on *x*-axis, the other measured on *y*-axis. Correlation between variables does not necessarily imply causation.

Misleading graphs often break the axes or stretch/compress measurement scales to exaggerate or understate variation. Always look closely at the values and labels on axes before interpreting a graph.

Graphs Used in Economic Models

Graphs showing relationships between variables fall into four categories:

- ♦ **Positive (direct) relationship**—variables move together in same direction: upward-sloping.
- ♦ **Negative (inverse) relationship**—variables move in opposite directions: downward-sloping.
- ♦ Relationships with a maximum/minimum:
  - Relationship slopes upward, reaches a maximum (zero slope), and then slopes downward.
  - Relationship slopes downward, reaches a minimum (zero slope), and then slopes upward.
- ♦ Unrelated (independent) variables—one variable changes while the other remains constant; graph is vertical or horizontal straight line.

The Slope of a Relationship

Slope of a relationship is change in value of variable on *y*-axis divided by change in value of variable on *x*-axis.

- ♦ Δ means "change in."
- ♦ Formula for slope is $\Delta y/\Delta x$ = rise/run.
- ♦ Straight line (**linear relationship**) has constant slope.
  - A positive, upward-sloping relationship has a positive slope.
  - A negative, downward-sloping relationship has a negative slope.
- ♦ Curved line has varying slope, which can be calculated
  - *at a point*—by drawing straight line tangent to the curve at that point and calculating slope of the line.
  - *across an arc*—by drawing straight line across two points on the curve and calculating slope of the line.

Graphing Relationships Among More Than Two Variables

Relationships among more than two variables can be graphed by holding constant the values of all variables except two. This is done by making a *ceteris paribus* assumption—"other things remain the same."

HELPFUL HINTS

1 Throughout the text, relationships among economic variables will almost invariably be represented and analyzed graphically. An early, complete understanding of graphs will greatly facilitate your mastery of the economic analysis of later chapters. Avoid the common mistake of assuming that a superficial understanding of graphs will be sufficient.

2 If you have limited experience with graphical analysis, this appendix is crucial to your ability to understand later economic analysis. You will likely find significant rewards in occasionally returning to this appendix for review. If you are experienced in constructing and using graphs, this appendix may be "old hat." Even so, you should skim it and work through the Self-Test in this *Study Guide*.

3 Slope is a *linear* concept since it is a property of a straight line. For this reason, the slope is constant along a straight line but is different at different points on a curved (nonlinear) line. For the slope of a curved line, we actually calculate the slope of a straight line. The text presents two alternatives for calculating the slope of a curved line: (1) slope at a point and (2) slope across an arc. The first of these calculates the slope of the *straight line* that just touches (is tangent to) the curve at a point. The second calculates the slope of the *straight line* formed by the arc between two points on the curved line.

4 A straight line on a graph can also be described by a simple equation (see Text Mathematical Note, pages 28–29). The general form for the equation of a straight line is

$$y = a + bx$$

If you are given such an equation, you can graph the line by finding the y-intercept (where the line intersects the vertical y-axis), finding the x-intercept (where the line intersects the horizontal x-axis), and then connecting those two points with a straight line:

To find the y-intercept, set $x = 0$.

$$y = a + b(0)$$
$$y = a$$

To find the x-intercept, set $y = 0$.

$$0 = a + bx$$
$$x = -a/b$$

Connecting these two points (($x = 0, y = a$) and ($x = -a/b, y = 0$)) or $(0, a)$ and $(-a/b, 0)$ allows you to graph the straight line. For any straight line with the equation of the form $y = a + bx$, the slope of the line is b. Figure A1.1 illustrates a line where b is a *negative* number, so there is a *negative* relationship between the variables x and y.

FIGURE A1.1

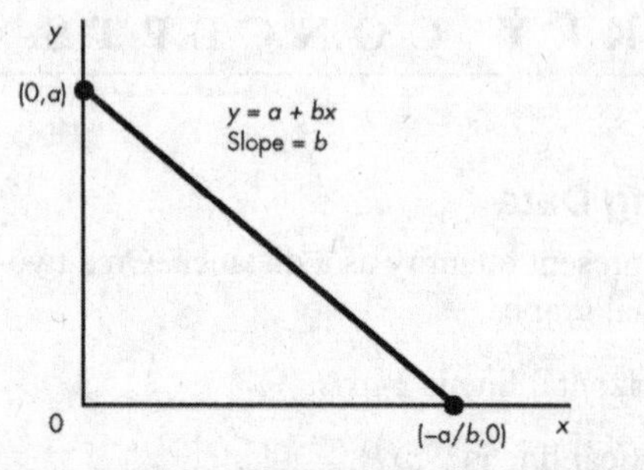

To see how to apply this general equation, consider this example:

$$y = 6 - 2x$$

To find the y-intercept, set $x = 0$.

$$y = 6 - 2(0)$$
$$y = 6$$

To find the x-intercept, set $y = 0$.

$$0 = 6 - 2x$$
$$x = 3$$

Connecting these two points, (0, 6) and (3, 0), yields the line in Figure A1.2.

FIGURE A1.2

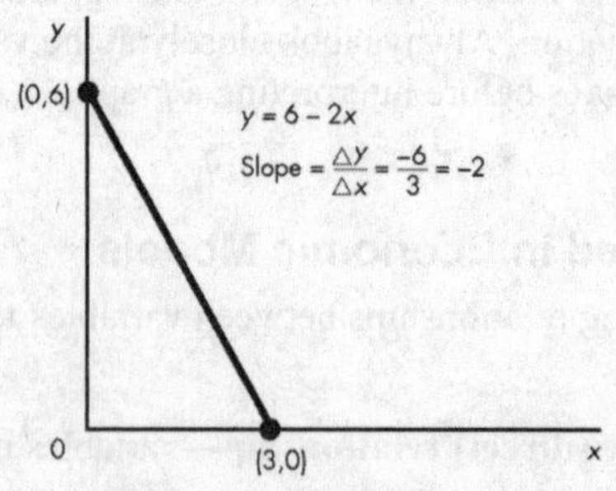

The slope of this line is –2. Since the slope is negative, there is a negative relationship between the variables x and y.

SELF-TEST

True/False and Explain

Graphing Data

1 A time-series graph shows the level of a variable across different groups at a point in time.

2 A graph with a break in the axes must be misleading.

3 If a scatter diagram shows a clear relationship between variables *x* and *y*, then *x* must cause *y*.

Graphs Used in Economic Models

4 If the graph of the relationship between two variables slopes upward (to the right), the graph has a positive slope.

5 The graph of the relationship between two variables that are in fact unrelated is always vertical.

6 In Figure A1.3, the relationship between *y* and *x* is first negative, reaches a minimum, and then becomes positive as *x* increases.

FIGURE **A1.3**

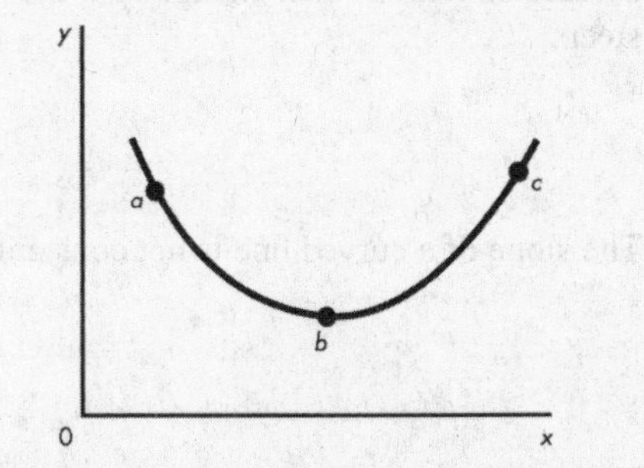

7 In Figure A1.3, the value of *x* is a minimum at point *b*.

The Slope of a Relationship

8 In Figure A1.3, the slope of the curve is increasing as we move from point *b* to point *c*.

9 In Figure A1.3, the slope of the curve is approaching zero as we move from point *a* to point *b*.

10 The slope of a straight line is calculated by dividing the change in the value of the variable measured on the horizontal axis by the change in the value of the variable measured on the vertical axis.

11 For a straight line, if a small change in *y* is associated with a large change in *x*, the slope is large.

12 For a straight line, if a large change in y is associated with a small change in x, the line is steep.

13 The slope of a curved line is not constant.

Graphing Relationships Among More Than Two Variables

14 *Ceteris paribus* means "other things change."

15 Relationships between three variables can be displayed on a two-dimensional graph.

Multiple-Choice

Graphing Data

1 Figure A1.4 is a time-series graph. The horizontal axis measures _________ and the vertical axis measures _________.

a time; the variable of interest
b time; slope
c the variable of interest in one year; the variable of interest in another year
d the variable of interest; time
e slope; time

FIGURE A1.4

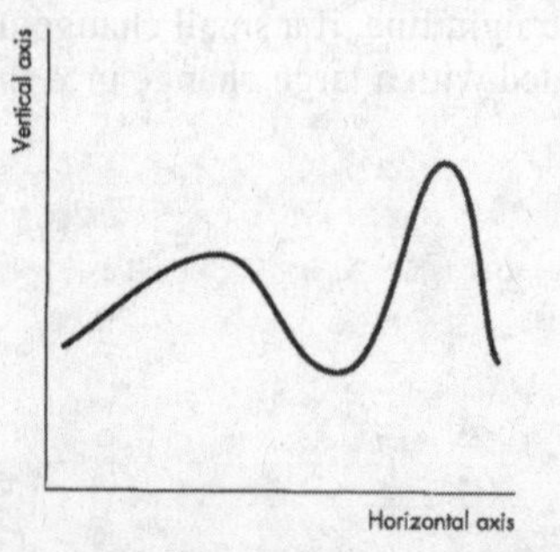

2 The tendency for a variable to rise or fall over time is called its

a slope.
b trend.
c y-coordinate.
d level.
e correlation.

3 Which type of graph can mislead?

a Time-series graphs only
b Cross-section graphs only
c Scatter diagrams only
d Graphs with correlations between variables only
e Any of the above

Graphs Used in Economic Models

4 From the data in Table A1.1, it appears that

a x and y have a negative relationship.
b x and y have a positive relationship.
c there is no relationship between x and y.
d there is first a negative and then a positive relationship between x and y.
e there is first a positive and then a negative relationship between x and y.

TABLE A1.1

Year	x	y
2004	6.2	143
2005	5.7	156
2006	5.3	162

5 If variables x and y move up and down together, they are said to be

a positively related.
b negatively related.
c conversely related.
d unrelated.
e trendy.

6 The relationship between two variables that move in opposite directions is shown graphically by a line that is

a positively sloped.
b relatively steep.
c relatively flat.
d negatively sloped.
e curved.

The Slope of a Relationship

7 In Figure A1.5 the relationship between x and y as x increases is
  a positive with slope decreasing.
  b negative with slope decreasing.
  c negative with slope increasing.
  d positive with slope increasing.
  e positive with slope first increasing then decreasing.

FIGURE **A1.5**

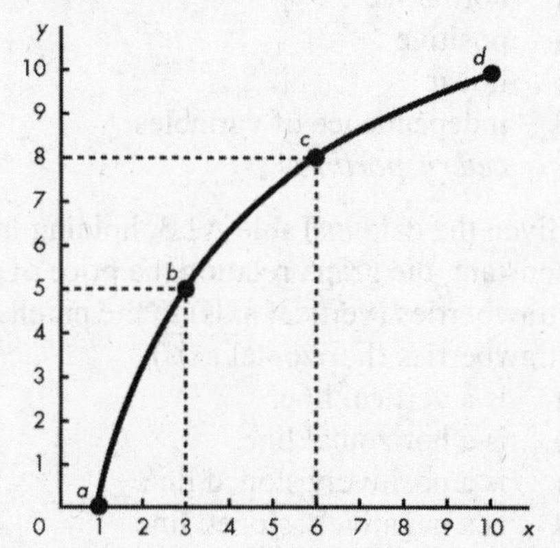

8 What is the slope across the arc between b and c in Figure A1.5?
  a 1/2
  b 2/3
  c 1
  d 2
  e 3

9 In Figure A1.5, consider the slopes of arc ab and arc bc. The slope at point b is difficult to determine exactly, but it must be
  a greater than 5/2.
  b about 5/2.
  c between 5/2 and 1.
  d about 1.
  e less than 1.

10 In Table A1.2, suppose that w is the independent variable measured along the horizontal axis. The slope of the line relating w and u is
  a positive with a decreasing slope.
  b negative with a decreasing slope.
  c positive with an increasing slope.
  d negative with a constant slope.
  e positive with a constant slope.

TABLE **A1.2**

w	2	4	6	8	10
u	15	12	9	6	3

11 Refer to Table A1.2. Suppose that w is the independent variable measured along the horizontal axis. The slope of the line relating w and u is
  a +3.
  b –3.
  c –2/3.
  d +3/2.
  e –3/2.

12 In Figure A1.6, if household income increases by $1,000, household expenditure will
  a increase by $1,333.
  b decrease by $1,333.
  c remain unchanged.
  d increase by $1,000.
  e increase by $750.

FIGURE **A1.6**

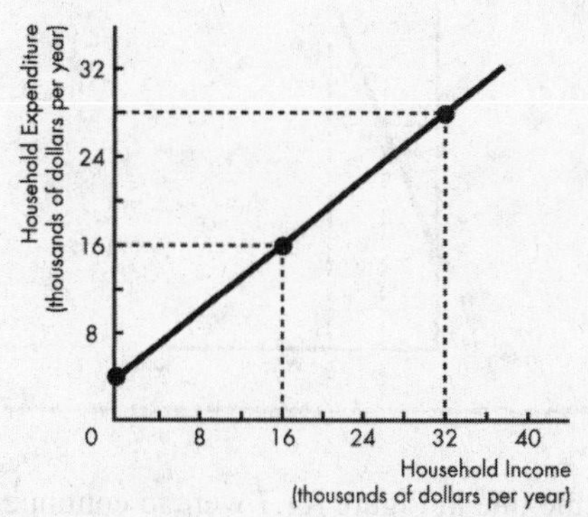

13 In Figure A1.6, if household income is zero, household expenditure is
  a 0.
  b –$4,000.
  c $4,000.
  d $8,000.
  e impossible to determine from the graph.

14 In Figure A1.6, if household expenditure is \$28,000, household income is
- **a** \$36,000.
- **b** \$32,000.
- **c** \$28,000.
- **d** \$25,000.
- **e** none of the above.

15 At all points along a straight line, slope is
- **a** positive.
- **b** negative.
- **c** constant.
- **d** zero.
- **e** none of the above.

16 What is the slope of the line in Figure A1.7?
- **a** 2
- **b** 1/2
- **c** 3
- **d** 1/3
- **e** –3

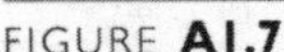

FIGURE **A1.7**

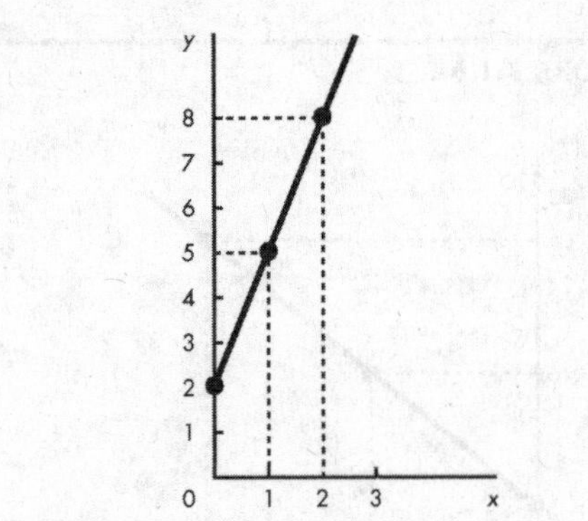

17 If the line in Figure A1.7 were to continue down to the x-axis, what would the value of x be when y is zero?
- **a** 0
- **b** 2
- **c** 2/3
- **d** –2/3
- **e** –3/2

18 If the equation of a straight line is $y = 6 + 3x$, the slope is
- **a** –3 and the y-intercept is 6.
- **b** –3 and the y-intercept is –2.
- **c** 3 and the y-intercept is 6.
- **d** 3 and the y-intercept is –2.
- **e** 3 and the y-intercept is –6.

19 If the equation of a straight line is $y = 8 - 2x$, then the slope is
- **a** –2 and the x-intercept is –4.
- **b** –2 and the x-intercept is 4.
- **c** –2 and the x-intercept is 8.
- **d** 2 and the x-intercept is –4.
- **e** 2 and the x-intercept is 4.

Graphing Relationships Among More Than Two Variables

20 To graph a relationship among more than two variables, what kind of assumption is necessary?
- **a** normative
- **b** positive
- **c** linear
- **d** independence of variables
- **e** *ceteris paribus*

21 Given the data in Table A1.3, holding income constant, the graph relating the price of strawberries (vertical axis) to the purchases of strawberries (horizontal axis)
- **a** is a vertical line.
- **b** is a horizontal line.
- **c** is a positively sloped line.
- **d** is a negatively sloped line.
- **e** reaches a minimum.

TABLE **A1.3**

Weekly Family Income (\$)	Price per Box of Strawberries (\$)	Number of Boxes Purchased per Week
300	\$1.00	5
300	\$1.25	3
300	\$1.50	2
400	\$1.00	7
400	\$1.25	5
400	\$1.50	4

22 Given the data in Table A1.3, suppose family income decreases from \$400 to \$300 per week. Then the graph relating the price of strawberries (vertical axis) to the purchases of strawberries (horizontal axis) will
- **a** become negatively sloped.
- **b** become positively sloped.
- **c** shift rightward.
- **d** shift leftward.
- **e** no longer exist.

23 Given the data in Table A1.3, holding price constant, the graph relating family income (vertical axis) to the purchases of strawberries (horizontal axis) is a

- **a** vertical line.
- **b** horizontal line.
- **c** positively sloped line.
- **d** negatively sloped line.
- **e** positively or negatively sloped line, depending on the price that is held constant.

24 In Figure A1.8, x is

- **a** positively related to y and negatively related to z.
- **b** positively related to both y and z.
- **c** negatively related to y and positively related to z.
- **d** negatively related to both y and z.
- **e** greater than z.

FIGURE **A1.8**

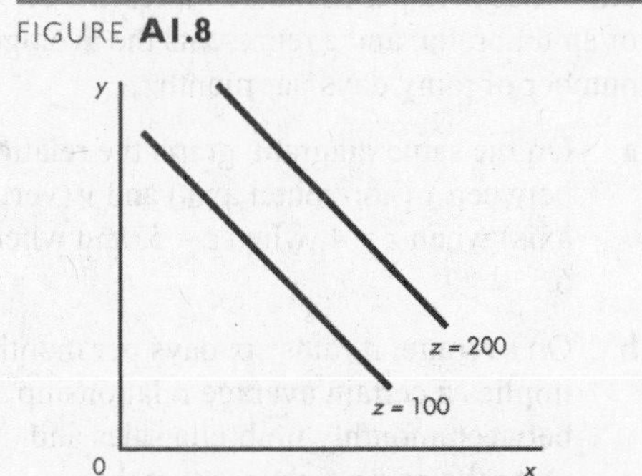

25 In Figure A1.8, a decrease in the value of z will cause, *ceteris paribus*,

- **a** a decrease in the value of x.
- **b** an increase in the value of x.
- **c** an increase in the value of y.
- **d** no change in the value of y.
- **e** no change in the value of x.

Short Answer Problems

1 Consider the data in Table A1.4.

- **a** Draw a time-series graph for the interest rate.
- **b** Draw a time-series graph for the inflation rate.
- **c** Draw a scatter diagram for the inflation rate (horizontal axis) and the interest rate (vertical axis).
- **d** Would you describe the general relationship between the inflation rate and the interest rate as positive, negative, or unrelated?

TABLE **A1.4**

Year	Inflation Rate (%)	Interest Rate (%)
1970	5.4	6.4
1971	3.2	4.3
1972	3.4	4.1
1973	8.3	7.0
1974	11.8	7.9
1975	6.7	5.8
1976	4.9	5.0
1977	6.5	5.3
1978	8.6	7.2
1979	12.3	10.0

2 Draw a graph of variables x and y that illustrates each of the following relationships:

- **a** x and y move up and down together.
- **b** x and y move in opposite directions.
- **c** as x increases y reaches a maximum.
- **d** as x increases y reaches a minimum.
- **e** x and y move in opposite directions, but as x increases y decreases by larger and larger increments for each unit increase in x.
- **f** y is unrelated to the value of x.
- **g** x is unrelated to the value of y.

3 What does it mean to say that the slope of a line is –2/3?

4 Compute the slopes of the lines in Figure A1.9(a) and (b).

FIGURE **A1.9**

(a)

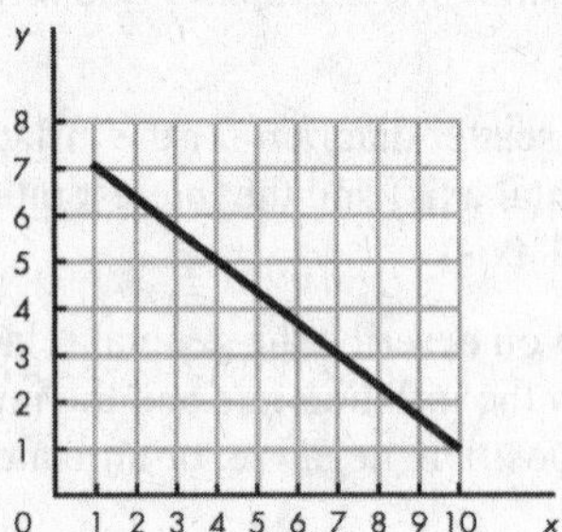

(b)

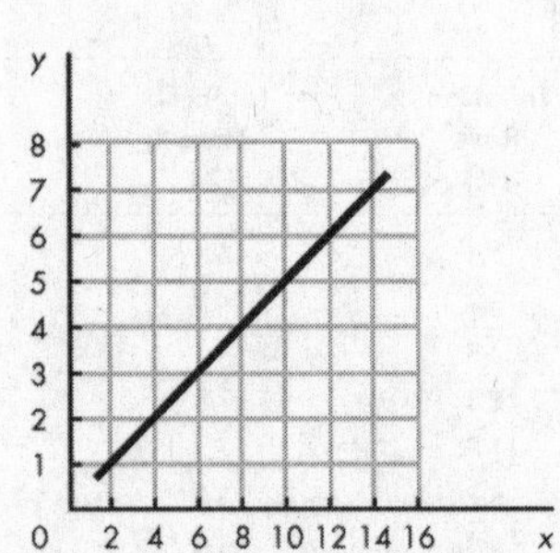

5 Draw each of the following:

a a straight line with slope –10 and passing through the point (2, 80).

b a straight line with slope 2 and passing through the point (6, 10).

6 The equation for a straight line is $y = 4 - 2x$.

a Calculate the y-intercept; the x-intercept; the slope.

b Draw the graph of the line.

7 Explain two ways to measure the slope of a curved line.

8 Use the graph in Figure A1.10 to compute the slope

a across the arc between points *a* and *b*.

b at point *b*.

c at point *c*, and explain your answer.

FIGURE **A1.10**

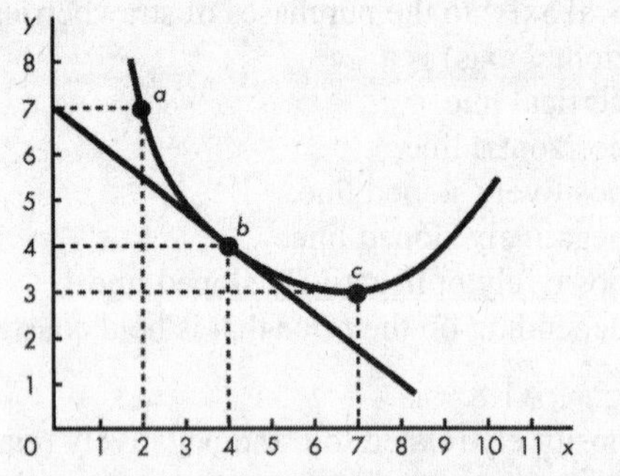

9 How do we graph a relationship among more than two variables using a two-dimensional graph?

10 In Table A1.5, x represents the number of umbrellas sold per month, y represents the price of an umbrella, and z represents the average number of rainy days per month.

a On the same diagram, graph the relationship between x (horizontal axis) and y (vertical axis) when $z = 4$, when $z = 5$, and when $z = 6$.

b On average, it rains six days per month. This implies a certain average relationship between monthly umbrella sales and umbrella price. Suppose that the "greenhouse effect" reduces the average monthly rainfall to four days per month. What happens to the graph of the relationship between umbrella sales and umbrella prices?

c On a diagram, graph the relationship between x (horizontal axis) and z (vertical axis) when $y = \$10$ and when $y = \$12$. Is the relationship between x and z positive or negative?

d On a diagram, graph the relationship between y (horizontal axis) and z (vertical axis) when $x = 120$ and when $x = 140$. Is the relationship between y and z positive or negative?

TABLE **A1.5**

Umbrellas Sold per Month (x)	Price per Umbrella (y)	Average Number of Rainy Days per Month (z)
120	$10	4
140	$10	5
160	$10	6
100	$12	4
120	$12	5
140	$12	6
80	$14	4
100	$14	5
120	$14	6

ANSWERS

True/False and Explain

1 F Definition of a cross-section graph. Time-series graph shows relationship between time (on *x*-axis) and other variable(s) (on *y*-axis). (18)

2 F Breaks in the axes may be misleading, or may bring information into clearer view. (20)

3 F *x* and *y* are correlated, but correlation does not guarantee causation. (20)

4 T Upward-sloping curves/lines have positive slopes. (20–21)

5 F Graph of unrelated variables may be vertical or horizontal. (23)

6 T Arc *ab* would have negative slope, arc *bc* positive slope. (22–26)

7 F Value of *y* is minimum at point *b*. (22–23)

8 T Curve becomes steeper, meaning Δy increasing faster than Δx, so slope increasing. (24–26)

9 T At *b*, tangent has slope = 0, since $\Delta y = 0$ along horizontal line through *b*. (24–26)

10 F Slope = (Δ variable on vertical (*y*) axis)/(Δ variable on horizontal (*x*) axis). (24–25)

11 F Large slope means large Δy associated with small Δx. (24–25)

12 T Steep line has large slope, meaning large Δy associated with small Δx. (24–25)

13 T Slope of straight line is constant. (24–25)

14 F "Other things remain the same." Only variables being studied are allowed to change. (26)

15 T See Text Figure A1.12. A *ceteris paribus* assumption holds one variable constant, allowing other two variables to be plotted in two dimensions. (26–27)

Multiple-Choice

1 a Time is measured on the *x*-axis and the variable in which we are interested on the *y*-axis. (18)

2 b Definition. (18)

3 e Any type of graph can mislead with breaks in the axes or stretched/compressed measurement scales. (20)

4 a Higher values *x* (6.2) associated with lower values *y* (143). (20–22)

5 a Definition. (20–22)

6 d Graph may be steep, flat, or curved, but must have negative slope. (21–22)

7 a Slope of arc *ab* = +2.5. Slope of arc *bc* = +1. (24–26)

8 c $\Delta y = 3(8 - 5)$; $\Delta x = 3(6 - 3)$. (25–26)

9 c 5/2 is slope of *ab*, while 1 is slope of *bc*. (25–26)

10 d As *w* increases, *u* decreases. $\Delta u/\Delta w$ is constant. (24–26)

11 e Between any two points, $\Delta u = 3$, $\Delta w = -2$. (24–26)

12 e Slope ($\Delta y/\Delta x$) = 3/4. If Δx (Δ household income) = $1,000, then Δy (Δ household expenditure) = $750 = ¾ of $1,000. (24–26)

13 c Where the line intersects the household expenditure (*y*) axis. (24–26)

14 b From $28,000 on vertical (expenditure) axis, move across to line, then down to $32,000 on horizontal (income) axis. (24–26)

15 c Along straight line, slope may or may not be **a**, **b**, or **d**. (24–25)

16 c Between any two points, $\Delta y = 3$ and $\Delta x = 1$. (24–25)

17 d Equation of line is $y = 2 + 3x$. Solve for x-intercept (set $y = 0$). (24–26, 28–29)

18 c Use formula $y = a + bx$. Slope = b, y-intercept = a. (24–26, 28–29)

19 b Use formula $y = a + bx$. Slope = b, x-intercept = $-a/b$. (24–26, 28–29)

20 e Must hold constant other variables to isolate relationship between two variables. (26–27)

21 d Look either at data in top 3 rows (income = 300) or data in bottom 3 rows (income = 400). Higher price associated with lower purchases. (26–27)

22 d At each price, fewer boxes will be purchased. (26–27)

23 c For $P = 1$, two points on line are (5 boxes, \$300) and (7 boxes, \$400). Same relationship for other prices. (26–27)

24 c Increased y causes decreased x holding z constant. Increased z causes increased x holding y constant. (26–27)

25 a Decreased z causes decreased x holding y constant. Decreased z causes decreased y holding x constant. (26–27)

Short Answer Problems

1 a A time-series graph for the interest rate is given in Figure A1.11(a).

b A time-series graph for the inflation rate is given in Figure A1.11(b).

c The scatter diagram for the inflation rate and the interest rate is given in Figure A1.11(c).

d From the graph in Figure A1.11(c), we see that the relationship between the inflation rate and the interest rate is generally positive (upward-sloping).

FIGURE **A1.11**

(a)

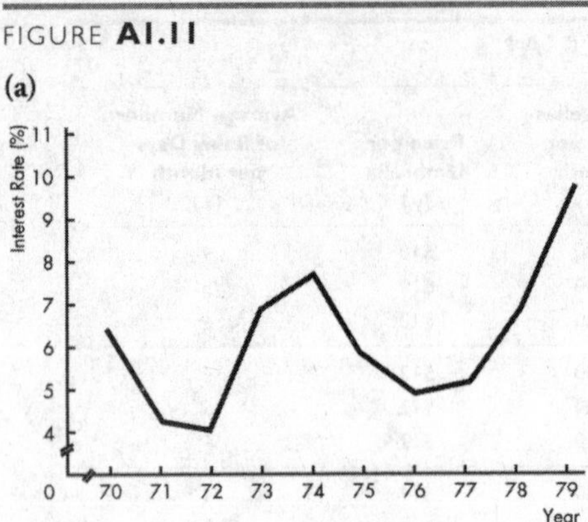

(b)

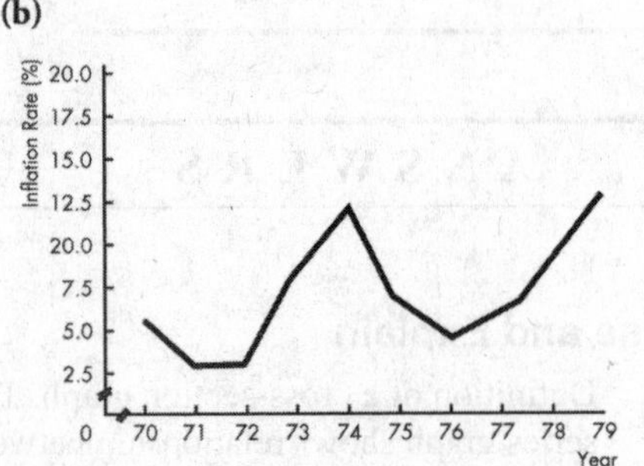

(c)

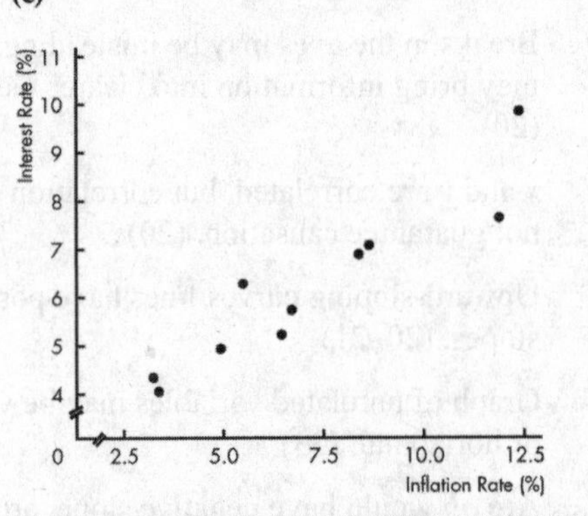

2 Figures A1.12(a) through (g) illustrate the desired graphs.

FIGURE **A1.12**

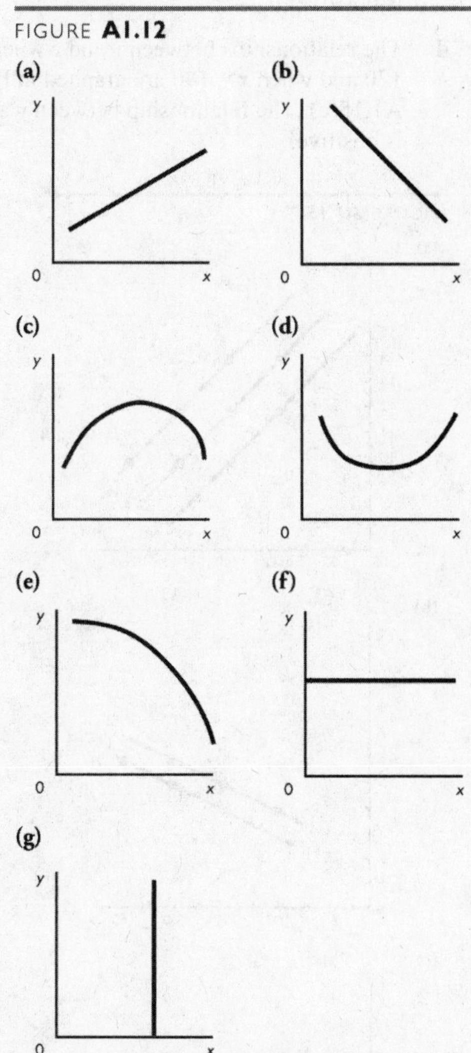

3 The negative sign in the slope of –2/3 means that there is a negative relationship between the two variables. The value of 2/3 means that when the variable measured on the vertical axis decreases by 2 units (the rise or Δy), the variable measured on the horizontal axis increases by 3 units (the run or Δx).

4 To find the slope, pick any two points on a line and compute $\Delta y/\Delta x$. The slope of the line in Figure A1.9(a) is –2/3, and the slope of the line in Figure A1.9(b) is 1/2.

5 a The requested straight line is graphed in Figure A1.13(a). First plot the point (2, 80). Then pick a second point whose y-coordinate decreases by 10 for every 1 unit increase in the x-coordinate, for example, (5, 50). The slope between the two points is –30/3 = –10.

b The requested straight line is graphed in Figure A1.13(b). First plot the point (6, 10). Then pick a second point whose y-coordinate decreases by 2 for every 1 unit decrease in the x-coordinate, for example, (5, 8). The slope between the two points is –2/–1 = 2.

FIGURE **A1.13**

(a)

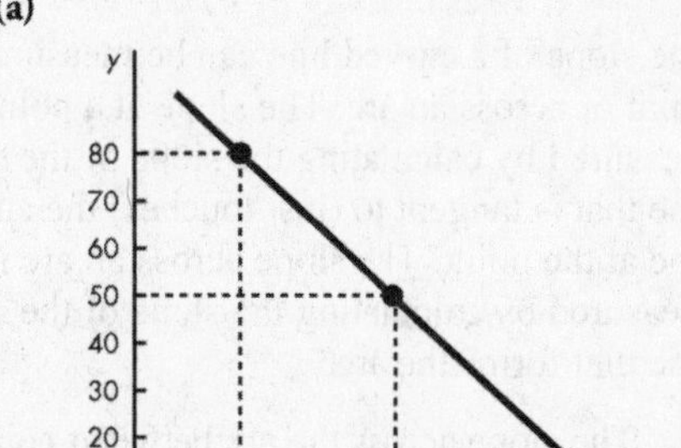

(b)

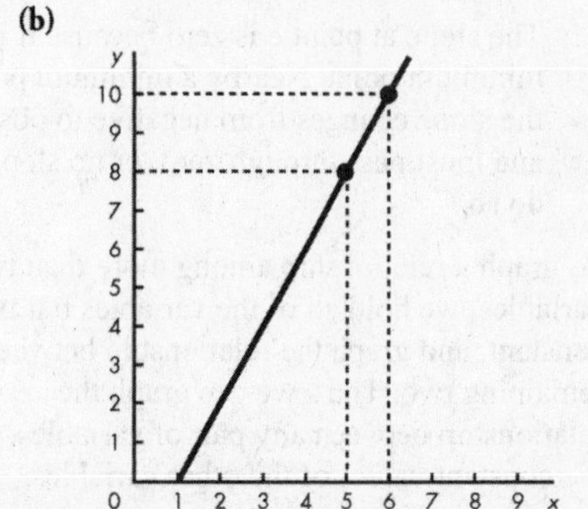

6 a To find the y-intercept, set $x = 0$.

$$y = 4 - 2(0)$$

$$y = 4$$

To find the x-intercept, set $y = 0$.

$$0 = 4 - 2x$$

$$x = 2$$

The slope of the line is –2, the value of the "b" coefficient on x.

b The graph of the line is shown in Figure A1.14.

FIGURE **A1.14**

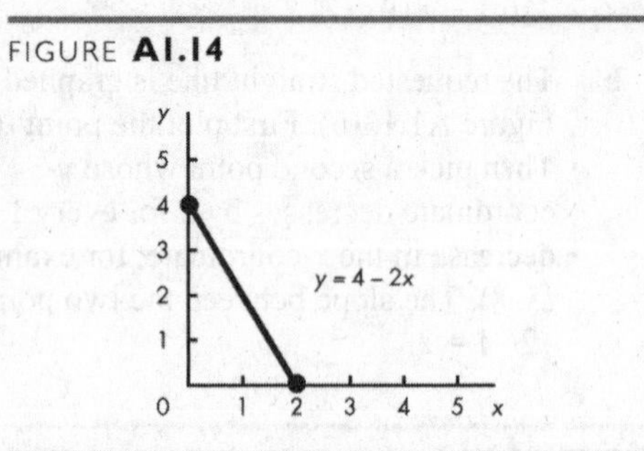

7 The slope of a curved line can be measured at a point or across an arc. The slope at a point is measured by calculating the slope of the straight line that is tangent to (just touches) the curved line at the point. The slope across an arc is measured by calculating the slope of the straight line that forms the arc.

8 a The slope across the arc between points *a* and *b* is –3/2.

b The slope at point *b* is –3/4.

c The slope at point *c* is zero because it is a minimum point. Nearby a minimum point the slope changes from negative to positive and must pass through zero, or no slope, to do so.

9 To graph a relationship among more than two variables, we hold all of the variables but two constant, and graph the relationship between the remaining two. Thus, we can graph the relationship between any pair of variables, given the constant values of the other variables.

10 a The relationships between *x* and *y* for $z = 4$, 5, and 6 are graphed in Figure A1.15(a).

b If the average monthly rainfall drops from 6 days to 4 days, the curve representing the relationship between umbrella sales and umbrella prices will shift from the curve labelled $z = 6$ to $z = 4$.

c The relationships between *x* and *z* when *y* is $10 and when *y* is $12 are graphed in Figure A1.15(b). The relationship between *x* and *z* is positive.

d The relationships between *y* and *z* when $x = 120$ and when $x = 140$ are graphed in Figure A1.15(c). The relationship between *y* and *z* is positive.

FIGURE **A1.15**

(a)

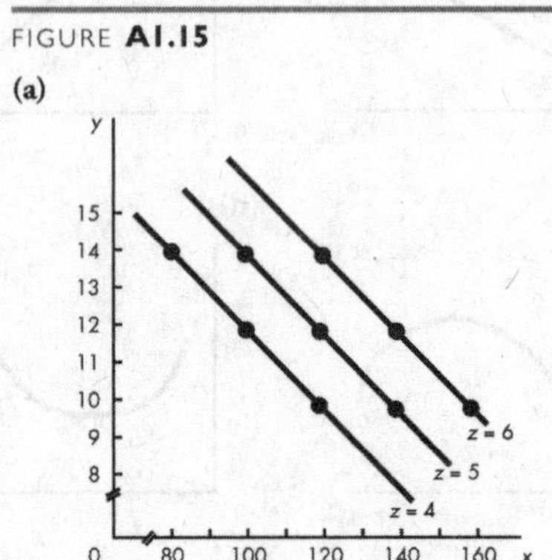

(b)

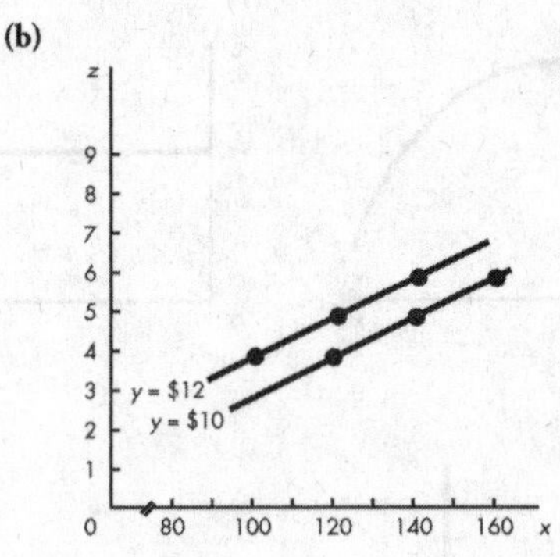

(c)

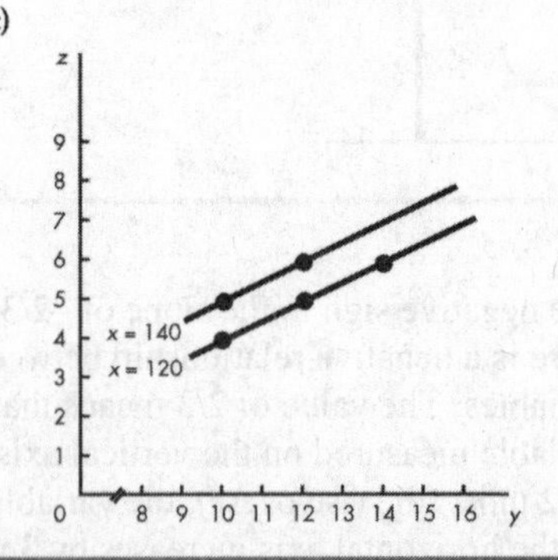

Chapter 2 The Economic Problem

KEY CONCEPTS

Production Possibilities and Opportunity Cost

The production possibility frontier (*PPF*)

- ♦ is the boundary between unattainable and attainable production possibilities.
- ♦ shows maximum combinations of outputs (goods and services) that can be produced with given resources and technology.

PPF characteristics:

- ♦ points on *PPF* represent **production efficiency**—more of one good cannot be produced without producing less of another good.
- ♦ points inside *PPF* are inefficient—attainable, but not maximum combinations of outputs; they represent unused or misallocated resources.
- ♦ points on *PPF* are preferred to points inside *PPF*.
- ♦ points outside *PPF* are unattainable.
- ♦ choosing among efficient points on *PPF* involves an *opportunity cost* and a *tradeoff*.

*PPF*s are generally bowed outward (concave), reflecting increasing opportunity costs as more of a good is produced.

- ♦ *PPF* is bowed outward because resources are not equally productive in all activities (nonhomogeneous). Resources most suitable for a given activity are the first to be used.
- ♦ Bowed-out-shaped *PPF* represents increasing opportunity cost—opportunity cost of good increases as its quantity produced increases.
- ♦ In moving between two points on *PPF* more good *X* can be obtained only by producing less good *Y*.

Opportunity cost on *PPF* of additional *X* is amount of *Y* forgone.

- ♦ No opportunity cost in moving from point inside *PPF* to point on *PPF*.

Using Resources Efficiently

To choose among points on *PPF*, compare

- ♦ **marginal cost**—opportunity cost of producing one more unit of a good.
  - marginal cost curve slopes upwards because of *increasing opportunity cost*.
- ♦ **marginal benefit**—benefit (measured in willingness to forgo other goods) from consuming one more unit of a good. Depends on a person's **preferences**—likes and dislikes.
  - **marginal benefit curve** slopes downwards because of *decreasing marginal benefit*.

We choose a point on *PPF* of **allocative efficiency**

- ♦ where we produce the goods and services valued most highly
- ♦ where marginal benefit = marginal cost.

Economic Growth

Economic growth is the expansion of production possibilities—an outward shift of *PPF*.

- ♦ *PPF* shifts from changes in resources or technology.
- ♦ **Capital accumulation** and **technological change** shift *PPF* outward—economic growth.
- ♦ Opportunity cost of increased goods and services in future (economic growth through capital accumulation and technological progress) is decreased consumption today.

Gains from Trade

Production increases if people *specialize* in the activity in which they have a comparative advantage.

- ♦ Person has **comparative advantage** in producing a good if she can produce at lower opportunity cost than anyone else.
- ♦ When each person specializes in producing a good at which she has comparative advantage and exchanges for other goods, there are gains from trade.
- ♦ Specialization and exchange allow consumption (not production) at points outside *PPF*.
- ♦ Person has **absolute advantage** in producing a good if, using the same quantity of resources, she can produce more than anyone else.
  - Absolute advantage is irrelevant for specialization and gains from trade.
  - Even a person with an absolute advantage in producing all goods gains by specializing in activity in which she has a comparative advantage and trading.
- ♦ **Dynamic comparative advantage** results from specializing in an activity, **learning-by-doing**, and over time becoming the producer with the lowest opportunity cost.

Economic Coordination

Gains from trade and specialization require coordination. Decentralized coordination through markets depends on the social institutions of

- ♦ **firms**—hire and organize factors of production to produce and sell goods and services. Firms coordinate much economic activity, but the efficient size of a firm is limited.
- ♦ **property rights**—governing ownership, use, and disposal of resources, goods, and services.
- ♦ **markets**—coordinating buying and selling decisions through price adjustments.
- ♦ **money**—any generally acceptable means of payment; makes trading more efficient.

HELPFUL HINTS

1 This chapter reviews the absolutely critical concept of opportunity cost—the best alternative forgone—that was introduced in Chapter 1. Opportunity cost is a *ratio*. A very helpful formula for opportunity cost, which works well in solving problems, especially problems that involve moving up or down a production possibility frontier (*PPF*), is:

$$\text{Opportunity Cost} = \frac{\text{Give Up}}{\text{Get}}$$

Opportunity cost equals the quantity of goods you must give up divided by the quantity of goods you will get. This formula applies to all *PPF*s, whether they are bowed out as in Text Figure 2.1 or linear as in Text Figure 2.7. To illustrate, look again at the bowed-out *PPF*.

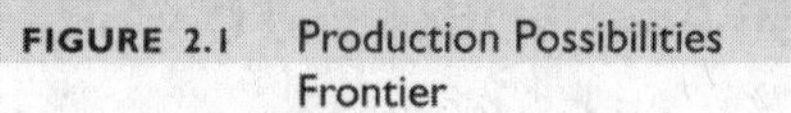

FIGURE 2.1 Production Possibilities Frontier

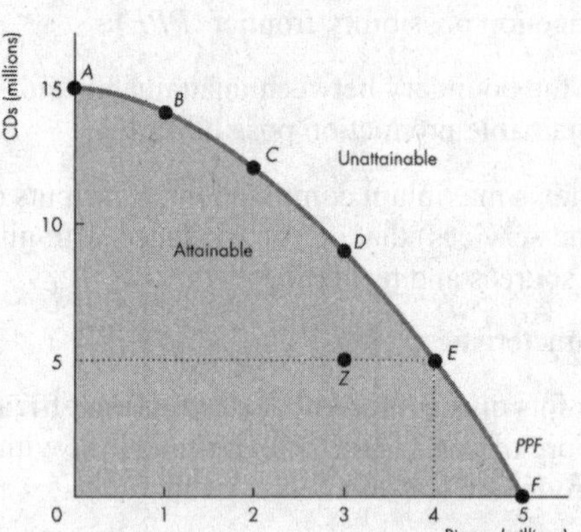

First, consider an example of moving down the *PPF*. In moving from *C* to *D*, what is the opportunity cost of an additional pizza? This economy must give up 3 CDs (12 – 9) to get 1 pizza (3 – 2). Substituting into the formula, the opportunity cost is:

$$\frac{3\text{ CDs}}{1\text{ pizza}} = 3\text{ CDs per pizza}$$

Next, consider an example of moving up the *PPF*. In moving from *D* to *C*, what is the opportunity cost of an additional CD? We must give up 1 pizza (3 – 2) to get 3 CDs (12 – 9). Substituting into the formula, the opportunity cost is:

$$\frac{1\text{ pizza}}{3\text{ CDs}} = \frac{1}{3}\text{ pizza per CD}$$

Opportunity cost is always measured in the units of the forgone good.

2 Opportunity cost can also be related to the slope of the *PPF*. As we move down between any two points on the *PPF*, the opportunity cost of an additional unit of the good on the horizontal axis is:

$$|\text{slope of } PPF|$$

The slope of the *PPF* is negative, but economists like to describe opportunity cost in terms of a positive quantity of forgone goods. Therefore, we must use the absolute value of the slope to calculate the desired positive number.

As we move up between any two points on the *PPF*, the opportunity cost of an additional unit of the good on the vertical axis is:

$$\left|\frac{1}{\text{slope of } PPF}\right|$$

This is the *inverse* relation we saw between possibilities *C* and *D*. The opportunity cost of an additional pizza (on the horizontal axis) between *C* and *D* is 3 CDs. The opportunity cost of an additional CD (on the vertical axis) between *D* and *C* is 1/3 pizza.

3 All points on a *PPF* achieve productive efficiency in that they fully employ all resources. But how do we pick a point on the *PPF* and decide *what* combination of goods we want? The *PPF* provides information about resources and *costs*. But choosing what goods we want also requires information about *benefits*.

This choice, like all economic choices, is made at the margin. To decide what goods we want, compare the marginal cost (*MC*) and marginal benefit (*MB*) of different combinations. Marginal cost is the opportunity cost of producing one more unit. The marginal cost of producing more of any good increases as we move along the *PPF*. Marginal benefit is the benefit received from consuming one more unit. Marginal benefit decreases as we consume more of any good.

If the marginal cost of a good exceeds the marginal benefit, we decrease production of the good. If the marginal benefit exceeds the marginal cost, we increase production. When marginal cost equals marginal benefit for every good, we have chosen the goods that we value most highly. The decision rule of $MB = MC$ yields an *efficient* allocation of resources.

Text Figure 2.4 is crucial for explaining all economic decisions. Make sure you spend time on it even though it may be hard to fully understand. You will understand Text Figure 2.4 better after we spend time in future chapters elaborating the concepts of marginal cost and marginal benefit.

4 The CDs and pizza production possibility frontier assumes that resources are *not* equally productive in all activities. Resources with such differences are also called nonhomogeneous resources. As a result of this assumption, opportunity cost increases as we increase the production of either good. In moving from possibility *C* to *D*, the opportunity cost per unit of pizza is 3 CDs. But in increasing pizza production from *D* to *E*, the opportunity cost per unit of pizza increases to 4 CDs. In producing the first 1 (million) pizzas, we use the resources best suited to pizza production. As we increase pizza production, however, we must use resources that are less well suited to pizza production—hence increasing opportunity cost. A parallel argument accounts for the increasing opportunity cost of increasing CD production.

It is also possible to construct an even simpler model of a *PPF* that assumes resources are equally productive in all activities, or homogeneous resources. As a result of this assumption, opportunity cost is constant as we increase production of either good. Constant opportunity cost means that the *PPF* will be a straight line (rather than bowed out). As you will see in some of the following exercises, such a simple model is useful for illustrating the principle of comparative advantage, without having to deal with the complications of increasing opportunity cost.

5 The text defines absolute advantage as a situation where one person is more productive than another in the producing one or more goods. We can also define *absolute advantage in the production of one good*. In comparing the productivity of two persons, this narrower concept of absolute advantage can be defined in terms of either greater output of the good per unit of resource inputs or fewer resource inputs per unit of output. It is useful to understand these definitions of absolute advantage only to demonstrate that absolute advantage has no role

in explaining specialization and trade. The gains from trade depend only on differing comparative advantages. People have a comparative advantage in producing a good if they can produce it at lower opportunity cost than others.

6 This chapter gives us our first chance to develop and use economic models. It is useful to think about the nature of these models in the context of the general discussion of models in Chapter 1. For example, one model in this chapter is a representation of the production possibilities in the two-person and two-good world of Liz and Joe. The model abstracts greatly from the complexity of the real world in which there are billions of people and numerous different kinds of goods and services. The model allows us to explain a number of phenomena that we observe in the world such as specialization and exchange.

The production possibilities model also has some implications or predictions. For example, countries that devote a larger proportion of their resources to capital accumulation will have more rapidly expanding production possibilities. The model can be subjected to "test" by comparing these predictions to the facts we observe in the real world.

SELF-TEST

True/False and Explain

Production Possibilities and Opportunity Cost

Refer to the production possibility frontier (*PPF*) in Figure 2.2 for Questions **1** to **4**.

FIGURE **2.2**

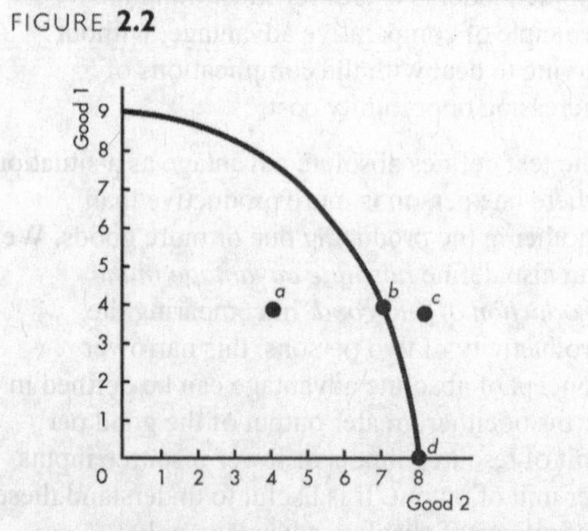

1 Point *a* is not attainable.

2 The opportunity cost of increasing the production of good 2 from 7 to 8 units is 4 units of good 1.

3 Point *c* is not attainable.

4 In moving from point *b* to point *d*, the opportunity cost of increasing the production of good 2 equals the absolute value of the slope of the *PPF* between *b* and *d*.

Using Resources Efficiently

5 The marginal cost of the 4th pizza is the cost of producing all 4 pizzas.

6 The marginal benefit of good *X* is the amount of good *Y* a person is willing to forgo to obtain one more unit of *X*.

7 The principle of decreasing marginal benefit states that the more we have of a good, the *less* we are willing to pay for an additional unit of it.

8 All points on a *PPF* represent both production efficiency and allocative efficiency.

Economic Growth

9 Economic growth, by shifting out the *PPF*, eliminates the problem of scarcity.

10 In a model where capital resources can grow, points on the *PPF* that have more consumption goods yield faster growth.

Gains from Trade

11 With specialization and trade, a country can produce at a point outside its *PPF*.

12 Canada has no incentive to trade with a cheap-labour country like Mexico.

13 Nadim definitely has a comparative advantage in producing skateboards if he can produce more than Elle.

Economic Coordination

14 The incentives for specialization and exchange do not depend on property rights but only on differing opportunity costs.

15 Price adjustments coordinate decisions in goods markets but not in factor markets.

Multiple-Choice

Production Possibilities and Opportunity Cost

1 If Harold can increase production of good *X* without decreasing the production of any other good, he
- **a** is producing on his *PPF*.
- **b** is producing outside his *PPF*.
- **c** is producing inside his *PPF*.
- **d** must have a linear *PPF*.
- **e** must prefer good *X* to any other good.

2 The bowed-out (concave) shape of a *PPF*
- **a** is due to the equal usefulness of resources in all activities.
- **b** is due to capital accumulation.
- **c** is due to technological change.
- **d** reflects the existence of increasing opportunity cost.
- **e** reflects the existence of decreasing opportunity cost.

3 The economy is at point *b* on the *PPF* in Figure 2.3. The opportunity cost of producing one more unit of *X* is
- **a** 1 unit of *Y*.
- **b** 20 units of *Y*.
- **c** 1 unit of *X*.
- **d** 8 units of *X*.
- **e** 20 units of *X*.

FIGURE **2.3**

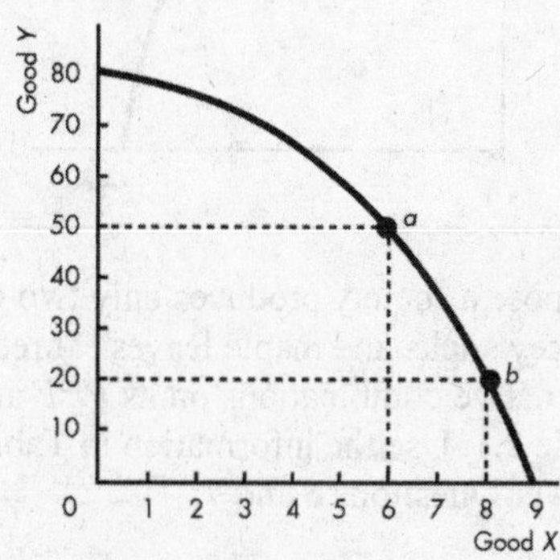

4 Refer to the *PPF* in Figure 2.3. Which of the following statements is *false*?
a Resources are not equally productive in all activities.
b Points inside the frontier represent unemployed resources.
c Starting at point *a*, an increase in the production of good *Y* will shift the frontier out.
d The opportunity cost of producing good *Y* increases as production of *Y* increases.
e Shifts in preferences for good *X* or good *Y* will not shift the frontier.

5 Refer to Figure 2.4, which shows the *PPF* for an economy without discrimination operating at maximum efficiency. If discrimination against women workers is currently occurring in this economy, the elimination of discrimination would result in a(n)
a movement from *a* to *b*.
b movement from *b* to *c*.
c movement from *a* to *c*.
d outward shift of the *PPF*.
e inward shift of the *PPF*.

FIGURE **2.4**

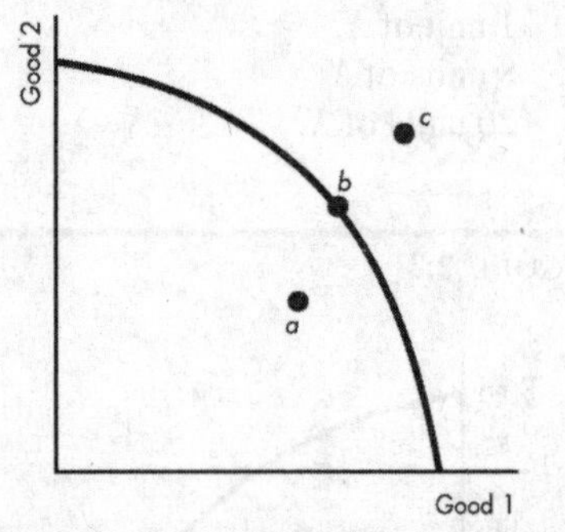

Suppose a society produces only two goods—hockey sticks and maple leaves. Three alternative combinations on its *PPF* are given in Table 2.1. Use the information in Table 2.1 to answer Questions **6** and **7**.

TABLE **2.1** PRODUCTION POSSIBILITIES

Possibility	Units of Hockey Sticks	Units of Maple Leaves
a	3	0
b	2	3
c	0	9

6 In moving from combination *c* to combination *b*, the opportunity cost of producing one additional hockey stick is
a 2 maple leaves.
b 1/2 maple leaves.
c 6 maple leaves.
d 1/6 maple leaves.
e 3 maple leaves.

7 According to this *PPF*
a resources are equally productive in all activities.
b a combination of 3 hockey sticks and 9 maple leaves is attainable.
c a combination of 3 hockey sticks and 9 maple leaves would not employ all resources.
d the opportunity cost of producing hockey sticks increases as more hockey sticks are produced.
e the opportunity cost of producing hockey sticks decreases as more hockey sticks are produced.

Using Resources Efficiently

8 The marginal benefit curve for a good
a shows the benefit a firm receives from producing one more unit.
b shows the amount a consumer is willing to pay for one more unit.
c is upward-sloping.
d is bowed out.
e is none of the above.

9 With increasing production of food, its marginal benefit
a increases and marginal cost increases.
b increases and marginal cost decreases.
c decreases and marginal cost increases.
d decreases and marginal cost decreases.
e decreases and marginal cost is constant.

10 Suppose the *PPF* for skirts and pants is a straight line. As the production of skirts increases, the marginal benefit of skirts
a increases and marginal cost is constant.
b is constant and marginal cost increases.
c decreases and marginal cost decreases.
d decreases and marginal cost increases.
e decreases and marginal cost is constant.

11 With allocative efficiency, for each good produced, marginal
a benefit equals marginal cost.
b benefit is at its maximum.
c benefit exceeds marginal cost by as much as possible.
d cost exceeds marginal benefit by as much as possible.
e cost is at its minimum.

Economic Growth

12 The *PPF* for wine and wool will shift if there is a change in
a the price of resources.
b the unemployment rate.
c the quantity of resources.
d preferences for wine and wool.
e all of the above.

13 A movement *along* a given *PPF* will result from
a technological change.
b change in the stock of capital.
c change in the labour force.
d all of the above.
e none of the above.

14 The opportunity cost of pushing the *PPF* outward is
a capital accumulation.
b technological change.
c reduced current consumption.
d the gain in future consumption.
e all of the above.

15 In general, the higher the proportion of resources devoted to technological research in an economy, the
a greater will be current consumption.
b faster the *PPF* will shift outward.
c faster the *PPF* will shift inward.
d closer it will come to having a comparative advantage in the production of all goods.
e more bowed out the shape of the *PPF* will be.

16 Refer to the *PPF* in Figure 2.5. A politician who argues that "if our children are to be better off, we must invest now for the future" is recommending a current point like
a *a.*
b *b.*
c *c.*
d *d.*
e *e.*

FIGURE **2.5**

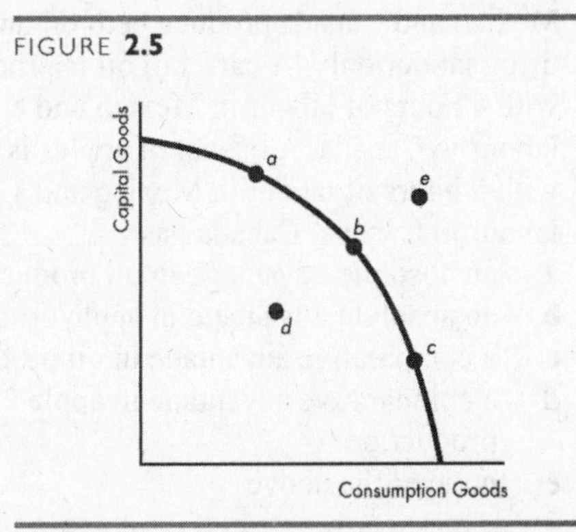

17 Refer to the *PPF* in Figure 2.5. The statement that "unemployment is a terrible waste of human resources" refers to a point like
a *a.*
b *b.*
c *c.*
d *d.*
e *e.*

Gains from Trade

In an eight-hour day, Andy can produce either 24 loaves of bread or 8 kilograms of butter. In an eight-hour day, Rolfe can produce either 8 loaves of bread or 8 kilograms of butter. Use this information to answer Questions **18** and **19**.

18 Which of the following statements is *true*?
a Andy has an absolute advantage in butter production.
b Rolfe has an absolute advantage in butter production.
c Andy has an absolute advantage in bread production.
d Andy has a comparative advantage in butter production.
e Rolfe has a comparative advantage in bread production.

19 Andy and Rolfe
a can gain from exchange if Andy specializes in butter production and Rolfe specializes in bread production.
b can gain from exchange if Andy specializes in bread production and Rolfe specializes in butter production.
c cannot gain from exchange.
d can exchange, but only Rolfe will gain.
e can exchange, but only Andy will gain.

20 Mexico and Canada produce both oil and apples using labour only. A barrel of oil is produced with 4 hours of labour in Mexico and 8 hours of labour in Canada. A bushel of apples is produced with 8 hours of labour in Mexico and 12 hours of labour in Canada. Canada has

a an absolute advantage in oil production.
b an absolute advantage in apple production.
c a comparative advantage in oil production.
d a comparative advantage in apple production.
e none of the above.

21 In Portugal, the opportunity cost of a bale of wool is 3 bottles of wine. In England, the opportunity cost of 1 bottle of wine is 3 bales of wool. Given this information,

a England has an absolute advantage in wine production.
b England has an absolute advantage in wool production.
c Portugal has a comparative advantage in wine production.
d Portugal has a comparative advantage in wool production.
e no trade will occur.

22 To gain from comparative advantage, countries must not only trade, they must also

a save.
b invest.
c engage in research and development.
d engage in capital accumulation.
e specialize.

23 Learning-by-doing is the basis of

a absolute comparative advantage.
b dynamic comparative advantage.
c intellectual property rights.
d financial property rights.
e none of the above.

Economic Coordination

24 Trade is organized using the social institutions of

a firms.
b property rights.
c money.
d markets.
e all of the above.

25 Markets

1 enable buyers and sellers to get information.

2 are defined by economists as geographical locations where trade occurs.

3 coordinate buying and selling decisions through price adjustments.

a 1 only
b 3 only
c 1 and 3 only
d 2 and 3 only
e 1, 2, and 3

Short Answer Problems

1 Why is a *PPF* negatively sloped? Why is it bowed out?

2 Suppose that an economy has the *PPF* shown in Table 2.2.

TABLE **2.2** PRODUCTION POSSIBILITIES

Possibility	Maximum Units of Butter per Week	Maximum Units of Guns per Week
a	200	0
b	180	60
c	160	100
d	100	160
e	40	200
f	0	220

a On graph paper, plot these possibilities, label the points, and draw the *PPF*. (Put guns on the *x*-axis.)

b If the economy moves from possibility *c* to possibility *d*, the opportunity cost *per unit of guns* will be how many units of butter?

c If the economy moves from possibility *d* to possibility *e*, the opportunity cost *per unit of guns* will be how many units of butter?

d In general terms, what happens to the opportunity cost of guns as the output of guns increases?

e In general terms, what happens to the opportunity cost of butter as the output of butter increases? What do the results in parts **d** and **e** imply about resources?

f If (instead of the possibilities given) the *PPF* were a straight line joining points *a* and *f*, what would that imply about opportunity costs and resources?

g Given the original *PPF* you have plotted, is a combination of 140 units of butter and 130 units of guns per week attainable? Would you regard this combination as an efficient one? Explain.

h Given the original *PPF*, is a combination of 70 units of butter and 170 units of guns per week attainable? Does this combination achieve productive efficiency? Explain.

3 If the following events occurred (each is a separate event, unaccompanied by any other event), what would happen to the *PPF* in Short Answer Problem **2**?

a A new, easily exploited, energy source is discovered.

b A large number of skilled workers immigrate into the country.

c The output of butter increases.

d A new invention increases output per person in the butter industry but not in the guns industry.

e A new law is passed compelling workers, who could previously work as long as they wanted, to retire at age 60.

4 The Borg produce only two goods—cubes and transwarp coils—and want to decide where on their *PPF* to operate. Table 2.3 shows the marginal benefit and marginal cost of cubes, measured in the number of transwarp coils per cube.

TABLE **2.3**

Borg Cubes	Marginal Benefit	Marginal Cost
1	12	3
2	10	4
3	8	5
4	6	6
5	4	7
6	2	8

a If the Borg are efficient (and they are!), what quantity of cubes will they produce?

b If the Borg were to produce one more cube than your answer in **a**, why would that choice be inefficient?

5 Suppose the country of Quark has historically devoted 10 percent of its resources to the production of new capital goods. Use *PPF* diagrams like Text Figures 2.5 and 2.6 on pages 40–41 to compare the consequences (costs and benefits) of each of the following:

a Quark continues to devote 10 percent of its resources to the production of capital goods.

b Quark begins now to permanently devote 20 percent of its resources to the production of capital goods.

6 Lawyers earn $200 per hour while secretaries earn $15 per hour. Use the concepts of absolute and comparative advantage to explain why a lawyer who is a better typist than her secretary will still specialize in doing only legal work and will trade with the secretary for typing services.

7 France and Germany each produce both wine and beer, using a single, homogeneous input—labour. Their production possibilities are:

- France has 100 units of labour and can produce a maximum of 200 bottles of wine or 400 bottles of beer.
- Germany has 50 units of labour and can produce a maximum of 250 bottles of wine or 200 bottles of beer.

a Complete Table 2.4.

TABLE **2.4**

	Bottles Produced by 1 Unit of Labour		Opportunity Cost of 1 Additional Bottle	
	Wine	Beer	Wine	Beer
France				
Germany				

Use the information in part **a** to answer the following questions.

ⓔ **b** Which country has an absolute advantage in wine production?

ⓔ **c** Which country has an absolute advantage in beer production?

d Which country has a comparative advantage in wine production?

e Which country has a comparative advantage in beer production?

f If trade is allowed, describe what specialization, if any, will occur.

ⓒⓣ **8** Tova and Ron are the only two remaining inhabitants of the planet Melmac. They spend their 30-hour days producing widgets and woggles, the only two goods needed for happiness on Melmac. It takes Tova 1 hour to produce a widget and 2 hours to produce a woggle, while Ron takes 3 hours to produce a widget and 3 hours to produce a woggle.

a For a 30-hour day, draw an individual *PPF* for Tova, then for Ron.

b What does the shape of the *PPF*s tell us about opportunity costs? about resources?

c Assume initially that Tova and Ron are each self-sufficient. Define self-sufficiency. Explain what the individual consumption possibilities are for Tova, then for Ron.

d Who has an absolute advantage in the production of widgets? of woggles?

e Who has a comparative advantage in the production of widgets? of woggles?

f Suppose Tova and Ron each specialize in producing only the good in which she/he has a comparative advantage (one spends 30 hours producing widgets, the other spends 30 hours producing woggles). What will be the total production of widgets and woggles?

g Suppose Tova and Ron exchange 7 widgets for 5 woggles. On your *PPF* diagrams, plot the new point of Tova's consumption, then of Ron's consumption. Explain how these points illustrate the gains from trade.

9 The Netsilik and Oonark families live on the Arctic coast, west of Hudson Bay. They often go fishing and hunting for caribou together. During an average working day, the Netsiliks can, at most, either catch 6 kilograms of fish or kill 6 caribou. The Oonarks can either catch 4 kilograms of fish or kill 4 caribou.

a Assuming linear *PPF*s, draw each family's *PPF* on the same diagram. Put fish on the horizontal axis and caribou on the vertical axis.

b Complete Table 2.5.

TABLE **2.5**

	Opportunity Cost of 1 Additional	
	Fish (kg)	**Caribou**
Netsiliks		
Oonarks		

c Which family has a comparative advantage in catching fish? in hunting caribou?

d Can specialization and trade increase the total output of fish and caribou produced by the two families? Explain.

10 Explain the interdependence that exists between households and firms in Text Figure 2.8 on page 47.

ANSWERS

True/False and Explain

1 F Attainable but not an efficient point. (34–35)

2 T Moving from *b* to *d*, production good 1 decreases by 4 units. (35–36)

3 T Outside *PPF*. (34–35)

4 T See Helpful Hint **2**. (35–36)

5 F Marginal cost is *additional* cost of producing the 4th pizza alone. (37)

6 T Marginal benefit is also the amount a person is willing to pay for one more unit, but payment in money ultimately represents an opportunity cost in goods forgone. (38)

7 T The more we have of a good, the smaller is the marginal benefit and hence the willingness to pay for it. (38)

8 F All points represent productive efficiency (efficient use of resources). But allocative efficiency only occurs at the single point (combination of goods) that we prefer above all others (where $MB = MC$). (39)

9 F Cost of growth is forgone current consumption. (40)

10 F Points with more capital goods yield faster growth. (40–41)

11 F Can *consume* at point outside *PPF*. (43–44)

12 F Mutually beneficial trade depends on comparative advantage, not absolute advantage. (42–45)

13 F Nadim has absolute advantage in skateboard production, but without information about opportunity costs, we don't know if he has comparative advantage. (45)

14 F Property rights are prerequisite for specialization and exchange. (46)

15 F Price adjustments coordinate buying and selling decisions in all markets. (46–47)

Multiple-Choice

1 c For 0 opportunity cost, must be unemployed resources. (34–35)

2 d **a** would be true if *un*equal resources; **b** and **c** shift *PPF*. (36)

3 b To increase quantity *X* to 9, must decrease quantity *Y* from 20 to 0. (35–36)

4 c Increased production *Y* moves up *along* *PPF*. (34–36)

5 a Discrimination causes underemployment of resources. Women not allowed to produce up to full abilities. (34–36)

6 e Give up 6 maple leaves to get 2 hockey sticks: 6/2 = 3 maple leaves per hockey stick. (35–36)

7 a Constant opportunity cost means resources equally productive for producing all goods—see Helpful Hint **4**. (34–36)

8 b Benefits apply to consumers; curve is downward-sloping. (38)

9 c Principles of diminishing marginal benefit and increasing marginal cost. (37–39)

10 e Diminishing marginal benefit, but linear *PPF* means constant opportunity and marginal costs. (37–39)

11 a Whenever $MB \neq MC$, efficiency improves by reallocating resources to produce more goods with high marginal benefits, causing a decrease in their marginal benefit and increase in marginal cost. (39)

12 c Only changes in resources or technology shift *PPF*. (40)

13 e **a**, **b**, and **c** all shift *PPF*. (40–41)

14 c **a** and **b** cause outward shift *PPF*, not opportunity cost; **d** effect of outward shift *PPF*. (40–41)

15 b Technological change shifts *PPF* outward at cost of current consumption. (40–41)

16 a Producing more capital goods now, shifts *PPF* outward in future. (40–41)

17 d Points inside *PPF* represent unemployed resources, whether labour, capital, or land. (34–35, 40–41)

18 c Andy produces 3 loaves bread per hour; Rolfe produces 1 loaf per hour—see Helpful Hint **5**. (42–45)

19 b Andy has comparative advantage (lower opportunity cost) bread, Rolfe has comparative advantage butter production. (42–45)

20 d Opportunity cost oil in bushels of apples—Canada 2/3, Mexico 1/2. Opportunity cost apples in barrels of oil—Canada 3/2, Mexico 2. (42–45)

21 c Opportunity cost wine in bales of wool—Portugal 1/3, England 3. Opportunity cost wool in bottles of wine—Portugal 3, England 1/3. (42–45)

22 e Gains from trade require specialization based on comparative advantage. **a**–**d** may increase productivity and absolute advantage, not necessarily comparative advantage. (42–45)

23 b Definition. (45)

24 e All 4 institutions required for gains from trade and specialization through decentralized coordination. (46)

25 c 2 is the ordinary meaning of markets, not the economist's definition. (45–46)

Short Answer Problems

1 The negative slope of the *PPF* reflects opportunity cost: in order to have more of one good, some of the other must be forgone. It is bowed out because the existence of resources not equally productive in all activities creates increasing opportunity cost as we increase the production of either good.

2 **a** The graph of the *PPF* is given in Figure 2.6.

FIGURE **2.6**

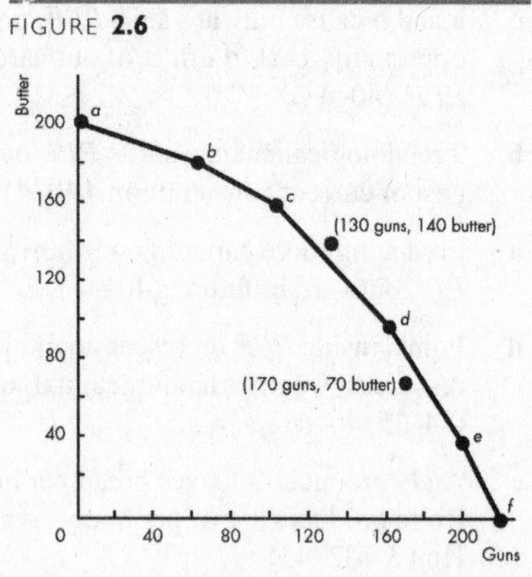

b In moving from *c* to *d*, in order to gain 60 units of guns, we must give up 160 – 100 = 60 units of butter. The opportunity cost per unit of guns is

$$\frac{60 \text{ units butter}}{60 \text{ units guns}} = 1 \text{ unit butter per unit of guns}$$

c In moving from *d* to *e*, in order to gain 40 units of guns, we must give up 100 – 40 = 60 units of butter. The opportunity cost per unit of guns is

$$\frac{60 \text{ units butter}}{40 \text{ units guns}} = 1.5 \text{ unit butter per unit of guns}$$

d The opportunity cost of producing more guns increases as the output of guns increases.

e Likewise, the opportunity cost of producing more butter increases as the output of butter increases. Increasing opportunity costs imply that resources are not equally productive in gun and butter production; that is, they are nonhomogeneous.

f Opportunity costs would always be constant, regardless of the output of guns or butter. The opportunity cost per unit of guns would be

$$200/220 = 10/11 \text{ units of butter}$$

The opportunity cost per unit of butter would be

$$220/200 = 1.1 \text{ units of guns}$$

Constant opportunity costs imply that resources are equally productive in gun and butter production; that is, they are homogeneous.

g This combination is outside the *PPF* and therefore is not attainable. Since the economy cannot produce this combination, the question of efficiency is irrelevant.

h This combination is inside the *PPF* and is attainable. It is inefficient because the economy could produce more of either or both goods without producing less of anything else. Therefore some resources are not fully utilized.

3 **a** Assuming that both goods require energy for their production, the entire *PPF* shifts out to the northeast as in Figure 2.7(a).

b Assuming that both goods use skilled labour in their production, the entire *PPF* shifts out to the northeast.

c The *PPF* does not shift. An increase in the output of butter implies a movement along the *PPF* to the left, not a shift of the *PPF* itself.

d The new invention implies that for every level of output of guns, the economy can now produce more butter. The *PPF* swings to the right, but remains anchored at point *f* as in Figure 2.7(b).

e The entire *PPF* shifts in toward the origin.

FIGURE **2.7**

(a)

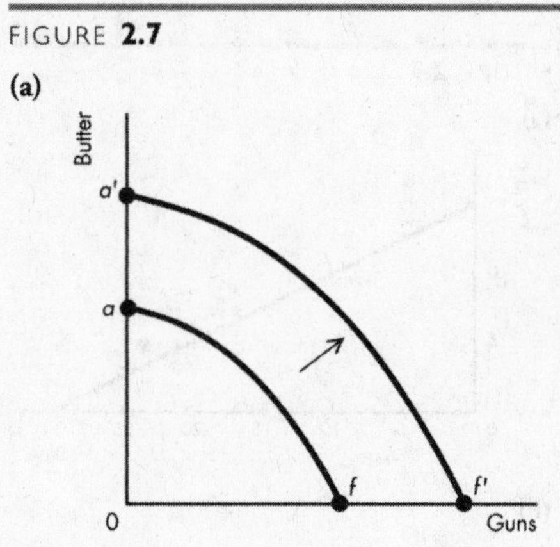

(b)

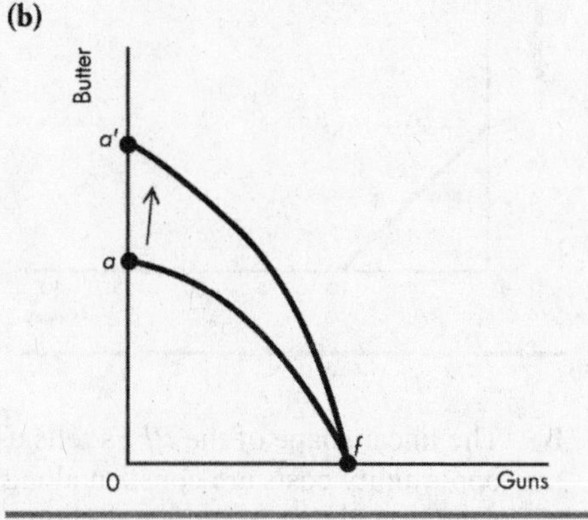

4 a At the efficient quantity of output, marginal benefit = marginal cost. The Borg will produce 4 cubes ($MB = MC = 4$ transwarp coils/cube).

b At 5 cubes, marginal benefit = 4 and marginal cost = 7. Since $MC > MB$, the Borg could get better use from their resources by shifting production out of cubes and into transwarp coils.

5 a The situation for Quark is depicted by Figure 2.8. Suppose Quark starts on PPF_1. If it continues to devote only 10 percent of its resources to the production of new capital goods, it is choosing to produce at a point like *a*. This will shift the *PPF* out in the next period, but only to the curve labelled 2 (where, presumably, Quark will choose to produce at point *b*).

FIGURE **2.8**

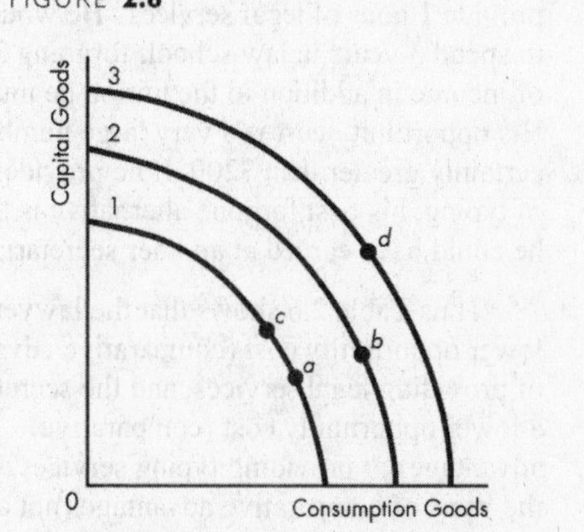

b Starting from the same initial *PPF*, if Quark now decides to increase the resources devoted to the production of new capital to 20 percent, it will be choosing to produce at a point like *c*. In this case, next period's *PPF* will shift further—to curve 3, and a point like *d*, for example.

Thus in comparing points *a* and *c*, we find the following costs and benefits: point *a* has the benefit of greater present consumption but at a cost of lower future consumption; point *c* has the cost of lower present consumption, but with the benefit of greater future consumption.

6 The lawyer has an absolute advantage in producing both legal and typing services relative to the secretary. Nevertheless, she has a comparative advantage in legal services, and the secretary has a comparative advantage in typing. To demonstrate these comparative advantages, we can construct Table 2.6 of opportunity costs.

TABLE **2.6**

	Opportunity Cost of 1 Additional Hour ($)	
	Legal Services	**Typing**
Lawyer	200	200
Secretary	>200	15

Consider first the lawyer's opportunity costs. The lawyer's best forgone alternative to providing 1 hour of legal services is the $200 she could earn by providing another hour of legal services. If she provides 1 hour of typing, she is also forgoing $200 (1 hour) of legal services.

What would the secretary have to forgo to provide 1 hour of legal services? He would have to spend 3 years in law school, forgoing 3 years of income in addition to the tuition he must pay. His opportunity cost is a very large number, certainly greater than $200. If he provides 1 hour of typing, his best forgone alternative is the $15 he could have earned at another secretarial job.

Thus Table 2.6 shows that the lawyer has a lower opportunity cost (comparative advantage) of providing legal services, and the secretary has a lower opportunity cost (comparative advantage) of providing typing services. It is on the basis of comparative advantage (not absolute advantage) that trade will take place from which both parties gain.

7 a The completed table is shown here as Table 2.4 Solution.

TABLE **2.4** SOLUTION

	Bottles Produced by 1 Unit of Labour		Opportunity Cost of 1 Additional Bottle	
	Wine	**Beer**	**Wine**	**Beer**
France	2	4	2.0 beer	0.50 wine
Germany	5	4	0.8 beer	1.25 wine

ⓔ b Germany, which can produce more wine (5 bottles) per unit of input, has an absolute advantage in wine production.

ⓔ c Neither country has an absolute advantage in beer production, since beer output (4 bottles) per unit of input is the same for both countries.

d Germany, with the lower opportunity cost (0.8 beer), has a comparative advantage in wine production.

e France, with the lower opportunity cost (0.5 wine), has a comparative advantage in beer production.

f The incentive for trade depends only on differences in comparative advantage. Germany will specialize in wine production and France will specialize in beer production.

ⓒⓣ 8 a The individual *PPF*s for Tova and Ron are given by Figure 2.9(a) and (b) respectively.

FIGURE **2.9**

(a)

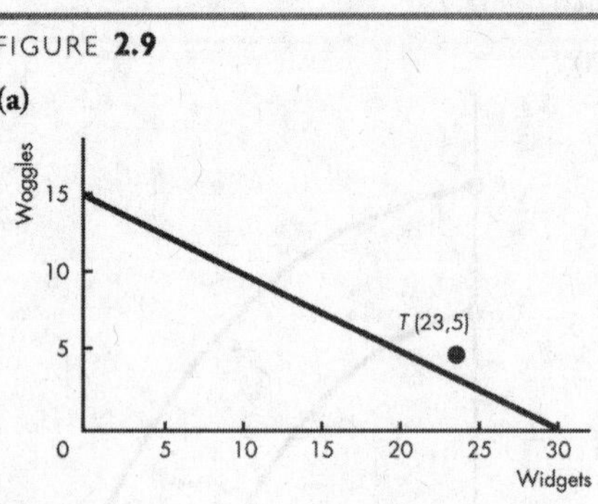

(b)

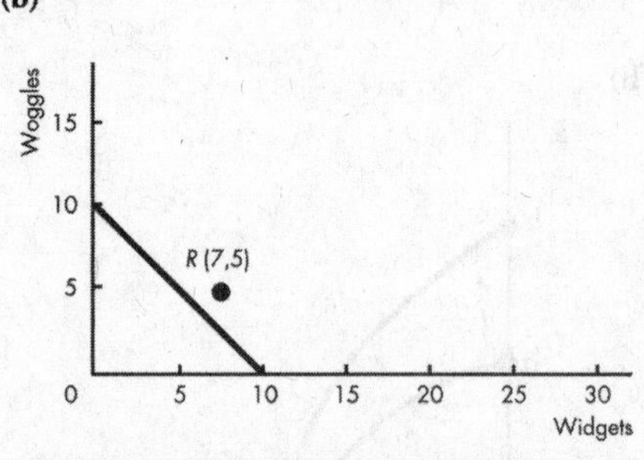

b The linear shape of the *PPF*s tells us that opportunity costs are constant along each frontier and that resources are homogeneous.

These linear *PPF*s with constant opportunity costs abstract from the complexity of the real world. The world generally has increasing opportunity costs, but that fact is not essential for understanding the gains from trade, which is the objective of this problem. Making the model more complex by including increasing opportunity costs would not change our results, but it would make it more difficult to see them.

c Individuals are self-sufficient if they consume only what they produce. This means there is no trade. Without trade, Tova's (maximum) consumption possibilities are exactly the same as her production possibilities—points along her *PPF*. Ron's (maximum) consumption possibilities are likewise the points along his *PPF*.

d Tova has an absolute advantage in the production of both widgets and woggles. Her absolute advantage can be defined either in terms of greater output per unit of inputs or fewer inputs per unit of output. A comparison of the *PPF*s in Figure 2.9 shows that, for given inputs of 30 hours, Tova produces a greater output of widgets than Ron (30 versus 10) and a greater output of woggles than Ron (15 versus 10). The statement of the problem tells us equivalently that, per unit of output, Tova uses fewer inputs than Ron for both widgets (1 hour versus 3 hours) and woggles (2 hours versus 3 hours). Since Tova has greater productivity than Ron in the production of all goods (widgets and woggles), we say that overall she has an absolute advantage.

e Tova has a comparative advantage in the production of widgets, since she can produce them at lower opportunity cost than Ron (1/2 woggle versus 1 woggle). On the other hand, Ron has a comparative advantage in the production of woggles, since he can produce them at a lower opportunity cost than Tova (1 widget versus 2 widgets).

f Tova will produce widgets and Ron will produce woggles, yielding a total production between them of 30 widgets and 10 woggles.

g After the exchange, Tova will have 23 widgets and 5 woggles (point *T*). Ron will have 7 widgets and 5 woggles (point *R*). These new post-trade consumption possibility points lie outside Tova's and Ron's respective pre-trade consumption (and production) possibilities. Hence trade has yielded gains that allow the traders to improve their consumption possibilities beyond those available with self-sufficiency.

9 a The *PPF*s of the Netsiliks and Oonarks are shown in Figure 2.10.

FIGURE **2.10**

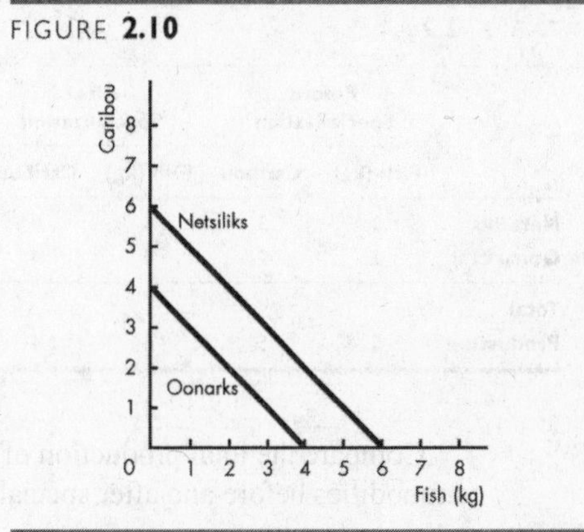

b The completed table is shown here as Table 2.5 Solution.

TABLE **2.5** SOLUTION

	Opportunity Cost of I Additional	
	Fish (kg)	**Caribou**
Netsiliks	I caribou	I kg fish
Oonarks	I caribou	I kg fish

c Neither family has a comparative advantage in catching fish, since the opportunity cost of fish is the same (1 caribou) for each family. Similarly, neither family has a comparative advantage in hunting caribou, since the opportunity cost of a caribou is the same (1 kilogram of fish) for each family.

d Gains from specialization and trade are due to the existence of comparative advantage. In this case, no family has a comparative advantage in either fishing or hunting, so there are no gains from specialization and trade.

To illustrate the absence of gains, suppose that initially each family devoted half of its time to each activity. Then suppose that the Netsiliks specialized completely in catching fish and the Oonarks specialized completely in hunting caribou. Production before and after specialization is shown in Table 2.7.

TABLE **2.7**

	Before Specialization		After Specialization	
	Fish (kg)	Caribou	Fish (kg)	Caribou
Netsiliks	3	3	6	0
Oonarks	2	2	0	4
Total Production	5	5	6	4

Compare the total production of both commodities before and after specialization.

Specialization has increased the total production of fish by 1 kilogram, but it has also led to a decrease in the total production of caribou by 1. There are no clear gains in consumption from specialization and trade.

10 Firms depend on households for the supply of factors of production. In exchange, households depend on firms for income. Households use that income to buy goods and services from firms, while firms depend on the money they get from household purchases to purchase more factors of production in the next period and renew the circular flow.

CHAPTERS 1–2

Part 1 Wrap Up

Understanding the Scope of Economics

PROBLEM

The economy is a mechanism that allocates scarce resources among competing uses. But how do those allocation decisions get made? In the Canadian economy, markets are the primary institutions that coordinate individual decisions through price adjustments.

Suppose, for simplicity, the Canadian economy produced only two outputs—child-care services and televisions. The production possibility frontier (*PPF*) for the economy appears in Figure P1.1 below. The economy is operating at point *a*, producing Q^0_{cc} units of child-care services and Q^0_{tv} televisions.

FIGURE **P1.1**

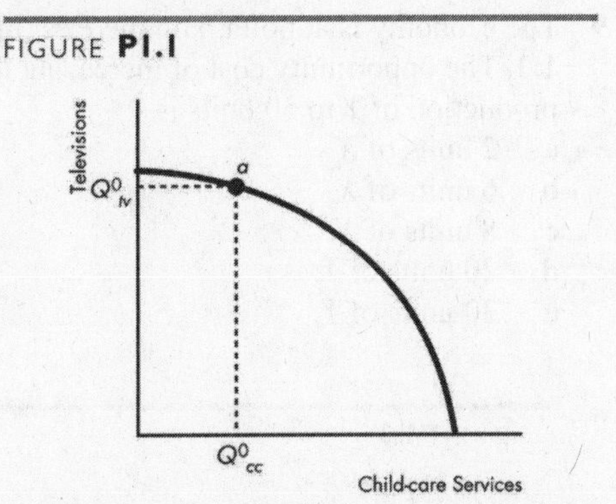

a What does the bowed-out (concave) shape of the *PPF* imply about resources? opportunity costs?

b As more women enter the labour force, there is increased demand for child-care services. As a result, the price and quantity of child-care services both increase. At the same time, the demand for televisions falls (perhaps to save money to pay for the additional child-care services). As a result, the price and quantity of televisions both decrease.

On the *PPF* in Figure P1.1, label as point *b* a new combination of child-care services and televisions reflecting the changes in demand.

c Explain how the economy came to produce these new quantities in response to the changing demands of households.

d What determines the distance of the *PPF* from the origin? What determines the precise point on the *PPF* at which the economy operates? What is the true cost of moving from point *a* to point *b* on the *PPF?*

MIDTERM EXAMINATION

You should allocate 30 minutes for this examination (15 questions, 2 minutes per question). For each question, choose the one *best* answer.

1 A *PPF* shows that
- **a** there is a limit to the production of any one good.
- **b** to produce more of one good, we must produce less of another good.
- **c** there are limits to total production with given resources and technology.
- **d** all of the above are true.
- **e** none of the above is true.

2 The graph showing the level of a variable across different groups at a point in time is a
- **a** linear graph.
- **b** time-series graph.
- **c** cross-section graph.
- **d** misleading graph.
- **e** scatter diagram.

Suppose a society produces only two goods—guns and butter. Three alternative combinations on its *PPF* are given in Table P1.1. Use the information in Table P1.1 to answer Questions **3** and **4**.

TABLE **P1.1** PRODUCTION POSSIBILITIES

Possibility	Units of Butter	Units of Guns
a	8	0
b	6	1
c	0	3

3 In moving from combination *b* to combination *c*, the opportunity cost of producing *one* additional unit of guns is
a 2 units of butter.
b 1/2 unit of butter.
c 6 units of butter.
d 1/6 unit of butter.
e 3 units of butter.

4 According to this *PPF*
a a combination of 6 butter and 1 gun would not employ all resources.
b a combination of 0 butter and 4 guns is attainable.
c resources are equally productive in all activities.
d the opportunity cost of producing guns increases as more guns are produced.
e the opportunity cost of producing guns decreases as more guns are produced.

5 Which of the following is a normative statement?
a Pollution is an example of an external cost.
b Pollution makes people worse off.
c Firms that pollute should be forced to shut down.
d Pollution imposes opportunity costs on others.
e None of the above.

6 The graph of the relationship between two variables that are negatively related
a is horizontal.
b slopes upward to the right.
c is vertical.
d slopes downward to the right.
e is linear.

7 In Figure P1.2, the slope of the line is
a 1.50.
b 1.25.
c 1.00.
d 0.75.
e 0.50.

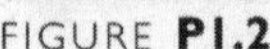

FIGURE **P1.2**

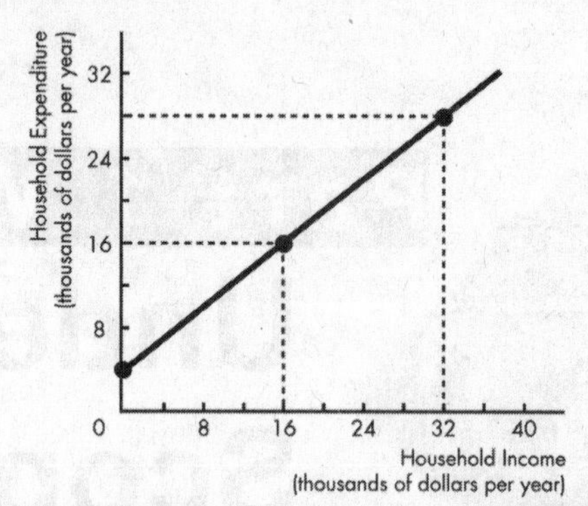

8 Other things being equal, which of the following statements is correct?

1 If unemployment increases, the opportunity cost of attending university decreases.

2 If men generally earn more than women in the labour market, the opportunity cost of attending university is higher for men than for women.

a 1 only
b 2 only
c 1 and 2
d Neither 1 nor 2
e Impossible to judge without additional information

9 The economy is at point *b* on the *PPF* in Figure 1.3. The opportunity cost of increasing the production of *Y* to 50 units is
a 2 units of *X*.
b 6 units of *X*.
c 8 units of *X*.
d 20 units of *Y*.
e 30 units of *Y*.

FIGURE **P1.3**

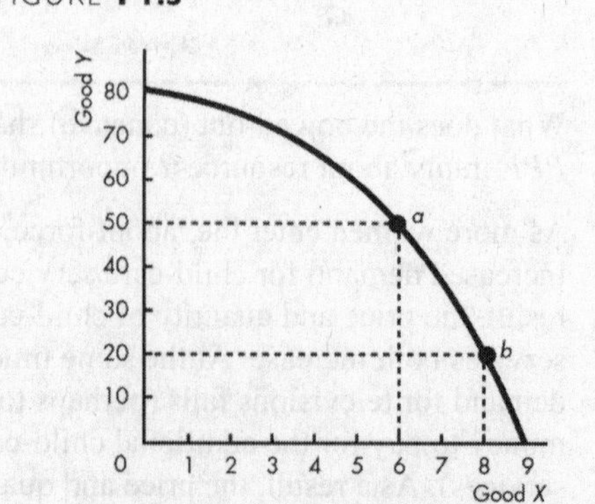

10 Because productive resources are scarce, we must give up some of one good in order to acquire more of another. This is the essence of the concept of
- **a** specialization.
- **b** monetary exchange.
- **c** comparative advantage.
- **d** absolute advantage.
- **e** opportunity cost.

11 The scarcity of resources implies that the *PPF* is
- **a** bowed inward (convex).
- **b** bowed outward (concave).
- **c** positively sloped.
- **d** negatively sloped.
- **e** linear.

12 If additional units of any good can be produced at a constant opportunity cost, the *PPF* is
- **a** bowed inward (convex).
- **b** bowed outward (concave).
- **c** positively sloped.
- **d** perfectly horizontal.
- **e** linear.

13 Marginal cost is the
- **a** total cost of an activity.
- **b** additional benefit of a decrease in an activity.
- **c** additional benefit of an increase in an activity.
- **d** opportunity cost of a decrease in an activity.
- **e** opportunity cost of an increase in an activity.

14 If variables *x* and *y* move in opposite directions, they are said to be
- **a** positively related.
- **b** negatively related.
- **c** intimately related.
- **d** unrelated.
- **e** siblings.

15 *Ceteris paribus* is a Latin term meaning
- **a** "After this, therefore because of this."
- **b** "What is true of the parts is true of the whole."
- **c** "What is true of the parts is *not* true of the whole."
- **d** "Other things being equal."
- **e** "Your place or mine."

ANSWERS

Problem

a The bowed-out shape of the *PPF* implies that resources are not equally productive in all activities; they are nonhomogeneous. With nonhomogeneous resources, there are increasing opportunity costs as production increases of either child-care services or televisions.

b See Figure P1.1 Solution.

FIGURE **P1.1** SOLUTION

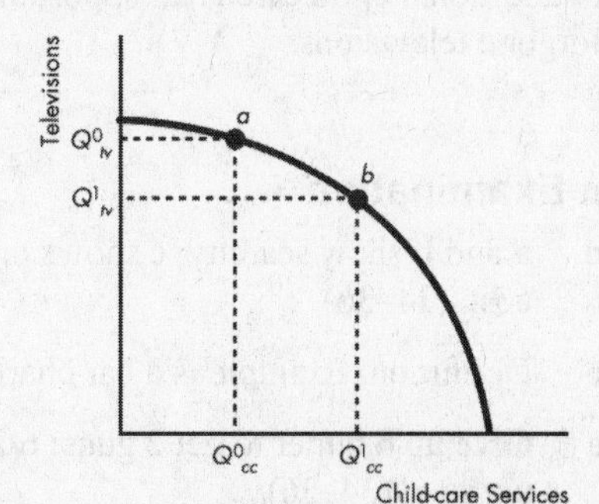

c The increased demand for child-care services puts upward pressure on the price of child-care services, making it more profitable to produce them. The higher price serves as a signal to firms to shift additional resources to producing child-care services.

Those additional resources come from the television market. The decreased demand for televisions puts downward pressure on the price of televisions, making it less profitable to produce them. The lower price serves as a signal to firms to shift resources to more profitable uses (in child care).

Thus the market economy responds to the changing demands of households by reallocating resources into child-care services from television production. Prices are the signals that coordinate the demand decisions of households with the resource allocation decisions of firms. The market—operating through a combination of price signals, self-interest, and competition—acts like an "invisible hand" to guide resources to the uses that households desire.

d The distance of the *PPF* from the origin is determined by the quantities of resources and the technology in the economy. The *PPF* shows maximum combinations of outputs (goods and services) that can be produced with given resources and technology.

The precise point on the *PPF* at which the economy operates (e.g., the combination at point *a* of child-care services and televisions) is determined by the demands of households.

The true cost of moving from point *a* to point *b* is the televisions that must be forgone as scarce resources are shifted to produce more child-care services. In other words, the true cost of additional child care is an opportunity cost—forgone televisions.

Midterm Examination

1 d **a** and **b** show scarcity, **c** shows opportunity cost. (34–36)

2 c Definition. Example is a bar chart. (18–20)

3 e Give up 6 butter to get 2 guns: 6/2 = 3 butter per gun. (34–36)

4 d Opportunity cost gun between *a* and *b* = 2 butter; between *b* and *c* = 3 butter. *a* on *PPF*, *b* outside *PPF*. (34–36)

5 c **a** is a true statement (definition); **d** and **b** are positive statements that can be tested. (12–13)

6 d As *x* increases, *y* decreases. (20–22)

7 d For example, using points (0, 4) and (16, 16): $\Delta y = 12$ (16 – 4), $\Delta x = 16$ (16 – 0). (24–26)

8 c Unemployment decreases expected average income from working. Higher opportunity cost for men may not be fair, but is a fact. (11)

9 a To move from *b* to *a*, quantity *X* decreases from 8 to 6. (35–36)

10 e Definition. (35–36)

11 d Scarcity implies opportunity cost, which involves a negative relationship—to get more of *X* you must give up *Y*. (34–36)

12 e Constant opportunity cost yields constant slope *PPF*. (36)

13 e Definition; **c** is marginal benefit, **b** and **d** are nonsense. (11, 37)

14 b Definition. (21–22)

15 d Definition; **a** is *post hoc ergo propter hoc*. (13–14)

Chapter 3 Demand and Supply

KEY CONCEPTS

Markets and Prices

Competitive market—many buyers and sellers so no one can influence prices.

Relative price of a good is

- its *opportunity cost*—the other goods that must be forgone to buy it.
- ratio of its **money price** to the money price of another good.
- determined by demand and supply.

Demand

The **quantity demanded** of a good is the amount consumers plan to buy during a given time period at a particular price. The **law of demand** states: "Other things remaining the same, the higher the price of a good, the smaller is the quantity demanded." Higher price reduces quantity demanded for two reasons:

- *substitution effect*—with an increase in the relative price of a good, people buy less of it and more of substitutes for the good.
- *income effect*—with an increase in the relative price of a good and unchanged incomes, people have less money to spend on all goods, including the good whose price increased.

The **demand curve** represents the inverse relationship between quantity demanded and price, *ceteris paribus*. The demand curve also is a willingness-and-ability-to-pay curve, which measures marginal benefit.

- A change in price causes movement along the demand curve. This is called a **change in the quantity demanded**. The higher the price of a good, the lower the quantity demanded.
- A shift of the demand curve is called a **change in demand**. The demand curve shifts from changes in
  - prices of related goods.
  - expected future prices.
  - income.
  - expected future income.
  - population.
  - preferences.
- Increase in demand—demand curve shifts rightward.
- Decrease in demand—demand curve shifts leftward.
- For an increase in
  - price of a **substitute**—demand shifts rightward.
  - price of a **complement**—demand shifts leftward.
  - expected future prices—demand shifts rightward.
  - income **(normal good)**—demand shifts rightward.
  - income **(inferior good)**—demand shifts leftward.
  - expected future income **(normal good)**—demand shifts rightward.
  - expected future income **(inferior good)**—demand shifts leftward
  - population—demand shifts rightward.
  - preferences—demand shifts rightward.

Supply

The **quantity supplied** of a good is the amount producers plan to sell during a given time period at a particular price. The **law of supply** states: "Other things remaining the same, the higher the price of a good, the greater is the quantity supplied." Higher price increases quantity supplied because marginal cost increases with increasing quantities. Price must rise for producers to be willing to increase production and incur higher marginal cost.

The **supply curve** represents the positive relationship between quantity supplied and price, *ceteris paribus*. The supply curve is also a minimum-supply-price curve, showing the lowest price at which a producer is willing to sell another unit.

- ♦ A change in price causes movement along the supply curve. This is called a **change in the quantity supplied**. The higher the price of a good, the greater the quantity supplied.
- ♦ A shift of the supply curve is called a **change in supply**. The supply curve shifts from changes in
  - prices of productive resources.
  - prices of related goods produced.
  - expected future prices.
  - number of suppliers.
  - technology.
- ♦ Increase in supply—supply curve shifts rightward.
- ♦ Decrease in supply—supply curve shifts leftward.
- ♦ For an increase in
  - prices of productive resources—supply shifts leftward.
  - price of a *substitute in production*—supply shifts leftward.
  - price of a *complement in production*—supply shifts rightward.
  - expected future prices—supply shifts leftward.
  - number of suppliers—supply shifts rightward.
  - technology—supply shifts rightward.

Market Equilibrium

The **equilibrium price** is where the demand and supply curves intersect, where quantity demanded equals quantity supplied.

- ♦ Above the equilibrium price, there is a surplus (quantity supplied > quantity demanded), and price will fall.
- ♦ Below the equilibrium price, there is a shortage (quantity demanded > quantity supplied), and price will rise.
- ♦ Only in equilibrium is there no tendency for the price to change. The **equilibrium quantity** is the quantity bought and sold at the equilibrium price.

Predicting Changes in Price and Quantity

For a single change *either* in demand *or* in supply, *ceteris paribus*, when

- ♦ demand increases, P rises and Q increases.
- ♦ demand decreases, P falls and Q decreases.
- ♦ supply increases, P falls and Q increases.
- ♦ supply decreases, P rises and Q decreases.

When there is a simultaneous change *both* in demand *and* supply, we can determine the effect on either price or quantity. But without information about the relative size of the shifts of the demand and supply curves, the effect on the other variable is ambiguous. *Ceteris paribus*, when

- ♦ both demand and supply increase, P may rise/fall/remain constant and Q increases.
- ♦ both demand and supply decrease, P may rise/fall/remain constant and Q decreases.
- ♦ demand increases and supply decreases, P rises and Q may rise/fall/remain constant.
- ♦ demand decreases and supply increases, P falls and Q may rise/fall/remain constant.

HELPFUL HINTS

1 When you are first learning about demand and supply, think of specific examples to help you understand how to use the concepts. For example, in analyzing complementary goods, think about hamburgers and french fries; in analyzing substitute goods, think of hamburgers and hot dogs. This will reduce the "abstractness" of the economic theory and make concepts easier to remember.

2 The statement that "price is determined by demand and supply" is a shorthand way of saying that price is determined by all of the factors affecting demand (prices of related goods, expected future prices, income, expected future income, population, preferences) and all of the factors affecting supply (prices of productive resources, prices of related goods produced, expected future prices, number of suppliers, technology). The benefit of using demand and supply curves is that they allow us to systematically sort out the influences on price of each of these separate factors. Changes in the factors affecting demand shift the demand curve and move us up or down the given supply curve. Changes in the factors affecting supply shift the supply curve and move us up or down the given demand curve.

Any demand and supply problem requires you to sort out these influences carefully. In so doing, *always draw a graph*, even if it is just a small graph in the margin of a true/false or multiple-choice problem. Graphs are a very efficient way to "see" what happens. As you become comfortable with graphs, you will find them to be effective and powerful tools for systematically organizing your thinking.

Do not make the common mistake of thinking that a problem is so easy that you can do it in your head, without drawing a graph. This mistake will cost you dearly on examinations. Also, when you do draw a graph, be sure to label the axes. As the course progresses, you will encounter many graphs with different variables on the axes. It is easy to become confused if you do not develop the habit of labelling the axes.

3 Another very common mistake among students is failing to *distinguish* correctly between *a shift in a curve* and *a movement along a curve*. This distinction applies both to demand and to supply curves. Many questions in the Self-Test are designed to test your understanding of this distinction, and you can be sure that your instructor will test you heavily on this. The distinction between "shifts in" versus "movements along" a curve is crucial for systematic thinking about the factors influencing demand and supply, and for understanding the determination of equilibrium price and quantity.

Consider the example of the demand curve. The quantity of a good demanded depends on its own price, the prices of related goods, expected future prices, income, expected future income, population, and preferences. The term "demand" refers to the relationship between the price of a good and the quantity demanded, holding constant all of the other factors on which the quantity demanded depends. This demand relationship is represented graphically by the demand curve. Thus, the effect of a change in price on quantity demanded is already reflected in the slope of the demand curve; the effect of a change in the price of the good itself is given by a movement along the demand curve. This is referred to as a **change in quantity demanded**.

On the other hand, if one of the other factors affecting the quantity demanded changes, the demand curve itself will shift; the quantity demanded *at each price* will change. This shift of the demand curve is referred to as a **change in demand**. The critical thing to remember is that a change in the price of a good will not shift the demand curve; it will only cause a movement along the demand curve. Similarly, it is just as important to distinguish between shifts in the supply curve and movements along the supply curve.

To confirm your understanding, consider the effect (draw a graph!) of an increase in household income on the market for compact discs (CDs). First note that an increase in income affects the demand for CDs and not supply. Next we want to determine whether the increase in income causes a shift in the demand curve or a movement along the demand curve. Will the increase in income increase the quantity of CDs demanded even if the price of CDs does not change? Since the answer to this question is yes, we know that the demand curve will shift rightward. Note further that the increase in the demand for CDs will cause the equilibrium price to rise. This price increase will be indicated by a movement along the supply curve (an increase in the quantity supplied) and will not shift the supply curve itself.

Remember: It is shifts in demand and supply curves that cause the market price to change, not changes in the price that cause demand and supply curves to shift.

4 When analyzing the shifts of demand and supply curves in related markets (for substitute goods like beer and wine), it often seems as though the feedback effects from one market to the other can go on endlessly. To avoid confusion, stick to the rule that each curve (demand and supply) for a given market can shift a maximum of *once*. (See Short Answer Problems **4** and **6** for further explanation and examples.)

5 The relationships between price and quantity demanded and supplied can be represented in three equivalent forms: demand and supply schedules, curves, and equations. Text Chapter 3 illustrates schedules and curves, but demand and supply equations are also powerful tools of economic analysis. The Mathematical Note to Chapter 3 provides the general form of these equations. The purpose of this Helpful Hint and the next is to further explain the equations and how they can be used to determine the equilibrium values of price and quantity.

Figure 3.1 presents a simple demand and supply example in three equivalent forms: (a) schedules, (b) curves, and (c) equations. The demand and supply schedules in (a) are in the same format as Text Figure 3.7. The price-quantity combinations from the schedules are plotted on the graph in (b), yielding linear demand and supply curves. What is new about this example is the representation of those curves by the equations in (c).

If you recall (Chapter 1 Appendix) the formula for the equation of a straight line ($y = a + bx$), you can see that the demand equation is the equation of a straight line. Instead of y, P is the dependent variable on the vertical axis, and, instead of x, Q_D is the independent variable on the horizontal axis. The intercept on the vertical axis a is +5, and the slope b is –1. The supply equation is also linear and graphed in the same way, but with Q_S as the independent variable. The supply curve intercept on the vertical axis is +1, and the slope is +1. The negative slope of the demand curve reflects the law of demand, and the positive slope of the supply curve reflects the law of supply.

You can demonstrate the equivalence of the demand schedule, curve, and equation by substituting various values of Q_D from the schedule into the demand equation, and calculating the associated prices. These combinations of quantity demanded and price are the coordinates (Q_D, P) of the points on the demand curve. You can similarly demonstrate the equivalence of the supply schedule, curve, and equation.

FIGURE **3.1**

(a) Demand and Supply Schedules

Price ($)	Q_D	Q_S	Shortage (–)/ Surplus (+)
1	4	0	–4
2	3	1	–2
3	2	2	0
4	1	3	+2
5	0	4	+4

(b) Demand and Supply Curves

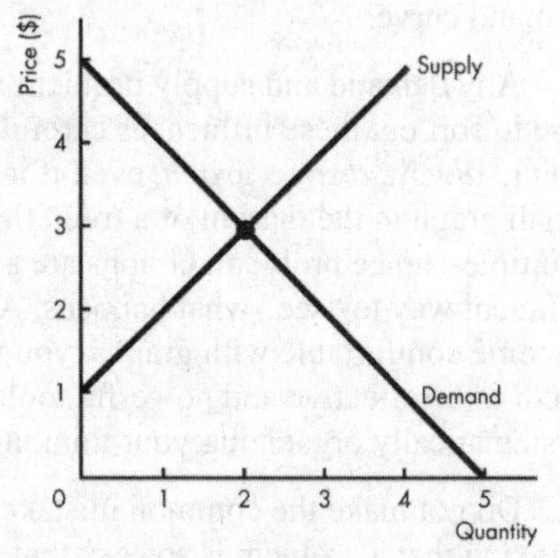

(c) Demand and Supply Equations

Demand: $P = 5 - 1Q_D$
Supply: $P = 1 + 1Q_S$

The demand and supply equations are very useful for calculating the equilibrium values of price and quantity. As the schedules and curves both show, two things are true in equilibrium: (1) the price is the same for consumers (the highest price they are willing to pay for the last unit) and producers (the lowest price they are willing to accept for the last unit) and (2) the quantity demanded equals the quantity supplied, so that there are no surpluses or shortages. In terms of the demand and supply equations, this means that, *in equilibrium*,

(1) The price in both equations is the same. We will denote the equilibrium price as P^*.

(2) $Q_D = Q_S$ = the equilibrium quantity bought and sold. We will denote the equilibrium quantity as Q^*.

In equilibrium, the equations become

Demand: $P^* = 5 - 1Q^*$

Supply: $P^* = 1 + 1Q^*$

These equilibrium equations constitute a simple set of simultaneous equations. Since there are two equations (demand and supply) and two unknowns (P^* and Q^*), we can solve for the unknowns.

Begin the solution by setting demand equal to supply:

$$5 - 1Q^* = 1 + 1Q^*$$

Collecting like terms, we find

$$4 = 2Q^*$$
$$2 = Q^*$$

Once we have Q^* (equilibrium quantity), we can solve for the equilibrium price using either the demand or the supply equations. Look first at demand:

$$P^* = 5 - 1Q^*$$
$$P^* = 5 - 1(2)$$
$$P^* = 5 - 2$$
$$P^* = 3$$

Alternatively, substituting Q^* into the supply equation yields the same result:

$$P^* = 1 + 1Q^*$$
$$P^* = 1 + 1(2)$$
$$P^* = 1 + 2$$
$$P^* = 3$$

Once you have solved for Q^*, the fact that substituting it into either the demand or the supply equation yields the correct P^* provides a valuable check on your calculations. If you make a mistake in your calculations, when you substitute Q^* into the demand and supply equations, you will get two different prices. If that happens, you know to recheck your calculations. If you get the same price when you substitute Q^* into the demand and supply equations, you know your calculations are correct.

6 Economists have developed the convention of graphing quantity as the independent variable (on the horizontal x-axis) and price as the dependent variable (on the vertical y-axis), and the foregoing equations reflect this. Despite this convention, economists actually consider real-world prices to be the independent variables and quantities the dependent variables. In that case, the equations would take the form

Demand: $Q_D = 5 - 1P$
Supply: $Q_S = -1 + 1P$

You can solve these equations for yourself to see that they yield exactly the same values for P^* and Q^*. (*Hint:* First solve for P^* and then for Q^*.) Whichever form of the equations your instructor may use, the technique for solving the equations will be similar and the results identical.

SELF-TEST

True/False and Explain

Markets and Prices

1 In a competitive market, every single buyer and seller influences price.

2 The relative price of a good is the other goods that must be forgone to buy it.

3 A good's relative price can fall even when its money price rises.

Demand

4 The law of demand tells us that as the price of a good rises, demand decreases.

5 The demand curve is a willingness-and-ability-to-pay curve that measures marginal cost.

6 Hamburgers and fries are complements. If Burger Bar reduces the price of fries, the demand for hamburgers increases.

7 A decrease in income always shifts the demand curve leftward.

Supply

8 A supply curve shows the maximum price at which the last unit will be supplied.

9 If *A* and *B* are substitutes, an increase in the price of *A* always shifts the supply curve of *B* leftward.

10 When a cow is slaughtered for beef, its hide becomes available to make leather. Thus beef and leather are substitutes in production.

11 If the price of beef rises, there will be an increase in both the supply of leather and the quantity of beef supplied.

Market Equilibrium

12 When the actual price is above the equilibrium price, a shortage occurs.

Predicting Changes in Price and Quantity

13 If the expected future price of a good increases, there will always be an increase in equilibrium price and a decrease in equilibrium quantity.

14 Suppose new firms enter the steel market. *Ceteris paribus*, the equilibrium price of steel will always fall and the quantity will rise.

15 Suppose the demand for personal computers increases while the cost of producing them decreases. The equilibrium quantity of personal computers will rise and the price will always fall.

Multiple-Choice

Markets and Prices

1 A relative price is
- **a** the ratio of one price to another.
- **b** an opportunity cost.
- **c** a quantity of a "basket" of goods and services forgone.
- **d** determined by demand and supply.
- **e** all of the above.

Demand

2 If an increase in the price of good *A* causes the demand curve for good *B* to shift leftward,
- **a** *A* and *B* are substitutes in consumption.
- **b** *A* and *B* are complements in consumption.
- **c** *A* and *B* are complements in production.
- **d** *B* is an inferior good.
- **e** *B* is a normal good.

3 Which of the following could *not* cause an increase in demand for a commodity?
- **a** an increase in income
- **b** a decrease in income
- **c** a decrease in the price of a substitute
- **d** a decrease in the price of a complement
- **e** an increase in preferences for the commodity

4 Some sales managers are talking shop. Which of the following quotations refers to a movement along the demand curve?
- **a** "Since our competitors raised their prices our sales have doubled."
- **b** "It has been an unusually mild winter; our sales of wool scarves are down from last year."
- **c** "We decided to cut our prices, and the increase in our sales has been remarkable."
- **d** "The Green movement has sparked an increase in our sales of biodegradable products."
- **e** none of the above.

5 If Hamburger Helper is an inferior good, then, *ceteris paribus*, a decrease in income will cause
a a leftward shift of the demand curve for Hamburger Helper.
b a rightward shift of the demand curve for Hamburger Helper.
c a movement up along the demand curve for Hamburger Helper.
d a movement down along the demand curve for Hamburger Helper.
e none of the above.

6 A decrease in quantity demanded is represented by a
a rightward shift of the supply curve.
b rightward shift of the demand curve.
c leftward shift of the demand curve.
d movement upward and to the left along the demand curve.
e movement downward and to the right along the demand curve.

7 Which of the following "other things" are *not* held constant along a demand curve?
a income
b prices of related goods
c the price of the good itself
d preferences
e all of the above

Supply

8 The fact that a decline in the price of a good causes producers to reduce the quantity of the good supplied illustrates
a the law of supply.
b the law of demand.
c a change in supply.
d the nature of an inferior good.
e technological improvement.

9 A shift of the supply curve for rutabagas will be caused by
a a change in preferences for rutabagas.
b a change in the price of a related good that is a substitute in consumption for rutabagas.
c a change in income.
d a change in the price of rutabagas.
e none of the above.

10 If a resource can be used to produce either good *A* or good *B*, then *A* and *B* are
a substitutes in production.
b complements in production.
c substitutes in consumption.
d complements in consumption.
e normal goods.

11 Which of the following will shift the supply curve for good *X* leftward?
a a decrease in the wages of workers employed to produce *X*
b an increase in the cost of machinery used to produce *X*
c a technological improvement in the production of *X*
d a situation where quantity demanded exceeds quantity supplied
e all of the above

12 Some producers are chatting over a beer. Which of the following quotations refers to a movement along the supply curve?
a "Wage increases have forced us to raise our prices."
b "Our new, sophisticated equipment will enable us to undercut our competitors."
c "Raw material prices have skyrocketed; we will have to pass this on to our customers."
d "We anticipate a big increase in demand. Our product price should rise, so we are planning for an increase in output."
e "New competitors in the industry are causing prices to fall."

13 If an increase in the price of good *A* causes the supply curve for good *B* to shift rightward,
a *A* and *B* are substitutes in consumption.
b *A* and *B* are complements in consumption.
c *A* and *B* are substitutes in production.
d *A* and *B* are complements in production.
e *A* is a factor of production for making *B*.

Market Equilibrium

14 If the market for Twinkies is in equilibrium,
a Twinkies must be a normal good.
b producers would like to sell more at the current price.
c consumers would like to buy more at the current price.
d there will be a surplus.
e equilibrium quantity equals quantity demanded.

15 The price of a good will tend to fall if
a there is a surplus at the current price.
b the current price is above equilibrium.
c the quantity supplied exceeds the quantity demanded at the current price.
d all of the above are true.
e none of the above is true.

16 A surplus can be eliminated by
a increasing supply.
b government raising the price.
c decreasing the quantity demanded.
d allowing the price to fall.
e allowing the quantity bought and sold to fall.

17 A shortage is the amount by which quantity
a demanded exceeds quantity supplied.
b supplied exceeds quantity demanded.
c demanded increases when the price rises.
d demanded exceeds the equilibrium quantity.
e supplied exceeds the equilibrium quantity.

Predicting Changes in Price and Quantity

18 Which of the following will definitely cause an increase in the equilibrium price?
a an increase in both demand and supply
b a decrease in both demand and supply
c an increase in demand combined with a decrease in supply
d a decrease in demand combined with an increase in supply
e none of the above

19 Coffee is a normal good. A decrease in income will
a increase the price of coffee and increase the quantity demanded of coffee.
b increase the price of coffee and increase the quantity supplied of coffee.
c decrease the price of coffee and decrease the quantity demanded of coffee.
d decrease the price of coffee and decrease the quantity supplied of coffee.
e cause none of the above.

20 An increase in the price of Pepsi (a substitute for coffee) will
a increase the price of coffee and increase the quantity demanded of coffee.
b increase the price of coffee and increase the quantity supplied of coffee.
c decrease the price of coffee and decrease the quantity demanded of coffee.
d decrease the price of coffee and decrease the quantity supplied of coffee.
e cause none of the above.

21 A technological improvement lowers the cost of producing coffee. At the same time, preferences for coffee decrease. The *equilibrium quantity* of coffee will
a rise.
b fall.
c remain the same.
d rise or fall depending on whether the price of coffee falls or rises.
e rise or fall depending on the relative shifts of demand and supply curves.

22 Since 1980, there has been a dramatic increase in the number of working mothers. On the basis of this information alone, we can predict that the market for child-care services has experienced a(n)
a increase in demand.
b decrease in demand.
c increase in quantity demanded.
d decrease in quantity supplied.
e increase in supply.

23 If *A* and *B* are complementary goods (in consumption) and the cost of a resource used in the production of *A* decreases, the price of
a both *A* and *B* will rise.
b both *A* and *B* will fall.
c *A* will fall and the price of *B* will rise.
d *A* will rise and the price of *B* will fall.
e *A* will fall and the price of *B* will remain unchanged.

24 The demand curve for knobs is $P = 75 - 6Q_D$ and the supply curve for knobs is $P = 35 + 2Q_S$. What is the equilibrium price of a knob?
a \$5
b \$10
c \$40
d \$45
e None of the above

25 The demand curve for tribbles is $P = 300 - 6Q_D$. The supply curve for tribbles is $P = 20 + 8Q_S$. If the price of a tribble was set at \$120, the tribble market would experience
a equilibrium.
b excess demand causing a rise in price.
c excess demand causing a fall in price.
d excess supply causing a rise in price.
e excess supply causing a fall in price.

Short Answer Problems

1 Explain the difference between wants and demands.

2 The price of personal computers has continued to fall even in the face of increasing demand. Explain.

ⓔ 3 A tax on crude oil would raise the cost of the primary resource used in the production of gasoline. A proponent of such a tax has claimed that it will not raise the price of gasoline using the following argument. While the price of gasoline may rise initially, that price increase will cause the demand for gasoline to decrease, which will push the price back down. What is wrong with this argument?

4 Brussels sprouts and carrots are substitutes in consumption and, since they can both be grown on the same type of land, substitutes in production too. Suppose there is an increase in the demand for brussels sprouts. Trace the effects on price and quantity traded in both the brussels sprout and the carrot market. (Keep in mind Helpful Hint **4**.)

5 The information given in Table 3.1 is about the behaviour of buyers and sellers of fish at the market on a particular Saturday.

TABLE **3.1** DEMAND AND SUPPLY SCHEDULES FOR FISH

Price (per fish)	Quantity Demanded	Quantity Supplied
$0.50	280	40
$1.00	260	135
$1.50	225	225
$2.00	170	265
$2.50	105	290
$3.00	60	310
$3.50	35	320

a On graph paper, draw the demand curve and the supply curve. Be sure to label the axes. What is the equilibrium price?

b We will make the usual *ceteris paribus* assumptions about the demand curve so that it does not shift. List six factors that we are assuming do not change.

c We will also hold the supply curve constant by assuming that five factors do not change. List them.

d Explain briefly what would happen if the price was initially set at $3.

e Explain briefly what would happen if the price was initially set at $1.

f Explain briefly what would happen if the price was initially set at $1.50.

6 The market for wine in Canada is initially in equilibrium with supply and demand curves of the usual shape. Beer is a close substitute for wine; cheese and wine are complements. Use demand and supply diagrams to analyze the effect of each of the following (separate) events on the equilibrium price and quantity in the Canadian wine market. Assume that all of the *ceteris paribus* assumptions continue to hold except for the event listed. For both equilibrium price and quantity you should indicate in each case whether the variable rises, falls, remains the same, or moves ambiguously (may rise or fall).

a The income of consumers falls (wine is a normal good).

b Early frost destroys a large part of the world grape crop.

c A new churning invention reduces the cost of producing cheese.

d A new fermentation technique is invented that reduces the cost of producing wine.

e A new government study is published that links wine drinking and increased heart disease.

f Costs of producing both beer and wine increase dramatically.

ⓔ 7 A newspaper reported, "Despite a bumper crop of cherries this year, the price drop for cherries won't be as much as expected because of short supplies of plums and peaches."

a Use a demand and supply graph for the cherry market to explain the effect of the bumper crop alone.

b On the same graph, explain the impact on the cherry market of the short supplies of plums and peaches.

8 Table 3.2 lists the demand and supply schedules for cases of grape jam.

TABLE **3.2** DEMAND AND SUPPLY SCHEDULES FOR GRAPE JAM PER WEEK

Price (per case)	Quantity Demanded (cases)	Quantity Supplied (cases)
\$70	20	140
\$60	60	120
\$50	100	100
\$40	140	80
\$30	180	60

a On the graph in Figure 3.2, draw the demand and supply curves for grape jam. Be sure to properly label the axes. Label the demand and supply curves D_0 and S_0 respectively.

FIGURE **3.2**

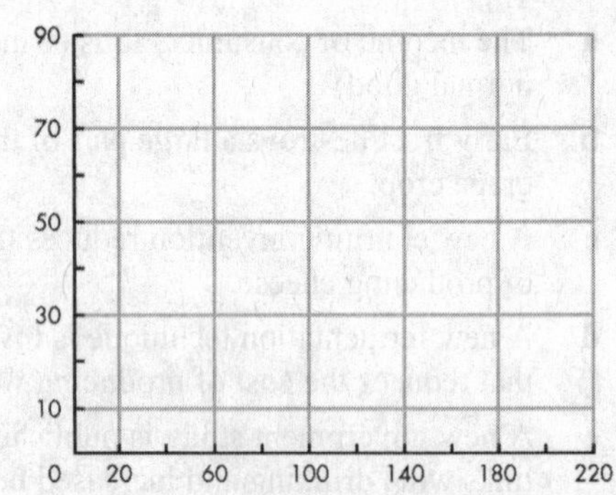

b What are the equilibrium price and quantity in the grape jam market? On your diagram, label the equilibrium point *a*.

c Is there a surplus or shortage at a price of \$40? How much?

d The demand and supply schedules can also be represented by the following demand and supply equations:

Demand: $P = 75 - 0.25Q_D$

Supply: $P = 0.5Q_S$

Use these equations to solve for the equilibrium quantity (Q^*); equilibrium price (P^*). (*Hint:* Your answers should be the same as those in **8b**.)

e Suppose the population grows sufficiently that the demand for grape jam increases by 60 cases per week at every price.

i Construct a table (price, quantity demanded) of the new demand schedule.

ii Draw the new demand curve on your original graph and label it D_1.

iii Label the new equilibrium point *b*. What are the new equilibrium price and quantity?

iv What is the new demand equation? (*Hints:* What is the new slope? What is the new price-axis intercept?)

9 The demand equation for dweedles is

$$P = 8 - 1Q_D$$

The supply equation for dweedles is

$$P = 2 + 1Q_S$$

where P is the price of a dweedle in dollars, Q_D is the quantity of dweedles demanded, and Q_S is the quantity of dweedles supplied. The dweedle market is initially in equilibrium and income is \$300.

a What is the equilibrium quantity (Q^*) of dweedles?

b What is the equilibrium price (P^*) of a dweedle?

c As a result of an increase in income to \$500, the demand curve for dweedles shifts (the supply curve remains the same). The new demand equation is

$$P = 4 - 1Q_D$$

Use this information to calculate the new equilibrium quantity of dweedles; calculate the new equilibrium price of a dweedle.

d On the graph in Figure 3.3, draw and label: (1) the supply curve, (2) the initial demand curve, (3) the new demand curve.

e Are dweedles a normal or inferior good? How do you know?

FIGURE **3.3**

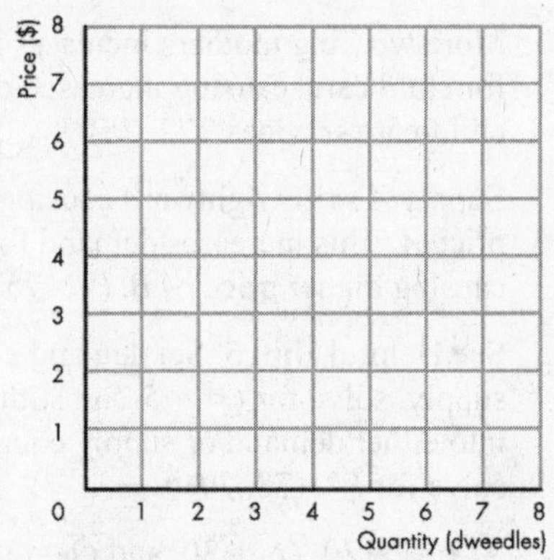

10 The demand equation for flubits is

$$P = 80 - 2Q_D$$

The supply equation for flubits is

$$P = 50 + 1Q_S$$

where P is the price of a flubit in dollars, Q_D is the quantity of flubits demanded, and Q_S is the quantity of flubits supplied. Assume that there are no changes in *ceteris paribus* assumptions.

a If the price of flubits was set at $56, calculate the exact surplus or shortage of flubits.

b Explain the adjustment process that will bring the situation above to equilibrium.

c What is the equilibrium quantity (Q^*) of flubits?

d What is the equilibrium price (P^*) of a flubit?

e Now assume that as a result of technological advance, the supply curve for flubits shifts (the demand curve remains the same). The new supply equation is

$$P = 20 + 1Q_S$$

Use this information to calculate the new equilibrium quantity of flubits; calculate the new equilibrium price of a flubit.

ANSWERS

True/False and Explain

1 F No single buyer or seller influences price. (60)

2 T Relative price is an opportunity cost. (60)

3 T If money prices of other goods rise even more, a good's relative price falls. If price of gum rises from $1 to $2, but price of coffee rises from $1 to $4, opportunity cost of pack of gum falls from 1 to 0.5 coffee forgone. (60)

4 F As price rises, *quantity demanded* decreases. (61)

5 F Measures marginal benefit. (62)

6 T Combined meal of hamburger and fries now cheaper. (63)

7 F Leftward shift for normal good, rightward shift for inferior good. (64)

8 F Supply curve shows minimum price at which last unit supplied. (67)

9 F True if A and B substitutes in production, but false if substitutes in consumption. (68–69)

10 F Beef and leather complements in production because produced together of necessity. (67–68)

11 T For complements in production, higher price for one good causes increased quantity supplied and increase in supply other good. (67–68)

12 F At $P >$ equilibrium P, there is surplus (quantity supplied > quantity demanded). (70–71)

13 F Higher expected future prices cause rightward shift demand and leftward shift supply. Price rises, but Δ quantity depends on relative magnitude shifts. (63–64, 68, 75)

14 T Increased number of firms causes rightward shift supply leading to fall in price and increased quantity. (73)

15 F Quantity will increase but Δ price depends on relative magnitude shifts in demand and supply. (75)

Multiple-Choice

1 e Definitions. (60)

2 b For example, higher-price fries causes decreased demand for hamburgers. (63)

ⓔ 3 c Both income answers could be correct if commodity were normal (**a**) or inferior (**b**). (63–64)

4 c Other answers describe shifts of demand curve. (63–65)

5 b Changes in income shift demand curve rather than causing movement along demand curve. (64)

6 d Decreased quantity demanded is movement up along demand curve. Could also be caused by leftward shift supply. (64–65)

ⓔ 7 c "Other things" shift demand curve. Only price can change along fixed demand curve. (65)

8 a Question describes movement down along supply curve. (66–67)

ⓔ 9 e Answers **a**, **b**, and **c** shift demand, while **d** causes movement along supply curve. (67–69)

10 a Definition of substitute in production. (67–68)

11 b Higher price productive resource shifts supply leftward. (67–68)

12 d Other answers describe shifts of supply curve. (68–69)

13 d Definition of complements in production. Price changes related goods in consumption shift demand. (67–68)

14 e At equilibrium price, plans producers and consumers match; quantity demanded = quantity supplied. (70–71)

15 d All answers describe price above equilibrium price. (70–71)

16 d Other answers make surplus (excess quantity supplied) larger. (70–71)

17 a Shortage is horizontal distance between demand and supply curves at price below equilibrium price. (70–71)

18 c Answers **a** and **b** have indeterminate effect on price, while **d** causes lower price. (74–75)

19 d Demand shifts leftward. (72–73)

20 b Demand shifts rightward. (72–73)

21 e Supply shifts rightward, demand shifts leftward, price definitely falls. (75)

22 a More working mothers increases preferences for child care, causing increased demand for child-care services. (72–75)

ⓔ 23 c Supply *A* shifts rightward causing lower-price *A*. This increases demand for *B*, causing higher price of *B*. (72–75)

ⓔ 24 d See Helpful Hint **5**. Set demand equal to supply, solve for $Q^* = 5$. Substitute $Q^* = 5$ into either demand or supply equation to solve for P^*. (78–79)

ⓔ 25 b At $P = \$120$, $Q_D = 30$, and $Q_S = 12.5$. Excess demand so price will rise. (71, 78–79)

Short Answer Problems

1 Wants are our unlimited desires for goods and services without regard to our ability or willingness to make the sacrifices necessary to obtain them. The existence of scarcity means that many of those wants will not be satisfied. On the other hand, if we demand something, then we want it, can afford it, and have made a definite plan to buy it. Demands reflect decisions about which wants to satisfy.

2 Due to the tremendous pace of technological advance, not only has the demand for personal computers been increasing, but the supply has been increasing as well. Indeed, supply has been increasing much more rapidly than demand, which has resulted in falling prices. Thus *much* (but not all) of the increase in sales of personal computers reflects a movement down along a demand curve rather than a shift in demand.

ⓔ **3** This argument confuses a movement along an unchanging demand curve with a shift in the demand curve. The proper analysis is as follows. The increase in the price of oil (the primary resource in the production of gasoline) will shift the supply curve of gasoline leftward. This will cause the equilibrium price of gasoline to increase and thus the quantity demanded of gasoline will decrease. Demand itself will not decrease—that is, the demand curve will not shift. The decrease in supply causes a movement along an unchanged demand curve.

4 The answer to this question requires us to trace through the effects on the two graphs in Figure 3.4: (a) for the brussels sprout market and (b) for the carrot market. The sequence of effects occurs in order of the numbers on the graphs.

Look first at the market for brussels sprouts. The increase in demand shifts the demand curve rightward from D_0 to D_1 (1), and the price of brussels sprouts rises. This price rise has two effects (2) on the carrot market. Since brussels sprouts and carrots are substitutes in consumption, the demand curve for carrots shifts rightward from D_0 to D_1. And, since brussels sprouts and carrots are substitutes in production, the supply curve of carrots shifts leftward from S_0 to S_1. Both of these shifts in the carrot market raise the price of carrots, causing feedback effects on the brussels sprout market. But remember the rule (Helpful Hint **4**) that each curve (demand and supply) for a given market can shift a maximum of *once*. Since the demand curve for brussels sprouts has already shifted, we can only shift the supply curve from S_0 to S_1 (3) because of the substitutes in production relationship. Each curve in each market has now shifted once and the analysis must stop. We can predict that the net effects are increases in the equilibrium prices of both brussels sprouts and carrots, and indeterminate changes in the equilibrium quantities in both markets.

FIGURE **3.4**

(a) Brussel Sprout Market

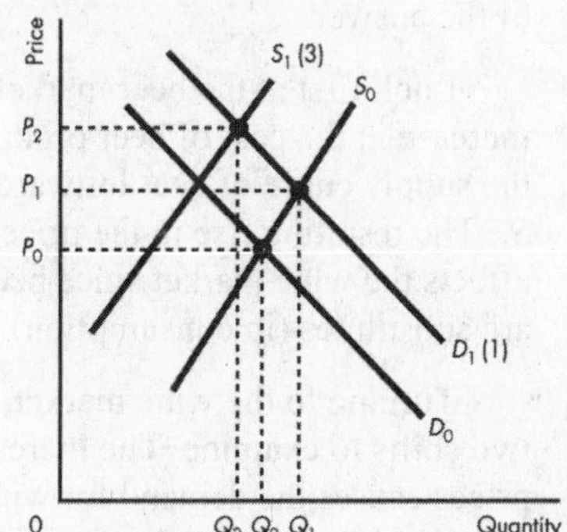

(b) Carrot Market

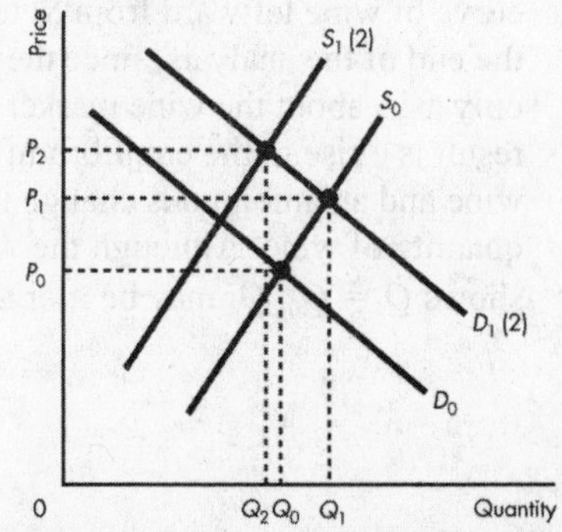

5 a The demand and supply curves are shown in Figure 3.5. The equilibrium price is $1.50 per fish.

FIGURE **3.5**

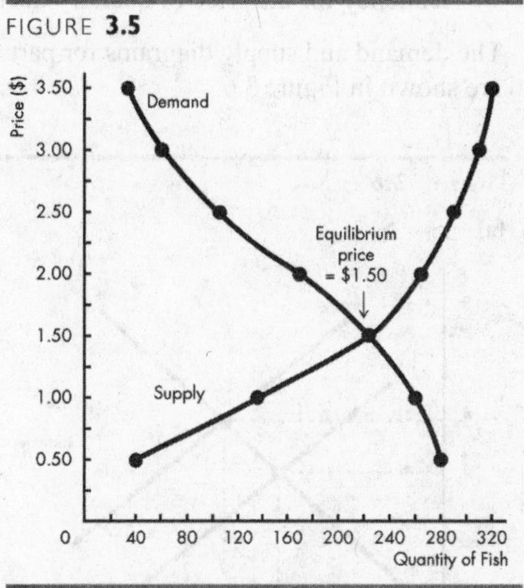

b Prices of related goods; expected future prices; income; expected future income; population; preferences.

c Prices of productive resources; prices of related goods produced; expected future prices; number of suppliers; technology.

d At a price of $3, quantity supplied (310) exceeds quantity demanded (60). Fish sellers find themselves with surplus fish. Rather than be stuck with unsold fish (which yields no revenue), some sellers cut their price in an attempt to increase the quantity of fish demanded. Competition forces other sellers to follow suit, and the price falls until it reaches the equilibrium price of $1.50, while quantity demanded increases until it reaches the equilibrium quantity of 225 units.

e At a price of $1, the quantity demanded (260) exceeds the quantity supplied (135)—there is a shortage. Unrequited fish buyers bid up the price in an attempt to get the "scarce" fish. As prices continue to be bid up as long as there is excess demand, quantity supplied increases in response to higher prices. Price and quantity supplied both rise until they reach the equilibrium price ($1.50) and quantity (225 units).

f At a price of $1.50, the quantity supplied exactly equals the quantity demanded (225). There is no excess demand (shortage) or excess supply (surplus), and therefore no tendency for the price or quantity to change.

6 The demand and supply diagrams for parts **a** to **e** are shown in Figure 3.6.

FIGURE **3.6**

(a)

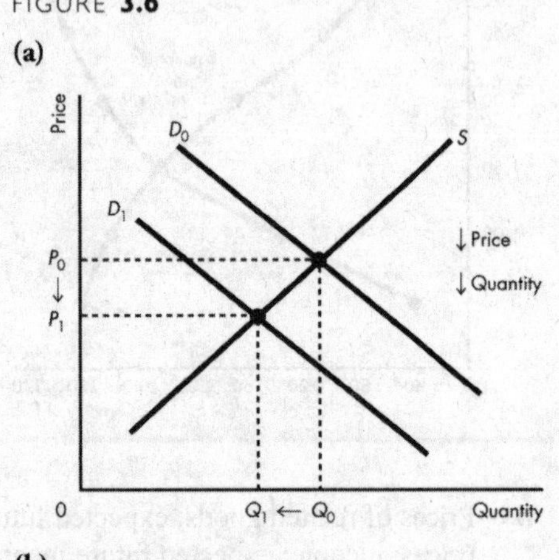

(b)

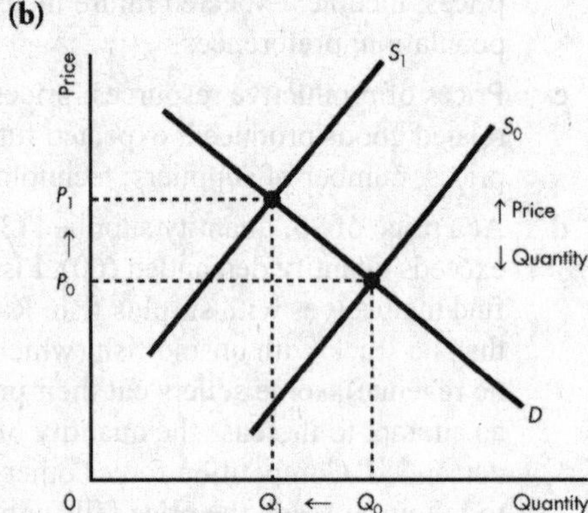

(c)

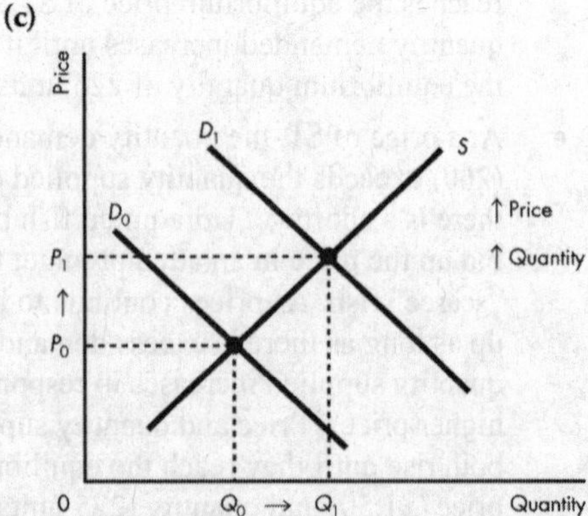

(d)

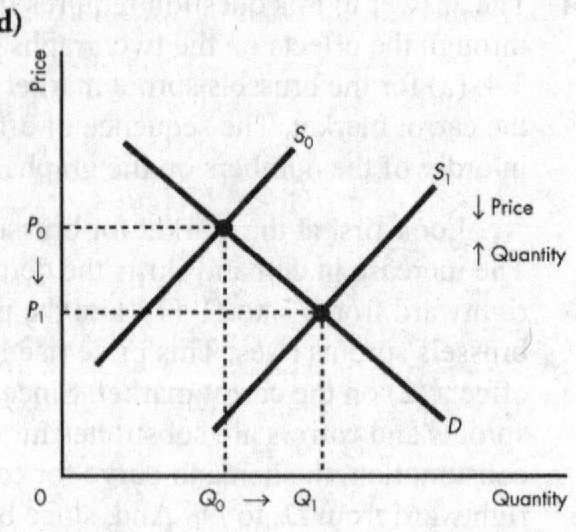

(e)

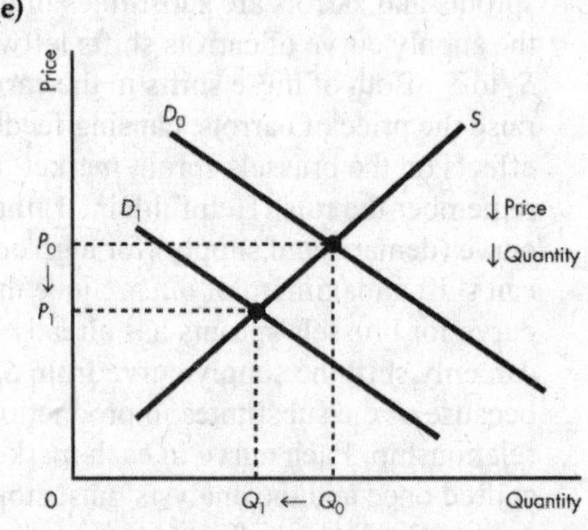

f Questions like this require the examination of two separate but related markets—the beer and wine markets. Since this kind of question often causes confusion for students, Figure 3.7 gives a more detailed explanation of the answer.

Look first at the beer market. The increase in the cost of beer production shifts the supply curve of beer leftward from S_0 to S_1. The resulting rise in the price of beer affects the wine market since beer and wine are substitutes (in consumption).

Turning to the wine market, there are two shifts to examine. The increase in beer prices causes the demand for wine to shift rightward from D_0 to D_1. The increase in the cost of wine production shifts the supply curve of wine leftward from S_0 to S_1. This is the end of the analysis, since the question only asks about the wine market. The final result is a rise in the equilibrium price of wine and an ambiguous change in the quantity of wine. Although the diagram shows $Q_1 = Q_0$, Q_1 may be $\geq$ or $\leq Q_0$.

FIGURE 3.7

(a) **Beer Market**

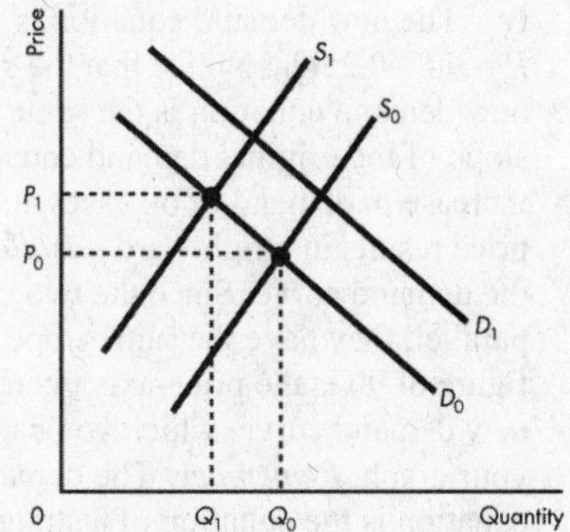

(b) **Wine Market**

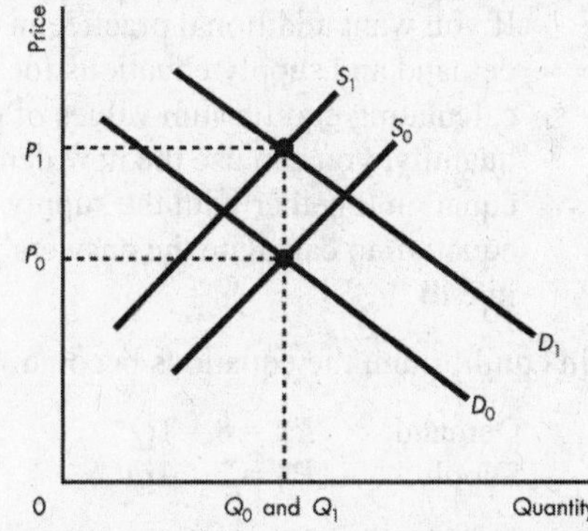

Many students rightfully ask, "But doesn't the rise in wine prices then shift the demand curve for beer rightward, causing a rise in beer prices and an additional increase in the demand for wine?" This question, which is correct in principle, is about the dynamics of adjustment, and these graphs are only capable of analyzing once-over shifts of demand or supply. We could shift the demand for beer rightward, but the resulting rise in beer prices would lead us to shift the demand for wine a *second time*. In practice, stick to the rule that each curve (demand and supply) for a given market can shift a maximum of *once*.

7 **a** The demand and supply curves for the cherry market are shown in Figure 3.8.

FIGURE 3.8

Cherry Market

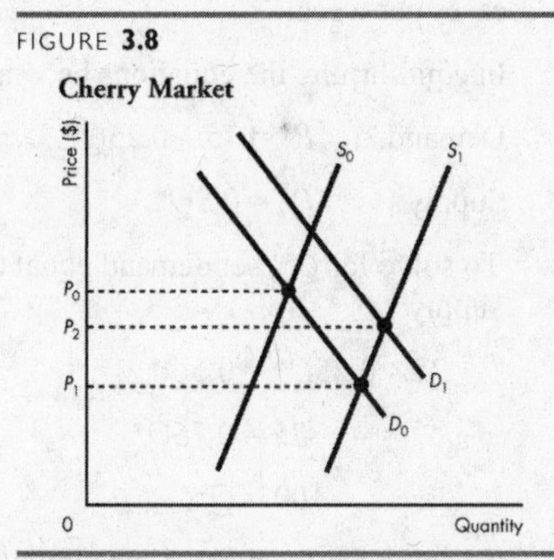

Suppose D_0 and S_0 represent the demand and supply curves for cherries last year. This year's bumper crop increases supply to S_1. Other things being equal, the price of cherries would fall from P_0 to P_1.

b But other things are not equal. Short supplies of plums and peaches (their supply curves have shifted leftward) drive up their prices. The increase in the prices of plums and peaches, which are substitutes in consumption for cherries, increases the demand for cherries to D_1. The net result is that the price of cherries only falls to P_2 instead of all the way to P_1.

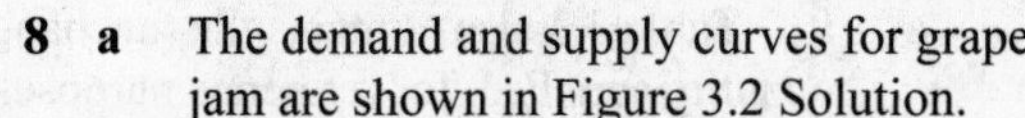

8 **a** The demand and supply curves for grape jam are shown in Figure 3.2 Solution.

FIGURE 3.2 SOLUTION

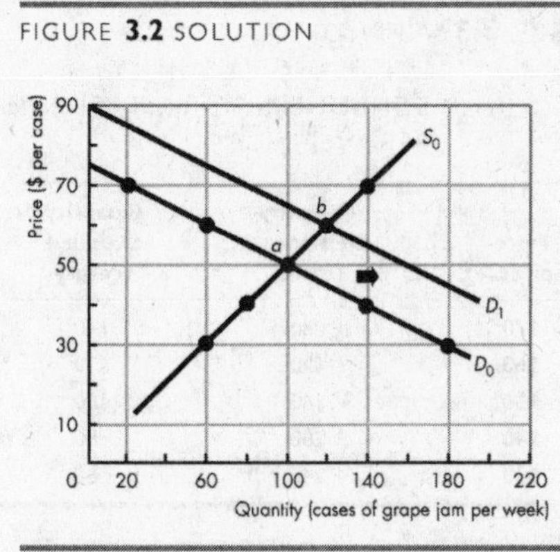

b The equilibrium is given at the intersection of the demand and supply curves (labelled point *a*). The equilibrium price is $50 per case and the equilibrium quantity is 100 cases per week.

c At a price of $40 there is a shortage of 60 cases per week.

d In equilibrium, the equations become:

Demand: $P^* = 75 - 0.25Q^*$

Supply: $P^* = 0.5Q^*$

To solve for Q^*, set demand equal to supply:

$$75 - 0.25Q^* = 0.5Q^*$$
$$75 = 0.75Q^*$$
$$100 = Q^*.$$

To solve for P^*, we can substitute Q^* into either the demand or supply equations. Look at demand first:

$$P^* = 75 - 0.25Q^*$$
$$P^* = 75 - 0.25(100)$$
$$P^* = 75 - 25$$
$$P^* = 50$$

Alternatively, substituting Q^* into the supply equation yields the same result:

$$P^* = 0.5Q^*$$
$$P^* = 0.5(100)$$
$$P^* = 50$$

e **i** Table 3.3 also contains the (unchanged) quantity supplied, for reference purposes.

TABLE **3.3** NEW DEMAND AND UNCHANGED SUPPLY SCHEDULES FOR GRAPE JAM PER WEEK

Price (per case)	Quantity Demanded (cases)	Quantity Supplied (cases)
$70	80	140
$60	120	120
$50	160	100
$40	200	80
$30	240	60

ii The graph of the new demand curve, D_1, is shown in Figure 3.2 Solution.

iii The new equilibrium price is $60 per case and the quantity is 120 cases of grape jam per week.

iv The new demand equation is $P = 90 - 0.25Q_D$. Notice that the slope of the new demand equation is the same as the slope of the original demand equation. An increase in demand of 60 cases at every price results in a rightward *parallel* shift of the demand curve. Since the two curves are parallel, they have the same slope. The figure of 90 is the price-axis intercept of the new demand curve, which you can see on your graph. *Remember:* The demand equation is the equation of a straight line ($y = a + bx$)—in this case, $a = 90$.

If you want additional practice in the use of demand and supply equations for calculating equilibrium values of price and quantity, you can use the new demand curve equation together with the supply curve equation to calculate the answers you found in **e iii**.

9 In equilibrium, the equations become

Demand: $P^* = 8 - 1Q^*$
Supply: $P^* = 2 + 1Q^*$

a To solve for Q^*, set demand equal to supply:

$$8 - 1Q^* = 2 + 1Q^*$$
$$6 = 2Q^*$$
$$3 = Q^*$$

b To solve for P^*, we can substitute Q^* into either the demand or supply equations. Look first at demand:

$$P^* = 8 - 1Q^*$$
$$P^* = 8 - 1(3)$$
$$P^* = 8 - 3$$
$$P^* = 5$$

Alternatively, substituting Q^* into the supply equation yields the same result:

$$P^* = 2 + 1Q^*$$
$$P^* = 2 + 1(3)$$
$$P^* = 2 + 3$$
$$P^* = 5$$

c In equilibrium, the equations are

Demand: $P^* = 4 - 1Q^*$
Supply: $P^* = 2 + 1Q^*$

To solve for Q^*, set demand equal to supply:

$$4 - 1Q^* = 2 + 1Q^*$$
$$2 = 2Q^*$$
$$1 = Q^*$$

To solve for P^*, we can substitute Q^* into either the demand or supply equations. Look first at demand:

$$P^* = 4 - 1Q^*$$
$$P^* = 4 - 1(1)$$
$$P^* = 4 - 1$$
$$P^* = 3$$

Alternatively, substituting Q^* into the supply equation yields the same result:

$$P^* = 2 + 1Q^*$$
$$P^* = 2 + 1(1)$$
$$P^* = 2 + 1$$
$$P^* = 3$$

d The supply curve, initial demand curve, and new demand curve for dweedles are shown in Figure 3.3 Solution.

FIGURE **3.3** SOLUTION

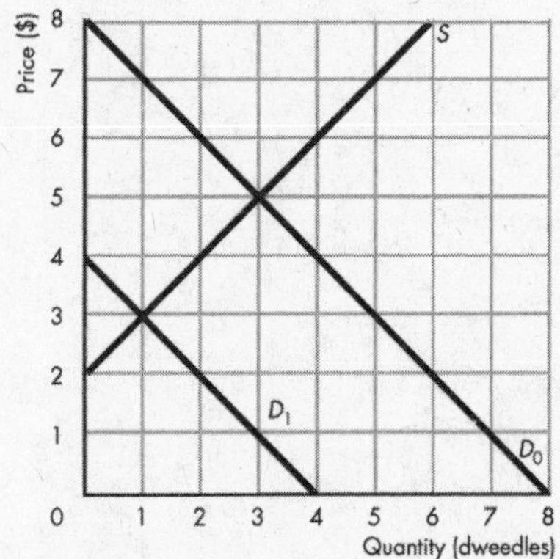

e Dweedles are an inferior good. An increase in income (from $300 to $500) caused a decrease in demand—the demand curve for dweedles shifted leftward.

10 a Substitute the price of $56 into the demand and supply equations to calculate the quantities demanded and supplied at that price. This is the mathematical equivalent of what you do on a graph when you identify a price on the vertical axis, move your eye across to the demand (or supply) curve, and then move your eye down to read the quantity on the horizontal axis.

Substituting into the demand equation, we find

$$P = 80 - 2QD$$
$$56 = 80 - 2QD$$
$$2QD = 24$$
$$QD = 12.$$

Substituting into the supply equation,

$$P = 50 + 1QS$$
$$56 = 50 + 1QS$$
$$6 = QS$$

Quantity demanded exceeds quantity supplied by 6 (12 – 6), so there is a shortage of 6 flubits.

b A shortage means the price was set below the equilibrium price. Competition between consumers for the limited number of flubits will bid up the price and increase the quantity supplied until we reach the equilibrium price and quantity.

c In equilibrium, the equations are

Demand: $P^* = 80 - 2Q^*$

Supply: $P^* = 50 + 1Q^*$

To solve for Q^*, set demand equal to supply:

$$80 - 2Q^* = 50 + 1Q^*$$
$$30 = 3Q^*$$
$$10 = Q^*$$

d To solve for P^*, substitute Q^* into the demand equation:

$$P^* = 80 - 2Q^*$$
$$P^* = 80 - 2(10)$$
$$P^* = 80 - 20$$
$$P^* = 60$$

You can check this answer yourself by substituting Q^* into the supply equation.

e The new equilibrium equations are

Demand: $P^* = 80 - 2Q^*$

Supply: $P^* = 20 + 1Q^*$

To solve for Q^*, set demand equal to supply:

$$80 - 2Q^* = 20 + 1Q^*$$

$$60 = 3Q^*$$

$$20 = Q^*$$

To solve for P^*, substitute Q^* into the supply equations:

$$P^* = 20 + 1Q^*$$

$$P^* = 20 + 1(20)$$

$$P^* = 20 + 20$$

$$P^* = 40$$

You can check this answer yourself by substituting Q^* into the demand equation.

Chapter 19 A First Look at Macroeconomics

KEY CONCEPTS

Origins and Issues of Macroeconomics

Modern macroeconomics was born during the **Great Depression** (a decade of high unemployment).

- ♦ Keynes' focus was the short-term problems of the Depression, which he thought were caused by too little spending.
- ♦ Once out of depression, the events of the 1960s–70s showed government spending contributed to long-term problems of inflation, and slow growth.
- ♦ Modern macroeconomics merges short-term and long-term problems in studying growth and fluctuations, unemployment, inflation, and deficits.

Growth and Fluctuations

Economic growth increases an economy's capacity to produce goods and services, measured by rise in real domestic product (real GDP).

- ♦ **Real GDP**—value of total production, measured in the prices of a single year.
- ♦ **Potential GDP**—real GDP when labour, capital, land, and entrepreneurial ability are fully employed.
- ♦ Economic growth in Canada has had two features:
  - Long-term economic growth—real GDP grew rapidly in the 1960s, followed by less rapid growth (a productivity growth slowdown) in the 1970s.
  - Business cycles—the periodic but irregular fluctuation of real GDP around potential GDP.
- ♦ Each cycle has two turning points (a **peak** and a **trough**), and two phases (**recession** when real GDP decreases for two or more quarters, and **expansion** when real GDP increases).
- ♦ The 1990–91 recession was mild but long compared to earlier recessions, much milder than the Great Depression of the 1930s.
- ♦ Compared to the world's largest economies, Canada has
  - Similar business cycles and **growth recessions** (slowdowns in the economic growth rate).
  - Slower growth of potential GDP than United States or Japan.
- ♦ Lower growth rates of real GDP per person relative to potential GDP lead to accumulated lost output (**Lucas wedge**):
  - Over the business cycle, real GDP – potential GDP = **output gap**.
  - Okun gap = negative output gap.
- ♦ Slow growth means fewer goods and services for individuals and governments.
- ♦ Fast economic growth also has costs—lower consumption from resources devoted to growth rather than consumption, and perhaps more rapid resource depletion and environmental pollution.

Jobs and Unemployment

Every year in Canada, many jobs are created and destroyed. Average net effect is 220,000 new jobs, but in recession, more jobs are destroyed than created, and vice versa in an expansion.

- ♦ **Unemployment** occurs when qualified workers seeking jobs cannot find any.
  - **Labour force**—sum of unemployed and employed.

   - **Unemployment rate**—percentage of labour force unemployed.
   - Unemployment rate underestimates actual unemployment due to exclusion of **discouraged workers** (those who wish to work but give up searching) and part-time workers (who desire full-time work).

- ♦ Unemployment has fluctuated greatly in Canadian history, with peaks occurring in 1930s, early 1980s, and early 1990s.
- ♦ Unemployment rises in recessions and falls in expansions.
- ♦ Costs of unemployment are lost production and incomes of unemployed and damaged job prospects due to lost human capital.

Inflation

Inflation is an increase in average level of prices (or **price level**), measured by the inflation rate (percentage change in price level).

- ♦ **Deflation**—price level is falling and inflation rate is negative.
- ♦ Inflation in Canada was low in the 1960s, rose through the 1970s, and is down since the early 1980s due to the actions of the Bank of Canada.
- ♦ Canada's inflation rate is historically similar to that of other industrial countries, but recently is lower.
- ♦ Unpredictable inflation
   - Creates winners/losers by creating unpredictable changes in the value of money.
   - Leads to resources diverted from productive activities to predicting inflation.
- ♦ Getting rid of inflation is costly, since it usually involves more unemployment.

Surpluses and Deficits

- ♦ **Government budget surpluses** occur when tax revenues exceed spending.
- ♦ **Government budget deficits** occur when government spending exceeds tax revenues.
- ♦ Canada's international deficit occurs when our imports exceed our exports.
   - The international deficit is often measured by the **current account**—exports minus imports and net interest payments to the rest of the world.
- ♦ Deficits of either kind mean governments and nations must borrow, and pay interest on debts. Borrowing can be a problem if it is for consumption purposes, but it can be an advantage if it is for productive purposes.

Macroeconomic Policy Challenges and Tools

Five main policy challenges are to reduce unemployment, increase economic growth, stabilize the business cycle, keep inflation low, and lower government and international deficits.

- ♦ Two main policy tools are
   - **Fiscal policy**—the government changing its tax rates and spending programs
   - **Monetary policy**—the Bank of Canada changing interest rates and the amount of money in the economy

HELPFUL HINTS

1 Note that to be unemployed, as officially measured by the Canadian Labour Force Survey, it is not enough to be without a job. One must also be "actively" seeking a job. Most university students are without jobs, but they are not counted as unemployed since they are not looking for jobs while they are attending school.

2 The variables we study in this chapter are interdependent—they affect and are affected by each other in economic interrelationships that we will learn about in subsequent chapters.

The most important relationship is the effect of the business cycle on other variables. Business cycles significantly affect the unemployment rate. In a recession, the unemployment rate rises, reaching its highest level when the economy is in the trough of the cycle. In an expansion, the unemployment rate falls, reaching its lowest level at the peak.

Government deficits are also affected strongly by business cycles. In a recession, real GDP falls and taxes collected fall, while government payments such as employment insurance and social assistance rise, creating a larger deficit. The opposite effects occur during an expansion.

There is also a strong relationship between business cycles and the current account. When exports are rising and we have a current account surplus, the surplus creates expansionary pressures on real GDP. On the other hand, as the economy expands, Canadians tend to buy more imported goods, pushing the current account toward a deficit.

3 The inflation rate is calculated as the percentage change in prices using the formula

$$\text{Inflation rate} = \frac{\text{Current year's price level} - \text{Last year's price level}}{\text{Last year's price level}} \times 100$$

For example, the average 1997 price level was 107.6, and the average 1996 price level was 105.8, allowing us to calculate the inflation rate for 1997:

$$\text{Inflation rate} = \frac{107.6 - 105.8}{105.8} \times 100 = 1.7\%$$

4 Inflation creates problems because it creates unpredictable changes in the value of money. The *value of money* is the quantity of goods and services that can be bought with a given amount of money. When an economy experiences inflation, the value of money falls—you cannot buy as many goods with a dollar this year as you could last year.

To illustrate this point, consider the data in Table 19.1 on the price of a chocolate bar in Canada over the past 52 years:

TABLE **19.1**

Year	Price of Chocolate Bar (¢)	Number of Bars $1 Buys
1950	10	10.00
1966	15	6.67
1976	30	3.33
1986	75	1.33
2002	100	1.00

Source: Statistics Canada, *The Consumer Price Index*, with calculations and extrapolation from 1989 by H. King.

The table shows us the strong cumulative impact of inflation over this time period, as well as the result that the value of a dollar has fallen enormously over this time period—it buys about 1/10th as many chocolate bars as it did in 1950. When your grandfather tells you "A dollar ain't worth what it used to be," he's telling the truth!

SELF-TEST

True/False and Explain

Origins and Issues of Macroeconomics

1 Macroeconomics focuses only on short-term problems such as unemployment.

Growth and Fluctuations

2 Higher economic growth is always good for an economy.

3 Potential GDP is the level of real GDP when labour, capital, land, and entrepreneurial ability are fully employed.

4 A growth recession means real GDP growth turns negative.

Jobs and Unemployment

5 In the recession phase of a business cycle, the unemployment rate is rising.

6 Discouraged workers are counted as unemployed but probably should not be.

7 Canadian unemployment is virtually identical to U.S. unemployment.

8 A university student seeking a job is counted as unemployed.

F

Inflation

9 If the price level was 130 in 1998 and 110 in 1997, the inflation rate in 1998 was 20 percent.

$\frac{130-110}{110} \times 100$ F

= 18%

10 Since inflation is costly, getting rid of it is always a good idea.

F

11 If the rate of inflation becomes more unpredictable, people will hold less money on average.

T

Surpluses and Deficits

12 If Canada sells more to the rest of the world than it buys from the rest of the world, Canada will have an international deficit.

F

13 A government budget deficit always creates problems for the government.

F

Macroeconomic Policy Challenges and Tools

14 In Canada, fiscal policy is implemented by the federal government.

T

15 One of the five main policy challenges is to increase inflation.

F

Multiple-Choice

Origins and Issues of Macroeconomics

1 Modern macroeconomics
- **a** was born during the 1960s–70s.
- **b** initially focused on long-term problems.
- **c** focuses only on short-term problems.
- **d** now merges both short-term and long-term problems.
- **e** focuses only on long-term problems.

2 Which of the following statements about long-term economic problems is *true*?
- **a** Keynes ignored them.
- **b** Keynes said they could be cured by increased government spending.
- **c** Economists consider them much less important than short-term problems.
- **d** They include inflation and slow economic growth.
- **e** The biggest long-term problem is business cycles.

Growth and Fluctuations

3 Comparing Canada's economic growth with other major industrial economies' growth shows that Canada
- **a** experienced a productivity growth slowdown, but others did not.
- **b** and the United States experienced a productivity growth slowdown, but Japan and Germany did not.
- **c** did not experience the productivity growth slowdown that others did.
- **d** always had a lower level of economic growth.
- **e** and all others experienced a slowdown in economic growth at about the same time.

4 Increasing potential GDP is
- **a** always beneficial since living standards rise.
- **b** always too costly since pollution and resource depletion rise.
- **c** beneficial only if pollution rises at less than 5 percent a year.
- **d** beneficial if the benefits of rising living standards outweigh the costs of higher pollution and resource depletion.
- **e** none of the above.

5 Which of the following statements by politicians is talking about the business cycle?
a "Canadian unemployment is falling due to the upturn in the economy."
b "Crime rates increase every spring as the school year ends."
c "An average of 220,000 new jobs are created each year in Canada."
d "More capital investment will create more jobs."
e "Business always rises just before Christmas."

6 Real GDP is defined as the yearly value of all
a goods produced in an economy.
b goods and services produced in an economy.
c goods and services produced in households.
d production when resources are fully employed.
e goods and services produced in an economy, measured in the prices of a single year.

7 In New Adanac, the average growth rates of potential GDP were 4 percent in the 1980s, but fell to 1 percent in the 1990s. Which of the following statements about this change is true?
a The Okun gap equals 3% of GDP for each of the 10 years.
b The Okun gap equals 1% of GDP for each of the 10 years.
c The Lucas wedge equals 3% of GDP for each of the 10 years.
d The Lucas wedge equals 1% of GDP for each of the 10 years.
e The Lucas wedge equals 4% of GDP for each of the 10 years.

8 In New Adanac, the percentage change in real GDP went from 5 percent in 2003 to 2 percent in 2004. What would an economist call this change in the growth rate?
a a growth recession
b a recession
c an expansion
d a trough
e a slowdown recession

Jobs and Unemployment

9 Compared to the U.S. unemployment rate, the Canadian unemployment rate moves
a independently of the U.S. rate.
b with the U.S. rate, but at a lower level recently.
c in the opposite direction to the U.S. rate.
d with the U.S. rate, but at a higher level recently.
e with the U.S. rate, at the same level.

10 The economic costs of unemployment include
a workers quitting and going to university.
b political problems for government.
c lost human capital of the unemployed.
d the creation of winners and losers due to job creation/destruction.
e the diversion of resources from productive activities to predicting unemployment.

11 In which year was the unemployment rate in Canada almost 20 percent?
a 1982
b 1976
c 1959
d 1933
e 1926

12 In a country with a population of 20 million, there are 9 million employed and 1 million unemployed. What is the labour force?
a 20 million
b 10 million
c 9 million
d 8 million
e 1 million

13 In a country with a population of 20 million, there are 9 million employed and 1 million unemployed. What is the unemployment rate?
a 11%
b 10%
c 8%
d 5%
e 1%

14 Including discouraged workers in the measured unemployment rate would
a not change the measured unemployment rate.
b lower the measured unemployment rate.
c lower the labour force.
d raise the measured unemployment rate only if there are no part-time workers.
e raise the measured unemployment rate.

Inflation

15 If the inflation rate is positive, the price level in an economy is
- **a** falling rapidly.
- **b** rising.
- **c** constant.
- **d** falling slowly.
- **e** zero.

16 How does an unpredictable inflation cause problems?
- **a** Business cycles become more variable.
- **b** The stock market falls in value.
- **c** The value of money rises.
- **d** Resources are diverted from productive activities to tax evasion.
- **e** Resources are diverted from productive activities to forecasting inflation.

17 Which of the following statements about Canada's inflation rate is *false*?
- **a** It is currently much lower than that of other industrial countries.
- **b** It was low in the 1960s.
- **c** It rose in the 1970s.
- **d** It fell in the 1980s due to the actions of the Bank of Canada.
- **e** Historically, it has always been around that of other industrial countries.

18 If a price index was 128 at the end of 1987 and 136 at the end of 1988, what was the rate of inflation for 1988?
- **a** 4.2%
- **b** 5.9%
- **c** 6.25%
- **d** 8%
- **e** 9.4%

19 If the price index in 1997 is equal to 130, and the inflation rate between 1997 and 1998 is 5 percent, what is the price index in 1998?
- **a** 136.5
- **b** 135
- **c** 125
- **d** 123.5
- **e** 105

Surpluses and Deficits

20 The government deficit will rise if
- **a** we buy more from other countries than we sell to them.
- **b** we sell more to other countries than we buy from them.
- **c** government revenues rise.
- **d** unemployment rises.
- **e** baby boomers continue to run the country.

21 In most years between 1975 and 1995, Canada's current account was
- **a** in deficit.
- **b** in surplus.
- **c** growing.
- **d** shrinking.
- **e** alternating between surpluses and deficits.

22 Deficits are a problem
- **a** if they are caused by economic growth.
- **b** only if they are international deficits, not government budget deficits.
- **c** only if they are government budget deficits, not international deficits.
- **d** only when they are caused by borrowing for consumption purposes.
- **e** only when they are caused by borrowing to buy income-generating assets.

23 Which of the following will *increase* the Canadian current account deficit?
- **a** Japan buys wheat from farmers in Canada.
- **b** Japan buys wheat from farmers in Australia.
- **c** Japan buys Canada Savings Bonds.
- **d** Canada buys Hondas from Japan.
- **e** Canada sells coal to Japan.

Macroeconomic Policy Challenges and Tools

24 An example of fiscal policy is changing the
- **a** interest rate.
- **b** money supply.
- **c** exchange rate.
- **d** tax rate.
- **e** all of the above.

25 Which of the following is *not* a policy challenge?
- **a** lowering unemployment
- **b** stabilizing the business cycle
- **c** keeping inflation low
- **d** lowering economic growth
- **e** lowering government deficits

Short Answer Problems

1 What are the economic costs of unemployment?

2 Go to the Statistics Canada World Wide Web site (**www.statcan.ca**) or the Statistics Canada publication *The Consumer Price Index*, and find out the price level in December of the most recent year available, as well as the previous year, and calculate the inflation rate over that year.

3 What is meant by the value of money? Why does the value of money fall when there is inflation?

ⓒⓣ 4 The federal government gives full-time students a tax credit per month of studies. In 1990, Tracy received this credit, which was worth $50 per month, whereas in 2006 Jennifer received a credit worth $200 per month. In 1990, the price level was 52.4, and in 2006 it was 116.5. Was the value of the tax credit money worth more to Jennifer or Tracy? (Ignore any changes in taxes, tuition, etc.)

5 What is the current account? What has its recent history been like?

6 During each of the four parts of the business cycle, what happens to real GDP compared to potential GDP, and to the unemployment rate?

7 Workers and managers in the ABC Company have negotiated a wage agreement under the expectation that the inflation rate will be zero over the period of the contract. In order to protect workers against unpredictable inflation, however, the contract states that at the end of each year, the wage rate will increase by the same percentage as the increase in the Consumer Price Index (CPI). At the beginning of the contract the CPI is 214 and the wage rate is set at $10 an hour. At the end of the first year the CPI is 225, and at the end of the second year the CPI is 234. What will the new wage rate become at the end of the first year? the second year?

8 Consider the following information about an economy: Population—25 million, employment—10 million, unemployment—1 million.

a What is the labour force in this economy?

b What is the unemployment rate?

9 Consider the following data on unemployment and the growth rate of real GDP from the country of Dazedland:

TABLE **19.2**

Year	Percentage Change in Real GDP	Unemployment Rate
1	2.0	7.0
2	3.0	6.0
3	1.0	7.8
4	0.0	9.0
5	–2.0	11.5
6	–0.3	9.5
7	3.0	6.5
8	1.5	7.5

The economy starts with real GDP equal to potential GDP. Potential GDP grows at a rate of 2 percent per year.

a Identify the peaks and troughs of the business cycle for this economy.

b In what years is this economy in recession?

c In which years did this economy have growth recessions?

d What is the relation between unemployment and the business cycle for this economy?

e In which years did this economy have an Okun gap?

ⓒⓣ 10 Is more economic growth good or bad for a society?

ANSWERS

True/False and Explain

1 F Recently macroeconomics merges short-term and long-term issues into a broad study. (446)

2 F Depends on benefits versus costs of higher growth. (452)

3 T Definition. (447)

4 F Real GDP growth still positive, but real GDP falls below potential GDP. (448)

5 T In recession, real GDP growth becomes negative, some workers become unemployed. (452)

6 F Not counted as unemployed, but probably should be. (453)

7 F Canadian and U.S. unemployment move together, but recently Canadian unemployment > U.S. unemployment. (454)

8 F Counted as out of the labour force (not actively seeking work). (452)

9 F Inflation = [(130 – 110)/110] × 100 = 18.2%. (455)

10 F Inflation is costly, but so is getting rid of it, which increases unemployment. It depends on the relative size of the costs. (457)

11 T Unpredictable changes in the value of money lead individuals to hold less money. (456)

12 F Sales > purchases implies international *surplus*. (457)

13 F Depends whether government borrows to increase consumption (bad) or investment (good). (458)

14 T It chooses spending, taxation, and deficits which is fiscal policy. (459)

15 F *Decrease* inflation. (459)

Multiple-Choice

1 d Born during the Great Depression, when it focused on short-term problems, but recently merges studies of both. (446)

2 d Keynes worried about them, noting they could be caused by too much government spending, but focused on short-term problems. **e** is short-term. (446)

3 e See Text Figure 19.4—all four countries had a substantial fall in their growth rates around 1970. (449–450)

4 d To decide, must weigh both costs and benefits and see which is higher. (452)

5 a Upturn implies expansion implies unemployment falls. **b** and **e** are irrelevant and seasonal, **c** is the average over the cycle, **d** is growth in potential GDP. (448)

6 e Definition. (447)

7 c We cannot tell what the Okun gap is in each year, as we do not know actual GDP. Lucas wedge = accumulated loss of output from a slowdown in real GDP growth = 4% – 1% = 3%. (451)

8 a Definition. (448)

9 d See Text Figure 19.7 and its discussion. (454)

10 c **a** is a gain, **b** is real but not economic cost, **d** is normal activity, **e** is nonsense. (454)

11 d During the Great Depression of the 1930s. (453)

12 b Labour force = unemployed + employed. (452)

13 b Unemployment rate = unemployed/labour force = 1/10. (452)

14 e It would add extra unemployed workers to the measured rate. (453)

15 b Positive inflation implies current price level – past price level > 0 by definition. (455)

16 e Forecasting inflation becomes important because unpredictable inflation leads to unpredictable winners and losers because the value of money *falls*. (456)

17 a See Text Figure 19.9. (456)

18 c 6.25% = [(136 – 128)/128] × 100. (452)

19 a Solve for P_{1998} in formula: inflation rate = $[(P_{1998} - P_{1997})/P_{1997}] \times 100$. $5 = [(P_{1998} - 130)/130] \times 100$. (452)

20 d **a**, **b**, **e** are irrelevant, while **c** lowers deficit. Rising unemployment implies more government spending and less tax revenues. (457)

21 a See Text Figure 19.10. (458)

22 d Both types of deficits can be problems, if they are for consumption, because they do not generate profits/income to help repay the resulting debts. **a** is irrelevant. (458)

23 d **a** and **e** lower the deficit, **b** and **c** are irrelevant. (457)

24 d **a** and **b** are monetary policy, **c** is neither. (459)

25 d Raising economic growth is a policy challenge. (459)

Short Answer Problems

1 The biggest cost of unemployment is the lost production and income. In addition, when workers are unemployed for long periods of time, their skills and abilities (human capital) deteriorate, and so do their future job prospects.

2 You should have used the following formula:

$$\text{Inflation rate} = \frac{\text{Current year's price level} - \text{Last year's price level}}{\text{Last year's price level}} \times 100$$

3 The value of money is the quantity of goods and services that can be purchased with one unit of money. Since inflation means that prices are rising on average, it means that one unit of money will buy less. Thus the value of money falls when there is inflation.

ⓒⓣ 4 There are two ways to answer this question. First, between 1990 and 2006 the tax credit has risen in value by 300 percent (= 150/50 × 100), while the price level has risen by 122 percent (= (116.5 – 52.4)/52.4 × 100). Clearly prices have risen less than the dollar value of the credit, raising the value of this money, so Jennifer gains more from it. Second, you could calculate the purchasing power of the tax credit in terms of how many goods it can purchase (remember, the price index measures the cost of a typical family's purchases). For Tracy the credit purchased 0.96 of a typical family's purchases (= 50/52.4), whereas for Jennifer it purchased 1.72 (= 200/116.5). Clearly Jennifer gained more from the credit.

5 The current account includes our exports minus our imports and also takes interest payments paid to and received from the rest of the world into account. As Text Figure 19.10 shows, Canada's current account had been fluctuating (but usually in deficit) since 1970 to the late 1990s, but since the late 1990s it has been mostly in surplus.

6 During the recession phase of the business cycle, the rate of growth of real GDP slows down and becomes negative, and real GDP falls below potential GDP. During this phase the unemployment rate is rising. At the trough, real GDP reaches its lowest point below potential GDP, and the unemployment rate is at its highest point over the cycle. The trough is a turning point between the recession phase and the expansion phase during which the rate of growth of real GDP increases and the unemployment rate falls. At the end of an expansion, the economy reaches the peak of the business cycle. The peak is characterized by real GDP at its highest point above potential GDP and the rate of unemployment is at its lowest point over the business cycle.

7 In order to determine the new wage rate at the end of the first year, we must determine the percentage increase in the CPI and apply that percentage change to the initial wage rate of $10 an hour. The percentage change in the CPI is [(225 – 214)/214] × 100, or 5.1 percent. Therefore, the new wage rate at the end of the first year will be $10 × 1.051 = $10.51. During the second year, the increase in the CPI is 4 percent. Thus the new wage rate at the end of the second year will be $10.51 × 1.04 = $10.93.

8 a The labour force is 11 million, the sum of employment and unemployment.

b The unemployment rate is 9.1 percent, the number of unemployed as a percentage of the labour force.

9 a Peaks occur when the percentage change in real GDP turns from positive to negative, year 4. Troughs occur when the percentage change in real GDP turns from negative to positive, between years 6 and 7.

b The economy is in recession when the growth rate of real GDP is negative, years 5 and 6.

c A growth recession occurs when economic growth is positive, but real GDP is below potential GDP. In Dazedland, this likely occurs in years 3, 4, and 8, when real GDP growth is below potential GDP growth.

d There is a rough inverse relationship between the two variables—when real GDP is rising, the unemployment rate is falling (between years 1 and 2), and when real GDP is falling, the unemployment rate is rising (between years 4 and 5).

e An Okun gap occurs when real GDP is less than potential GDP. In this economy, an Okun gap likely occurs when real GDP growth is less than potential GDP growth of 2 percent. This situation happens in years 3, 4, and 8.

ⓒⓣ 10 There is no correct answer to this question, since it depends on the balance of the costs versus the benefits of more growth—it is a normative question. However, a society would need to weigh the costs (lost current consumption because of resources devoted to growth rather than current consumption, and potentially more rapid resource depletion and environmental pollution) against the benefits (an increase in consumption possibilities of individuals and governments) and make a judgment.

Chapter 20 Measuring GDP and Economic Growth

KEY CONCEPTS

Gross Domestic Product

Gross domestic product (GDP) is the market value of all final goods and services produced within a country in a given time period.

- ♦ Total production is measured by the market value of each good.
- ♦ Only new **final goods** (those bought by their final users) are measured, not **intermediate goods** (those bought by firms from each other and used as inputs in production).
- ♦ GDP measures total production *and* total income *and* total expenditure.

The *circular flow* of expenditure and income shows four economic sectors (firms, households, governments, rest of world) operating in three key markets (goods markets, factor markets, financial markets).

- ♦ Households sell factor services to firms in return for income—total household income = aggregate income (Y).
- ♦ Household income is spent on taxes (to government), on **consumption expenditure** (C) on goods and services, and on **saving** (S = Income – Net taxes – Consumption) in financial markets.
- ♦ Firms produce goods and services, and sell C to households, **investment** (I = purchase of *new* capital) to other firms, **government expenditures** (G) to governments, and **net exports** = (exports (X)—imports (M)) to the rest of world.
- ♦ Governments interact with households and firms to buy goods and services, collect taxes, provide transfer payments (**Net taxes** (NT) = taxes – transfer payments – government debt interest payments), and borrow (to cover budget deficits).
- ♦ The rest of world buys our **exports** and sells us **imports**, and borrows and lends to us in financial markets.

Circular flow shows that aggregate income = aggregate production = aggregate expenditure:

$$Y = C + I + G + X - M$$

- ♦ Circular flow also shows how I is financed by private saving (S) + government saving ($NT - G$) + borrowing from rest of world ($M - X$):

$$I = S + (NT - G) + (M - X)$$

- ♦ If $NT > G$, the government can lend some of its surplus.
- ♦ If foreigners sell Canadians more goods than they buy from us ($M > X$), we must borrow this amount from them to finance it, so part of their savings flows to us for investment purposes.
- ♦ I is financed by **national saving** (= $S + (NT - G)$) + foreign borrowing.

GDP is a flow (quantity per unit of time). A stock is a quantity at a point in time.

- ♦ A key stock is **wealth** (value of all things people own), and Δ wealth = saving.
- ♦ The capital stock is plant, equipment, buildings, and inventories used to produce goods and services.
  - Investment (I) = purchase of *new* capital.
  - **Depreciation** = fall in stock of capital because of wear and tear = **capital consumption**.
  - **Gross investment** = net investment + replacing depreciated capital.
  - Δ capital stock = **net investment** = gross investment – depreciation.

Measuring Canada's GDP

Statistics Canada measures GDP two ways on the basis of the following equality:

income = production = expenditure

- ♦ Expenditure approach measures $C + I + G + X - M$.
- ♦ *Income approach* adds up all incomes paid from firms to households (with some adjustments).
  - Net domestic income at factor cost = wages, etc. + profits + interest/investment income + farmers' income + nonfarm unincorporated business income.
  - Net domestic product at market prices = net domestic income + indirect taxes – subsidies.
  - GDP = net domestic product + depreciation.

Real GDP and the Price Level

GDP increases from production of more goods and services, or from higher prices for goods and services.

- ♦ **Nominal GDP** is the value of final goods and services produced in a given year when valued at that year's prices = the sum of expenditures on goods and services.
- ♦ **Real GDP** is the value of final goods and services produced in a given year when valued at constant prices. Real GDP measures changes in production only.
- ♦ Real GDP is calculated using the **chain-weighted output index** method:
  - First, calculate the value of the current year's quantities and the previous year's quantities using the prices of the *previous* year, and calculate the resulting increase in value from the previous year.
  - Second, calculate the value of the current year's quantities and the previous year's quantities using the prices of the *current* year, and calculate the resulting increase in value from the previous year.
  - Third, take the average of the two increases in value—this is the increase in real GDP from the previous year.

The average level of prices is the **price level**.

- ♦ **GDP deflator** is an average of current year prices expressed as a percent of base-year prices =

$$\frac{\text{Nominal GDP}}{\text{Real GDP}} \times 100$$

Measuring Economic Growth

Economic growth rate = annual percentage change in quantity of goods and services produced =

$$\frac{\text{Real GDP this year} - \text{Real GDP last year}}{\text{Real GDP last year}} \times 100$$

- ♦ Real GDP is used to assess **economic welfare** (measure of economic well-being), make international comparisons, and assess business cycles.
- ♦ Real GDP as a measure of economic welfare is flawed because
  - Price indexes overadjust for inflation.
  - Real GDP does not include factors that increase economic welfare (household production, underground economic activity, health and life expectancy, leisure, political freedom, and social justice).
  - Real GDP does not include factors that lower economic welfare (pollution).
  - International comparisons of real GDP per capita are further flawed by currency conversion problems.
- ♦ Despite flaws, real GDP is a reasonably accurate indicator of recessions/expansions, but it probably overstates fluctuations in economic welfare by ignoring household production and leisure time.

HELPFUL HINTS

1 Studying the circular flow and the national accounts can be boring, but it is useful for several reasons. First, they provide crucial equalities that are the starting point for our economic model—studying this material will help you pass the course! Second, many current debates involve tradeoffs between economic growth and environmental damage. Understanding what GDP does and does not measure is crucial to this debate. Third, in macroeconomics we study how several markets operate simultaneously in a joint, interrelated equilibrium—the circular flow gives us our first taste of this interrelation.

2 One of the key equations in this and future chapters is the identity:

$$Y = C + I + G + X - M$$

which underlies Chapters 23 and 24.

Macroeconomics tries to understand what affects GDP, and we start in this chapter by measuring production (GDP). However, we cannot directly measure production that easily. The circular flow helps us measure it indirectly. In the circular flow, production is purchased by the four economic decision makers (measured by expenditure), and the money earned from these sales is used to pay incomes. Therefore, production can be measured in three equivalent ways:

income = expenditure = value of production (GDP)

Therefore:

Y (income) = $C + I + G + X - M$ (expenditure)

3 Be sure to distinguish carefully between intermediate goods and investment goods. Both are goods sold by one firm to another, but they differ in terms of their use. Intermediate goods are processed and then resold, while investment goods are final goods. Also note that the national income accounts include purchases of residential housing as investment because housing, like business capital stock, provides a continuous stream of value over time.

4 Note the difference between government expenditures on goods and services (G) and government transfer payments. Both involve payments by the government, but transfer payments are not payments for currently produced goods and services. Instead, they are simply a flow of money, just like taxes. Think of transfer payments as negative taxes. We define net taxes (NT) as taxes minus transfer payments minus interest payments on government debt.

5 It is very important to understand the difference between real and nominal GDP. Nominal GDP is the value, *in current prices*, of the output of final goods and services in the economy in a year. Real GDP evaluates those final goods and services *at the prices prevailing in a base year (constant prices)*.

Nominal GDP can rise from one year to the next, either because prices rise or because the output of goods and services rises. A rise in real GDP, however, means that the output of goods and services has risen.

If we had a simple economy that produced only pizzas, this rise in real GDP would be easy to measure—are there more pizzas to eat? In a multiple-good economy, we have a more complex task, and must turn to a weighted average of the goods and services we produce.

6 The chain-weighted output index method is the method Statistics Canada uses to measure real GDP. It is a difficult concept, and it is worth summarizing the steps:

a Calculate the value of the current year's quantities and the previous year's quantities using the *previous* year's prices, and calculate the percentage change in the value of the quantities from last year to this year (define %Δ as percentage change):

$$\%\,\Delta \text{ in value of production at previous prices} = \frac{\text{Sum of current quantities at previous prices} - \text{Sum of previous quantities at previous prices}}{\text{Sum of previous quantities at previous prices}} \times 100$$

b Calculate the value of the current year's quantities and the previous year's quantities using the *current* year's prices, and calculate the percentage change in the value of the quantities from last year to this year:

$$\%\,\Delta \text{ in value of production at current prices} = \frac{\text{Sum of current quantities at current prices} - \text{Sum of previous quantities at current prices}}{\text{Sum of previous quantities at current prices}} \times 100$$

c Take the average of these two percentage changes, and this is the percentage change in real GDP:

$$\%\,\Delta \text{ in real GDP} = \frac{\%\,\Delta \text{ in value of production at previous prices} + \%\,\Delta \text{ in value of production at current prices}}{2}$$

d Apply this percentage change to last year's real GDP to get this year's real GDP:

This year's real GDP = last year's real GDP × [1 + (%Δ in real GDP)/100]

e By applying this method to each year's quantities, we can link each year's real GDP back to the base year. For example, next year's real GDP would be calculated from the change in real GDP between this year and next year, using this year and next year's prices.

SELF-TEST

True/False and Explain

Gross Domestic Product

1 Wage payments to households are an example of a real flow from firms to households.

2 A higher government deficit lowers investment, other things being equal.

3 Net investment gives the net addition to the capital stock.

4 In the aggregate economy, income is equal to expenditure and to GDP.

5 If exports currently equal imports, then GDP must equal consumption plus investment plus government expenditures.

6 Net exports are positive if the expenditure by foreigners on goods and services produced in Canada are greater than the expenditure by Canadian citizens on goods and services produced in other countries.

Measuring Canada's GDP

7 If there were only households and firms and no government, market price and factor cost would be equal for any good.

8 Net exports are used in the income approach to measuring GDP.

9 Profits are part of the income approach to measuring GDP.

Real GDP and the Price Level

10 If you are interested in knowing whether the economy is producing more output, you would look at real GDP rather than nominal GDP.

11 The GDP deflator is real GDP divided by nominal GDP, multiplied by 100.

12 The chain-weighted output index method for measuring real GDP calculates the changes in value of the quantities produced using only the previous year's prices.

13 If real GDP this year is $116 billion, and last year it was $113 billion, then the economic growth rate was 3 percent.

Measuring Economic Growth

14 If underground economic activity was included in GDP calculations, measured GDP levels would be higher.

15 If two economies have the same real GDP per person, the standard of living must be the same in each economy.

Multiple-Choice

Gross Domestic Product

1 The capital stock in the year 2006 equals the capital stock in the year 2005
- **a** minus depreciation.
- **b** plus net investment plus depreciation.
- **c** plus gross investment.
- **d** plus net investment.
- **e** plus net investment minus depreciation.

2 Which of the following is a *real* flow from households to firms?
- **a** goods and services
- **b** factor services
- **c** payments for goods and services
- **d** payments for factor services
- **e** loans

3 For the aggregate economy, income equals
- **a** expenditure, but these are not generally equal to GDP.
- **b** GDP, but expenditure is generally less than these.
- **c** expenditure equals GDP.
- **d** expenditure equals GDP only if there are no government or foreign sectors.
- **e** expenditure equals GDP only if there is no depreciation.

4 Which of the following is *false*?
- **a** $Y = C + I + G + M - X$
- **b** $I = S + (NT - G) + (M - X)$
- **c** $Y = C + S + NT$
- **d** $Y + M = C + I + G + X$
- **e** $Y = C + I + G + X - M$

5 The capital stock does *not* include the
- **a** inventory of raw cucumbers ready to be made into pickles by the Smith Pickle Company.
- **b** Smith family holdings of stock in the Smith Pickle Company.
- **c** pickle factory building owned by the Smith family.
- **d** pickle-packing machine in the pickle factory building owned by the Smith family.
- **e** pickle inventories in the pickle factory building owned by the Smith family.

6 Saving can be measured as income minus
- **a** taxes.
- **b** transfer payments.
- **c** net taxes minus consumption expenditure.
- **d** consumption expenditure.
- **e** net taxes plus subsidies.

7 Investment is financed by
- **a** $C + I + G + X - M.$
- **b** $C + S + NT.$
- **c** $S + NT + M.$
- **d** $S + (NT - G) + (X - M).$
- **e** $S + (NT - G) + (M - X).$

8 Which of the following is a consumption expenditure?
- **a** Spending by the CBC on children's programs
- **b** Welfare payments to single mothers
- **c** The purchase of a new car by the IPSCO steel company
- **d** The purchase of a new car by the Singh household
- **e** The purchase of a computer by the IPSCO steel company

9 Which of the following will happen if the government sector's deficit increases?
- **a** More funds will be available to lend to the rest of the world.
- **b** More funds will be available to finance investment.
- **c** In the circular flow, consumption expenditure will fall.
- **d** GDP will be higher.
- **e** Less funds will be available to finance investment.

Measuring Canada's GDP

10 To obtain the factor cost of a good from its market price
- **a** add indirect taxes and subtract subsidies.
- **b** subtract indirect taxes and add subsidies.
- **c** subtract both indirect taxes and subsidies.
- **d** add both indirect taxes and subsidies.
- **e** subtract depreciation.

11 Interest plus miscellaneous investment income is a component of which approach to measuring GDP?
- **a** income approach
- **b** expenditure approach
- **c** injections approach
- **d** output approach
- **e** opportunity cost approach

12 From the data in Table 20.1, what is net investment in Eastland?
a –$160
b $160
c $240
d $400
e $500

TABLE 20.1 DATA FROM EASTLAND

Item	Amount ($)
Wages, salaries, and supplementary labour income	800
Farm income	80
Government expenditures on goods and services	240
Capital consumption	240
Gross private domestic investment	400
Personal income taxes net of transfer payments	140
Corporate profits	80
Indirect taxes	120
Net exports	80
Consumption expenditures	640
Interest and miscellaneous investment income	100

13 From Table 20.1, what additional data are needed to compute net domestic income at factor cost?
a income of nonfarm unincorporated businesses
b transfer payments
c subsidies
d depreciation
e net taxes

14 From the data in Table 20.1, what is GDP in Eastland?
a $1,120
b $1,180
c $1,360
d $1,420
e not calculable with the given information

Real GDP and the Price Level

15 From the data in Table 20.2, compute Southton's nominal GDP in the current year.
a $197
b $198
c $208
d $209
e cannot be calculated given the data

TABLE 20.2 DATA FROM SOUTHTON

Item	Price ($) Base	Price ($) Current	Quantity Base	Quantity Current
Rubber ducks	1.00	1.25	100	100
Beach towels	7.00	6.00	12	14

16 From the data in Table 20.2, compute Southton's nominal GDP in the base year.
a $184
b $197
c $198
d $209
e cannot be calculated given the data

17 From the data in Table 20.2, compute Southton's real GDP in the base year.
a $184
b $197
c $198
d $209
e cannot be calculated given the data

18 What is the correct definition of the chain-weighted output index method of calculating real GDP in 2006?
a The value of the final goods and services produced in 2006 valued at the prices that prevailed in 2006.
b The value of the final goods and services produced in 2006 valued at the prices that prevailed in the base year.
c Nominal GDP in 2006 multiplied by the GDP deflator.
d The value of final goods and services produced in the base year valued at the 2006 prices.
e Take 2005's real GDP and add the average of the increases in real GDP calculated using the 2005 prices and the 2006 prices.

19 From the data in Table 20.3, what is Northton's GDP deflator in 2006?
a 250
b 200
c 160
d 125
e 80

TABLE 20.3 DATA FROM NORTHTON

Year	Nominal GDP	Real GDP	GDP Deflator (1996 = 100)
1996	125	125	100
2006	250	200	
2007	275		122.22

20 Use the Northton data in Table 20.3. What is real GDP in 2007?
a 336.2
b 275
c 225
d 220
e 110

Measuring Economic Growth

21 Consider the data in Table 20.3. What is the growth rate of real GDP between 2006 and 2007?
- a –2.8%
- (b) 12.5%
- c 22.2%
- d 25%
- e 100%

22 The underground economy is all economic activity that
- a produces intermediate goods or services.
- b is not taxed.
- (c) is legal but unreported or is illegal.
- d has negative social value.
- e is conducted underground.

23 Given that pollution is a byproduct of some production processes,
- a GDP accountants adjust GDP downward.
- b GDP accountants adjust GDP upward.
- c GDP accountants do not adjust GDP unless pollution is a serious problem.
- (d) GDP tends to overstate economic welfare.
- e GDP tends to understate economic welfare.

24 Which of the following is *not* a reason for GDP incorrectly measuring the value of total output?
- a leisure time
- b household production
- c underground economic activity
- (d) capital consumption
- e environmental quality

25 Which of the following is the major reason China's measured GDP might be underestimated?
- a It includes replacement of depreciated capital stock.
- b It includes production processes that create pollution as a side-effect.
- c It ignores decreases in health and life expectancy.
- (d) It does not use purchasing power parity prices.
- e It ignores human rights and political freedoms.

Short Answer Problems

ct 1 How can we measure gross domestic product by using either the expenditure or the income approach, when neither of these approaches actually measures production?

2 Suppose nominal GDP rises by 75 percent between year 1 and year 2.
- a If the average level of prices has also risen by 75 percent between year 1 and year 2, what has happened to real GDP?
- b If the average level of prices has risen by less than 75 percent between year 1 and year 2, has real GDP increased or decreased?

3 What *productive* activities are *not* measured and thus are *not* included in GDP? Is this lack of measurement a serious problem?

4 Use the data for Northland given in Table 20.4 to compute the following:

TABLE 20.4 DATA FROM NORTHLAND

Item	Amount (billions of $)
Consumption expenditure (*C*)	600
Taxes (*Tax*)	400
Transfer payments (*TR*)	250
Exports (*X*)	240
Imports (*M*)	220
Government expenditure on goods and services (*G*)	200
Gross investment (*I*)	150
Depreciation (*Depr*)	60

- a GDP
- b net investment
- c net exports
- d after-tax income
- e saving
- ct f the value of each of the three sources of financing for investment

5 Use the data for the same economy given in Table 20.5 to compute:

TABLE 20.5 DATA FOR NORTHLAND

Item	Amount (billions of $)
Wages, salaries, and supplementary labour income	550
Indirect taxes	120
Subsidies	20
Farmers' income	20
Corporate profits	80
Interest and miscellaneous investment income	90
Depreciation	60
Income of nonfarm unincorporated businesses	70

- a net domestic income at factor cost
- b net domestic product at market prices
- c GDP

6 Table 20.6 gives data for Easton, where there are three final goods included in GDP: pizzas, beer, and CDs.
  a Calculate nominal GDP in 2006 and 2007.
  b What is real GDP in 2006?
  c Using the chain-weighted method, what is real GDP in 2007?
  d What is the GDP deflator in 2007?

TABLE **20.6**

	2007		2006 (Base Period)	
Goods	**Output**	**Price ($)**	**Output**	**Price ($)**
Pizza	110	8	105	6
Beer	50	10	55	8
CDs	50	9	40	10

7 Table 20.7 gives data for the country of Weston.

TABLE **20.7** DATA FOR WESTON

Year	Nominal GDP	Real GDP	GDP Deflator
2005	3,055		94
2006		3,170	100
2007	3,410	3,280	
2008		3,500	108

  a Complete Table 20.7.
  b What is the base year for the GDP deflator?
  c Calculate the percentage change in nominal GDP, real GDP, and the GDP deflator between 2007 and 2008. Was the increase in nominal GDP due mostly to an increase in real GDP or to an increase in the price level?

8 Figure 20.1 shows the circular flow for Northweston. All amounts are in thousands of dollars.

FIGURE **20.1**

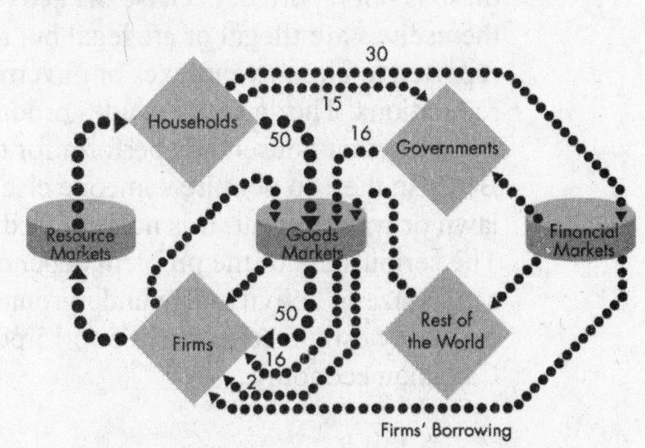

Use Figure 20.1 to calculate, for Northweston,
  a GDP.
  b aggregate expenditure.
  c investment.
  d aggregate income.
  e household saving.
  f government borrowing or saving.
  g foreign borrowing or saving.
  h firms' borrowing.

9 Consider the following list of economic activities. Identify which of the three markets in the circular flow that each activity belongs to. Give a one-line reason for your answer in each case.
  a Fred of the Forest buys a new loincloth in preparation for his date with Angela.
  b Fred goes back to school at the University of Sandhurst to get his BA in Vine Swinging.
  c While in school, Fred receives student loans.
  d Fred has graduated, and is getting paid to knock down trees by Treetop City.
  e Fred pays income taxes on his income from his new job.
  f Fred goes on a holiday in the United States.

10 Consider the list of economic activities in Short Answer Problem 9 above. Identify whether the activity involves expenditures, and, if so, which component of expenditures each activity belongs to (C, I, G, X, M).

ANSWERS

True/False and Explain

1 **F** It is a money flow in payment for real flow. (467)

2 **T** Higher deficit implies lower ($NT - G$), which implies lower $I = S + (NT - G) + (M - X)$. (469)

3 **T** Net investment nets out depreciation (replacement of worn-out capital), leaving only new capital additions. (469)

4 **T** From circular flow, firm production is sold (expenditure) and earnings used to pay out incomes. (468)

5 **T** If $X = M$, then $X - M = 0$, and $Y = C + I + G + 0$. (468)

6 **T** By definition of exports (goods and services sold to the rest of the world) and imports (goods bought from the rest of the world), and net exports = exports – imports. (468)

7 **T** Market price = factor cost + taxes – subsidies. (472)

8 F They are an expenditure, used in the expenditure approach. (471)
9 T Definition. (471–472)
10 T Real GDP measures the quantity of goods and services, while nominal measures current dollar value and includes price level increases. (473)
11 F GDP deflator = [(nominal GDP)/(real GDP)] × 100. (474)
12 F It calculates the average of this change *and* the changes using the current year's prices. (474)
13 F Economic growth = [(real GDP this year – real GDP last year)/(real GDP last year)] × 100 = [(116 – 113)/113] × 100 = 2.7%. (476)
14 T Since they are omitted, and they are a productive activity, real GDP would be higher if they were included. (477)
15 F Real GDP is imperfect measure of standard of living; answer depends on factors such as exchange rates between each country's currency. (478–479)

Multiple-Choice

1 d Definition. (469)
2 b **a** is in opposite direction, others are money flows. (467)
3 c Expenditure = money earned by sales of produced goods which is used to pay incomes (including profits). (468)
4 a Should be $X - M$ and not $M - X$. (467–468)
5 b Equity is financial asset, not capital. (469)
6 c From $S = (Y - NT) - C$. (468)
7 e Definition. (468)
8 d **a** is government expenditure, **b** is transfer payment, **c** and **e** are investment. (467–468)
9 e A higher deficit means $NT - G$ is smaller, so $I = S + (NT - G) + (M - X)$ is smaller. (468–469)
10 b Market price = factor cost + indirect taxes – subsidies, so factor cost = market price – indirect taxes + subsidies. (472)
11 a Definition. (472)
12 b Net investment = gross investment – capital consumption. (469)
13 a Table lists the other four components of factor incomes. (472)
14 c $Y = C + I + G + X - M = 640 + 400 + 240 + 80 = 1{,}360$. (471)
15 d Nominal GDP = sum of dollar value (= current price × current quantity) of all goods = ($1.25 × 100) + ($6 × 14) = 209. (473–474)
16 a Nominal GDP = sum of current price × current quantity of all goods = ($1 × 100) + ($7 × 12) = 184. (473–474)
17 a In base year, real GDP = nominal GDP. (473–474)
18 e Definition. (473–474)
19 d GDP deflator = [(nominal GDP)/(real GDP)] × 100. (474–475)
20 c Real GDP = [(nominal GDP)/(GDP deflator)] × 100. (474–475)
21 b Growth rate of real GDP = [(real GDP in 2007) – (real GDP in 2006)]/(real GDP in 2006) × 100. (476)
22 c Definition. (477)
23 d No such adjustment occurs, so GDP overstates economic welfare. (477)
24 d Capital consumption is depreciation and is part of GDP. (476–478)
25 d See text discussion. (478–479)

Short Answer Problems

ct **1** The analysis of the circular flow showed that firms produce goods and services (what we wish to measure), sell them (what the expenditure approach measures), and then use the proceeds to pay for factor incomes, rents, profits, etc. (what the income approach measures). Therefore expenditure = production = income.

2 a Real GDP is unchanged. The increased value of goods and services is only because of increased prices.

b The fact that prices have risen less in proportion to the increase in nominal GDP means that real GDP has increased.

3 Activities that produce goods and services that are not included in GDP are underground economic activity and household production. The first of these is not reported, because the activities themselves are illegal or are legal but are not reported to circumvent taxes or government regulations. The second includes productive activities that households perform for themselves. Because they do not hire someone else to mow the lawn or wash the car, it is not included in GDP. The seriousness of the problem depends on the actual size of activity. The underground economy is usually estimated as about 5 to 15 percent of the Canadian economy.

4 a GDP = $C + I + G + (X - M)$ = $970 billion.
b Net $I = I - Depr$ = $90 billion.
c Net exports = $X - M$ = $20 billion.
d After-tax income = GDP + $TR - Tax$ = $820 billion.
e Saving = after-tax income – C = $220 billion.
ⓒⓣ **f** $I = S + (NT - G) + (M - X)$ or 150 = 220 + (150 – 200) + (220 – 240). Saving contributes $220 billion, the government budget deficit reduces investment by $50 billion, and the net export surplus reduces investment by $20 billion.

5 a Net domestic income at factor cost = wages, salaries, and supplementary labour income + interest and miscellaneous investment income + corporate profits + farmers' income + income of nonfarm unincorporated business = $810 billion.

b Net domestic product at market prices = net domestic product at factor cost + indirect taxes – subsidies = $910 billion.

c GDP = net domestic product at market prices + depreciation = $970 billion.

6 a Nominal GDP is the sum of the expenditures on all goods in the year in question. For 2006, Nominal GDP = ($6 × 105) + ($8 × 55) + ($10 × 40) = $1,470. For 2007, Nominal GDP = ($8 × 110) + ($10 × 50) + ($9 × 50) = $1,830.

b Since 2006 is the base period, Nominal GDP = Real GDP = $1,470.

c First, calculate real GDP in 2007 by using the 2006 prices and the 2007 quantities: ($6 × 110) + ($8 × 50) + ($10 × 50) = $1,560. Percentage change in the value of production = [(1,560 – 1,470)/1,470] × 100 = +6.1%.

Second, calculate the value of the 2006 quantities using 2007 prices: ($8 × 105) + ($10 × 55) + ($9 × 40) = $1,750. At 2006 prices, the value of production increased from $1,750 to $1,830, an increase of +4.6% (= [(1,830 – 1,750)/1,750] × 100).

Finally, average the two increases: (6.1 + 4.6)/2 = 5.35%. Real GDP in 2007 is 5.35 percent higher than in 2006. Real GDP in 2006 was $1,470, so real GDP in 2007 is $1,548.65 (= $1,470 × 1.0535).

d The GDP deflator = [(nominal GDP)/(real GDP)] × 100 = (1,830/1,548.65) × 100 = 118.

7 a Table 20.7 is completed here as Table 20.7 Solution. The following equation is used: GDP deflator = (nominal GDP/real GDP) × 100.

TABLE **20.7** SOLUTION

Year	Nominal GDP	Real GDP	GDP Deflator
2005	3,055	3,250	94
2006	3,170	3,170	100
2007	3,410	3,280	104
2008	3,780	3,500	108

b The base year is 2006—GDP deflator is 100.
c Percentage change in nominal GDP = [(3,780 – 3,410)/3,410] × 100 = 10.9%. Percentage change in real GDP = [(3,500 – 3,280)/3,280] × 100 = 6.7%. Percentage change in GDP deflator = [(108 – 104)/104] × 100 = 3.8%. Since the percentage change in real GDP is higher than the percentage change in the GDP deflator, most of the increase in nominal GDP is due to an increase in real GDP.

8 a GDP can be calculated from how households spend their income: $Y = C + S + NT$ = 50 + 30 + 15 = $95,000.
b Aggregate expenditure = GDP = $95,000.
c Investment is the only missing component of aggregate expenditure, and can be deduced from the equation $Y = C + I + G + X - M$ or 95 = 50 + I + 16 + 2, implying I = $27,000. (Note that the components of aggregate expenditure must all flow through the goods market.)
d Aggregate income paid to households must equal aggregate expenditure earned by firms, so it equals $95,000.
e Household saving goes from households to financial markets, and equals $30,000.
f Government borrowing or saving = $NT - G$ = 15 – 16 = –$1,000, borrowing.
g From examining the goods market, foreign borrowing or saving = $X - M$ = $2,000 of borrowing.
h Firms' borrowing comes from the fact that saving = firms' borrowing + government borrowing + foreign borrowing, or 30 = firms' borrowing + 1 + 2, so that firms' borrowing = $27,000.

9 a Goods and service market—purchase of a good.
b Goods and service market—purchase of an educational service.
c Financial market—household borrowing.
d Factor market—Fred is working for wage income.
e Not part of any market, a direct flow to the government.
f Goods and services market—import expenditure, since the money flows to the United States.

10 a Expenditure (*C*).
b Expenditure (*C*).
c Not an expenditure, a financial flow.
d Not an expenditure, a factor service purchase.
e Not an expenditure, a flow to the government.
f Expenditure (*M*).

Chapter 21 Monitoring Cycles, Jobs, and the Price Level

KEY CONCEPTS

The Business Cycle

The **business cycle** is the periodic, irregular up-and-down movement in production and jobs.

- Each cycle has a peak of activity, followed by a recession (a significant decline in economic activity) that ends in a trough. The trough is followed by an expansion when real GDP increases.
- A **growth rate cycle downturn** is a persistent decline in the growth rate of aggregate economic activity.

Jobs and Wages

Employment is a key feature in determining the onset of recession. Statistics Canada surveys households to estimate job status.

- **Working-age population** = Number of people 15 years and over.
- **Labour force** = employed + unemployed
  - Employed = those with full-time and part-time jobs.
  - Unemployed = without work, actively seeking within last four weeks, waiting to be called back after layoff, or waiting to start new job within four weeks.
- **Unemployment rate** = Percentage of labour force who are unemployed. Increases in recessions, but no trend recently.
- Involuntary part-time rate = percentage of labour force who are part-time but want full-time. Increases in recessions.
- **Labour force participation rate** = percentage of working-age population who are in labour force. Strong upward trend, but decreases in recessions because of **discouraged workers** (people who temporarily leave labour force in a recession).
- **Employment-to-population ratio** = percentage of working-age population with jobs. Increased overall since 1960s (many new jobs created), but decreases in recessions.
- Participation and employment rates down for men and up (strongly) for women since 1960s, creating increase in both overall rates.
- To see quantity of labour employed, examine **aggregate hours** = total hours worked.
  - Upward trend, decreases in recessions.
  - Hours per worker has downward trend, with faster decreases in recessions.
- **Real wage rate** = quantity of goods an hour's work can buy = **money wage rate** (dollars per hour)/price level. Upward trend, but at slower rate since early 1970s.

Unemployment and Full Employment

- People become unemployed when they
  - are laid off (**job losers**).
  - voluntarily quit (**job leavers**).
  - enter (**entrants**) or re-enter (**re-entrants**) the labour force to search for jobs.
- People end unemployment when they are hired, recalled, or withdraw from the labour force.

- ♦ Primary source of unemployment is job loss, which fluctuates strongly with business cycle.
- ♦ Wide range in duration of unemployment, higher in recessions.
- ♦ Unemployment rate is higher for younger people.

The types of unemployment are frictional, structural, seasonal, and cyclical.

- ♦ **Frictional unemployment**—normal turnover and a healthy part of a dynamic economy. Depends on the number of entrants/re-entrants and job creation/destruction. Higher in Canada than in the United States due to Canada's employment insurance generosity.
- ♦ **Structural unemployment**—job losses in industries/regions that are declining due to technological change or international competition. Tends to last longer than frictional unemployment.
- ♦ **Seasonal unemployment**—jobs decreases in certain seasons.
- ♦ **Cyclical unemployment**—fluctuations in unemployment over the business cycle. Increases in recession, decreases in expansion.

Full employment—only frictional, structural, and seasonal unemployment occurring (no cyclical unemployment).

- ♦ Unemployment rate at full employment is called the **natural rate**.
- ♦ Actual unemployment rate fluctuates around the natural rate, as real GDP fluctuates around **potential GDP** (quantity of real GDP at full employment).
  - When real GDP < potential GDP, unemployment rate > natural rate.
  - When real GDP > potential GDP, unemployment rate < natural rate.

The Consumer Price Index

The **Consumer Price Index (CPI)** measures the average of prices paid for a fixed basket of consumer goods and services.

- ♦ CPI = 100 for the **base period**.
- ♦ CPI basket is constructed from surveys of consumers' spending habits, with prices surveyed monthly.
- ♦ $\text{CPI} = \dfrac{\text{Cost of CPI basket at current prices}}{\text{Cost of CPI basket at base-period prices}} \times 100.$
- ♦ **Inflation rate** = Percentage change in the price level
- ♦ CPI overstates the inflation rate (biased upward) because
  - new goods replace old goods.
  - quality improvements create some part of price rises.
  - consumers change consumption towards cheaper goods not reflected in fixed-basket price index.
  - consumers substitute toward discount outlets not covered in CPI surveys.
- ♦ Magnitude of CPI bias probably low in Canada, but it will lead to distorted contracts, more government outlays, and incorrect wage bargaining.

HELPFUL HINTS

1 In a dynamic economy, some unemployment is efficient. There are economic benefits of frictional unemployment to the individual and to society. Younger workers typically experience periods of unemployment trying to find jobs that match their skills and interests. The benefit of the resulting frictional unemployment is a more satisfying and productive work life. Society benefits because the frictional unemployment that accompanies such a job-search process allows workers to find jobs in which they are more productive. As a result, the total production of goods and services in the economy increases. (Compare this case with the case for graduates in the Republic of China up until the 1990s. They were assigned jobs upon graduation, with very little personal input about type of job or location.)

On the other hand, structurally unemployed workers will not get a new job without retraining or relocation. This fact means a much greater cost to the worker and society—structurally unemployed workers are typically unemployed for much longer time periods. These workers bear much of the cost of restructuring industries in our economy, although society gains in the long run from the shift of labour and other productive resources to the new industries.

2 The term "full employment," or its equivalent "the natural rate of unemployment," does not mean that everyone has a job. Rather, it means

that the only unemployment is frictional, structural, and seasonal—there is no cyclical unemployment. (Note this definition implies the natural rate is higher in the wintertime!)

It is possible for the actual rate of unemployment to be less than the natural rate of unemployment, because it is possible for the level of employment to exceed full employment. In these situations, people are spending too little time searching for jobs, and therefore less-productive job matches are being made.

3 There are four different types of unemployment, but defining these types does not explain them. Explanations of how unemployment occurs is a goal of the remaining chapters in the textbook!

SELF-TEST

True/False and Explain

The Business Cycle

1 A recession is a persistent decline in the growth rate of aggregate economic activity.

2 The correct order of a business cycle is expansion, peak, recession, trough.

Jobs and Wages

3 The employment-to-population ratio is the percentage of working-age population in the labour force.

4 If the employment-to-population ratio increases, unemployment always decreases.

5 If the number of discouraged workers decreases, the employment-to-population ratio decreases as they begin to look for jobs.

6 George was laid off last month, and is waiting to be recalled to his old job, so he is not actively seeking work. George is *not* counted as unemployed.

7 The real wage rate has an upward trend since the 1970s.

Unemployment and Full Employment

8 Being unemployed for a few months after graduating from university always hurts the graduate.

9 A decline in the number of jobs in the automobile sector matched by an equal increase in the number of jobs offered in the banking sector will not alter the unemployment rate.

10 At full employment, there is no unemployment.

11 Bill has just graduated from high school and is looking for his first job. Bill is frictionally unemployed.

12 Fluctuations in unemployment over the business cycle create frictional unemployment.

The Consumer Price Index

13 The CPI overstates the inflation rate because it ignores substitution toward higher-quality goods by households.

14 The market basket used in calculating the CPI changes each year.

15 The magnitude of the CPI bias in Canada is quite high.

Multiple-Choice

The Business Cycle

1 In 2005, real GDP growth was +4% in the first quarter, +3% in the second quarter, +2% in the third quarter, and +1% in the fourth quarter of the year. In 2005, this economy

- **a** suffered a recession.
- **b** reached a trough in the final quarter.
- **c** reached a peak in the final quarter.
- **d** suffered a growth rate cycle downturn.
- **e** showed no evidence of a business cycle.

2 During a recession, real GDP __________ and employment __________.

- **a** increases; increases
- **b** increases; decreases
- **c** decreases; increases
- **d** decreases; decreases
- **e** decreases; stays constant

Jobs and Wages

3 Including discouraged workers in the measured unemployment rate would

- **a** not change the measured unemployment rate.
- **b** lower the measured unemployment rate.
- **c** raise the natural rate of unemployment.
- **d** raise the full employment rate.
- **e** raise the measured unemployment rate.

4 In a country with a working-age population of 20 million, 13 million are employed, 1.5 million are unemployed, and 1 million of the employed are working part time, half of whom wish to work full time. The size of the labour force is

- **a** 20 million.
- **b** 15.5 million.
- **c** 14.5 million.
- **d** 13 million.
- **e** 11.5 million.

5 In a country with a working-age population of 20 million, 13 million are employed, 1.5 million are unemployed, and 1 million of the employed are working part-time, half of whom wish to work full-time. The labour force participation rate is

- **a** 75.5%.
- **b** 72.5%.
- **c** 65%.
- **d** 57.5%.
- **e** none of the above.

6 In a country with a working-age population of 20 million, 13 million are employed, 1.5 million are unemployed, and 1 million of the employed are working part time, half of whom wish to work full time. The unemployment rate is

- **a** 10%.
- **b** 10.3%.
- **c** 11.5%.
- **d** 15.4%.
- **e** none of the above.

7 Who of the following would be counted as unemployed in Canada?

- **a** Doris only works five hours a week, but is looking for a full-time job.
- **b** Kanhaya has stopped looking for work, since he was unable to find a suitable job during a two-month search.
- **c** Sharon is a college student with no job.
- **d** Maurice has been laid off from his job for 20 weeks, but expects to be called back soon.
- **e** Bogdan has been laid off from his job, but does not expect to be called back and is not looking.

8 If the number of discouraged workers increases, all else unchanged, the

- **a** unemployment rate will increase.
- **b** employment-to-population ratio will decrease.
- **c** labour force participation rate will increase.
- **d** labour force participation rate will decrease.
- **e** employment-to-population ratio will increase.

9 Initially the money wage rate is $10 per hour, and the price level is 100. If the money wage rate increases to $20 per hour and the price level increases to 125, what happens to the real wage rate?
- **a** It stays the same.
- **b** It doubles in value.
- **c** It decreases in value.
- **d** It increases in value, but by less than double.
- **e** It increases in value, by more than double.

10 If the employment-to-population ratio increases,
- **a** the unemployment rate *must* decrease.
- **b** the labour force participation rate *must* increase.
- **c** the labour force participation rate will be unaffected.
- **d** aggregate hours worked *must* increase.
- **e** none of the above.

11 The increase in the Canadian labour force participation rate since the 1960s is largely due to the
- **a** increase in female labour force participation.
- **b** increase in male labour force participation.
- **c** decrease in the number of baby boomers.
- **d** increase in youth labour force participation.
- **e** decrease in the number of discouraged workers.

Unemployment and Full Employment

12 Which of the following events would raise cyclical unemployment?
- **a** Real GDP growth slows down or turns negative.
- **b** Unemployment benefits increase.
- **c** The pace of technological change increases.
- **d** Both job destruction and job creation increase.
- **e** All of the above.

13 Unemployment will increase if there is an increase in the number of people
- **a** retiring.
- **b** withdrawing from the labour force.
- **c** recalled from layoffs.
- **d** leaving jobs to go to school.
- **e** leaving school to find jobs.

14 Who of the following would be considered structurally unemployed?
- **a** a Saskatchewan farmer who has lost her farm and is unemployed until retrained
- **b** a Nova Scotia fishery worker who is searching for a better job closer to home
- **c** a steelworker who is laid off but who expects to be called back soon
- **d** an office worker who has lost her job because of a general slowdown in economic activity
- **e** none of the above

15 Who of the following would be considered cyclically unemployed?
- **a** a Saskatchewan farmer who has lost her farm and is unemployed until retrained
- **b** a Nova Scotia fishery worker who is searching for a better job closer to home
- **c** a steelworker who is laid off but who expects to be called back soon
- **d** an office worker who has lost her job because of a general slowdown in economic activity
- **e** none of the above

16 Who of the following would be considered frictionally unemployed? A steelworker who
- **a** loses her job because of technological change.
- **b** is laid off but expects to be called back within a week.
- **c** gives up her job because she retires.
- **d** decides to leave the labour force and become a full-time ballet student.
- **e** becomes discouraged and stops looking for a job.

17 In a recession, what is the largest source of the increase in unemployment?
- **a** job leavers
- **b** job losers
- **c** new entrants to the labour force
- **d** re-entrants to the labour force
- **e** involuntary part-time workers

18 At full employment, there is no
- **a** natural unemployment.
- **b** unemployment.
- **c** cyclical unemployment.
- **d** structural unemployment.
- **e** frictional unemployment.

19 Unemployment caused by permanently decreased demand for horse-drawn carriages is an example of
- **a** cyclical unemployment.
- **b** seasonal unemployment.
- **c** frictional unemployment.
- **d** structural unemployment.
- **e** discouraged unemployment.

20 The natural rate of unemployment is
  a the rate at which unemployment equals 0%.
  b the same as cyclical unemployment.
  c the rate at which cyclical unemployment equals 6%.
  d the rate at which cyclical unemployment equals 0%.
  e none of the above.

21 The duration of a spell of unemployment typically
  a decreases in recession and increases in expansion.
  b decreases in recession and in expansion.
  c increases in recession and in expansion.
  d increases in recession and decreases in expansion.
  e does not change during recessions and expansions.

The Consumer Price Index

TABLE **21.1** DATA FROM SOUTHTON

Item	Price ($) Base	Price ($) Current	Quantity Base	Quantity Current
Rubber ducks	1.00	1.25	100	100
Beach towels	9.00	6.00	12	14

22 From the data in Table 21.1, what is Southton's consumer price index for the current year?
  a 112
  b 105.6
  c 100.5
  d 100
  e 94.7

23 Refer to the data in Table 21.1. Between the base year and the current year, the relative price of rubber ducks
  a remained unchanged.
  b fell.
  c rose.
  d cannot be determined with the amount of information given.
  e depends on whether overall inflation was positive.

24 Which of the following is *not* a reason the Consumer Price Index overstates inflation?
  a New goods of higher quality and prices replace old goods.
  b Quality improvements create some part of price rises in existing goods and services.
  c Consumers change their consumption basket toward cheaper goods not reflected in the fixed-basket price index.
  d Consumers substitute toward using discount outlets not covered in CPI surveys.
  e It does not measure the underground economy.

25 The technique used to calculate the CPI implicitly assume that consumers buy
  a relatively more of goods with relative prices that are increasing.
  b relatively less of goods with relative prices that are decreasing.
  c the same relative quantities of goods as in a base year.
  d goods and services whose quality improves at the rate of growth of real GDP.
  e more computers and CD players and fewer black-and-white TVs.

Short Answer Problems

(ct) 1 Explain why an economy does not have 0 percent unemployment when it has full employment.

(ct) 2 Should the government try to force the unemployment rate down as close to zero as possible? Discuss some problems such a policy might create.

3 Consider the following information about an economy: working-age population—20 million; full-time employment—8 million; part-time employment—2 million (1 million of whom wish they had full-time jobs); unemployment—1 million.
  a What is the labour force in this economy? What is the labour force participation rate?
  b What is the unemployment rate?
  c What is the involuntary part-time rate?
  d What is the employment-to-population ratio?
  e If 0.6 million of those unemployed are frictionally, structurally, and seasonally unemployed, what is the natural rate of unemployment?

f What is the amount of cyclical unemployment?

g Can you tell if this economy is in recession or expansion?

4 Consider the economy described in Short Answer Problem 3. Over the next year, there is no change in the working-age population, but the number of unemployed rises to 1.5 million, while the number of full-time employed rises to 8.5 million. There are no changes in part-time employment.

a Calculate the new labour force participation rate, the new employment-to-population ratio, and the new unemployment rate.

b How is it possible that all three of these rates rose at the same time? Explain briefly. (*Hint:* What do you think has happened to the number of discouraged workers over this time period?)

5 In Chapter 19 we learned about the costs of unemployment. Are they more severe for frictional or structural unemployment?

6 Explain the difference between cyclical and structural unemployment. How would you tell a cyclically unemployed person from a structurally unemployed person?

7 Table 21.2 gives data for Southland, where there are three consumption goods: bananas, coconuts, and grapes.

TABLE **21.2** DATA FOR SOUTHLAND

Goods	Quantity in Base-Period Basket	Base Period Price ($)	Base Period Expenditure ($)	Current Period Price ($)	Current Period Expenditure ($)
Bananas	120	6		8	
Coconuts	60	8		10	
Grapes	40	10		9	

a Complete the table by computing expenditures for the base period and expenditures for the same quantity of each good in the current period.

b What is the value of the basket of consumption goods in the base period? in the current period?

c What is the Consumer Price Index for the current period?

ⓒⓣ **d** On the basis of the data in this table, would you predict consumers would make any substitutions between goods between the base period and the current period? If so, what kind of problems would this create for your measurement of the CPI?

8 Examine each of the following changes in John Carter's labour market activity, and explain whether they constitute unemployment, employment, or being out of the labour force. If unemployment, which of the four types of unemployment is represented?

a John graduates from Barsoom High and starts looking for a job.

b John has no luck finding the full-time job he wants and takes a part-time job cleaning out the canals.

c Canal-cleaning doesn't work out for John because of unforeseen allergies, so he quits.

d Discouraged by the lack of work, John stops looking and stays home watching his favourite soap opera, *As Mars Turns*.

e John sees an advertisement on TV for the Barsoom Swordfighter School, and enrols to get his BSF.

f John graduates at the top of his class and joins up with Princess Dejah Thoris' guard.

g An inventor at Barsoom University comes up with a new laser personal defence system, and the Princess disbands her guard—John spends a long time looking for work.

h John gets a job cleaning up after the sandstorms, but once the wet season comes along, he is laid off.

i John sees an advertisement seeking someone to help explore the ruins of the lost city of Rhiannon and signs up as security—the six-armed tribes are particularly ferocious there.

ⓒⓣ **9** Consider the data from 1995 in Table 21.3 on Canada as a whole and Newfoundland specifically.

TABLE 21.3

Economy	Labour Force Participation Rate	Unemployment Rate	Employment-to-Population Ratio
Canada	64.8	9.5	58.6
Newfoundland	53.1	18.3	43.3

Source: Statistics Canada, *Labour Force Review.*

Newfoundland has twice the unemployment of Canada, as well as a radically lower employment-to-population ratio and labour force participation rate. By examining these, can you get any insight into the impact of such a high unemployment rate on the labour market in Newfoundland? Why is the gap in the employment-to-population ratio (15.3 points) so much bigger than the unemployment gap (8.8 points)?

ct **10** Consider the data in Table 21.4 below on the economic growth of an imaginary country.

TABLE **21.4**

Year: Quarter	2004: 1	2004: 2	2004: 3	2004: 4	2005: 1	2005: 2	2005: 3	2005: 4
Real GDP Growth	+4%	+5%	+2%	−3%	−2%	−1%	+3%	+5%

a Identify the peak of this business cycle, any growth rate cycle downturns, the recessionary phase, the trough, and the expansionary phase.

b Are there any problems with using real GDP growth to identify the business cycle?

ANSWERS

True/False and Explain

1 F This defines a growth rate cycle downturn. (486–487)

2 T Definition. (486–487)

3 F Percentage of working-age population with jobs. (489–490)

4 F True if participation decreases or does not increase by much, otherwise false. (489–490)

5 F This change will only change labour force participation. (489–490)

6 F Since waiting for recall, he is counted. (489–490)

7 T See text discussion. (492)

8 F It depends on whether time unemployed leads to better job. (495–496)

9 F Workers retrain/relocate leading to more structural unemployment. (495–496)

10 F Full employment implies we still have frictional, structural, and seasonal unemployment. (495–496)

11 T Searching for jobs = frictionally unemployed. (495–496)

12 F Create *cyclical* unemployment. (497)

13 T See text discussion. (501)

14 F Changed every 10 years. (499–500)

15 F Low due to Statistics Canada's corrections. (501)

Multiple-Choice

1 d Persistent decline in the growth rate of aggregate economic activity. (486–487)

2 d A recession is a decline in aggregate economic activity (usually measured by real GDP), accompanied by a decline in employment. (486–487)

3 e It would add extra unemployed workers to the measured rate. (489–490)

4 c Employed + unemployed. (489–490)

5 b Labour force/working-age population = 14.5/20 = 72.5%. (489–490)

6 b Unemployed/labour force = 1.5/14.5 = 10.3%. (489–490)

7 d Doris is employed, Kanhaya isn't looking for work, Sharon is out of labour force, Bogdan does not expect to be called back. (489–490)

8 d Discouraged workers were unemployed, but stop looking and exit labour force, so unemployment rate decreases, labour force participation decreases, employment-to-population ratio unchanged. (489–490)

9 d Money wage doubles, but since the price level increases by 25 percent, real wage doesn't double. (489–490)

10 e Any of **a** to **d** *might* occur, but they do not *have* to occur. (489–492)

11 a See Text Figure 21.4 and discussion. (490)

12 a **b** to **d** raise frictional or structural unemployment, but if real GDP growth slows down, cyclical unemployment increases. (495–496)

13 e Others all lower unemployment. (493–496)

14 a Structural unemployment includes having wrong skills. Others are frictional or cyclical unemployment. (495–496)

15 d Cyclical unemployment is due to economy-wide slowdowns. (495–496)

16 b a is structural, rest are not officially unemployed. (493–496)

17 b See text discussion. (493–495)

18 c Definition. (496–497)

19 d Definition—unemployment caused by structural change. (495–496)

20 d Definition. (496–497)

21 d See Text Figure 21.9. (494)

ⓒⓣ **22 e** CPI = [(sum of current prices × base quantities)/(sum of base prices × base quantities)] × 100. (499–500)

23 c Ratio *P*(ducks)/*P*(towels) has risen. (499–500)

24 e This problem is for real GDP. (501)

25 c Because it assumes a fixed basket. (501)

Short Answer Problems

ⓒⓣ **1** An economy always has some unemployment, of people searching for jobs—frictional, structural, and seasonal unemployment. We define full as when there is zero cyclical unemployment, but still some frictional, structural, and seasonal unemployment.

ⓒⓣ **2** Pushing down the unemployment rate would entail stopping frictional unemployment, which would reduce the number of good job matches, and stopping structural unemployment, which would likely prevent the kind of structural readjustment the economy needs. Therefore it does not seem like a good idea to get unemployment as close to zero as possible!

3 a The labour force is 11 million, the sum of employment and unemployment. Labour force participation rate = percentage of working-age population who are in the labour force = 11/20 or 55 percent.

b The unemployment rate is 9.1 percent, the number of unemployed as a percentage of the labour force.

c It is 9.1 percent, the percentage of the labour force who are part time and want full time.

d It is 50 percent, percentage of working-age population with a job.

e The natural unemployment is frictional plus structural plus seasonal unemployment. In our case, it is the rate of unemployment if unemployment were only 0.6 million. Thus the natural rate of unemployment is 5.45 percent.

f Cyclical unemployment is actual unemployment minus natural unemployment, or 0.4 million.

g Since there is positive cyclical unemployment, real GDP is below potential GDP. It is possible we have a recession (negative real GDP growth), but the economy could be expanding out of the recession.

4 a Labour force participation rate = percentage of working-age population who are employed + unemployed = (1.5 + 8.5 + 2)/20 = 60 percent. The employment-to-population ratio is the percentage of the population with a job = 52.5 percent. The unemployment rate is the percentage of the labour force without a job = 12.5 percent.

b One million more people entered the labour force (participation rate increases), half of whom found a job (employment-to-population ratio increases) and half of whom did not (unemployment rate increases). It seems likely this change is due to discouraged workers now retrying to find jobs because the overall economy is improving.

5 The costs of unemployment include the lost output of the unemployed, and the deterioration of skills and abilities; in other words, human capital erodes. These costs will be higher for structural unemployment because it lasts longer, and often the workers' human capital becomes worthless in the marketplace.

6 Cyclical unemployment is caused by a downturn in the economy, when there is a decrease in demand for all products. Structural unemployment is caused by structural changes in a specific industry or region, and there is a decrease in demand for a certain type of labour whose skills are no longer desired.

Cyclical unemployment will end when the economy turns up. Structural unemployment will end when the workers retrain or move.

7 a Table 21.2 is completed here as Table 21.2 Solution. Note that the base-period quantities are evaluated at current prices to find the value of quantities in the current period.

TABLE **21.2** SOLUTION

Goods	Quantity in Base-Period Basket	Base Period Price ($)	Base Period Expenditure ($)	Current Period Price ($)	Current Period Expenditure ($)
Bananas	120	6	720	8	960
Coconuts	60	8	480	10	600
Grapes	40	10	400	9	360

b The value of the basket of consumption goods in the base period is the sum of the expenditures in that period: $1,600. The value of the basket of consumption goods in the current period is obtained as the sum of the values of quantities in that period: $1,920.

c The Consumer Price Index is the ratio of the value of quantities in the current period to the base period expenditure, times 100: CPI = (1,920/1,600) × 100 = 120.

ⓒⓣ d Since the price of grapes has fallen relative to the prices of bananas and coconuts, we would expect that consumers would substitute toward the cheaper grapes and away from bananas and coconuts. This substitution means that our CPI measure will be biased upward.

8 a He is an entrant, and is frictionally unemployed.

b He is now employed, although he is also involuntarily part time.

c He is a job leaver, and is frictionally unemployed.

d He is a discouraged worker, but technically out of the labour force.

e He is still out of the labour force.

f He is employed.

g He is structurally unemployed.

h He is initially employed, but then is seasonally unemployed.

i He is employed again.

ⓒⓣ 9 The higher unemployment rate in Newfoundland has pushed many workers out of the labour force—they have become discouraged workers and are not even attempting to find work. (We can see this in the lower participation rate.) The bigger gap in the employment-to-population ratio reflects this exiting, because it includes the measured unemployed and the discouraged workers.

ⓒⓣ 10 a The peak would be at the highest *level* of real GDP, just before we move toward negative economic growth. The peak occurs in 2004:3. A growth rate cycle downturn occurs when the growth rate is positive but declining, which occurs in 2004:3. This is followed by a recessionary phase with negative real GDP growth in 2004:4–2005:2. The trough is the lowest *level* of real GDP, so it would be in the last quarter of negative growth in 2005:2, followed by the expansion of positive growth in 2005:3 and 2005:4.

b We are implicitly identifying our business cycle by only using real GDP growth. However, since this data is released only quarterly, the ECRI and the NBER look at a variety of monthly measures of economic activity, including employment, to try and identify the business cycle.

Chapter 22 Aggregate Supply and Aggregate Demand

KEY CONCEPTS

Aggregate Supply

The *AS–AD* model enables us to understand how equilibrium real GDP and the price level are determined and fluctuate.

Quantity of *real GDP supplied* (Y) depends on quantities of labour (L), capital (K), and technology (T) as described by **aggregate production function**: $Y = F(L, K, T)$.

- ♦ At a given time, only quantity of labour can vary.
- ♦ Full employment occurs at the wage rate where quantity of labour demanded = quantity of labour supplied.
- ♦ Even at full employment, there is some unemployment due to labour market turnover.
- ♦ Unemployment rate at full employment is the **natural rate of unemployment**.
- ♦ Potential GDP is quantity of real GDP supplied at full employment.
  - Over business cycle, employment fluctuates around full employment, as real GDP fluctuates around potential GDP.

Two separate *AS* concepts: long-run (*LAS*) and short-run (*SAS*).

- ♦ **Macroeconomic long run** is long enough time frame so that real GDP = potential GDP. **Macroeconomic short run** is a period during which real GDP is above or below potential GDP.
- ♦ **Long-run aggregate supply (*LAS*)** is relationship between quantity of real GDP supplied and price level when real GDP = potential.
  - *LAS* curve is vertical at potential GDP—increase in P leads to equivalent percentage increase in resource prices, which means profits and real wages remain constant—no Δ employment, no Δ quantity supplied Y.
  - *LAS* shifts rightward when potential GDP increases, due to increase in full employment quantity of labour, increase in capital stock, technological advance.
- ♦ **Short-run aggregate supply (*SAS*)** is relationship between quantity of real GDP supplied and price level when the money wage rates and other resource prices are held constant.
  - *SAS* curve is upward-sloping—increase in P leads to an increase in profits and employment and an increase in quantity supplied Y.
- ♦ *SAS* shifts along with *LAS*, but also shifts if Δ resource prices.

Aggregate Demand

Quantity of real GDP demanded is total amount of final goods and services produced in Canada that economic agents plan to buy. It depends on price level, expectations, fiscal/monetary policy, and world economy.

- ♦ **Aggregate demand (*AD*)** is total quantity real GDP demanded ($Y = C + I + G + X - M$) at given price level (P).
- ♦ Increase in P decreases quantity real GDP demanded, represented by movement up along *AD* curve because of *wealth* and *substitution effects*.
- ♦ Changes in other factors *shift AD* curve.
  - If **fiscal policy** cuts taxes (which increases **disposable income**) or increases government expenditure, *AD* increases.

- If **monetary policy** decreases interest rates or increases quantity of money, *AD* increases.
- If exchange rate decreases or foreign income increases, *AD* increases.
- Increase in expectations of future disposable income or future inflation or future profits increases *AD*.

Macroeconomic Equilibrium

There are two different types of macroeconomic equilibriums. Long-run equilibrium is state toward which the economy is heading. Short-run equilibrium is the normal state of the economy, and occurs at each point in time along path to long-run equilibrium.

- ♦ **Long-run macroeconomic equilibrium** occurs when real GDP = potential GDP—when *AD* = *SAS* = *LAS*.
- ♦ **Short-run macroeconomic equilibrium** occurs where *AD* = *SAS*, with *P* adjusting to achieve equilibrium.
- ♦ Economic growth results from *LAS* shifting rightward on average, due to increase in labour, capital, and technology advances.
- ♦ Persistent inflation occurs when *AD* grows faster than *LAS*.
- ♦ Growth in *Y* is not steady, but goes in cycles because *AD* and *SAS* do not shift at same pace.
- ♦ Over the business cycle, short-run equilibrium may occur at
  - Long-run equilibrium.
  - **Below full-employment equilibrium**—*AD* = *SAS* left of *LAS*, real GDP < potential by amount of **recessionary gap** (= Okun gap).
  - **Above full-employment equilibrium**—*AD* = *SAS* right of *LAS*, real GDP > potential by amount of **inflationary gap**.
- ♦ Economy fluctuates in short run because of fluctuations in *AD* and *SAS*.
- ♦ If *AD* increases so *Y* > potential, economy does not stay in above full-employment equilibrium—upward pressures on the money wage rate shifts *SAS* leftward toward long-run equilibrium.
- ♦ If resource prices increase so *SAS* shifts leftward and *Y* < potential, then *stagflation* results (*P* higher, *Y* lower).

Canadian Economic Growth, Inflation, and Cycles

Y and *P* have changed dramatically over time in Canadian economy with economic growth, inflation, and business cycles.

- ♦ In 1970s, inflation increased and growth decreased due to massive increase in oil prices, and increase in quantity of money.
- ♦ Central banks responded by restraining *AD*, leading to deep recession in 1981–82.
- ♦ Through 1980s, steady growth and inflation as *LAS* shifted rightward.
- ♦ In 1991, decreasing *AD* led to recession. Since then, economic growth, low inflation, return to full employment.

HELPFUL HINTS

1 The aggregate demand and aggregate supply model introduced in this chapter (and developed in detail throughout this book) is an insightful method of analyzing complex macroeconomic events. In order to sort out these complex events, it is helpful if *you always draw a graph*—even if it is a small graph in the margin of a multiple-choice question. Graphs are powerful and effective tools for analyzing economic events, and you should become familiar with using them as soon as possible.

2 When using graphs, two factors often confuse students:

a Sometimes graphs are based on explicit numerical or algebraic models, where the intercepts, slopes, sizes of shifts, etc. have explicit values. Often these numbers are based on real-world values, but sometimes they are just "made-up" numbers that the instructor has picked to illustrate the point (although they are still economically logical). Do *not* get caught up in the exact values of the numbers. Concentrate on the basic economic results—for example, an increase in *AD* leads to an increase in the price level and real GDP.

b One common student mistake is failing to *distinguish between a shift in a curve versus a movement along a curve*. This distinction is crucial in understanding the factors that influence *AD* and *AS*, and you can be sure that your instructor will test you on it! The slope of the *AD* curve reflects the impact of a change in the price level on aggregate demand. A change in the price level produces a *movement along* the *AD* curve. A change in one of the factors affecting the *AD* curve other than price is reflected by a *shift* in the entire *AD* curve. Similarly, a change in price produces a *movement along* the *SAS* or the *LAS* curve and does not lead to a shift in the curves.

3 A change in price will not shift the *AD* or the *AS* curves. To cement the previous point, consider Figure 22.1. The initial long-run equilibrium is at the point *a*. (For the moment, ignore the SAS_1 curve.)

What happens in our model when there is a decrease in expected future disposable income and profits (such as happened in the 1990–91 recession)? This decrease in expected income and profits leads to a decrease in consumption and investment, and a decrease in aggregate demand, shown as the shift from AD_0 to AD_1.

To understand what happens next, imagine that the AD_0 and SAS_1 curves are peeled off the page (remember, we are ignoring SAS_1 for the moment). This removal leaves us with the curves SAS_0 and AD_1, and with a price level of P_0. At P_0, there is a surplus of goods and services (the quantity of real GDP supplied is equal to Y_0 [at *a*], greater than the quantity of real GDP demanded of Y_c [at *c*]), so that firms find their inventories piling up. In this case, they cut prices and decrease production.

This decrease in price eliminates the surplus in two ways. First, as price decreases, firms supply fewer goods and services: a movement along the *SAS* curve from *a* to *b*. (Be careful—the price change does *not* shift the *SAS* curve.) Second, the decrease in price leads to an increase in the quantity demanded: a movement along AD_1 from *c* to *b*. (Note there is no shift in the *AD* curve as price changes.)

FIGURE **22.1**

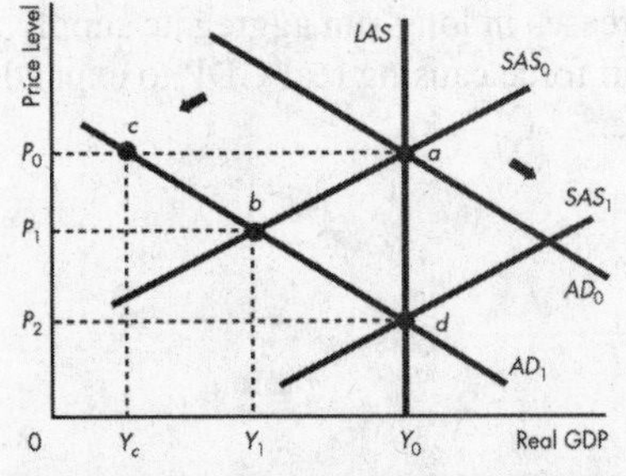

The end result is the new below full-employment equilibrium at *b*, with a lower price level (P_1) and a lower level of real GDP (Y_1).

4 In Figure 22.1, point *b* is a short-run, below full-employment equilibrium, but it is not a long-run equilibrium, since $Y_1 < Y_0$ (potential). There are two possible adjustments back from Y_1 to Y_0. First, the government or central bank could intervene with an expansionary fiscal or monetary policy, raising *AD* back to AD_0—the economy will move back to a full-employment, long-run equilibrium at *a* with $Y = Y_0$ (potential). Second, if the government does nothing, the unemployment at *b* will lead to downward pressures on the money wage rate and other resource prices (although this adjustment can be very slow). As the money wage rates decrease, the *SAS* curve shifts slowly rightward, eventually reaching SAS_1, with a full-employment, long-run equilibrium at *d* with $Y = Y_0$ (potential).

5 On the supply side, a crucial (and often hard to understand) distinction occurs between suppliers' behaviour in the short run and the long run. The short run and long run are not lengths of calendar time, but are defined in terms of whether resource prices change. In the short run, the prices of productive resources do not change; in the long run, they do.

To see what this difference implies for the supply decision, consider what happens when the price level increases. In the short run, resource prices stay unchanged. As a result, per-unit revenues are increasing, while per-unit costs are unchanged. Therefore profit-maximizing firms react by hiring more productive resources and supplying more real GDP as the price level increases—the short-run aggregate supply curve is upward-sloping.

In the long run, resource prices adjust by the same amount as the price level, which means that the costs of each unit of production have increased by the same percentage as the revenue. These two effects offset each other, there is no change in profits, and firms do not change their supply decision as the price level increases—the long-run aggregate supply curve is vertical.

This distinction between the short run and the long run also applies to the influences that affect the short-run and long-run aggregate supply curves. Since prices of productive resources are held constant for the short-run aggregate supply curve but not for the long-run aggregate supply curve, a change in the prices of productive resources will shift *SAS* but not *LAS*.

SELF-TEST

True/False and Explain

Aggregate Supply

1 As the price level increases, in the long run the aggregate quantity of goods and services supplied increases.

2 Any factor that shifts the short-run aggregate supply curve rightward also shifts the long-run aggregate supply curve rightward.

3 A significant technological advance (other things remaining unchanged) will shift the long-run aggregate supply curve rightward, but the short-run aggregate supply curve will not shift.

4 If the wage rate decreases (other things remaining unchanged), both the long-run aggregate supply curve and the short-run aggregate supply curve will shift rightward.

Aggregate Demand

5 An increase in the foreign exchange value of the dollar will increase aggregate demand in Canada.

6 An increase in the expected rate of inflation will decrease aggregate demand.

7 An increase in the quantity of money increases the quantity of real GDP demanded.

8 If the price level increases, the quantity of real GDP demanded will decrease.

Macroeconomic Equilibrium

9 A shift rightward in the aggregate demand curve leads to an increase in the price level, which in turn shifts the short-run aggregate supply curve rightward in the short run.

10 If the aggregate demand curve and the short-run aggregate supply curve both shift rightward at the same time, but the aggregate demand curve shifts further rightward, the price level increases.

11 An economy is initially in short-run equilibrium and then expected future profits decrease. The new short-run equilibrium will always be a below full-employment equilibrium.

12 If the economy is in an above full-employment equilibrium, the long-run aggregate supply curve will shift rightward until the economy is in full-employment equilibrium.

13 If real GDP is higher than potential GDP, the money wage rate will rise.

Canadian Economic Growth, Inflation, and Cycles

14 Increases in long-run aggregate supply are the main force causing real GDP to expand over time.

15 During the 1980s in Canada, inflation rates were high and increasing.

Multiple-Choice

Aggregate Supply

1 A technological improvement will shift

a both *SAS* and *AD* rightward.
b both *SAS* and *LAS* leftward.
c *SAS* rightward but leave *LAS* unchanged.
d *LAS* rightward but leave *SAS* unchanged.
e both *SAS* and *LAS* rightward.

2 An increase in the money wage rate will shift

a both *SAS* and *LAS* rightward.
b both *SAS* and *LAS* leftward.
c *SAS* leftward, but leave *LAS* unchanged.
d *LAS* rightward, but leave *SAS* unchanged.
e *SAS* rightward, but leave *LAS* unchanged.

3 Long-run aggregate supply will increase for all of the following reasons *except*

a a fall in the money wage rate.
b a rise in human capital.
c the introduction of new technology.
d more aggregate labour hours.
e more capital stock.

4 Potential GDP is the level of real GDP at which

a aggregate demand equals short-run aggregate supply.
b there is full employment.
c there is a recessionary gap.
d there is over full employment.
e prices are sure to increase.

5 The short-run aggregate supply curve is the relationship between the price level and the quantity of real GDP supplied, holding constant the

a wage rate only.
b quantities of productive resources.
c level of government expenditures.
d price level.
e prices of productive resources.

6 Consider Figure 22.2. Which graph illustrates what happens when resource prices decrease?

a (a)
b (b)
c (c)
d (d)
e none of the above

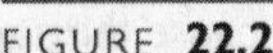

FIGURE **22.2**

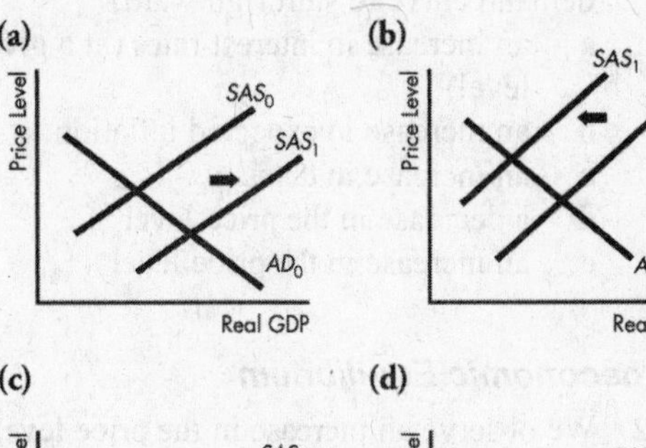

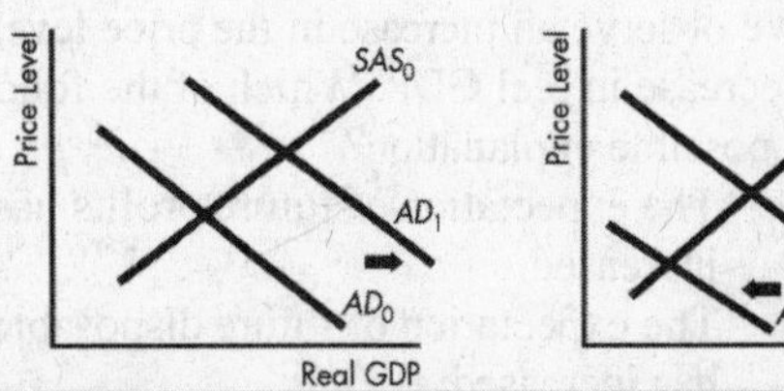

Aggregate Demand

7 Consider Figure 22.2. Which graph illustrates what happens when government expenditures increase?

a (a)
b (b)
c (c)
d (d)
e none of the above

8 Consider Figure 22.2. Which graph illustrates what happens when the quantity of money decreases?

a (a)
b (b)
c (c)
d (d)
e none of the above

9 Consider Figure 22.2. Which graph illustrates what happens when expected future disposable income increases?

a (a)
b (b)
c (c)
d (d)
e none of the above

10 Which of the following is a reason for the downward slope of the aggregate demand curve?
a the wealth effect
b the expectations effect
c the expected inflation effect
d the nominal balance effect
e none of the above

11 Which of the following will cause the aggregate demand curve to shift rightward?
a an increase in interest rates (at a given price level)
b an increase in expected inflation
c an increase in taxes
d a decrease in the price level
e an increase in the price level

Macroeconomic Equilibrium

12 We observe an increase in the price level and a decrease in real GDP. Which of the following is a possible explanation?
a The expectation of future profits has increased.
b The expectation of future disposable income has increased.
c The price of raw materials has increased.
d The stock of capital has increased.
e The money supply has increased.

13 Short-run macroeconomic equilibrium *always* occurs when the
a economy is at full employment.
b economy is below full employment.
c economy is above full employment.
d quantity of real GDP demanded equals the quantity of real GDP supplied.
e *AD* curve intersects the *LAS* curve.

14 Consider the economy represented in Table 22.1. In short-run macroeconomic equilibrium, the price level is ________ and the level of real GDP is ________ billion dollars.
a 120; 600
b 120; 500
c 125; 550
d 130; 600
e 130; 500

TABLE 22.1

Price Level	Aggregate Demand (billions of 1997 $)	Short-Run Aggregate Supply (billions of 1997 $)	Long-Run Aggregate Supply (billions of 1997 $)
100	800	300	600
110	700	400	600
120	600	500	600
130	500	600	600
140	400	700	600

15 Consider the economy represented in Table 22.1. The economy is in a(n)
a long-run equilibrium and resource prices will not change.
b above-full-employment equilibrium, and resource prices will increase.
c above-full-employment equilibrium, and resource prices will decrease.
d below-full-employment equilibrium, and resource prices will decrease.
e below-full-employment equilibrium, and resource prices will increase.

16 Consider the economy represented in Table 22.1. There is
a an inflationary gap equal to $100 billion.
b an inflationary gap equal to $50 billion.
c a recessionary gap equal to $50 billion.
d a recessionary gap equal to $100 billion.
e no gap; the economy is at full employment.

17 The economy cannot remain at a level of real GDP above long-run aggregate supply (*LAS*) because prices of productive resources will
a decrease, shifting *LAS* rightward.
b decrease, shifting *SAS* rightward.
c increase, shifting *LAS* leftward.
d increase, shifting *SAS* leftward.
e increase, shifting *SAS* rightward.

18 Consider an economy starting from a position of full employment. Which of the following changes does *not* occur as a result of a decrease in aggregate demand?
a The price level decreases.
b The level of real GDP decreases in the short run.
c A recessionary gap arises.
d Resource prices decrease in the long run, shifting the short-run aggregate supply curve rightward.
e The long-run aggregate supply curve shifts leftward to create the new long-run equilibrium.

19 If prices of productive resources remain constant, an increase in aggregate demand will cause a(n)
- **a** increase in the price level and an increase in real GDP.
- **b** increase in the price level and a decrease in real GDP.
- **c** decrease in the price level and an increase in real GDP.
- **d** decrease in the price level and a decrease in real GDP.
- **e** increase in the price level but no change in real GDP.

20 Which of the graphs in Figure 22.3 illustrates a below full-employment equilibrium?
- **a** (a) only
- **b** (b) only
- **c** (c) only
- **d** (d) only
- **e** both (c) and (d)

FIGURE **22.3**

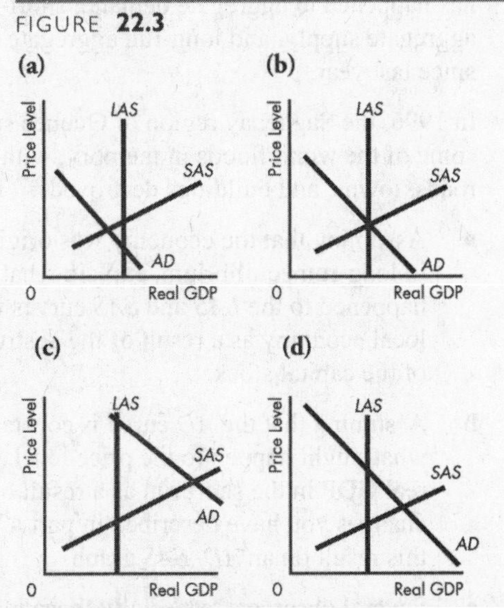

21 Which of the graphs in Figure 22.3 illustrates an above full-employment equilibrium?
- **a** (a) only
- **b** (b) only
- **c** (c) only
- **d** (d) only
- **e** both (c) and (d)

22 If real GDP is greater than potential GDP, the economy is
- **a** not in short-run equilibrium.
- **b** in a recessionary equilibrium.
- **c** in an above-full-employment equilibrium.
- **d** in a below-full-employment equilibrium.
- **e** in long-run equilibrium.

23 Which one of the following newspaper quotations best describes a movement along an *SAS* curve?
- **a** "The decrease in consumer spending may lead to a recession."
- **b** "The increase in consumer spending is expected to lead to inflation, without any increase in real GDP."
- **c** "Recent higher wage settlements are expected to cause higher inflation this year."
- **d** "Growth has been unusually high the last few years due to more women entering the workforce."
- **e** "The recent tornadoes destroyed many factories in Calgary and Edmonton."

Canadian Economic Growth, Inflation, and Cycles

24 The fact that the short-run aggregate supply and aggregate demand curves do not shift at a fixed, steady pace explains why we observe
- **a** persistent inflation.
- **b** business cycles.
- **c** economic growth.
- **d** large government budget deficits.
- **e** persistent unemployment.

25 *Persistent* inflation is caused by
- **a** shifts rightward in aggregate demand.
- **b** shifts rightward in short-run aggregate supply.
- **c** shifts rightward in short-run aggregate supply accompanied by shifts leftward in aggregate demand.
- **d** the tendency for long-run aggregate supply to increase faster than aggregate demand.
- **e** the tendency for aggregate demand to increase faster than long-run aggregate supply.

Short Answer Problems

1 The substitution effects imply that an increase in the price level will lead to a decrease in the aggregate quantity of goods and services demanded. Explain.

2 Why is the *LAS* curve vertical?

3 Why is the *SAS* curve positively sloped?

4 What are the most important factors in explaining the steady and persistent increases in the price level over time in Canada?

5 Suppose the economy is initially in long-run equilibrium. Graphically illustrate the short-run effects of an increase in the money wage rate. What happens to the price level and the level of real GDP?

6 Consider an economy that is in above full-employment equilibrium due to an increase in *AD*. Prices of productive resources have not changed. With the help of a graph, discuss how the economy returns to long-run equilibrium, with no government intervention.

7 Table 22.2 below shows the aggregate demand and short-run aggregate supply schedule for an economy. Long-run aggregate supply is equal to 1.1 trillion 1997 $.

TABLE 22.2

Price Level	Aggregate Demand (trillions of 1997 $)	Short-Run Aggregate Supply (trillions of 1997 $)
100	1.3	0.9
105	1.2	1.0
110	1.1	1.1
115	1.0	1.2
120	0.9	1.3

a Graph this economy's *AD*, *SAS*, and *LAS* curves, and show the original macroequilibrium. What kind of equilibrium is this—below full employment, above full employment, or full employment? If there is an inflationary or recessionary gap, identify how large it is.

b Next, suppose that at every price level, the quantity of real GDP demanded falls by $200 billion. Plot the new aggregate demand curve on your graph, and show the new short-run equilibrium. What kind of equilibrium is this—below full employment, above full employment, or full employment? If there is an inflationary or recessionary gap, identify how large it is.

c Suppose that the government does not take any action and that the cause of the decrease in aggregate demand remains unchanged. What kind of adjustments occur in the long run? Explain what happens to the price level, real GDP, *AD*, and *AS* during this adjustment, illustrating the changes on your graph.

8 With the aid of a graph, illustrate the case of an economy that has persistent inflation and positive economic growth over a three-year period.

ⓒⓣ 9 Consider an economy for which economists have estimated that last year's real GDP was $800 billion, equal to potential GDP. The price level was 105. Suppose that this year the economists estimate that potential GDP has increased by 10 percent. However, actual real GDP has decreased by 5 percent, while the price level has also decreased by 5 percent.

Draw an *AD–AS* graph that shows last year's equilibrium, as well as last year's aggregate demand, aggregate supply (short-run and long-run), price level, and real GDP level. Next, given the information above, show what has happened to the price level and the level of real GDP this year (show this year's equilibrium), plus what has happened to aggregate demand, short-run aggregate supply, and long-run aggregate supply since last year.

ⓒⓣ 10 In 1996, the Saguenay region of Quebec suffered some of the worst floods in memory, with many roads, towns, and buildings destroyed.

a Assuming that the economy was originally in long-run equilibrium, explain what has happened to the *LAS* and *SAS* curves in the local economy as a result of the destruction of the capital stock.

b Assuming that the *AD* curve is constant, what might happen to the price level and real GDP in the short run as a result of the changes you have described in part **a**? Show this result on an *AD–SAS* graph.

c Several observers, especially those in the construction industry, argued that the rebuilding of the destroyed capital stock would strongly stimulate the local economy. What component of aggregate demand is affected by this rebuilding? What will happen to aggregate demand as a result of this rebuilding?

d Some observers implied the local economy was better off, in a purely economic sense, as a result of the floods and the resulting rebuilding process. Do you agree?

ANSWERS

True/False and Explain

1 F In the long run, the money wage rates increase as well, leaving profits, real wages, and production unchanged. (508–509)

2 F Changes in resource prices shift only *SAS* and not *LAS*. (511–512)

3 F Anything that shifts *LAS* also shifts *SAS*. (511–512)

4 F Only the *SAS* shifts in response to a wage change. (511–512)

5 F Increase in value of dollar makes Canadian exports more expensive and imports cheaper, decreasing demand for Canadian goods. (514–516)

6 F If individuals expect an increased inflation rate, they will spend more today to avoid higher future prices. (514–516)

7 T Higher quantity of money increases spending. (514–516)

8 T Movement along the *AD* curve due to wealth and substitution effects. (513–514)

9 F Increase in *P* leads to movement along *SAS* curve, not shift in it. (520–521)

10 T Try drawing a graph. (520–521)

ⓒ **11 F** It depends on where initial equilibrium is and on size of decrease in *AD* that results from decrease in future profits—try drawing a graph or two. (520–521)

12 F *SAS* shifts in this type of situation, not *LAS*. (517–521)

13 T Unemployment below the natural rate, upward pressure on the money wage rate. (520–521)

14 T Increase in population, capital stock, human capital, and technology advances shift *LAS* rightward over time. (522–523)

15 F See text discussion. (522–523)

Multiple-Choice

1 e Technological improvements means same inputs can produce more output, leading to increase in quantity supplied in both short and long run. (508–516)

2 c Wage rate is held constant along given *SAS*; if the money wage rate increases, production is less at every price level leading to *SAS* shifting leftward. (511–512)

3 a Changes in the money wage rates change *SAS* only, not *LAS*. (511–512)

4 b Definition. (508)

5 e Short run is defined as time period where resource prices are constant. (509–510)

6 a When resource prices decrease, firms produce more at every price level shifting *SAS* rightward. (511–512)

7 c Increase in government expenditures leads to increase in aggregate spending, shifting *AD* rightward. (513–516)

8 d Decrease in quantity of money leads to decrease in aggregate spending, shifting *AD* leftward. (513–516)

9 c Increase in expected future disposable income leads to increase in household consumption, shifting *AD* rightward. (513–516)

10 a **b** and **c** shift *AD* curve, and **d** doesn't exist. (513–516)

11 b Answers **a** and **c** cause it to shift leftward, while **d** and **e** are movements along *AD* curve. (513–516)

ⓒ **12 c** Answers **a**, **b**, and **e** increase *AD* leading to increase in real GDP, while **d** shifts *LAS* rightward, leading to increase in real GDP. **c** shifts *SAS* leftward leading to increase in *P*, decrease in real GDP (try drawing a graph). (520–521)

13 d Short-run macroeconomic equilibrium always occurs where *AD* = *SAS*; equilibrium *may* occur at answers **a–c** and **e**, but it doesn't *always* occur there. (520–521)

14 c Short-run equilibrium occurs where *AD* = *SAS*, which occurs at $P = 125$ and real GDP = 550—halfway between $P = 120$ and $P = 130$. (516–517)

15 d Real GDP = 550 billion < potential GDP of 600 billion which is below full-employment equilibrium, so unemployed workers eventually offer to work for less. (516–521)

16 c Actual real GDP = 550 billion, which is 50 billion less than potential GDP of 600 billion. (516–517)

17 d Above long-run aggregate supply, extra demand for resources leads to increase in their prices leading to increase in cost of production leading to *SAS* shifting leftward. (516–521)

18 e Decrease in *AD* creates recession, leading to decrease in resource prices, shifting *SAS* rightward, pushing economy back to *LAS*. (520–521)

19 a Increase in *AD* leads to shortages, leading to increase in prices, leading to increase in aggregate quantity supplied in short run, so increase in *P* and increase in real GDP. (520–521)

20 a Below-full-employment equilibrium occurs when *AD* = *SAS* to left of *LAS*. (516–517)

21 e Above-full-employment equilibrium occurs when *AD* = *SAS* to right of *LAS*. (516–517)

22 c Equilibrium is with *AD* = *SAS*; if *Y* is > *LAS* then an above-full-employment equilibrium. (516–517)

ⓒⓣ **23 a** Decrease in consumer spending leads to shift leftward in *AD* leading to movement down an *SAS* curve in short-run leading to decrease in *P* and decrease in *Y*. (516–521)

24 b Sometimes curves shift leftward (creating recession) and sometimes rightward (creating boom). (522–523)

25 e Combination of these shifts leads to shortages leading to increase in *P*. **a**, **b**, and **c** may lead to increase in *P*, while **d** leads to decrease in *P*. (522–523)

Short Answer Problems

1 There are two substitution effects. First, if the prices of domestic goods increase and foreign prices remain constant, domestic goods become relatively more expensive, and so households will buy fewer domestic goods and more foreign goods. This decline in spending means that there will be a decrease in the quantity of real GDP demanded. Thus, an increase in the price level (the prices of domestic goods) will lead to a decrease in the aggregate quantity of (domestic) goods and services demanded.

Second, the increase in the price level increases the rate of interest, which increases saving and decreases spending. This decline in spending also means that there will again be a decrease in the quantity of real GDP demanded.

2 Long-run aggregate supply is the level of real GDP supplied when there is full employment. Since this level of real GDP is independent of the price level, the long-run aggregate supply curve is vertical. This level of real GDP is that attained when prices of productive resources are free to adjust so as to clear resource markets.

3 The short-run aggregate supply curve is positively sloped because it holds prices of productive resources constant. When the price level increases, firms see the prices of their output (revenues) increasing, but the prices of their input (costs) remain unchanged. With profits increasing, each firm has an incentive to increase output and so aggregate output increases.

4 The price level can increase either as the result of an increase in aggregate demand or as the result of a decrease in aggregate supply. Both of these forces have contributed to periods of an increasing price level. The steady and persistent increases in the price level, however, have been the result of a tendency for aggregate demand to increase faster than aggregate supply.

5 In Figure 22.4, the economy is initially at point *a* on the SAS_0 curve. An increase in the money wage rate will shift the *SAS* curve leftward to SAS_1. At the new equilibrium, point *b*, the price level has increased and the level of real GDP has decreased.

FIGURE **22.4**

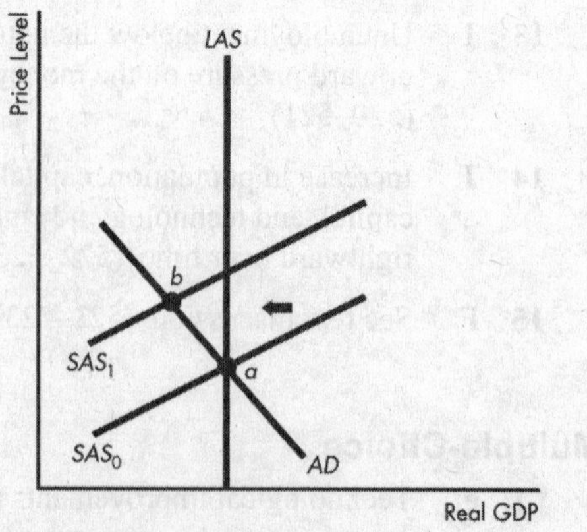

6 In Figure 22.5, the increase in *AD* from AD_0 to AD_1 results in the above-full-employment equilibrium at point *b* and causes the price level to increase. Since the money wage rates have not changed, the real cost of labour to firms has decreased, profits rise, and output is stimulated as indicated by the movement along the SAS_0 curve from point *a* to point *b*. Furthermore, the purchasing power of workers' money wage rates has decreased.

Workers will eventually demand higher money wage rates and firms will be willing to pay them. Similarly, other prices of productive resources will increase as well. This increase in prices of productive resources will shift the *SAS* curve leftward, which results in a new equilibrium. There will continue to be pressure for the money wage rates and other prices of productive resources to increase until the *SAS* curve shifts all the way to SAS_1, where the purchasing power of the money wage rates and other prices of productive resources has been restored and the economy is again at full employment, point *c*.

FIGURE **22.5**

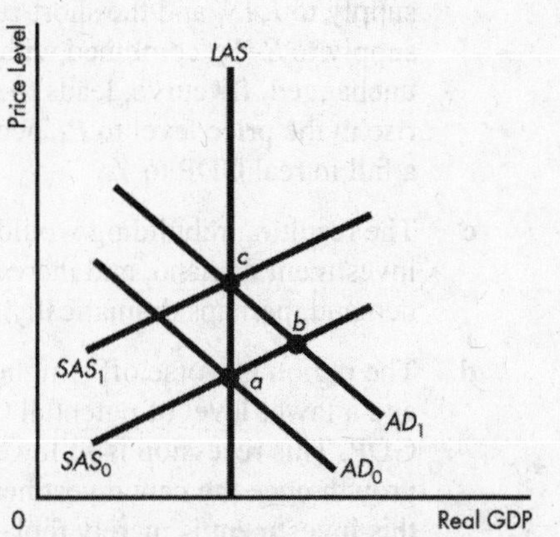

7 a The economy's AD_0, SAS_0, and *LAS* curves are graphed in Figure 22.6 (ignore the AD_1 and SAS_1 curves for now). The macroeconomic equilibrium occurs when the *AD* and *SAS* curves cross, at a price level of 110 and real GDP of 1.1 trillion 1997 $. Since this level of real GDP equals the level of potential GDP, this economy is in a full-employment equilibrium, with no type of gap.

FIGURE **22.6**

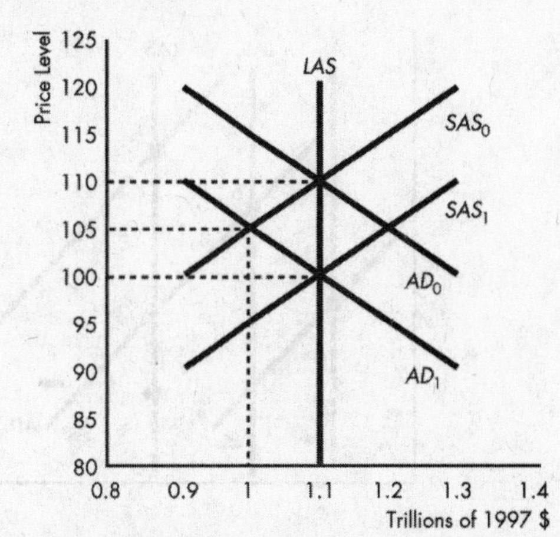

b This decrease in aggregate demand leads to a new short-run equilibrium where the new AD_1 crosses SAS_0, at a price level of 105 and real GDP of 1 trillion 1997 $. Since real GDP is less than potential GDP, the economy is in a below-full-employment equilibrium, and there is a recessionary gap (or an Okun gap) equal to the difference between real GDP and potential GDP, a gap of $100 billion.

c Since real GDP is below potential GDP, unemployment is above the natural rate. Eventually unemployed resources start offering to work for lower resource prices, which shifts the *SAS* curve rightward to SAS_1, raising aggregate supply, lowering prices even more, and leading to a new long-run equilibrium where SAS_1 crosses AD_1 and *LAS* at the point where the price level is 100 and real GDP is back at potential GDP ($1.1 trillion).

8 In order to have these two events, long-run aggregate supply is growing (shifting rightward), and aggregate demand is shifting rightward as well, but at a faster pace. Figure 22.7 illustrates such a case, with the points *a*, *b*, and *c* showing the three years. (The *SAS* curves have been omitted from the graph for simplicity.)

FIGURE 22.7

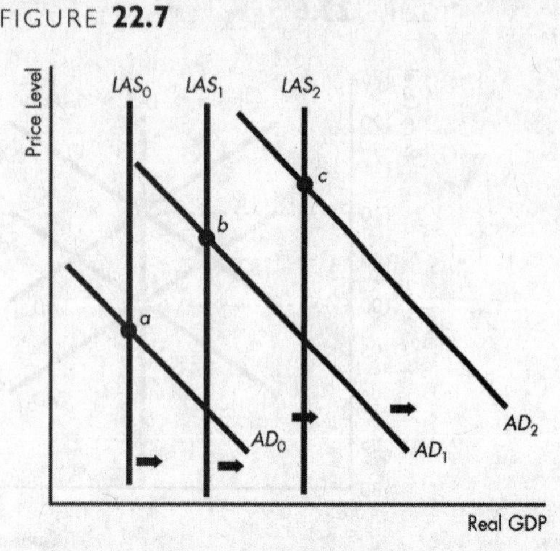

9 Figure 22.8 shows the original full-employment equilibrium, at last year's equilibrium price level of 105 and income level of 800.

FIGURE 22.8

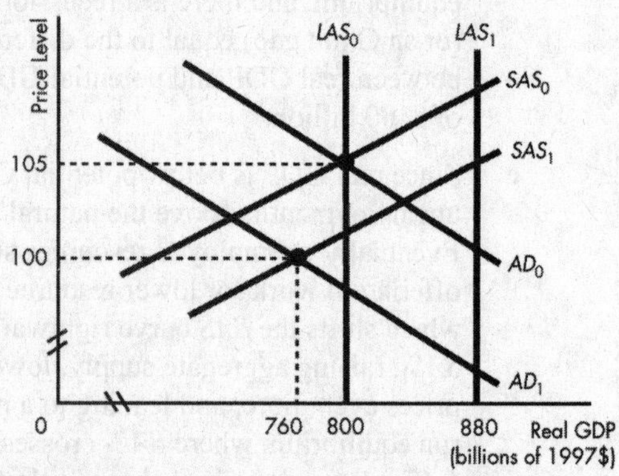

For the current year, the *LAS* curve has shifted rightward to LAS_1, a value of 880, and the *SAS* curve shifts with it to SAS_1, all else equal. The new short-run equilibrium must be along the intersection of SAS_1 and an *AD* curve. Since prices are 5 percent lower at 100, and real GDP is 5 percent lower at 760, the new *AD* curve must have shifted leftward as shown.

(*Hint:* To decide where AD_1 should be, first find the intersection of $P = 100$ and $Y = 760$ on the new *SAS* curve, and then draw in the *AD* curve to go through this point.)

10 a The destruction of towns, roads, etc. is a destruction of the capital stock, which would lower potential GDP, and shift the *LAS* curve leftward, shifting the *SAS* curve leftward as well.

b Figure 22.9 shows the original long-run equilibrium at Y_0 and P_0.

FIGURE 22.9

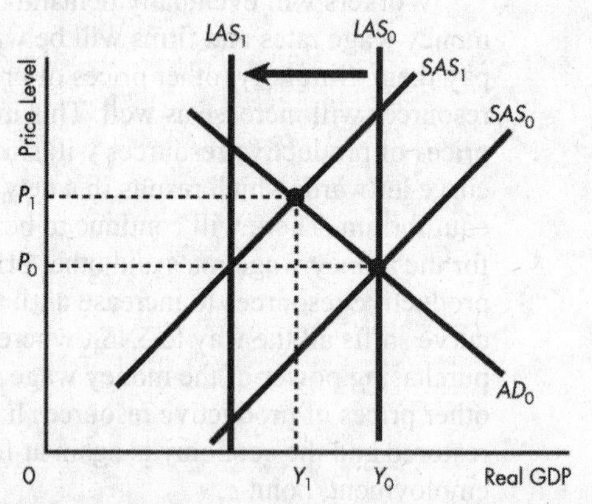

The shift leftward in the long-run aggregate supply to LAS_1 and the short-run aggregate supply to SAS_1, combined with the unchanged *AD* curve, leads to stagflation—a rise in the price level to P_1, accompanied by a fall in real GDP to Y_1.

c The resulting rebuilding would stimulate investment demand, and increase aggregate demand, perhaps dramatically.

d The region is worse off—higher inflation, and a lower level of potential GDP and real GDP. This recession is followed by higher growth once the new investment starts, *but* this investment is merely replacing lost capital, and is not adding new capital stock.

CHAPTERS 19–22

Part 7 Wrap Up Understanding the Themes of Macroeconomics

PROBLEM

a Consider the following data for the economy of Autoland for 2003 and 2004. Calculate the value of nominal GDP for each year.

TABLE P7.1 2003

Item	Amount (billions of $)
Government expenditures on goods and services	60
Government transfer payments	30
Income taxes	80
Wages, etc., paid to labour	200
Export earnings	30
Consumption expenditure	180
Import payments	25
Net investment expenditure	15
Depreciation	5

TABLE P7.2 2004

Item	Amount (billions of $)
Wages, etc., paid to labour	200
Indirect taxes	20
Profits	20
Subsidies	5
Interest and miscellaneous investment income	5
Depreciation	10
Farmers' income	10
Income of nonfarm unincorporated business	10

b Using your data from **a**, complete the following table:

TABLE P7.3

Year	Nominal GDP (billions of $)	Price Level	Real GDP (billions of 1997 $)
2003		132.5	
2004		140.0	

ct **c** Draw an *AD–AS* graph that represents the Autoland economy for 2003 and 2004, on the basis of the data in Table P7.3, and explain what has happened to the economy over this time period.

d If the economy was in long-run equilibrium in 2003, what has happened to cyclical unemployment between 2003 and 2004?

e Calculate the inflation rate, the growth rate in real GDP, and the growth rate in nominal GDP over this time period.

MIDTERM EXAMINATION

You should allocate 32 minutes for this examination (16 questions, 2 minutes per question). For each question, choose the one *best* answer.

1 Which of the following people would be counted as unemployed in Canada?
- a Doris only works 20 hours a week and is not looking for a full-time job.
- b Kanhaya has stopped looking for work since he has retired.
- c Sharon is a college student with no job.
- d Maurice is working in his garden while looking for work.
- e Taylor is on disability leave.

2 Which of the following is *not* an example of investment in the expenditure approach to measuring GDP? General Motors
- a buys a new auto stamping machine.
- b adds 500 new cars to inventories.
- c buys Canadian government bonds.
- d builds another assembly plant.
- e replaces worn-out stamping machines.

3 The changes represented in Figure P7.1 *must*
- a not occur in the real world, because *AD* and *SAS* cannot change at the same time.
- b create an inflationary gap.
- c create a recessionary gap.
- d create inflation.
- e do none of the above.

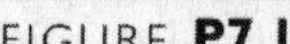

FIGURE **P7.1**

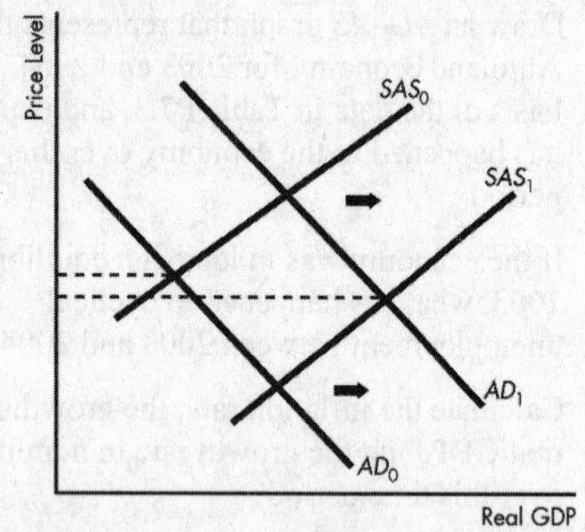

4 In a country with a working-age population of 20 million, 13 million are employed, 1.5 million are unemployed, and 1 million of the employed are working part-time, half of whom wish to work full-time. The employment-to-population ratio is
- a 57.5%.
- b 65%.
- c 72.5%.
- d 75.5%.
- e none of the above.

5 Which of the following statements about nominal and real GDP is *incorrect*?
- a The chain-weighted output index is used to calculate real GDP.
- b The GDP deflator equals (nominal GDP)/(real GDP) × 100.
- c Increases in total expenditures can be due to increases in production, or increases in prices for goods and services.
- d If total expenditures on goods and services (measured at constant prices) is higher this year compared to last year, this indicates positive economic growth.
- e If total expenditures on goods and services is higher this year compared to last year, this indicates positive economic growth.

6 Which of the following is *not* part of the incomes approach to GDP?
- a net exports
- b wages, salaries, and supplementary labour income
- c corporate profits
- d farmers' income
- e income of nonfarm unincorporated businesses

7 The technique used to calculate the CPI implicitly assumes that consumers buy
- a relatively more goods with relative prices that are rising.
- b relatively fewer goods with relative prices that are rising.
- c the same relative quantities of goods as in a base year.
- d goods and services whose quality improves at the rate of growth of real income.
- e more computers and CD players and fewer black-and-white TVs.

8 If a price index was 150 at the end of 2000 and 165 at the end of 2001, what was the rate of inflation for 2001?
- a 9.1%
- b 10%
- c 15%
- d 50%
- e 65%

9 If the money wage rate decreases,
- a *AD* shifts rightward.
- b firms hire less labour.
- c only *LAS* shifts rightward.
- d only *SAS* shifts rightward.
- e both *SAS* and *LAS* shift rightward.

10 The aggregate demand curve illustrates that, as the price level decreases, the
a quantity of real GDP demanded increases.
b quantity of real GDP demanded decreases.
c quantity of nominal GDP demanded increases.
d quantity of nominal GDP demanded decreases.
e value of assets decrease.

11 We observe an increase in the price level and an increase in real GDP. A possible explanation is that the
a quantity of money has fallen.
b expectation of future disposable income has decreased.
c price of raw materials has increased.
d stock of capital has increased.
e expectation of future profits has increased.

12 In the circular flow, the flows of investment and saving interact with the flows of income and consumption to determine
a total production.
b aggregate income.
c aggregate expenditure.
d all of the above.
e none of the above.

13 Who of the following would be considered seasonally unemployed?
a a Saskatchewan farmer who has lost her farm and is unemployed until retrained
b a Nova Scotia fishery worker who is laid off during the winter
c a steelworker who is laid off but who expects to be called back soon
d an office worker who has lost her job because of a general slowdown in economic activity
e none of the above

14 Unemployment caused by an economy-wide decrease in the demand for goods and services is known as
a cyclical unemployment.
b seasonal unemployment.
c frictional unemployment.
d structural unemployment.
e natural unemployment.

15 Macroeconomic policy challenges include
a keeping the deficit high if borrowing is for consumption.
b stabilizing the business cycle.
c keeping inflation at the current level.
d ignoring inflation if unemployment is a problem.
e none of the above.

16 A business cycle is the
a increase in real GDP for more than two periods.
b decrease in real GDP for more than two periods.
c increase in the economic potential to produce goods and services.
d irregular fluctuation of potential GDP around real GDP.
e irregular fluctuation of real GDP around potential GDP.

ANSWERS

Problem

a For 2003, calculate nominal GDP as the sum of $C + I + G + X - M$. For G, you must use only expenditures on goods and services, and you need to calculate gross investment (= net investment + depreciation, or \$20 billion). Thus nominal GDP = 180 + 20 + 60 + 30 – 25 = \$265 billion for 2003.

For 2004, you need to use the incomes approach. First, calculate Net domestic income at factor cost = wages, etc. + profits + interest and miscellaneous investment income + farmers' income + income of nonfarm unincorporated business = 200 + 20 + 5 + 10 + 10 = \$245 billion. Next, to get net domestic product you must add indirect taxes and subtract subsidies from net domestic income, or 245 + 20 – 5 =\$260 billion. Finally, to get gross domestic product, you must add depreciation to net domestic product, or 260 + 10 = \$270 billion for 2004.

b Table P7.3 is completed here as Table P7.3 Solution, using the formula real GDP = (nominal GDP/price level) × 100.

TABLE **P7.3** SOLUTION

Year	Nominal GDP (billions of \$)	Price Level	Real GDP (billions of 1997 \$)
2003	265	132.5	200.0
2004	270	140.0	192.9

ⓒ **c** Figure P7.2 shows the Autoland economy in 2003 and 2004. The exact sizes of shifts in *AD* and *SAS* depends on assumptions about their slopes, but the relative types of shifts must be as shown in order to get the simultaneous increase in the price level and decrease in real GDP that occurred from 2003 to 2004. As the graph shows, the likely changes were a shift leftward in *SAS* and a shift leftward in *AD*, with the shift leftward in *SAS* larger (it is this shift that results in the price level increasing).

FIGURE **P7.2**

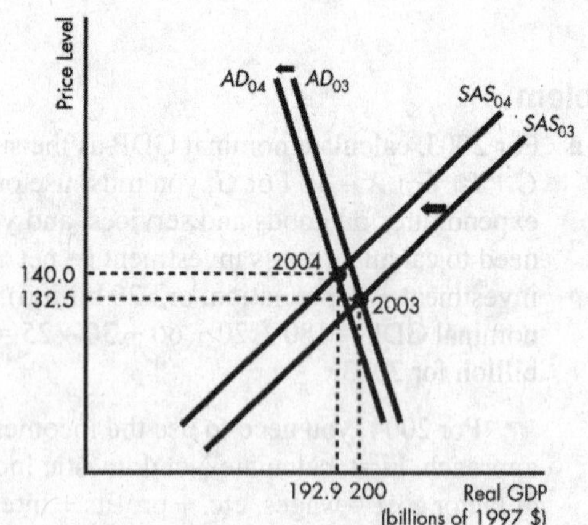

d If the economy was in long-run equilibrium in 2003, then real GDP = potential GDP and there was zero cyclical unemployment. The decrease in real GDP to below potential GDP means that unemployment must be above the natural rate, so that cyclical unemployment has increased in 2004.

e The inflation rate is equal to

$$5.7\% = \frac{140.0 - 132.5}{132.5} \times 100$$

The growth rate of real GDP is equal to

$$-3.6\% = \frac{192.9 - 200}{200} \times 100$$

The growth rate of nominal GDP is equal to

$$1.9\% = \frac{270 - 265}{265} \times 100$$

Midterm Examination

1 d Doris is employed part time, Kanhaya is not looking for work (discouraged worker), Sharon and Taylor are out of labour force. (452–453)

2 c This is purchase of financial assets, not capital stock. (467)

3 e These changes could occur. Whether there is a gap cannot be determined without *LAS* curve. (522–523)

4 b Employed/working-age population × 100 = 13/20 × 100 = 65%. (489–490)

5 e This definition is for nominal GDP, and it might be higher either due to higher prices or higher production of goods and services. Only the latter represents positive economic growth. (473–475)

6 a Part of expenditure approach. (471–472)

7 c CPI assumes fixed basket of goods for years being compared. (499–501)

8 b 10% = [(165 – 150)/150] × 100. (455)

9 d If money wage rate decreases, cost of production decreases, firms hire more labour, supply more goods and services, represented by (only) *SAS* shifting rightward. (516–521)

10 a *AD* curve is downward-sloping due to wealth and substitution effects. Real GDP by definition, not nominal, and asset values increase here. (513–516)

11 e Answer **e** shifts *AD* rightward, leading to an increase in *P* and real GDP. **a** and **b** shift *AD* leftward, while **c** shifts *SAS* leftward, leading to decrease in *Y*, and **d** shifts *LAS* rightward, which decreases *P* (try drawing a graph). (516–521)

12 d Expenditure = money earned by sales of produced goods, and is used to pay incomes (including profits). (467–470)

13 b Job not available in winter. (495–496)

14 a Definition. (495–496)

15 b It should be reducing the deficit and keeping inflation low. (459)

16 e Definition. (448)

Chapter 23 Expenditure Multipliers

KEY CONCEPTS

Expenditure Plans and GDP

Components of aggregate expenditure are consumption (C), investment (I), government expenditures (G), and exports (X) minus imports (M), which sum to real GDP (Y).

- ♦ C, M depend on real GDP (Y), so that an increase in Y increases AE, and increase in AE increases Y.

Consumption and saving depend primarily on **disposable income** (YD) = real GDP – net taxes (NT).

- ♦ **Consumption function** shows increase in YD leads to increase in consumption.
- ♦ **Saving function** shows increase in YD leads to increase in saving, with $\Delta C + \Delta S = \Delta YD$.
- ♦ **Marginal propensity to consume** (MPC) = fraction of ΔYD that is consumed = $\Delta C/\Delta YD$ = slope of consumption function.
- ♦ **Marginal propensity to save** (MPS) = fraction of ΔYD that is saved = $\Delta S/\Delta YD$ = slope of saving function.
- ♦ $MPC + MPS = 1$.

Influences other than ΔYD *shift* the functions.

- ♦ Increase in *expected future disposable* income shifts S function downward, C function upward.
- ♦ Increase in the *real interest rate* shifts S function upward, C function downward.
- ♦ Increase in *wealth* shifts S function downward, C function upward.
- ♦ Consumption and saving are a function of real GDP, since increase in real GDP leads to increase in YD.

Import function is relationship between imports and real GDP.

- ♦ **Marginal propensity to import** is fraction of ΔY spent on imports = $\Delta M/\Delta Y$.
- ♦ Other variables, such as implementing trade agreements, also influence imports.

Equilibrium Expenditure at a Fixed Price Level

In the very short term, the price level is fixed—aggregate demand determines aggregate quantity sold.

- ♦ To understand AD, we study the aggregate expenditure model.
- ♦ **Aggregate planned expenditure** (AE) = planned C + planned I + planned G + planned X – planned M.

Components of aggregate expenditure interact to determine Y, and AE is influenced by Y.

- ♦ AE can be represented by graph or schedule. Increase in Y leads to increase in AE.
- ♦ Aggregate planned expenditure has two parts:
  - **Autonomous expenditure** (A) = part of AE that does *not* vary with income.
  - **Induced expenditure** (N) = part of AE that *does* vary with income.
- ♦ Actual aggregate expenditure may not equal planned expenditure if level of real GDP is not consistent with plans.
- ♦ **Equilibrium expenditure** occurs when AE = real GDP.
  - On graph this point occurs when AE curve crosses 45° line.
  - If real GDP above equilibrium value, AE < real GDP. Firms cannot sell all their production, leading to unplanned increase in inventories.

Firms lower production, leading to decrease in real GDP and convergence to equilibrium.

- If real GDP below equilibrium value, *AE* > real GDP. Firms sell all their production and more, leading to unplanned decrease in inventories. Firms increase production to restore inventories, leading to increase in real GDP and convergence to equilibrium.

The Multiplier

The **multiplier** is the amount by which change in autonomous expenditure is multiplied to determine change in equilibrium expenditure and real GDP.

♦ Increase in autonomous expenditure leads to primary effect of increased aggregate planned expenditure, leading to increase in real GDP, leading to further (secondary) increase in aggregate planned expenditure, leading to further increases in real GDP, etc.

♦ Secondary, *induced* effects means total Δ real GDP > initial Δ autonomous expenditure.

♦ Multiplier = (Δ real GDP)/(Δ autonomous expenditure) = 1/(1 – slope of *AE* function).

- Multiplier > 1 because of induced effects.
- Higher slope of *AE* function implies larger induced effects and larger multiplier.
- Multiplier is higher if *MPC* is higher, or marginal tax rate is lower or marginal propensity to import is lower.

♦ Recessions and depressions begin with expenditure fluctuations magnified by multiplier effect.

The Multiplier and the Price Level

Aggregate demand curve shows relationship between real GDP demanded and price level, other things remaining the same, and can be derived from *AE* curve.

♦ Increase in price level shifts *AE* curve downward (due to wealth and substitution effects), lowers equilibrium real GDP, shown by movement up and to left on *AD* curve.

♦ Δ nonprice variables (autonomous expenditures) shifts both *AE* and *AD* curves.

♦ In short run, increase in *AE* leads to shift rightward in *AD* curve, which increases price level, which lowers *AE* somewhat, offsetting increase in *Y* somewhat, so multiplier is smaller.

♦ In long run, vertical *LAS* means there is large enough increase in price level to create decrease in *AE* that totally offsets initial increase, so that multiplier = 0.

HELPFUL HINTS

1 The 45° line is important for understanding the consumption function and the expenditure function. It is a *reference line* on a graph, showing the points where the two variables on the axes of the graph have the same value.

FIGURE **23.1**

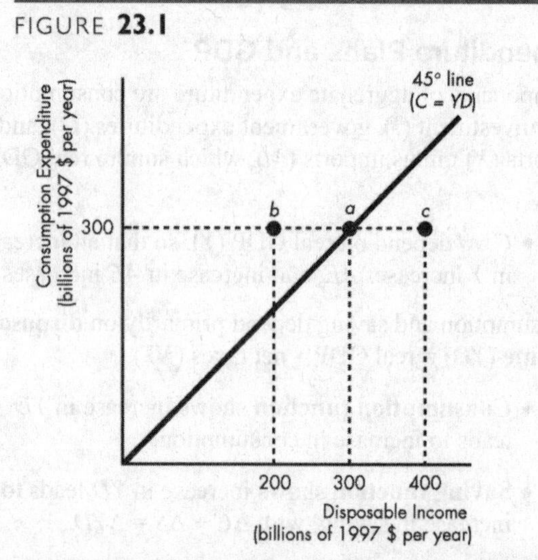

Consider the graph of consumption and disposable income illustrated in Figure 23.1. Along the 45° line, consumption equals disposable income at all points. For example, at point *a*, *C* = *YD* = $300 billion.

Consider point *b*. Consumption is still equal to $300 billion, but now disposable income is only $200 billion. To the left of the 45° line, variables measured on the vertical axis (here, consumption) are greater than variables measured on the horizontal axis (here, disposable income).

Next, consider point *c*. Consumption is still equal to $300 billion, but now disposable income is $400 billion. To the right of the 45° line, variables measured on the vertical axis are less than variables measured on the horizontal axis.

To summarize, consider the consumption function (*CF*) shown in Figure 23.2. Using the

45° line as our reference, any point on the consumption function to the left of the 45° line has consumption greater than disposable income (and therefore saving (= $YD - C$) is negative). Any point on the consumption function to the right of the 45° line has consumption less than disposable income (and saving is positive).

FIGURE **23.2**

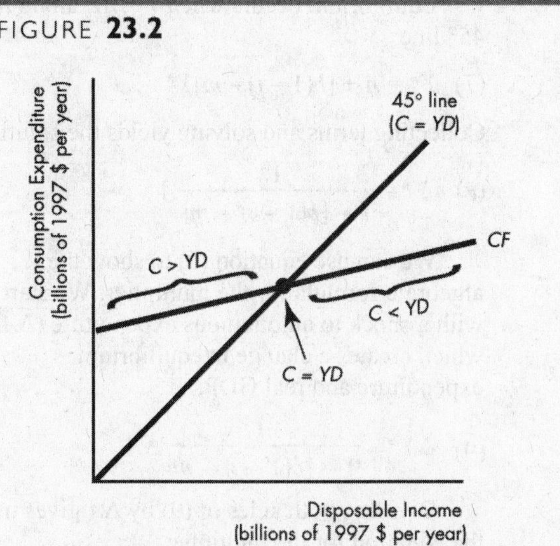

To make sure you understand, draw the graph of the aggregate expenditure function, with a 45° line, and identify the points on your graph where aggregate expenditure is greater than income, equal to income, or less than income. *Note:* For the consumption function, the 45° line is a pure reference line—it is possible in equilibrium for consumption to be greater than, less than, or equal to disposable income. However, for the aggregate expenditure function, the point on the 45° line where $AE = Y$ is more than just a reference point; it shows the point of *equilibrium expenditure.*

2 Aggregate demand is the relationship between the price level and the quantity of goods and services demanded; in other words, it is the relationship between the price level and the level of planned aggregate expenditure. One purpose of this chapter is to help you understand planned aggregate expenditure by separating and examining its individual components. In particular, consumption expenditure, investment, and net exports—the three components of private aggregate expenditure—are examined. As you put the discussion of this chapter and the next in perspective, remember that the ultimate objective is a more complete understanding of aggregate demand (and what shifts it), which combines these expenditure components with government expenditure on goods and services. This understanding of the components such as consumption will help you in later chapters to understand the potential causes of past and future recessions.

Be sure you can distinguish the *AD* curve from the *AE* curve—they are based on different thought experiments. Each *AE* curve holds constant the price level, and represents only a single point on an *AD* curve, while the *AD* curve allows the price level to vary. Changing the price level will shift the *AE* curve, but create a movement along the *AD* curve.

3 This chapter distinguishes between *autonomous* expenditure and *induced* expenditure. Autonomous expenditure is independent of changes in real GDP, whereas induced expenditure will vary as real GDP varies. In general, a change in autonomous expenditures creates a change in real GDP, which in turn creates a change in induced expenditure. As the flow graph in Figure 23.3 illustrates, these changes are at the heart of the multiplier effect.

FIGURE **23.3**

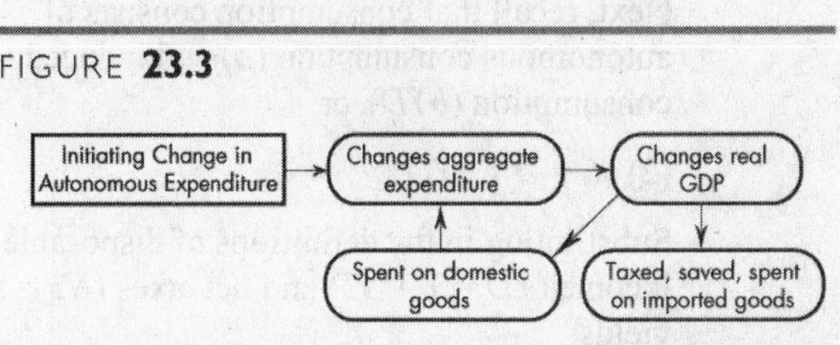

(It is important to realize, however, that even though autonomous expenditure may be independent of changes in real GDP, it will not be independent of changes in other variables—for example, the price level.)

4 The concept of the multiplier is very important. It results from the interaction of the components of aggregate expenditure. An initial increase in autonomous expenditure directly increases real GDP, but that is not the end of the story. As shown in Figure 23.3, that initial increase in real GDP generates an increase in *induced* expenditure, which further increases real GDP, and induces further increases in expenditure. The total effect on real GDP is larger than the initial increase in autonomous expenditure, because there is induced expenditure. You should become thoroughly familiar with both the intuition and the mathematics behind the multiplier.

5 The multiplier shows the change in equilibrium expenditure, and the change in equilibrium real GDP, price level held constant—it shows the shift rightward or leftward in the *AD* curve. However, the price level normally will change with a shift in the *AD* curve, the size of the change depending on the *AS* curve. In the short run, the change in the price level creates an opposite change in aggregate expenditure, one that somewhat offsets the initial change in aggregate expenditure, so that the total change in real GDP is less than the initial shift in *AD* would indicate. In the long run, this offsetting effect is 100 percent.

ⓔ 6 The mathematical note to Chapter 23 on the algebra of the multiplier will be covered by some students' instructors, and this material is worth reviewing if you are one of those students.

To start, recall that aggregate planned expenditure (*AE*) is equal to the sum of components' planned levels:

(1) $AE = C + I + G + X - M$

Next, recall that consumption consists of autonomous consumption (a) and induced consumption (bYD), or

(2) $C = a + bYD$

Substituting in the definitions of disposable income ($YD = Y - NT$) and net taxes ($NT = tY$) yields:

(3) $C = a + b(Y - NT) = a + b(1 - t)Y$

Next, recall that imports also depend on real GDP.

(4) $M = mY$

Next, substitute the consumption function (equation (3)) and the import function (equation (4)) into the aggregate planned expenditure function:

(5) $AE = a + b(1 - t)Y + I + G + X - mY$

Collecting terms:

(6) $AE = [a + I + G + X] + [b(1 - t) - m]Y$

or

(6a) $AE = A + [b(1 - t) - m]Y$

A is autonomous expenditure and $[b(1 - t) - m]$ is the slope of the aggregate planned expenditure function.

Equilibrium occurs when $Y = AE$ along the 45° line:

(7) $Y^* = A + [b(1 - t) - m]Y^*$

Collecting terms and solving yields the solution:

(8) $Y^* = \frac{1}{1 - [b(1 - t) - m]}A$

We can use equation (8) to show the algebraic formula for the multiplier. We start with a shock to autonomous expenditure (ΔA) which creates a change in equilibrium expenditure and real GDP:

(9) $\Delta Y^* = \frac{1}{1 - [b(1 - t) - m]}\Delta A$

Dividing both sides of (9) by ΔA gives us the equation for the multiplier:

(10) $\frac{\Delta Y^*}{\Delta A} = \frac{1}{1 - [b(1 - t) - m]}$

$= \frac{1}{1 - \text{Slope of } AE \text{ function}}$

SELF-TEST

True/False and Explain

Expenditure Plans and GDP

1 The sum of the marginal propensity to consume and the marginal propensity to save equals 1.

2 A change in disposable income will shift the consumption function.

3 An increase in expected future disposable income will shift both the consumption and saving functions upward.

4 Net taxes increase as real GDP increases.

Equilibrium Expenditure at a Fixed Price Level

5 When aggregate planned expenditure exceeds real GDP, inventories will increase more than planned.

6 Equilibrium expenditure occurs when aggregate planned expenditure equals real GDP.

7 Induced expenditure is that part of aggregate expenditure that varies as real GDP varies.

8 The aggregate expenditure schedule lists the level of aggregate planned expenditure that is generated at each level of real GDP.

The Multiplier

9 If the slope of the *AE* function is 0.75, the multiplier is equal to 3.

10 If the marginal tax rate increases, the multiplier will be higher.

11 If the marginal propensity to import decreases, the multiplier will be higher.

The Multiplier and the Price Level

12 An increase in the price level shifts the aggregate expenditure curve upward.

13 An increase in autonomous expenditure generates an increase in equilibrium real GDP in the short run.

14 An increase in autonomous expenditure generates an increase in equilibrium real GDP in the long run.

15 The higher the marginal propensity to consume, the higher the multiplier in the long run.

Multiple-Choice

Expenditure Plans and GDP

1 The fraction of the last dollar of disposable income saved is the
- **a** marginal propensity to consume.
- **b** marginal propensity to save.
- **c** marginal propensity to dispose.
- **d** marginal tax rate.
- **e** saving function.

2 Consider Table 23.1. Autonomous consumption is equal to
- **a** $0.
- **b** $65.
- **c** $100.
- **d** $260
- **e** $400.

TABLE 23.1

Disposable Income (1997 $)	Consumption Expenditure (1997 $)
0	100
100	165
200	230
300	295
400	360

3 Consider Table 23.1. The marginal propensity to consume is
a 0.35.
b 0.65.
c 1.15.
d 1.65.
e not calculable with the information given.

4 In Table 23.1, at which level(s) of *YD* is there positive saving?
a 0
b 100
c 200
d 300
e all of the above levels

5 Which of the following events would shift the consumption function upward?
a An increase in disposable income
b A decrease in disposable income
c An increase in the real interest rate
d A decrease in expected future disposable income
e An increase in wealth

Equilibrium Expenditure at a Fixed Price Level

6 The aggregate expenditure curve shows the relationship between aggregate planned expenditure and
a disposable income.
b real GDP.
c the interest rate.
d consumption expenditure.
e the price level.

7 If there is an unplanned increase in inventories, aggregate planned expenditure is
a greater than real GDP and firms will increase output.
b greater than real GDP and firms will decrease output.
c less than real GDP and firms will increase output.
d less than real GDP and firms will decrease output.
e less than real GDP and firms will decrease investment.

8 If $AE = 50 + 0.6Y$ and $Y = 200$, unplanned inventory
a increases are 75.
b increases are 30.
c decreases are 75.
d decreases are 30.
e changes are 0 and equilibrium exists.

9 Autonomous expenditure is *not* influenced by
a the interest rate.
b the foreign exchange rate.
c real GDP.
d the price level.
e any variable.

10 In Figure 23.4, the marginal propensity to consume is
a 0.3.
b 0.6.
c 0.9.
d 1.0.
e none of the above.

FIGURE **23.4**

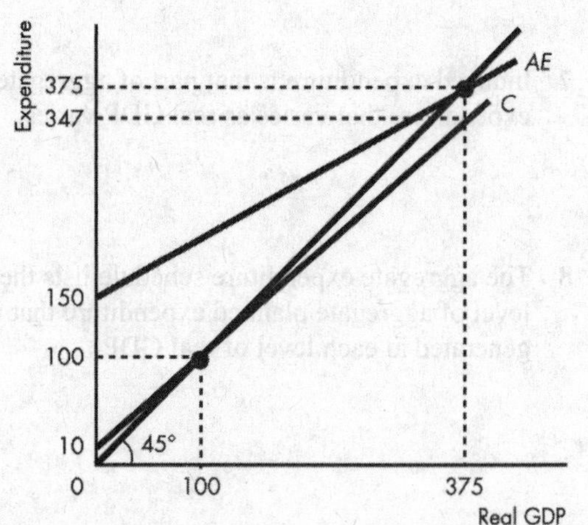

Note: There are no taxes in this economy.

11 In Figure 23.4, *autonomous* aggregate expenditure is
a 10.
b 100.
c 150.
d 347.
e 375.

12 In Figure 23.4, *equilibrium* expenditure is
a 10.
b 100.
c 150.
d 347.
e 375.

13 In Figure 23.4, at the equilibrium level of real GDP, *induced* expenditure is
- **a** 28.
- **b** 150.
- **c** 225.
- **d** 347.
- **e** 375.

14 In Figure 23.4, the marginal propensity to import is
- **a** 0.
- **b** 0.1.
- **c** 0.25.
- **d** 0.3.
- **e** 0.6.

The Multiplier

15 In Figure 23.4, the multiplier is
- **a** 0.25.
- **b** 1.
- **c** 1.60.
- **d** 2.50.
- **e** 10.

16 An increase in expected future disposable income leads to a(n)
- **a** increase in consumption and a decrease in aggregate expenditure.
- **b** increase in both consumption and aggregate expenditure.
- **c** decrease in both consumption and aggregate expenditure.
- **d** decrease in consumption and an increase in aggregate expenditure.
- **e** increase in consumption and either an increase or a decrease in aggregate expenditure, depending on what happens to saving.

17 Which of the following quotations illustrates the idea of the multiplier?
- **a** "The new stadium will generate $200 million in spinoff spending."
- **b** "Higher expected profits are leading to higher investment spending by business, and will lead to higher consumer spending."
- **c** "The projected cuts in government jobs will hurt the local retail industry."
- **d** "Taking the grain elevator out of our small town will destroy all the jobs."
- **e** All of the above.

18 The value of the multiplier increases with
- **a** an increase in the marginal propensity to import.
- **b** an increase in the marginal tax rate.
- **c** a decrease in the marginal propensity to consume.
- **d** a decrease in the marginal propensity to save.
- **e** an increase in the marginal propensity to save.

The Multiplier and the Price Level

19 An increase in the price level will
- **a** shift the *AE* curve upward and increase equilibrium expenditure.
- **b** shift the *AE* curve upward and decrease equilibrium expenditure.
- **c** shift the *AE* curve downward and increase equilibrium expenditure.
- **d** shift the *AE* curve downward and decrease equilibrium expenditure.
- **e** have no impact on the *AE* curve.

20 A decrease in the price level will
- **a** increase aggregate expenditure and thus produce a movement along the aggregate demand curve.
- **b** increase aggregate expenditure and thus produce a rightward shift in the aggregate demand curve.
- **c** increase aggregate expenditure and thus produce a leftward shift in the aggregate demand curve.
- **d** have no effect on aggregate expenditure.
- **e** increase aggregate expenditure, but produce no effect on the aggregate demand curve.

21 Suppose that investment increases by $10 billion. If the multiplier is 2, the *AD* curve will
- **a** shift rightward by the horizontal distance of $20 billion.
- **b** shift rightward by a horizontal distance greater than $20 billion.
- **c** shift rightward by a horizontal distance less than $20 billion.
- **d** not be affected.
- **e** shift upward by a vertical distance equal to $20 billion.

22 Suppose the multiplier is 2 and the short-run aggregate supply curve is positively sloped. If investment increases by $10 billion, equilibrium real GDP will
- **a** increase by $20 billion.
- **b** increase by more than $20 billion.
- **c** decrease by less than $20 billion.
- **d** be unaffected.
- **e** increase by less than $20 billion.

23 Suppose the multiplier is 2 and investment increases by $10 billion. In the long run, equilibrium real GDP will
- **a** increase by $20 billion.
- **b** increase by more than $20 billion.
- **c** decrease by less than $20 billion.
- **d** be unaffected.
- **e** increase by less than $20 billion.

Mathematical Note to Chapter 23: The Algebra of the Multiplier

24 Consider Fact 23.1. What is the equation for the aggregate expenditure function of this economy?
- **a** $AE = 16 + 0.7Y$
- **b** $AE = 36 - 0.7Y$
- **c** $AE = 26 + 0.8Y$
- **d** $AE = 36 + 0.9Y$
- **e** $AE = 36 + 0.7Y$

FACT 23.1

The economy of Beverly Hills has a consumption function of $C = 10 + 0.8Y$, investment equal to 6, government expenditures on goods and services equal to 10, exports equal to 10, and an import function of $M = 0.1Y$.

25 Consider Fact 23.1. What is equilibrium real GDP in this economy?
- **a** 36
- **b** 120
- **c** 130
- **d** 360
- **e** None of the above

Short Answer Problems

1 Explain how studying the circular flow in Chapter 20 helps us to understand the multiplier process of Chapter 23.

2 Suppose aggregate planned expenditure is greater than real GDP. Explain how equilibrium expenditure is achieved.

3 Define and explain what autonomous expenditure is, and what induced expenditure is, and what role each plays in the multiplier process.

4 Explain (without algebraic expressions) why the multiplier is larger if the marginal propensity to consume is higher.

5 Explain how the effects of price level changes on the *AE* curve will generate an *AD* curve.

6 Table 23.2 illustrates the consumption function for a very small economy.

TABLE 23.2

Disposable Income (1997 $)	Consumption Expenditure (1997 $)	Saving (1997 $)
0	3,000	
3,000	5,250	
6,000	7,500	
9,000	9,750	
12,000	12,000	
15,000	14,250	

- **a** Compute the economy's saving at each level of disposable income by completing Table 23.2.
- **b** Compute the economy's *MPC* and *MPS*.
- **c** From the information given and computed, draw the economy's consumption and saving functions.
- **d** Write out the equations of the consumption and saving functions.

7 Consider an economy with the following components of aggregate expenditure:
- Consumption function: $C = 20 + 0.8Y$
- Investment function: $I = 30$
- Government expenditures: $G = 8$
- Export function: $X = 4$
- Import function: $M = 2 + 0.2Y$

(There are no taxes, so $YD = Y$.)
- **a** What is the marginal propensity to consume in this economy?
- **b** What is the equation of the aggregate expenditure function in this economy?
- **c** What is the slope of the *AE* function?
- **d** Find this economy's equilibrium aggregate expenditure and real GDP by completing the columns of Table 23.3.

TABLE 23.3

Y	C	I	G	X	M	AE
0						
30						
60						
90						
120						
150						
180						

e Using the equation of the aggregate function you derived in **b**, solve mathematically for the equilibrium aggregate expenditure and real GDP.

f What is the multiplier for this economy?

8 Consider an economy with the following characteristics:

- Autonomous part of consumption expenditure = \$10 billion
- Investment = \$5 billion
- Government expenditures of goods and services = \$40 billion
- Exports = \$5 billion
- Slope of the *AE* function = 0.5
- There are no autonomous imports.

(Assume that the price level is constant.)

a What is autonomous expenditure in this economy?

b What is the equation of the *AE* function?

c Draw a graph containing the *AE* curve for this economy (label it AE_0) as well as a 45° line.

d What is equilibrium expenditure?

ⓒⓣ **e** What is induced expenditure in equilibrium?

9 Return to the economy of Short Answer Problem **8**. Now suppose that the government decides to increase its expenditures on goods and services to \$60 billion.

a Using the graph from Short Answer Problem **8c**, draw the new *AE* curve and label it AE_1.

ⓒⓣ **b** What is the new equilibrium expenditure? Solve for this value using both the graphical approach and the mathematical approach.

c What is the multiplier?

ⓒⓣ **d** After the increase in government expenditures, were there increases or decreases in autonomous expenditure, induced expenditure, consumption, imports, and investment?

10 Explain carefully what an increase in expected future disposable income will do to the consumption function, the saving function, the aggregate expenditure curve, and the aggregate demand curve.

ANSWERS

True/False and Explain

1 T Last dollar of *YD* is either spent or saved. (538–539)

2 F Change in *YD* leads to movement along consumption function. (536–540)

3 F Shifts upward the consumption function—more consumption expenditure at each level of *current YD*, but given constant current *YD*, this increase in consumption means less saving. (539–540)

4 T Due to induced income taxes. (540)

5 F *AE* > real GDP creates excess sales, leading to falling inventories. (544–545)

6 T Definition. (544–545)

7 T Definition. (543)

8 T Definition. (543)

9 F Multiplier = 1/(1 – slope of *AE* function) = 1/(1 – 0.75) = 1/0.25 = 4. (546–548)

ⓒⓣ **10 F** A higher marginal tax rate lowers the slope of the *AE* curve and the size of the multiplier. (548–549)

11 T A lower marginal propensity to import increases the slope of the *AE* curve and the size of the multiplier. (548–549)

12 F Increase in price level lowers *AE* through wealth and substitution effects. (551–553)

13 T The increase in *AE* shifts the *AD* curve rightward, movement along *SAS* in the short run with an increase in real GDP. (553–555)

14 F Same initial effect as for **13**, but given the vertical *LAS* curve, there is no increase in real GDP. (553–555)

15 F In the long run, the multiplier is zero due to the vertical *LAS* curve. (553–555)

Multiple-Choice

1 b Definition. (538–539)

2 c The level of consumption when disposable income is zero. (536)

3 b $MPC = \Delta C/\Delta YD = (165 - 100)/(100 - 0) = 0.65$. (538)

4 d Only here is $YD > C$. (536–537)

5 e **a** and **b** are movements along the curve, **c** and **d** shift it downward. (539–540)

6 b Definition. (543)

ⓒⓣ **7 d** Increase in inventories means $AE <$ real GDP and decreases in firms' sales, so they decrease production in response. (544–545)

ⓒⓣ **8 b** $Y = 200$ implies $AE = 50 + 0.6(200) = 170$. Unplanned inventories $= Y - AE = +30$. (544–545)

9 c Definition. (543)

10 c MPC = slope of consumption function = $\Delta C/\Delta Y = 90/100 = 0.9$. (538)

11 c Intercept of AE function. (543)

12 e Where the AE curve crosses the 45° line. (543–545)

13 c Induced = aggregate – autonomous = 375 – 150 = 225. (543–545)

ⓒⓣ **14 d** Marginal propensity to import = MPC – slope of AE curve = 0.9 – 0.6 = 0.3, where the slope of AE curve = $\Delta AE/\Delta Y = 225/375 = 0.6$. (543–545)

15 d Multiplier = 1/(1 – slope of AE function) = 1/(1 – 0.6) = 1/0.4 = 2.5. (548)

16 b Increase in expected future disposable income leads to more consumption spending, less saving, and an increase in autonomous expenditure. (539–547)

17 e All of the choices discuss secondary, induced effects. (546–547)

ⓒⓣ **18 d** This change raises MPC and multiplier. Others lower multiplier. (547–549)

19 d Increase in price level leads to decrease in aggregate expenditure due to wealth and substitution effects, leading to new equilibrium at lower real GDP = equilibrium expenditure. (551–553)

20 a Decrease in price level leads to increase in aggregate expenditure due to three effects, leading to movement along AD curve. (551–553)

21 a Multiplier effect raises AE and Y by 2 times original Δ autonomous expenditure, which leads to shift rightward by same amount in AD curve. (551–553)

22 e Multiplier effect of Question **21** is reduced by increase in price level due to positively sloped SAS curve. (551–555)

23 d Vertical LAS curve means that there is no increase in real GDP after the shift rightward in AD. (551–555)

24 e $AE = 10 + 0.8Y + 6 + 10 + 10 - 0.1Y = 36 + 0.7Y$. (558–559)

25 b Solve $Y^* = 36 + 0.7Y^*$, which leads to $Y^*(1 - 0.7) = 36$, and therefore $Y^* = 36/0.3 = 120$. (558–559)

Short Answer Problems

1 The circular flow shows us that firms produce goods and services, sell them on the market to consumers, investors, governments, and the rest of the world, and use the money earned to pay factors of production, who in turn buy goods and services. The circular flow thus shows us the secondary, induced effects of the multiplier process in action. An initial increase in autonomous expenditure means more sales for firms, which means more household income, which means more consumption expenditure, etc.

2 If aggregate planned expenditure is greater than real GDP, inventories decrease more than planned, and firms will increase output to replenish those depleted inventories. As a result, real GDP increases. This procedure continues as long as real GDP is less than aggregate planned expenditure. It will stop only when equilibrium is attained—when real GDP equals aggregate planned expenditure.

3 Autonomous expenditure is the part of aggregate expenditure that does not vary with real GDP, but varies as a result of changes in other variables such as the real interest rate. Induced expenditure is the part of aggregate expenditure that does vary with real GDP. The multiplier process starts out with a change in autonomous expenditure that changes aggregate expenditure, which in turn changes real GDP. This change in real GDP creates secondary effects by changing induced expenditure in the same direction, which in turn changes aggregate expenditure and real GDP, leading to a total effect that is a multiple of the initial change in autonomous expenditure.

4 Any initial stimulus to autonomous expenditure will generate a direct increase in real GDP. The basic idea of the multiplier is that this initial increase in real GDP generates further increases in real GDP as increases in consumption expenditure are induced. At each round of the multiplier process, the increase in spending, and thus the further increase in real GDP, are partially determined by the marginal propensity to consume. Since a larger marginal propensity to consume means a larger increase in real GDP at each round, the total increase in real GDP will also be greater. Thus the multiplier will be larger if the marginal propensity to consume is larger.

5 The aggregate demand curve illustrates the relationship between the price level and aggregate expenditures. The aggregate expenditure diagram shows the level of equilibrium expenditure holding the price level constant. If the price level changes, the *AE* curve will shift and a new level of equilibrium expenditure will result. Thus, for each price level, there is a different level of equilibrium expenditure. These combinations of price level and corresponding aggregate expenditure are points on the aggregate demand curve. For example, if the price level increases, autonomous expenditure will decline, and the *AE* curve will shift downward. This shift will lead to a decrease in equilibrium expenditure. Since an increase in the price level is associated with a reduction in equilibrium expenditure, the *AD* curve is negatively sloped.

6 **a** The answers to **a** are shown in Table 23.2 Solution, where saving = *YD* – *C*.

TABLE **23.2** SOLUTION

Disposable Income (1997 $)	Consumption Expenditure (1997 $)	Saving (1997 $)
0	3,000	–3,000
3,000	5,250	–2,250
6,000	7,500	–1,500
9,000	9,750	–750
12,000	12,000	0
15,000	14,250	+750

b The *MPC* = (Δ consumption)/(Δ disposable income). Using the first two entries in the table, we can see that change in consumption is 2,250, and the change in disposable income is 3,000, so that the *MPC* = 0.75 = 2,250/3,000. The *MPS* = (Δ saving)/(Δ disposable income). Using the first two entries in the table, we can see that Δ saving is +750, and Δ disposable income is 3,000, so that the *MPS* = 0.25 = 750/3,000. Using any other two adjacent entries in the table will yield the same result.

c The consumption function is shown in Figure 23.5, and the saving function is illustrated in Figure 23.6.

FIGURE **23.5**

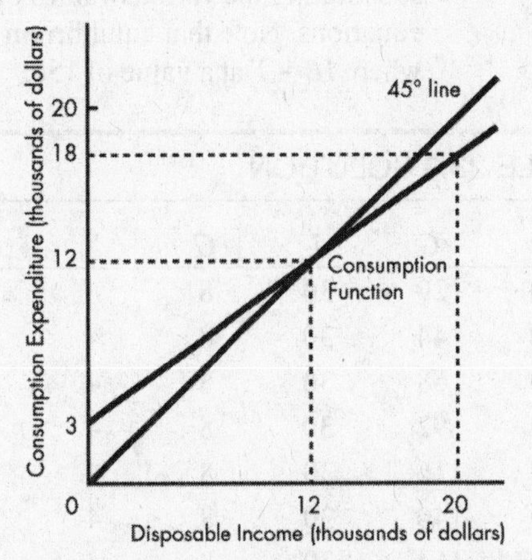

FIGURE **23.6**

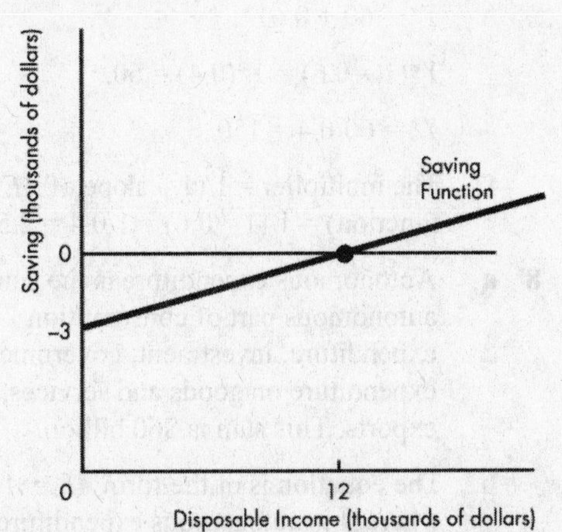

d The equation of the consumption function is based on an intercept of 3,000 and the slope (*MPC*) of 0.75. $C = 3{,}000 + 0.75YD$. Similarly, for the saving function, $S = -3{,}000 + 0.25YD$.

7 a From the consumption function equation we know this value is $0.8 = \Delta C/\Delta Y$.

b Substitute the various equations into:

$AE = C + I + G + X - M,$

$AE = 20 + 0.8Y + 30 + 8 + 4 - 2 - 0.2Y,$

$AE = 60 + 0.6Y.$

c The slope of the *AE* function comes from the equation and equals $\Delta AE/\Delta Y = 0.6$.

d The answer is presented in Table 23.3 Solution below. The table is constructed by substituting the various values of *Y* into the equations. Note that equilibrium occurs when $AE = Y$ at a value of 150.

TABLE **23.3** SOLUTION

Y	*C*	*I*	*G*	*X*	*M*	*AE*
0	20	30	8	4	2	60
30	44	30	8	4	8	78
60	68	30	8	4	14	96
90	92	30	8	4	20	114
120	116	30	8	4	26	132
150	140	30	8	4	32	150
180	164	30	8	4	38	168

e Equilibrium occurs when

$Y = AE,$

$Y^* = 60 + 0.6Y^*,$

$Y^*(1 - 0.6) = Y^*(0.4) = 60,$

$Y^* = 60/0.4 = 150$

f The multiplier = 1/(1 – slope of *AE* function) = 1/(1 – 0.6) = 1/0.4 = 2.5.

8 a Autonomous expenditure is the sum of the autonomous part of consumption expenditure, investment, government expenditure on goods and services, and exports. This sum is $60 billion.

b The equation is of the form $AE = A + eY$, where *A* is autonomous expenditure and *e* is the slope of the *AE* function. In this case, the equation is $AE = 60 + 0.5Y$, where units are billions of dollars.

c See the curve labelled AE_0 in Figure 23.7. The curve was drawn by noting that the amount of autonomous expenditure ($60 billion) gives the vertical intercept and that the slope of the *AE* function is 0.5.

FIGURE **23.7**

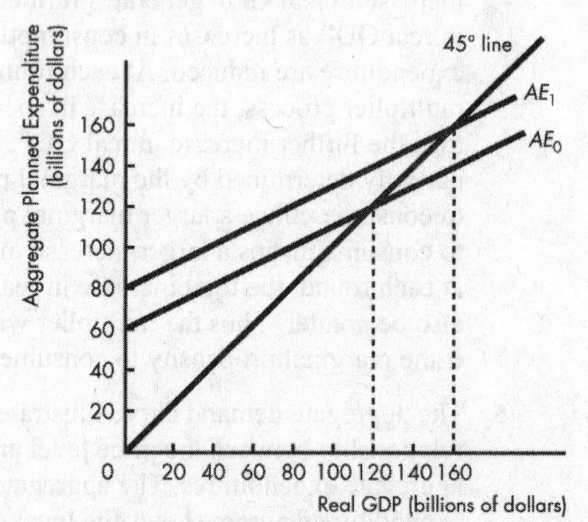

d Equilibrium expenditure can be solved one of two ways. First, equilibrium expenditure occurs at the intersection of the AE_0 curve and the 45° line. Equilibrium expenditure is $120 billion. Second, it can be calculated by solving the $AE = Y$ equation:

$Y^* = 60 + 0.5Y^*,$

$Y^*(1 - 0.5) = 60,$

$Y^* = 60/0.5 = 120.$

ⓒⓣ **e** Induced expenditure = total expenditure – autonomous expenditure = 120 – 60 = 60 in this case.

9 a See the curve labelled AE_1 in Figure 23.7. The new curve reflects the fact that autonomous expenditure increases by $20 billion but the slope of the *AE* function remains unchanged.

ⓒⓣ **b** The new equilibrium expenditure is $160 billion. This answer is given by the intersection of the AE_1 curve with the 45° line, or by solving the new equilibrium condition:

$Y^* = 80 + 0.5Y^*,$

$Y^*(1 - 0.5) = 80,$

$Y^* = 80/0.5 = 160.$

c Since a $20 billion increase in autonomous expenditure generated a $40 billion increase in equilibrium expenditure, the multiplier is 2. This value can be obtained by using the formula that the multiplier = 1/(1 – slope of *AE* function).

ⓒⓣ **d** The total change in real GDP is $40 billion. First, we can note that the change in autonomous expenditure is just the increase in government expenditures of $20 billion, and we can further note:

Δ total expenditure = Δ autonomous expenditure + Δ induced expenditure

or

+$40 billion = +$20 billion + $20 billion,

so that the change in induced expenditure is also $20 billion.

Second, since real GDP has increased, this increases both consumption and imports, because they are part of induced expenditure. However, investment being autonomous, it is not affected by the change in real GDP.

10 An increase in expected future disposable income leads to less saving (so that the saving function shifts downward at each level of disposable income) and more consumption out of current disposable income (so that the consumption function shifts upward). This change is an increase in autonomous consumption, and is therefore an increase in aggregate expenditure, and leads to a shift upward in the aggregate expenditure function. This shift creates multiplier effects and a shift rightward in the aggregate demand curve at the current price level.

Chapter 24 Fiscal Policy

KEY CONCEPTS

Government Budgets

The **federal budget** is annual statement of revenue and outlays of government of Canada (**provincial budget** is for provincial governments).

- ♦ Budgets finance government activities and achieve macroeconomic policy objectives (**fiscal policy**).
- ♦ Fiscal policy is made by government and Parliament, in consultation with bureaucrats, provincial governments, and business and consumer groups.
- ♦ Budgetary revenues—personal income taxes, corporate income taxes, indirect taxes (GST), investment income.
- ♦ Budgetary outlays—transfer payments, expenditures on goods and services, debt interest payments.
- ♦ Budget balance = revenues – outlays
  - **Budget surplus** when revenues > outlays.
  - **Budget deficit** when revenues < outlays.
  - **Balanced budget** when revenues = outlays.
- ♦ **Government debt** = total borrowing by governments = sum of past deficits – sum of past surpluses
  - Persistent deficits of the 1980s increased borrowing, which increased interest payments and increased deficit, etc.
  - Balanced budget of 1997 stopped this cycle—government debt is falling.
- ♦ Provincial government outlays are almost as large as federal, focused on hospitals, schools, and colleges/universities.
- ♦ Canada's budget surplus is unusual compared to those of other industrial nations.

Fiscal Policy Multipliers

Fiscal policy actions can either be **discretionary** (initiated by Parliament, involves Δ government outlays, taxes), or **automatic** (triggered by state of economy).

- ♦ Initially, assume a model economy with only **autonomous taxes** (do *not* vary with real GDP), and no exports or imports.
- ♦ Government expenditures multiplier
  = (Δ real GDP)/(Δ government expenditures)
  = 1/(1 – slope of the *AE* curve) > 1.
- ♦ Initial increase in *G* increases real GDP, which leads to secondary, induced effects.
- ♦ **Autonomous tax multiplier** = (Δ real GDP)/(Δ taxes) = –*MPC*/(1 – slope of the *AE* curve) < 0.
- ♦ Increase in *NT* decreases *YD*, decreases *C*, and therefore decreases real GDP, which leads to secondary, induced effects.
  - Since some of tax change affects saving, initial Δ*C* = –*MPC* × Δ taxes.
- ♦ Autonomous transfers multiplier = *MPC*/(1 – slope of the *AE* curve) since transfers are negative taxes.

Induced taxes, transfer payments, and imports are **automatic stabilizers**—mechanisms that reduce fluctuations in real GDP automatically.

- ♦ **Induced taxes** and induced transfer payments vary with real GDP.
  - The larger the marginal tax rate, the smaller the multipliers.
- ♦ Higher marginal propensity to import also reduces multiplier effects.

Budget deficits fluctuate with business cycle due to cyclical fluctuations in net taxes.

- ♦ **Structural surplus or deficit** is budget balance when real GDP = potential.
- ♦ **Cyclical surplus or deficit** = actual balance – structural balance.

♦ Cyclical surplus or deficit is due only to fact that real GDP ≠ potential.

Fiscal Policy Multipliers and the Price Level

Price level adjustments change outcome of fiscal policy.

♦ **Expansionary fiscal policy** (increased *G* or decreased *NT*) shifts *AD* curve rightward.

♦ **Contractionary fiscal policy** (decreased *G* or increased *NT*) shifts *AD* curve leftward.

♦ In short run, expansionary policy has positive but reduced effects because increase in *AD* increases price level, which decreases *AE*, creating movement along *AD*, partially offsetting initial effect.

♦ If real GDP at potential, increase in price level fully offsets initial effect.

♦ Even short-run fiscal policy is limited by

- Slowness of the legislative process.
- Difficulties in telling if real GDP is above or below potential GDP.

Supply-Side Effects of Fiscal Policy

Cutting tax rates might increase potential GDP and shift *LAS* rightward.

♦ Higher income taxes decrease incentives to work and save, which decreases labour supply and capital supply.

♦ Tax cut shifts *AD* curve rightward *and* shifts *SAS* rightward due to increased incentives.

♦ Size of rightward *SAS* shift is politically controversial. Conservatives tend to believe that supply-side effects are large; liberals that the effects are small.

HELPFUL HINTS

1 It is crucial to distinguish between two types of autonomous shocks. One type adds to the instability of the economy; it includes changes in autonomous consumption, investment, and exports. The other is planned in order to (hopefully) reduce the instability of the economy; it includes fiscal policy—changes in government expenditures and taxes. Because the two shocks work through the same multiplier process, the same process that creates instability can also help to reduce instability.

2 The size of the fiscal policy multipliers depends on the sizes of the *MPC*, the marginal tax rate, and the marginal propensity to import. Figure 24.1 below shows why. A crucial part of the multiplier process is the changes in induced expenditure in the second round of the multiplier. These induced expenditures are reduced as income is siphoned off for saving, to pay for taxes, or to buy imported goods!

FIGURE **24.1**

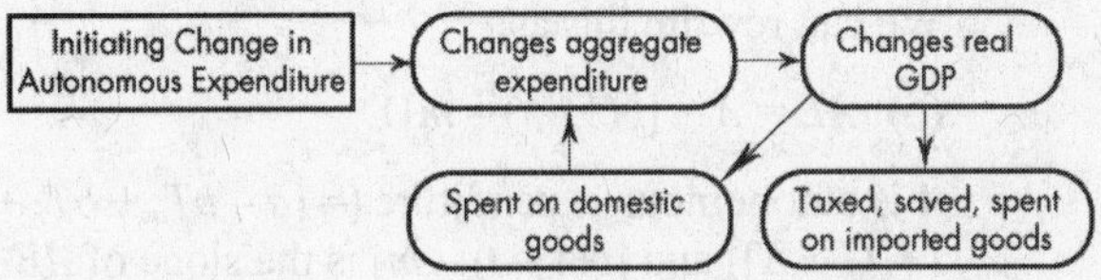

3 Helpful Hint **4** in Chapter 20 emphasized the difference between government expenditure on goods and services and government transfer payments. The difference is crucial once again in understanding why the government expenditures multiplier (= 1/(1 – slope of the *AE* curve)) is larger than the autonomous transfer payments multiplier (= *MPC*/(1 – slope of the *AE* curve)).

A \$1 increase in government expenditures on goods and services directly raises autonomous expenditure by \$1 in the first round of the multiplier. However, a \$1 increase in spending on autonomous transfer payments raises consumers' disposable income by \$1, and some of this extra income is saved, so that only \$1 × *MPC* is consumed, and autonomous expenditure increases by \$*MPC* < \$1 in the first round of the multiplier.

4 The mathematical note on the algebra of fiscal multipliers will be covered by some students' instructors, and is worth reviewing if you are one of those students.

First, aggregate planned expenditure (*AE*) is defined as in (1) below:

(1) $AE = C + I + G + X - M$

Second, net taxes (*NT*) are defined as autonomous taxes (T_a) – autonomous transfer payments (T_r) + induced taxes (tY):

(2) $NT = T_a - T_r + tY$

Consumption depends on disposable income:

(3) $C = a + b(Y - NT)$

Substituting (2) into (3):

(4) $C = a - bT_a + bT_r + b(1 - t)Y$

Imports depend on real GDP:

(5) $M = mY$

Substitute (4) and (5) into (1):

$AE = a - bT_a + bT_r + b(1 - t)Y + I + G + X - mY$

Collecting terms:

$AE = [a - bT_a + bT_r + I + G + X] + [b(1 - t) - m]Y$

We can rewrite this as:

(6) $AE = A + [b(1 - t) - m]Y$

A is autonomous expenditure ($= [a - bT_a + bT_r + I + G + X]$) and $[b(1 - t) - m]$ is the slope of AE curve. Equilibrium occurs when $Y = AE$ along the 45° line.

(7) $Y^* = A + [b(1 - t) - m]Y^*$

This equation can be solved for equilibrium real GDP:

(8) $$Y^* = \frac{A}{1 - [b(1 - t) - m]}$$

An increase in government expenditures affects A directly ($\Delta A = \Delta G$):

$$\Delta Y = \frac{1}{1 - [b(1 - t) - m]}\Delta G$$

Dividing both sides by ΔG yields the government expenditures multiplier:

(9) $$\frac{\Delta Y}{\Delta G} = \frac{1}{1 - [b(1 - t) - m]}$$

An increase in autonomous taxes affects A indirectly ($\Delta A = -b\Delta T_a$):

$$\Delta Y = \frac{-b}{1 - [b(1 - t) - m]}\Delta T_a$$

Dividing both sides by ΔT_a yields the autonomous tax multiplier:

(10) $$\frac{\Delta Y}{\Delta T_a} = \frac{-b}{1 - [b(1 - t) - m]}$$

Similarly, the autonomous transfer payments multiplier can be solved for:

(11) $$\frac{\Delta Y}{\Delta T_r} = \frac{b}{1 - [b(1 - t) - m]}$$

SELF-TEST

True/False and Explain

Government Budgets

1 The federal deficit is the total amount of borrowing that the federal government has undertaken.

2 Only government expenditures on goods and services, not transfer payments, are crucial in analyzing the federal deficit.

3 A government starts out with a balanced budget. In the next year, the percentage growth in outlays is higher than the percentage growth in revenues. It will now have a deficit.

4 Government investment income is an example of a budgetary outlay.

Fiscal Policy Multipliers

5 An increase in autonomous transfer payments matched by an increase in autonomous taxes will lead to an increase in real GDP equal to the size of the increase in transfer payments.

6 Taxes and transfer payments that vary with income act as automatic stabilizers in the economy.

7 The autonomous transfer payments multiplier is smaller than the government expenditures multiplier.

8 If real GDP increases, so do autonomous taxes.

9 If an economy has a structural deficit, the budget balance at potential GDP is negative.

Fiscal Policy Multipliers and the Price Level

10 If the price level is variable, an increase in government expenditures will never lead to an increase in real GDP.

11 A cut in autonomous taxes will increase equilibrium real GDP in the short run.

12 An increase in autonomous taxes will decrease equilibrium real GDP in the long run, if there are no incentive effects.

13 An increase in government expenditures will shift the *AE* curve upward and shift the *AD* curve rightward.

Supply-Side Effects of Fiscal Policy

14 Cutting income taxes will shift the *AD* curve rightward, but shift the *SAS* curve leftward.

15 An increase in income taxes will decrease potential GDP.

Multiple-Choice

Government Budgets

1 Provincial government outlays
- **a** are small and irrelevant to the economy.
- **b** are an important source of fiscal policy.
- **c** are always equal to provincial government revenues.
- **d** are focused on transfer payments to individuals, such as employment insurance.
- **e** tend to fluctuate with federal outlays.

2 Which of the following would *not* increase the budget deficit?
- **a** an increase in interest on the government debt
- **b** an increase in government expenditures on goods and services
- **c** an increase in government transfer payments
- **d** an increase in indirect business taxes
- **e** a decrease in government investment income

3 The budget deficit grew as a percentage of GDP after 1974 because
- **a** government expenditures on goods and services rose, while tax revenues remained constant.
- **b** government expenditures on goods and services remained constant, while tax revenues fell.
- **c** debt interest payments rose, while tax revenues remained constant.
- **d** debt interest payments rose, while tax revenues fell.
- **e** none of the above.

4 Which of the following groups does *not* influence federal fiscal policy?
- **a** government bureaucrats
- **b** provincial governments
- **c** Parliament
- **d** business and consumer groups
- **e** government unions

5 Which of the following is a budgetary outlay?
- **a** personal income taxes
- **b** government investment income
- **c** debt interest payments
- **d** indirect taxes
- **e** corporate income taxes

Fiscal Policy Multipliers

6 Which of the following happens *automatically* if the economy goes into a recession?
   - a Only government outlays increase.
   - b Only net taxes increase.
   - c The deficit increases.
   - d The deficit decreases.
   - e Both government outlays and net taxes increase, and the deficit stays the same.

7 During an expansion, tax revenue
   - a and government outlays decline.
   - b declines and government outlays increase.
   - c increases and government outlays decline.
   - d and government outlays increase.
   - e stays constant and government outlays increase.

8 Consider the economy of NoTax, where the slope of the *AE* curve is 0.6. If the government desires to shift the *AD* curve rightward by $5 billion, the correct increase in government expenditures is
   - a $2 billion.
   - b $2.5 billion.
   - c $3 billion.
   - d $7.5 billion.
   - e $8.33 billion.

9 How does an increase in the marginal tax rate affect the size of the multiplier?
   - a It has no impact.
   - b It makes the multiplier larger.
   - c It makes the multiplier smaller.
   - d It makes the multiplier smaller, but only if the new tax rate is larger than the *MPC*.
   - e It makes the multiplier smaller, but only if the new tax rate is smaller than the *MPC*.

10 A cyclical deficit is when
   - a government outlays are greater than revenues.
   - b government outlays are less than revenues.
   - c there is a deficit due to the fact real GDP is greater than potential GDP.
   - d there is a deficit due to the fact real GDP is less than potential GDP.
   - e there is a deficit even when real GDP equals potential GDP.

11 Currently the country of Ricardia has a budget plan with constant government outlays equal to $100 billion and taxes related positively to real GDP by the equation: Taxes = $25 billion + 0.1*Y*. If the structural deficit is $10 billion, what is potential GDP in this economy?
   - a $65 billion
   - b $75 billion
   - c $650 billion
   - d $750 billion
   - e $850 billion

12 If the slope of the *AE* function is 0.40, and the *MPC* is 0.75, what is the government expenditures multiplier?
   - a 0.60
   - b 1.2525
   - c 1.67
   - d 2.5
   - e 4

13 If the slope of the *AE* function is 0.40, and the *MPC* is 0.75, what is the autonomous tax multiplier?
   - a −1.67
   - b −1.2525
   - c −0.60
   - d 1.2525
   - e 1.67

14 If the slope of the *AE* function is 0.40, and the *MPC* is 0.75, what is the change in *Y* if *both* government expenditures and autonomous taxes increase by $200?
   - a 0
   - b $83.50
   - c $200
   - d $800
   - e not calculable with the information given

15 If the slope of the *AE* function is 0.40, and the *MPC* is 0.75, what is the autonomous transfer payments multiplier?
   - a −1.67
   - b −1.2525
   - c −0.60
   - d 1.2525
   - e 1.67

Fiscal Policy Multipliers and the Price Level

16 An *expansionary* fiscal policy leads to a(n)
- a rightward shift in the *AD* curve equal to the multiplier times the policy change.
- b leftward shift in the *AD* curve equal to the multiplier times the policy change.
- c leftward shift in the *SAS* curve.
- d increase in Y equal to the multiplier times the policy change, in the short run.
- e increase in Y equal to the multiplier times the policy change, in the long run.

17 Short-run fiscal policy is limited by the fact that
- a the *LAS* curve is vertical.
- b the legislative process is slow.
- c real GDP is typically not equal to potential GDP.
- d the policy might shift the *SAS* curve to the right.
- e the policy might shift the *SAS* curve to the left.

18 Which of the following is an example of an *expansionary* fiscal policy?
- a increasing debt interest payments
- b increasing taxes
- c decreasing transfer payments
- d increasing transfer payments
- e decreasing government expenditures on goods and services

19 Which of the following policies will *not* shift the *AD* curve rightward?
- a increasing government expenditures on goods and services
- b decreasing autonomous taxes
- c increasing autonomous transfer payments
- d increasing government expenditures on goods and services *and* increasing autonomous taxes by the same amount
- e decreasing government expenditures on goods and services *and* decreasing autonomous taxes by the same amount

Supply-Side Effects of Fiscal Policy

20 Which of the following quotations correctly refers to the effects of fiscal policy in the *long run*?
- a "The increase in taxes will increase real GDP."
- b "The increase in taxes will raise prices only."
- c "A change in the budget has no impact on real GDP unless it changes aggregate supply."
- d "A change in the budget has no impact on real GDP."
- e "An increase in government expenditures on goods and services will increase real GDP."

21 Which of the following quotations correctly refers to the effects of fiscal policy in the *short run*?
- a "The increase in taxes will increase real GDP."
- b "The increase in taxes will raise prices only."
- c "A change in the budget has no impact on real GDP unless it changes aggregate supply."
- d "A change in the budget has no impact on real GDP."
- e "The increase in government expenditures on goods and services will increase real GDP."

22 Suppose that the autonomous tax multiplier is –2. If autonomous taxes decrease by $4 billion and incentives to work and save are affected, in the long run real GDP will
- a decrease by $8 billion.
- b increase by $8 billion.
- c be unaffected.
- d increase, but by how much is unclear.
- e decrease, but by how much is unclear.

Mathematical Note to Chapter 24: The Algebra of the Fiscal Policy Multipliers

23 The formula for the tax function is
- a $G = G_a + gY$.
- b $M = mY$.
- c $NT = T_a - T_r + tY$.
- d $NT = 1/(1 - [b(1 - t) + m])$.
- e none of the above.

Fact 24.1

The economy of New Estevan has the following consumption and tax functions:
Consumption: $C = a + 0.5(Y - NT)$
Net taxes: $NT = T_a - T_r + 0.5Y$
This economy has no exports or imports.

---

24 Consider Fact 24.1. The government expenditures multiplier for this economy is
- a 0.25.
- b 0.5.
- c 1.33.
- d 2.0.
- e not calculable with the given information.

25 Consider Fact 24.1. The autonomous tax multiplier for this economy is
- **a** –0.667.
- **b** –1.0.
- **c** –1.33.
- **d** –2.0.
- **e** 0.667.

Short Answer Problems

1 What changes in the components of the federal government budget after 1974 were the principal causes of continuing large government deficits?

2 During the summer of 1995, Saskatchewan had a provincial election. A central plank of the Saskatchewan Liberal Party's election strategy was a promise to cut taxes dramatically, stating that these cuts would create 50,000 new jobs (about 10 percent of the labour force) over the next five years. Critics claimed that this policy would have only a small effect in Saskatchewan, that most of the new jobs from the tax cuts would show up in other provinces.
- **a** What economic concept underlies the Liberals' promise?
- **b** What economic concept underlies the critics' argument?
- **c** The Liberals lost the election, so we do not get to see if the tax cuts would have had the promised effect. But what do you think would have happened?

3 Suppose you are visiting the town of Elbow, Saskatchewan, which is suffering a depressed economy due to low wheat prices. You spend \$100 on accommodation and another \$100 golfing and dining at the excellent local golf club.
- **a** What factors will influence how much extra real GDP will be generated within Elbow by your \$200 of expenditure? (Treat Elbow as if it were a separate economy.)
- **b** What does your answer imply for the argument made by the Elbow town council that the Saskatchewan government should shift a government department to the town in order to stimulate the town's economy?

4 Explain why the multiplier of an expansionary fiscal policy is smaller once we consider the aggregate supply curve. What happens if there are incentive effects on *AS*?

5 Explain whether the following events will shift the *AE* curve and/or the *AD* curve and briefly explain your answer. (For each case, assume that the other variables are not changing.)
- **a** an increase in the price level
- **b** an increase in expected future profits for businesses
- **c** a cut in autonomous taxes
- **d** an increase in government expenditures

ⓒⓣ **6** Some politicians and economists argue tax cuts are beneficial for the economy in the short run *and* the long run. Explain their arguments, and evaluate them briefly.

ⓔ **7** You may wish to review the mathematical notes to Chapters 23 and 24 before doing this problem. Consider the expenditure functions for the following economy:

Consumption:	$C = 4{,}000 + 0.7(Y - NT) - 20P$
Investment:	$I = 2{,}000$
Government:	$G = 5{,}000$
Exports:	$X = 400$
Imports:	$M = 0.1Y$
Taxes:	$NT = 2{,}000$

where *P* is the price level.
- **a** What is the equation of the aggregate expenditure function? What is autonomous expenditure in this economy? What is the slope of the *AE* function?
- **b** Assume that the price level is equal to 100. Calculate equilibrium real GDP, consumption, and imports.
- **c** If the price level is now equal to 200, what is the new equilibrium real GDP?
- **d** Using your information from **b** and **c**, sketch the *AD* curve for this economy.
- **e** Calculate the government expenditures multiplier, the autonomous tax multiplier, and the autonomous transfer payments multiplier for this economy.
- **f** Suppose that the price level is equal to 100, and that government expenditures increase by 2,000. What is the resulting change in real GDP demanded, holding constant the price level?
- **g** Suppose that the change in real GDP demanded raises the price level by 100. What is the overall change in real GDP from

the two effects? What is the multiplier after the two effects have worked through the economy? Why is your answer different from **e**?

8 As finance minister for the government of Adanac, your crack team of economists has estimated the economy's *MPC* to be 0.75, price level held constant. (There are no induced taxes or imports, so that the slope of the *AE* curve = the *MPC*.) You are confident that this estimate is correct, since you threatened to exile the economists to the North Pole should they err. You have decided that in order to get reelected next year, you need to raise real GDP by $200 billion.

a If you decide to change only government expenditures, how much change is required to accomplish your goal?

b If you decide to change only autonomous taxes, how much change is required to accomplish your goal?

c Having selected method **a**, you find that the increase in real GDP is less than $200 billion, jeopardizing your chance for reelection. Before you exile the poor economists to the North Pole, is there any excuse for their mistake? (In other words, what went wrong?)

9 Suppose that the economy is in equilibrium at the point where the *AD* curve crosses the *SAS* curve. (Assume that the economy stays in the short run for the rest of this question, and ignore any incentive effects.) Suppose that the government raises autonomous taxes dramatically.

a Initially, assume the price level is held constant. Carefully explain what happens to aggregate expenditure, aggregate demand, and real GDP as a result of this autonomous shock. Draw a two-part graph as part of your answer, showing aggregate expenditure and the 45° line on the top, and the *AD–SAS* curves on the bottom.

ⓒⓣ **b** What happens to the levels of the components of aggregate expenditure after this shock?

c Next, show on the graph from **a** what happens when the price level changes. Explain the overall effect on aggregate expenditure, aggregate demand, short-run aggregate supply, the price level, and real GDP from the combined effects of the shock and the resulting change in the price level.

10 In the economy of Paridisio, government outlays are related to the level of real GDP by the formula: Outlays = 500 – 0.6*Y*, while tax revenues are related to the level of real GDP by the formula: Taxes = 100 + 0.4*Y*.

a Complete Table 24.1.

TABLE **24.1**

Real GDP	Outlays	Revenues	Budget Balance
0			
100			
200			
300			
400			
500			
600			

b If potential GDP is 300, what is the structural balance for Paridisio?

c If real GDP is currently 200, what are the values of the cyclical deficit, the structural deficit, and the actual deficit?

d Is the tax structure in this economy acting as an automatic stabilizer?

ANSWERS

True/False and Explain

1 F Deficit is when outlays > revenues in current year. (565)

2 F Government expenditures on goods, transfer and interest payments are all part of outlays. (565)

3 T If outlays grow faster than taxes, outlays > taxes next year and therefore there is a deficit. (565)

4 F Example of revenue. (564–565)

5 F They exactly offset each other (Δ net taxes = 0), so Δ real GDP = 0. (572–573)

6 T If income decreases, this leads to decrease in taxes + increase in transfers, and so an increase in disposable income, which increases aggregate expenditure, leading to increase in income, potentially offsetting initial decrease. (573–576)

7 T Since $MPC < 1$, government multiplier [1/(1 – slope of the *AE* curve)] > transfer multiplier [*MPC*/(1 – slope of the *AE* curve)]. (570–573)

8 F Autonomous is not affected by real GDP. (573)

9 T Definition. (574–576)

10 F In short run, increase in *G* leads to rightward shift in *AD*, and increase in real GDP. (576–578)

11 T Shifts *AD* rightward. (576–579)

12 F Vertical *LAS* curve means only price is affected by the shift in *AD*. (576–579)

13 T Increase in government expenditures = increase in autonomous expenditure, so *AE* curve shifts upward, leading to higher level of *AD*, same price level. (576–578)

14 F Income tax cut raises *YD* and shifts *AD* rightward, and it raises incentives to work and save, shifting *SAS* curve *rightward*. (579–580)

15 T Due to negative incentive effects. (579–580)

Multiple-Choice

1 e They may have a deficit, they are not really used for fiscal policy, they are almost as large as the federal government outlays, and *federal* government does employment insurance. (568–569)

2 d This effect is increase in revenue. (564–565)

3 c See text discussion. (566–568)

4 e See text discussion. (564–565)

5 c Others are sources of revenue. (564–565)

6 c In recession, decrease in *Y* leads to decrease in taxes and increase in spending on employment insurance, etc., which leads to increase in deficit. (564–566)

7 c Increase in real GDP leads to increase in tax revenue. Decrease in unemployment leads to decrease in transfer payments. (564–566)

ⓒⓣ **8 a** Government expenditures multiplier = 1/(1 – slope of the *AE* curve) = 1/(1 – 0.6) = 2.5. Invert ΔY = multiplier × ΔG: ΔG = ΔY/multiplier = 5/2.5 = 2. (570–572)

9 c It decreases *YD* at each stage of the multiplier process, reducing the amount of extra consumption spending. (573)

10 d Definition. (574–576)

ⓒⓣ **11 c** $10 billion = *G* – *NT* = $100 billion – $25 billion – 0.1 (potential GDP), therefore potential GDP = (100 – 25 – 10)/0.1 = $650 billion. (574–576)

12 c Multiplier = 1/(1 – slope of the *AE* curve) = 1/(1 – 0.40) = 1.67. (570–572)

13 b Autonomous tax multiplier = –*MPC*/(1 – slope of the *AE* curve) = –0.75/(1 – 0.40) = –1.2525. (572–573)

14 b Impact of government expenditures multiplier is 1.67 × $200 = $334, impact of autonomous tax multiplier is –1.2525 × $200 = – $250.50, total impact = $334 – $250.50 = $83.50. (570–573)

15 d Autonomous transfer payments multiplier = *MPC*/(1 – slope of the *AE* curve) = 0.75/(1 – 0.40) = 1.2525. (572–573)

16 a Increase in government expenditures or tax cut shifts *AD* curve rightward by this amount. The *SAS* curve would shift *rightward* if there are incentive effects; and the ΔY is smaller than this amount due to the increase in the price level. (576–578)

17 b Others are irrelevant or not limitations. (579)

18 d Definition. (576–578)

19 e The decrease in *G* shifts *AD* leftward by the government expenditures multiplier, the decrease in taxes shifts *AD* rightward by the autonomous tax multiplier, which has a smaller impact. (570–573)

20 c In the long run, changes in fiscal policy have an impact only if they change potential GDP (aggregate supply). (576–579)

21 e Shift rightward in *AD* increases real GDP in the short run. (576–578)

22 d Only the incentive effects on potential GDP matter, but their size is uncertain. (579–581)

23 c Definition. (584–585)

24 c Multiplier = $1/(1 - [b(1 - t) - m]) = 1/(1 - [0.5(1 - 0.5)]) = 1.33$. (584–585)

25 a Autonomous multiplier = $-MPC/(1 - [b(1 - t) - m]) = -0.5/(1 - 0.25) = -0.667$. (584–585)

Short Answer Problems

1 The deficit increased because the level of government outlays as a percentage of GDP increased, while taxes as a percentage of GDP fell during the late 1970s and then slowly increased. The components of spending that showed the most consistent growth were transfer payments and interest payments on government debt.

2 a The Liberals are counting on the autonomous tax multiplier to boost aggregate expenditure and create new jobs.

b The critics are arguing that most of the new expenditure would be on products from outside the province—they are arguing that the marginal propensity to import for a province is very high, so that the multipliers are very low.

c It is likely that fiscal policy multipliers are low for individual provinces due to high marginal propensities to import. For your information, imports in Saskatchewan were about 62 percent (= 15.14 billion/24.28 billion) of provincial real GDP in 1995. (*Source:* Statistics Canada, CANSIM matrices D21425 and D31874.)

3 a Your $200 will trigger a multiplier process—the owners of the factors of production at the golf course will spend their extra income, for example. This spending induces second-round increases in consumption expenditure, leading to a final change in real GDP in Elbow that is a multiple of $200. The size of the multiplier effect will be determined by two things. First, the larger the marginal propensity to consume in Elbow and the smaller the marginal propensity to import (from outside Elbow), the larger the multiplier will be. In a small town, the marginal propensity to import from outside the town is likely to be quite high, making the multiplier much smaller. Second, the effect is smaller if the aggregate supply curve is steeper—the increase in aggregate demand gets reduced by an increase in the price level.

b Clearly, such a shift might stimulate the town's economy, since the annual increase in government expenditures will create multiplier effects. The usefulness of this endeavour is limited by the factors mentioned that might reduce the size of the multiplier. (This policy was actual government policy in Saskatchewan until the Conservatives were defeated in 1991, at least partially because of this policy.)

4 The multiplier tells us the size of the change in real GDP (the shift in the *AD* curve) relative to the size of an initial change in government expenditure or autonomous taxes, holding constant the price level. Once we consider the *AS* curve, we know the price level will increase as aggregate demand increases—the increase in the price level being higher, the steeper the *AS* curve. This increase in the price level lowers aggregate expenditure, shown by the movement up the *AD* curve, leading to a smaller increase in real GDP.

Incentive effects would potentially shift the *AS* curve rightward, increasing the value of the multiplier.

5 Any change that does not initiate as a change in real GDP will shift the *AE* curve. Therefore all four changes will shift the *AE* curve. Any change in autonomous expenditure that is not caused by a change in the price level will shift the *AD* curve. Therefore **a** involves a movement along an *AD* curve, while **b**–**d** involve shifts in the *AD* curve.

ⓒⓣ **6** A cut in taxes will increase disposable income, and shift the *AD* curve rightward in the normal multiplier manner. However, supply-side economists argue that tax cuts will also increase the after-tax returns to work and saving, which in turn will lead to an increase in labour supply and saving, shifting the *AS* curves rightward.

An evaluation is still somewhat premature. As the text points out, it is still a matter of political opinion whether the *AS* effects are small or large. So far, there is no hard empirical evidence one way or the other.

7 a The equation can be found by totalling the components of aggregate expenditure:

$AE = 4{,}000 + 0.7(Y - 2{,}000) - 20P + 2{,}000 + 5{,}000 + 400 - 0.1Y$, or

$AE = 10{,}000 - 20P + 0.6Y$

Autonomous expenditure, which does not depend on real GDP, is $10{,}000 - 20P$. The slope is 0.6.

b Substitute $P = 100$ into the AE function, and solve for $Y^* = AE$:

$Y^* = 10{,}000 - 20(100) + 0.6Y^*$, or

$Y^*(1 - 0.6) = 8{,}000$, or

$Y^* = 8{,}000/0.4 = 20{,}000$

Equilibrium consumption equals $4{,}000 + 0.7(20{,}000 - 2{,}000) - 20(100) = 14{,}600$.

Imports $= 0.1(20{,}000) = 2{,}000$.

c Substitute $P = 200$ into the AE function from **a**:

$Y^* = 10{,}000 - 20(200) + 0.6Y^*$, or

$Y^*(0.4) = 6{,}000$, or

$Y^* = 6{,}000/0.4 = 15{,}000$

d One point on the curve is $P = 100$, $Y = 20{,}000$ and another point is $P = 200$, $Y = 15{,}000$. These points are illustrated in Figure 24.2.

FIGURE **24.2**

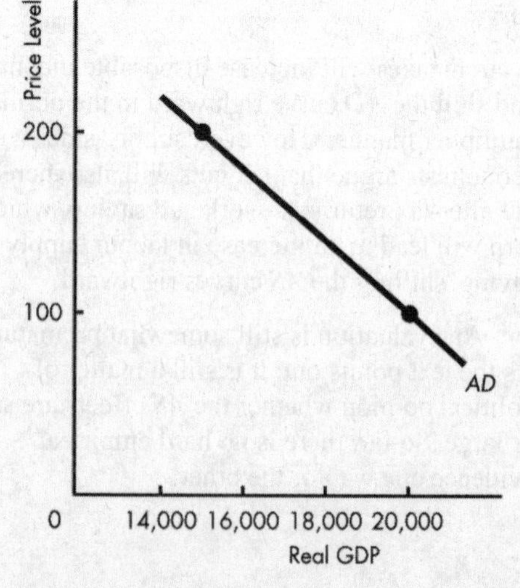

e The government expenditures multiplier = $1/(1 -$ slope of the AE function$) =$

$1/(1 - 0.6) = 2.5$

The autonomous tax multiplier =

$-MPC/(1 -$ slope of the AE function$) =$

$-0.7/(1 - 0.6) = -1.75$

The transfer payments multiplier =

$MPC/(1 -$ slope of the AE function$) =$

$0.7/(1 - 0.6) = 1.75$.

f The change in real GDP demanded equals the change in government expenditures times the government expenditures multiplier, or $2{,}000 \times 2.5 = 5{,}000$.

g If the price level increases by 100, then autonomous expenditure decreases by 5,000, as we saw in **d**. This decrease completely offsets the increase in real GDP due to the increase in government expenditures on 2,000. Therefore the overall change in real GDP is equal to zero, and the multiplier is equal to zero. The answer is different here compared with part **f**, because the price level is allowed to adjust, which leads to the offsetting effects.

8 a The government expenditures multiplier equals $1/(1 -$ slope of the AE curve$) = 1/(1 - 0.75) = 4$ in this case, so in order to raise real GDP by \$200 billion you need to increase government expenditures by \$50 billion = \$200/4 billion.

b The autonomous tax multiplier equals $-MPC/(1 -$ slope of the AE curve$) = -0.75/(1 - 0.75) = -3$ in this case, so in order to raise real GDP by \$200 billion you need to lower taxes by \$66.6 billion = \$200/3 billion.

c The multiplier effects we have been analyzing are based on the assumption that the price level is constant. In the real world, the stimulation of aggregate demand that you have carried out would raise the price level, which would lower aggregate expenditure, and partially (or completely) offset the increase in real GDP from your policy.

9 a Figure 24.3 shows what happens to aggregate expenditure (top of the graph) and to aggregate demand and supply (bottom). As taxes increase, disposable income decreases, and household consumption decreases, leading to a decrease in autonomous expenditure, shown by the shift downward in aggregate expenditure from AE_0 to AE_b. This decrease leads to a decrease in real GDP (holding constant the price level) from Y_0 to Y_b, with the new equilibrium at the point *b*, which is shown in the bottom graph as the shift leftward in the *AD* curve from AD_0 to AD_1.

FIGURE **24.3**

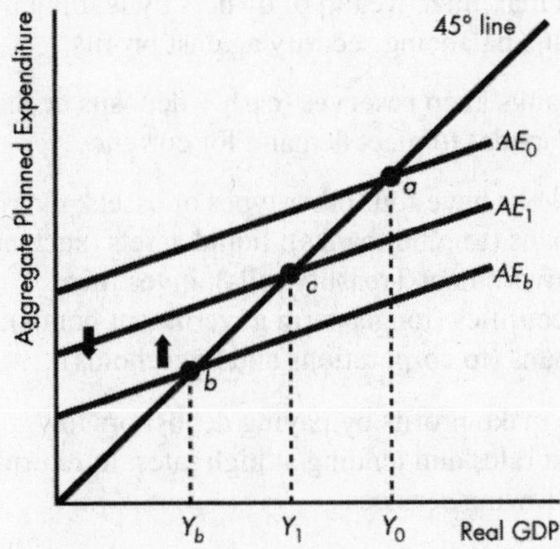

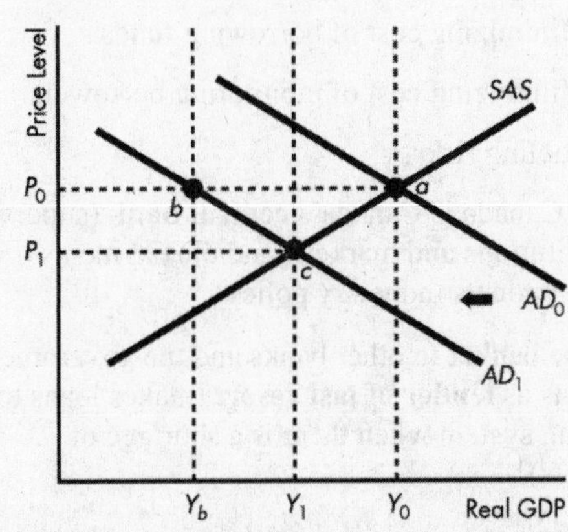

b Since the decrease in real GDP equals the decrease in aggregate expenditure, we know that the five components of aggregate expenditure have decreased in total value. Since government expenditures, investment, and exports are autonomous, they are unchanged. Consumption will have decreased for two reasons—the decrease in autonomous expenditure that initiated the changes, plus a decrease in induced consumption due to the decrease in real GDP. Imports will have decreased due to the decrease in real GDP.

c At the original price level P_0, there is excess supply. This surplus leads to firms cutting their prices, leading to a decrease in the price level. This decrease gets rid of the excess supply, leading to a new equilibrium at the point *c*. The decrease in the price level raises aggregate expenditure back upward to the level AE_1, which also shows up as the movement along the curve AD_1 from *b* to *c*. The decrease in the price level leads to a movement along the *SAS* curve from point *a* to point *c*. At the new equilibrium, the overall effect of the shock is a lower level of aggregate expenditure, a lower level of aggregate demand, a lower level of aggregate supply, a lower price level, and a lower level of real GDP.

10 a Table 24.1 is completed as Table 24.1 Solution below, using the two formulas plus the fact that the budget balance = revenues – outlays.

TABLE 24.1 SOLUTION

Real GDP	Outlays	Revenues	Budget Balance
0	500	100	–400
100	440	140	–300
200	380	180	–200
300	320	220	–100
400	260	260	0
500	200	300	100
600	140	340	200

b The structural balance is the surplus or deficit that would exist with the existing budget structure at potential GDP, and is equal to a deficit of 100.

c The structural deficit is still 100, the actual deficit is 200 at real GDP of 200, and the cyclical deficit = actual – structural = 100.

d Yes it is, since as real GDP decreases, tax revenues decrease and outlays increase, creating upward pressure on aggregate expenditure.

Chapter 25 Money, Banking, and Interest Rates

KEY CONCEPTS

What Is Money?

Money is something acceptable as a **means of payment** (method of settling a debt), and has three functions—medium of exchange, unit of account, store of value.

- ♦ Medium of exchange—accepted in exchange for goods and services
  - Better than **barter** (direct exchange of goods for goods)—guarantees double coincidence of wants.
- ♦ Unit of account—agreed measure for prices.
- ♦ Store of value—exchangeable at a later date.

Money today is **currency** (coins + Bank of Canada notes) and deposits (can be converted into currency and used to pay debts).

- ♦ Cheques are only an instruction to bank.
- ♦ Debit cards are like cheques, while credit cards are ID cards for loans—neither is money.

There are two official measures of money:

- ♦ **M1**: currency outside banks + private demand deposits at banks.
- ♦ **M2+**: M1 + personal savings deposits at banks + nonpersonal notice deposits at banks + all deposits at other financial institutions.
- ♦ Currency plus some deposits are means of payments; other deposits are not, but have **liquidity** (quickly convertible into means of payments).

The Banking System

The banking system consists of the depository institutions, the Bank of Canada, and the payments system.

- ♦ **Depository institutions** take deposits from households and firms, and make loans to others.
  - Three main types are **chartered banks** (chartered under Bank Act), **credit unions** and caisses populaires, and **trust and mortgage loan companies**.
- ♦ Banks maximize wealth of owners by lending out deposits, balancing security against profits.
  - Banks keep **reserves** (cash + deposits at Bank of Canada) to meet demand for currency.
  - Banks have four other types of assets: overnight loans (to other banks); liquid assets (such as government Treasury bills); investment securities (longer-term government bonds); and loans (to corporations and households).
- ♦ Banks make profits by paying depositors low interest rates and lending at high rates, in return for the following services:
  - Creating liquid assets.
  - Minimizing cost of borrowing funds.
  - Minimizing cost of monitoring borrowers.
  - Pooling risks.

The Bank of Canada is Canada's **central bank** (supervises financial institutions and markets, and the payments system, and conducts monetary policy).

- ♦ It is the banker to other banks and the government, and acts as **lender of last resort** (makes loans to the banking system when there is a shortage of reserves).
- ♦ The Bank of Canada is the sole issuer of bank notes.
- ♦ Bank of Canada balance sheet shows assets (government securities and loans to banks, usually zero) and liabilities (bank notes and deposits of banks and government).
  - Chartered bank deposits at the Bank of Canada are part of bank reserves.

The **payments system** allows banks to settle inter-bank transactions, and has two components.

- ♦ **Large Value Transfer System (LVTS)** is an electronic payments system for chartered banks, with continuous payments throughout the day and net payments at end of the day financed by overnight loans.
- ♦ **Automated Clearing Settlement System (ACSS)** involves smaller payments than LVTS, with net payments only at end of the day.

How Banks Create Money

Banks create money (deposits) when they lend out excess reserves.

- ♦ The quantity of deposits that can be created is limited by the monetary base, the level of desired reserves, and the desired currency holding.
- ♦ The **monetary base** = sum of Bank of Canada notes outside the Bank, banks' deposits at the Bank, and coins in circulation. It limits deposit creation as it limits amount available for desired reserves and desired currency holding.
- ♦ People desire to hold some portion of their money as currency—the **currency drain ratio** = currency/deposits.
- ♦ If a bank gets new deposit, this creates **excess reserves** (actual reserves – desired reserves).
  - **Reserve ratio** = reserves/total deposits.
  - **Desired reserve ratio** = ratio of reserves to total deposits banks wish to hold.
- ♦ Banks loan out excess reserves.
  - Borrower spends loan (and keeps some as currency), recipient of spent money deposits it at her bank.
  - New bank has more reserves, some desired, but some are excess reserves, leading to further steps in deposit multiplier process.
- ♦ Total Δ quantity of money = increase in currency + increase in deposits.

The **money multiplier** = (Δ quantity of money)/(Δ monetary base).

- ♦ Total Δ quantity of money (*M*) = money multiplier × initial Δ monetary base (*MB*).
  - Size of money multiplier depends on desired reserve ratio (*b*) and currency drain ratio (*a*): $M = (1 + a)/(a + b) \times MB$.
  - Larger desired reserve ratio (*b*) means smaller money multiplier.
  - Larger currency drain ration (*a*) means smaller money multiplier.

The Demand for Money

People choose money holdings based on price level, interest rate, real GDP, financial innovation.

- ♦ People hold money for its buying power.
  - Therefore, an increase in price level (*P*) causes equal increase in nominal money demanded (*M*), so no change in real money demanded (*M/P*).
- ♦ **Interest rate** = opportunity cost of holding money.
  - Higher interest rate decreases quantity of real money demanded.
  - **Demand for money curve** (*MD*) is relationship between quantity of real money demanded and interest rate, holding constant real GDP and **financial innovation.**
- ♦ Increase in real GDP shifts *MD* curve rightward.
- ♦ Financial innovation has ambiguous effect on *MD* curve.
  - Financial innovation decreased demand for M1 in 1980s, but partially reversed that shift in 1990s.
  - Financial innovation increased demand for M2+ in 1970s, but partially reversed in 1990s.
  - Such shifts make quantity of money an unreliable predictor of changes in aggregate demand.

Interest Rate Determination

People divide their wealth between bonds and money.

- **Interest rate** is amount paid by borrower to lender = percentage of loan.

Bond prices are inversely related to interest rates.

- The supply of and demand for money determine the interest rate.
- The actions of the Bank of Canada determine the supply of money.

The Bank of Canada can either target the quantity of money or the interest rate.

- If the Bank of Canada targets the quantity of money, the money supply curve is vertical.
  - Changes in the interest rate create equilibrium in money market.
  - If the interest rate is above equilibrium, people have excess money holdings.
  - Therefore, they buy financial assets, which increases price of financial assets, and decreases interest rates toward equilibrium.
- If the Bank of Canada targets the interest rate, the quantity of money supplied is determined by the quantity of money demanded at the target interest rate.

HELPFUL HINTS

1 What is money? In one sense, whatever meets the functions of money is money. For example, cigarettes fulfilled the functions of money in prisoner-of-war camps and similar situations. However, you should be able to answer this question on several levels. First, at the level of general definition: money is a medium of exchange. Second, at the level of classification: chequable deposits are money but savings deposits are not. Third, at the level of specific definitions: M1 and M2+ are official definitions of money.

We often refer to our income earnings as the "money we make working." However, in economics, money means the *stock* of money we are holding in currency plus deposits (M1 or M2+). It does *not* mean the *flow* of income earnings—be careful of this distinction.

Another important distinction is between the act of holding money and the act of consumption spending. In this situation, we are dealing with money markets, not goods and services markets. The choice for households modelled in this chapter is between holding bonds and holding money. The choice for consumer spending involves saving versus spending.

2 As we work through the text, notice the important role of changes in interest rates and the exchange rate in creating shifts in aggregate demand, and therefore business cycle shocks.

Chapters 25, 26, and 28 begin the process of learning what affects the values of the interest and exchange rates, showing that the money market plays a crucial role. Chapter 25 explains the demand for money, and part of the supply of money. Chapter 26 explains exchange rate determination, and the role of the Bank of Canada in that determination. Chapter 28 explains how the supply of money is determined by the actions of the Bank of Canada and the deposit creation process.

3 An important concept in Chapter 25 is the money multiplier process by which banks create money. Become thoroughly familiar with this process.

There are two fundamental facts that allow banks to create money. First, banks create money by creating new chequable deposits. Second, banks hold fractional reserves. Fractional reserves mean that when a bank receives a deposit, it only holds part of it as reserves and lends the rest. Note that the bank is not indulging in a scam—it is still maintaining assets (reserves plus loans) to match its liabilities (deposits). When that loan is spent, at least part of the proceeds will likely be deposited in another bank, creating a new deposit (money).

The deposit multiplier process follows from this last fact: banks make loans when they receive new deposits. These loans are spent—some leaves the process as currency drain, and the rest returns to another bank, creating another new deposit. The process then repeats itself, adding more deposits (but in progressively smaller amounts) in each round. Practise going through examples until the process becomes second nature. As you go, note the role played by the profit-seeking behaviour of the banks. It is this profit seeking that leads them to turn reserves, which earn no revenues, into loans, which do earn revenues.

SELF-TEST

True/False and Explain

What Is Money?

1 Money is anything generally acceptable as a means of payment.

2 A notice deposit at a chartered bank is part of M1.

3 If the public shifts their deposits from their chequing accounts to their savings accounts, M1 will decrease and M2+ increase.

The Banking System

4 Since banks are profit-seeking institutions, they will loan out as much of their deposits as they can.

5 One of the key economic functions of banks is acting as a lender of last resort.

6 Individual households are generally better at pooling risk than are depository institutions.

How Banks Create Money

7 Bank reserves consist of cash in the bank's vault plus its deposits at the Bank of Canada.

8 The size of the monetary base is a limit to the amount of deposit creation in the money creation process.

9 If a depositor uses a debit card to buy something, their bank's actual reserve ratio declines.

10 If the desired reserve ratio is 0.1 and the currency drain ratio is 0.2, the money multiplier would be 3.67.

The Demand for Money

11 If the price level increases, there will be an increase in the quantity of real money people will want to hold.

12 If interest rates increase, the quantity of real money demanded decreases.

13 The development of near-money deposits and growth in the use of credit cards in the 1980s caused the demand for M2+ to shift rightward.

Interest Rate Determination

14 If households or firms have more money than they want to hold, they will buy financial assets, causing asset prices to increase and the interest rate to decrease.

15 If the price of a bond increases, the interest rate earned on the bond decreases.

Multiple-Choice

What Is Money?

1 Which of the following is a function of money?
a medium of exchange
b measure of liquidity
c pooling risk
d store of exchange
e reducing transactions costs

2 Which of the following is a component of M2+ but *not* of M1?
a currency in circulation
b personal demand deposits at chartered banks
c personal savings deposits at chartered banks
d currency in bank vaults
e Canada Savings Bonds

3 Which of the following is *most* liquid?
a demand deposits
b real estate
c government bonds
d savings deposits
e cheques

4 Which of the following is *not* a store of value?
a credit cards
b demand deposits
c term deposits
d other chequable deposits
e savings deposits

The Banking System

5 Which of the following statements about depository institutions is *false*?
a They maximize their owner's wealth, ignoring all else.
b They keep reserves to meet cash withdrawals.
c A credit union is a depository institution.
d They pool and therefore reduce risk.
e They borrow at low interest rates and lend at higher interest rates.

6 Which of the following is an economic service provided by a depository institution?
a borrowing low and lending high
b keeping cash reserves
c pooling liquidity
d minimizing the cost of borrowing funds
e creating liquid liabilities

7 When a bank receives short-term deposits and issues long-term loans, this is an example of
a being a lender of last resort.
b minimizing the cost of borrowing.
c creating liquidity.
d taking unnecessary risks.
e pooling risk.

8 Which of the following is an asset of the Bank of Canada?
a Currency in circulation
b Government securities held in the Bank of Canada
c Deposits of chartered banks at the Bank of Canada
d Coins in circulation
e Deposits of governments at the Bank of Canada

9 Which of the following actions occurs if a bank has net payments owing on inter-bank transactions at the end of the day?
a It lends money to other banks.
b It borrows money from other banks.
c It deposits money at the Bank of Canada.
d The Bank of Canada acts as a lender of last resort.
e Nothing, this happens all the time.

How Banks Create Money

10 The Bank of Speedy Creek currently has actual (and desired) reserves of $40, loans of $460 and deposits of $500. What is their desired reserve ratio?
a 4%
b 8%
c 12.5%
d 25%
e 40%

11 The Bank of Speedy Creek currently has actual (and desired) reserves of $40, loans of $460 and deposits of $500. Huck Finn comes along and deposits $10. After Huck's deposit, but before any other actions have occurred, the total amount of *monetary base* in the economy
a is unchanged, with currency $10 higher and deposits $10 lower.
b has increased by $10.
c has decreased by $10.
d is unchanged, but with deposits $10 higher and currency $10 lower.
e may or may not have changed, depending on if Huck deposited his money in a savings deposit or a demand deposit.

12 The Bank of Speedy Creek currently has actual (and desired) reserves of $40, loans of $460 and deposits of $500. Huck Finn comes along and deposits $10. After Huck's deposit, but before any other actions have occurred, the total amount of *money* in the economy has
- a stayed the same, with currency and deposits unchanged.
- b stayed the same, with currency falling and deposits rising.
- c decreased, with currency falling and deposits staying the same.
- d increased, with currency unchanged and deposits rising.
- e decreased, with currency falling and deposits unchanged.

13 The Bank of Speedy Creek currently has actual (and desired) reserves of $40, loans of $460 and deposits of $500. Huck Finn comes along and deposits $10. After Huck's deposit, but before any other actions have occurred, the Bank of Speedy Creek will have excess reserves of
- a zero.
- b $9.
- c $9.20.
- d $10.
- e $40.

14 The Bank of Speedy Creek currently has actual (and desired) reserves of $40, loans of $460 and deposits of $500. Huck Finn comes along and deposits $10. After Huck's deposit, given that the Bank of Speedy Creek is profit-seeking, what is the amount of new loans it will make?
- a zero
- b $9
- c $9.20
- d $10
- e $40

15 The Bank of Speedy Creek currently has actual (and desired) reserves of $40, loans of $460 and deposits of $500. Huck Finn comes along and deposits $10. After Huck's deposit, and after the Bank of Speedy Creek has lent the amount it wishes to lend, the total amount of reserves in the bank will be $________, the total amount of loans will be $________, and the total amount of deposits will be $________.
- a 40.80; 469.20; 510
- b 40; 460; 500
- c 50; 470; 520
- d 41; 469; 510
- e 42.50; 467.50; 510

16 If new deposits are made in the banking system, which of the following will limit the amount of the new money created?
- a The desired reserve ratio only.
- b The currency drain ratio only.
- c The monetary base only.
- d The desired reserve ratio and the currency drain ratio, but not the monetary base.
- e The desired reserve ratio, the currency drain ratio and the monetary base.

17 The money multiplier will be larger if
- a the interest rate is higher.
- b liquidity is higher.
- c the desired reserve ratio is higher.
- d the monetary base is higher.
- e the desired reserve ratio is lower.

18 Which of the following steps in the description of the money multiplier process is *wrong*?
- a Banks lend out excess reserves.
- b Bank deposits increase.
- c The deposits are spent.
- d Some new spending returns as deposits, and currency comes in as new deposits.
- e Banks once again have excess reserves, and the process continues.

The Demand for Money

19 Consider Figure 25.1. Which of the following best describes the response of this household to an *increase* in their annual income?
- a movement from *a* to *f*
- b movement from *a* to *c*
- c movement from *e* to *a*
- d movement from *b* to *a*
- e movement from *a* to *e*

FIGURE **25.1** THE DEMAND FOR REAL MONEY BALANCES BY AN INDIVIDUAL HOUSEHOLD

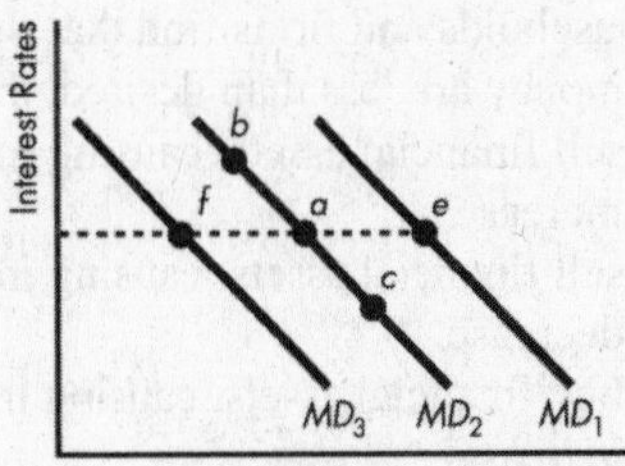

20 Consider Figure 25.1. Which of the following best describes the response of this household to a *decrease* in the market price of bonds?
a movement from *a* to *b*
b movement from *a* to *c*
c movement from *a* to *f*
d movement from *a* to *e*
e movement from *e* to *a*

21 Which of the following could cause the demand curve for M1 to shift leftward?
a increase in real GDP
b decrease in interest rates
c expanded use of credit cards
d increase in quantity of money supplied
e increase in the price level

22 Real money is equal to nominal money
a divided by real GDP.
b minus real GDP.
c divided by the price level.
d minus the price level.
e divided by velocity.

Interest Rate Determination

23 If the interest rate is above the equilibrium rate, how is equilibrium achieved in the money market?
a People buy goods to get rid of excess money, lowering the price of goods, and lowering the interest rate.
b People sell goods to get rid of excess money, lowering the price of goods, and lowering the interest rate.
c People sell bonds to get rid of excess money, lowering the price of bonds, and lowering the interest rate.
d People sell bonds to get rid of excess money, raising the price of bonds, and lowering the interest rate.
e People buy bonds to get rid of excess money, raising the price of bonds, and lowering the interest rate.

24 If households and firms find that their holdings of real money are less than desired, they will
a sell financial assets, causing interest rates to increase.
b sell financial assets, causing interest rates to decrease.
c buy financial assets, causing interest rates to increase.
d buy financial assets, causing interest rates to decrease.
e buy goods, causing the price level to increase.

25 Money market equilibrium occurs
a when interest rates are constant.
b when the level of real GDP is constant.
c when quantity of real money supplied equals real money demanded.
d only under a fixed exchange rate.
e when bond prices are constant.

Short Answer Problems

1 Banks can no longer issue their own paper money, but can create deposit money by crediting people's deposits. Since there is no paper money deposited to back up this creation, is this created money real? Is it acceptable in society? Why or why not?

2 Briefly explain how and why banks create new money during the deposit multiplier process (in a multibank system).

3 Why do people care about the quantity of real money they hold rather than the quantity of nominal money?

4 Suppose that Bank 1 has excess reserves equal to $1,000. (In Chapter 27 we will see how such a situation might arise from the actions of the Bank of Canada.) Assume that the desired reserve ratio for all banks in the multibank system is 20 percent (0.2). There is a currency drain ratio of 33 percent (0.33). Table 25.1 gives information for the first round of the money creation process that will be generated by this new deposit.

a Follow the next five rounds of the money creation process by completing Table 25.1.

TABLE 25.1 MONEY CREATION PROCESS

Bank Number	Initial Deposit = New Reserves	Desired Reserves	Excess Reserves	New Loans	Withdrawals Leading To: New Currency	Withdrawals Leading To: New Deposit	Total Increase in Money
1	1,000	0	1,000	1,000	250	750	1,000
2							
3							
4							
5							
6							

b What is the total increase in the quantity of money after six rounds?

5 a For the banking system in Short Answer Problem **4**, what is the money multiplier?

b After all rounds have been completed, what will be the total increase in the quantity of money?

ⓒⓣ c How much of this increase in money is new currency in circulation, and how much is new deposits?

6 For the entire banking system in Short Answer Problem **4**, compared to the starting point of $1,000 in excess reserves, what are the final total amounts of desired/actual reserves, loans, and deposits?

7 There is only one chartered bank in the country of Adanac, and it has the following assets and liabilities:

Currency reserves	$20 million
Reserves held at the Bank of Adanac	$10 million
Loans	$700 million
Securities	$20 million
Deposits	$750 million

a Assuming that the bank has freely chosen its reserves, what is its desired reserve ratio?

b If the amount of currency in circulation is $50 million, what is the monetary base? What is the money supply?

c What is the currency drain ratio?

d What is the money multiplier?

8 Assume that the central bank targets the quantity of money.

a What happens to the money supply in a case like this?

Show on a graph and briefly explain what each of the following will do (in sequence) to the demand for real money (defined as M1) and therefore the equilibrium interest rate. Assume that the real money supply remains constant.

b The price level rises.

c There is a financial innovation (the widespread adoption of electronic funds transfers) that reduces the need to use chequing accounts.

d Real GDP falls during a recession.

9 Consider the situation in Short Answer Problem **8**. Now assume that the central bank targets the interest rate.

a What happens to the money supply curve in this situation? (No graphs needed.)

b Redo part **b** from Short Answer Problem **8** in this situation, focusing on what happens to the money supply. (No graphs needed.)

c Redo part **c** from Short Answer Problem **8** in this situation, focusing on what happens to the money supply. (No graphs needed.)

d Redo part **d** from Short Answer Problem **8** in this situation, focusing on what happens to the money supply. (No graphs needed.)

10 Briefly explain the role of the Bank of Canada in the banking system.

ANSWERS

True/False and Explain

1 **T** Basic function of money. (590–591)

2 **F** See definition of M1. (591–592)

ⓒⓣ 3 **F** M1 will decrease as chequing accounts (demand deposits) decrease, but since chequing and saving accounts are part of M2+ there is no change in M2+. (591–592)

4 **F** They are restrained by need to balance security versus profit. (593)

5 **F** This is function of central bank. (594–595)

6 **F** Large size allows banks to pool risk. (594)

7 **T** Definition. (596–597)

8 **T** Limits amount available for desired reserves and desired currency holdings. (596–597)

9 **T** Withdrawal leads to decrease in reserves = decrease in deposits, which leads to decrease in reserve/deposit ratio. (598–599)

10 **F** Money multiplier = (1 + 0.2)/(0.1 + 0.2) = 4. (599–600)

11 **F** Real money demand independent of price level. (601)

12 **T** Increase in interest rate increase opportunity cost of holding money, leading to decrease in quantity money demanded. (601-602)

13 T Shifts toward notice accounts—see text discussion. (603)

14 T Agents substitute toward bonds, leading to increase in bond demand, leading to increase in bond price, which implies decrease in bond interest rate. (605)

15 T Price of bond and its interest rate are inversely related. (604)

Multiple-Choice

1 a See text discussion. (590)

2 c Definition. (591–592)

3 a Most readily changed into currency. (592)

4 a Credit cards not guaranteed for future purchases—credit card company might cancel your card. (591)

5 a Must be prudent about risk too. (593–594)

6 d See text discussion. (594)

7 c Short-term deposits are more liquid for depositors than long-term loans. (594–595)

8 b Definition. (595)

9 b Must borrow to cover its net LTVS position. (595–596)

10 b Desired reserve ratio = chosen reserves/deposits = 40/500 = 0.08. (597)

11 d Decrease in currency in circulation = increase in bank deposits. (597)

12 b Decrease in currency as deposit made = Increase in deposits. (597–600)

13 c Excess = actual ($50) – desired ($40.80 = 0.08 × $510). (597)

14 c Banks will lend the amount of excess reserves. (598–600)

ⓒⓣ **15 a** The $10 deposit is divided between the new desired reserves (0.08 × $10) and new loans. (598–600)

ⓒⓣ **16 e** The monetary base limits the possible amount of new reserves and new currency in circulation. The higher the desired reserve ratio, the more money banks hold back at each stage. The higher the currency drain ratio, the more households hold back at each stage. (598–600)

17 e The lower the desired reserve ratio (b), the bigger the formula money multiplier = $(1 + a)/(a + b)$. Other variables do not affect money multiplier. (599–600)

18 d Some of the new spending is kept back as currency and not deposited. (598–600)

19 e *a* to *f*, *e* to *a* are decreases in income, others are Δ interest rates. (602)

20 a Decrease in price of bonds leads to increase in interest rates. *a* to *f*, *a* to *e*, *e* to *a*, are income changes, *a* to *c* is decrease in interest rates. (602–605)

21 c Financial innovation means people use less money. Other changes create rightward shift or no shift. (602)

22 c Definition. (601)

ⓒⓣ **23 e** If interest rate > equilibrium, this implies too much money, which implies buying bonds, leading to increase in price of bonds and therefore decrease in interest rates. (605)

24 a They substitute money for bonds, extra sales leads to decrease in price of bonds and increase in interest rates. (605)

25 c Definition. (605)

Short Answer Problems

1 This created money is real, because it is backed by the assets of the bank, which consist of the bank's reserves, loans, and holdings of securities.

Deposit money is generally accepted in society (you can buy goods, pay debts, etc., with it) because people know that the banks will provide currency upon demand.

2 Banks create money by making new loans. When banks get a new deposit, this deposit leaves them with excess reserves. Their desire to make profits (maximize owners' wealth) leads banks to lend out the excess reserves, creating a matching deposit, which is new money. When the proceeds of these loans are spent, the person receiving the money will deposit much of it in a bank deposit, creating excess reserves so that the process continues.

3 Nominal money is simply the number of dollars, while real money is a measure of what money will buy. Real money will decrease if the price level rises, and if the number of dollars is constant. What matters to people is the quantity of goods and services that money will buy, not the number of dollars. If the price level rises by 10 percent, people will want to hold 10 percent more dollars (given a constant real income and interest rates) in order to retain the same purchasing power.

4 a Table 25.1 is completed here as Table 25.1 Solution. Note that 80 percent of each new deposit will be lent and 20 percent will be held as reserves. Of the borrowed money, one-quarter is kept as currency and three-quarters is spent and ends up being deposited in the next bank, where it becomes a new deposit.

TABLE **25.1** SOLUTION

					Withdrawals Leading To:		
Bank Number	Initial Deposit = New Reserves	Desired Reserves	Excess Reserves	New Loans	New Currency	New Deposits	Total Increase in Money
1	1,000	0	1,000	1,000	250	750	1,000
2	750	150	600	600	150	450	1,600
3	450	90	360	360	90	270	1,960
4	270	54	216	216	54	162	2,176
5	162	32.40	128.60	128.60	32.15	96.45	2,304.60
6	128.60	25.72	108.88	102.88	25.72	77.16	2,407.48

b After six rounds, the total (cumulative) increase in the quantity of money is $2,407.48, as shown in the Table.

5 a The money multiplier can be calculated from the formula $(1 + a)/(a + b)$, where a is the currency drain ratio (0.33 in this case) and b is the desired reserve ratio (0.2 in this case). Substitution of these values in the formula yields an answer of $(1 + 0.33)/(0.2 + 0.33) = 2.51$.

b The total increase in money will be 2.51 × the initial amount of new reserves, or $2,501.

ⓒⓣ **c** Given that currency drain ratio of 0.33, then amount of currency must be one-quarter (25%) of the amount of new money (0.33 = 25/75), or roughly $625.25. The amount of new deposits is therefore 75 percent of the amount of new money, or $1875.75.

6 The total change in reserves will be 20 percent of the new deposits, or $375.15. We have already stated that the total amount of new deposits is $1,875.75. The amount of new loans will be the difference between these two numbers, or $1,500.50. *Note:* This value follows from the requirement that the total amounts of new assets held by the chartered banks (loans and reserves) equals the total amount of new liabilities (the deposits).

7 a The desired reserve ratio = desired reserves/deposits = 30/750 = 0.04.

b The monetary base = reserves + currency in circulation = $80 million. The money supply = currency in circulation + deposits = $800 million.

c The currency drain ratio = (currency in circulation)/(deposits) = 50/750 = 1/15 = 0.0667.

d The money multiplier can be calculated in one of two ways. First, as the ratio of the money supply to the monetary base = 800/80 = 10. Second, from the formula $(1 + a)/(a + b)$ where a is the currency drain ratio and b is the desired reserve ratio. This formula gives the answer as $(1 + 0.0667)/(0.04 + 0.0667) = 10$.

8 a If the central bank is targeting the quantity of money, the quantity of money supplied is fixed, and the money supply curve is vertical (at *MS* in Figure 25.2 below).

FIGURE **25.2**

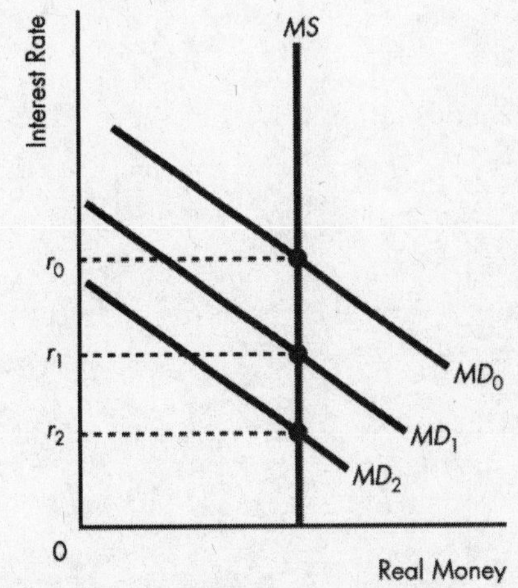

b A change in the price level will have no impact on real money demand, and therefore no impact on the equilibrium interest rate (r). In Figure 25.2, demand for real money remains at MD_0, and the interest rate remains at r_0.

c This financial innovation would reduce the need to use chequing accounts, which are part of M1. Therefore the demand for real money falls to MD_1, and the equilibrium interest rate falls to r_1 in Figure 25.2.

d The decrease in real GDP lowers the demand for real money to MD_2, and the equilibrium interest rate falls to r_2 in Figure 25.2.

9 a If the interest rate is targeted, the quantity of money supplied is the quantity demanded at the Bank's chosen interest rate.

b A change in the price level will have no impact on real money demand, and therefore no impact on the money supply.

c Financial innovation reduces the need to use chequing accounts, which are part of M1. Therefore the demand for real money falls. In order to keep the interest rate at its target, the Bank of Canada must reduce the quantity of money in an equivalent manner.

d The decrease in real GDP lowers the demand for real money. Once again, in order to keep the interest rate at its target, the Bank of Canada must reduce the quantity of money in an equivalent manner.

10 The Bank of Canada supervises financial institutions and markets and the financial system, and conducts monetary policy. It acts as the banker to other banks and to the government, and acts as a lender of last resort by making loans to the banking system when there is a shortage of reserves. It is also the sole issuer of bank notes.

Chapter 26

The Exchange Rate

KEY CONCEPTS

Currencies and Exchange Rates

To buy foreign goods or assets, Canadians need **foreign currency** (foreign notes, coins, bank deposits).

- ♦ To buy Canadian goods or assets, foreigners need Canadian dollars.
- ♦ Foreigners and Canadians exchange dollars for foreign currency in the **foreign exchange market**.
- ♦ **Foreign exchange rate** = price at which one currency exchanges for another (number of U.S. cents per Canadian dollar).
  - **Currency depreciation** is decrease in value of Canadian dollar in terms of another currency.
  - **Currency appreciation** is increase in value of Canadian dollar in terms of another currency.
- ♦ Since 1985, the Canadian dollar has fluctuated versus the U.S. dollar, but has been steady versus other major currencies.

The Foreign Exchange Market

The exchange rate is determined by supply and demand in the foreign exchange market.

- ♦ Demand for Canadian dollars by foreigners is matched by a supply of their currency. Supply of Canadian dollars by Canadians is matched by a demand for foreign currency.

Quantity of Canadian dollars demanded in the foreign exchange market = amount traders plan to buy at a given price, on the basis of demands for Canadian exports and Canadian assets.

- ♦ Quantity of Canadian dollars demanded depends on
  - Exchange rate.
  - World demand for Canadian exports.
  - Interest rates in Canada and other countries.
  - Expected future exchange rate.
- ♦ Increase in exchange rate decreases quantity demanded of Canadian dollars (movement up to the left along demand curve), because
  - Exports become more expensive for foreigners, decreasing demand for exports and therefore demand for dollars.
  - Expected profits decrease from buying Canadian dollars and holding them until they appreciate.

Quantity of Canadian dollars supplied in foreign exchange market = amount traders plan to sell at a given price, in order to buy other currencies to buy imports and foreign assets.

- ♦ Quantity of Canadian dollars supplied depends on
  - Exchange rate.
  - Canadian demand for imports.
  - Interest rates in Canada and other countries.
  - Expected future exchange rate.
- ♦ Increase in exchange rate increases quantity supplied of Canadian dollars (movement up to the right along supply curve), because
  - Imports become cheaper for Canadians, increasing demand for imports and therefore demand for foreign currency = increase in supply of Canadian dollars.
  - Expected profits increase from buying foreign currency and holding it until it appreciates, increasing demand for foreign currency = increase in supply of Canadian dollars.

Market equilibrium (without Bank of Canada action) determined by demand and supply, with exchange rate adjusting as required.

- ♦ Digital information flows in the foreign exchange market mean instant adjustments to equilibrium for all exchange rates.

Changes in Demand and Supply: Exchange Rate Fluctuations

The demand curve for Canadian dollars shifts *rightward* if

- ♦ World demand for Canadian exports increases.
- ♦ **Canadian interest rate differential** (Canadian interest rate – foreign interest rate) increases, increasing demand for Canadian assets.
- ♦ Expected future exchange rate increases, increasing expected profits from buying Canadian dollars and holding them until they appreciate.

The supply curve of Canadian dollars shifts *leftward* if

- ♦ Canadian demand for imports decreases.
- ♦ Canadian interest rate differential increases, decreasing demand for foreign assets = decrease in supply of Canadian dollar.
- ♦ Expected future exchange rate increases, decreasing expected profits from selling Canadian dollars, buying foreign currency and holding it until Canadian dollar depreciates.

Expectations of Δ exchange rate are due to the forces of **purchasing power parity** (two currencies have the same value or purchasing power) and **interest rate parity** (two currencies earn the same interest rate, adjusted for expected exchange rate changes).

- ♦ If purchasing power parity does not hold, and Canadian dollar buys more than the U.S. dollar, people expect it to appreciate, which increases demand for Canadian dollar, decreases supply—it does appreciate.
- ♦ Interest rate parity always holds (adjusted for risk), but if returns are higher in Canada, increased demand for Canadian dollar instantly increases exchange rate.

Exchange Rate Policy

Four different exchange rate policies.

- ♦ **Flexible exchange rate** policy lets exchange rate be determined by supply and demand.
  - This policy is the current Bank of Canada policy.
  - No direct intervention by Bank of Canada, but changes in Canadian interest rates unintentionally influence the exchange rate.
- ♦ **Fixed exchange rate** policy pegs the exchange rate at a target value.
  - If exchange rate falls in value, Bank of Canada must buy Canadian dollars to push up demand (paying for them out of its foreign currency holdings).
  - If exchange rate rises in value, Bank of Canada must sell Canadian dollars to push up supply (taking in foreign currency).
  - Bank of Canada cannot offset permanent shifts in the exchange rate because it has limited foreign currency reserves.
- ♦ **Crawling peg** policy selects a target *path* (a changing target rate), with intervention to achieve that path.
- ♦ **Currency union** is merger of two or more countries' currencies to form a single money.
- ♦ Benefits of a currency union:
  - Transparency and competition improve.
  - Transactions costs of converting currencies disappear.
  - Risk of foreign exchange rate fluctuations is eliminated.
  - Real interest rates fall due to the elimination of foreign exchange rate risk.
- ♦ Costs of a currency union:
  - Single currency means a single monetary policy, which may not be appropriate for all members of the union.
  - Members of the union give up some sovereignty over monetary policy and sometimes fiscal policy.

HELPFUL HINTS

1 There is an important difference between trade within a single country and trade between countries—currency. Individuals trading in the same country use the same currency, and trade is straightforward. International trade (which will be examined in more detail in Chapter 32) is complicated by the fact that individuals in

different countries use different currencies. A Japanese vendor selling goods will want payment in Japanese yen, but a Canadian buyer will likely be holding only Canadian dollars. This chapter addresses this complication by examining the foreign exchange market.

2 Think of foreign exchange rates as prices determined by supply and demand. They are prices of currency determined in markets for currency. The demand for Canadian dollars in the foreign exchange market arises from the desire on the part of foreigners to purchase Canadian goods and services (which requires dollars) and Canadian financial or real assets.

The supply of Canadian dollars is a special type of supply, because the offer to sell a Canadian dollar is equivalent to an offer to buy foreign currency. Therefore it depends on the desire of Canadians to buy foreign goods and services (which requires foreign currency), and to buy foreign assets. Remembering that the supply of Canadian dollars equals the demand for foreign currency will help you to understand many of the shifts in the supply of Canadian dollars.

As an example, think about what happens if currency speculators learn new information that makes them think the Canadian dollar will appreciate next month (which also implies foreign currencies will depreciate next month). They will plan to buy Canadian dollars *this* month, and sell foreign currencies this month, in order to make a profit. Thus, the demand for the Canadian dollar shifts rightward this month, and the supply of foreign exchange shifts leftward.

3 The exchange rate is volatile because supply and demand often shift in a reinforcing manner, since they are both affected by the same changes in expectations. These changes in expectations are driven by two forces: purchasing power parity and interest rate parity. Each of these is a version of the law of one price, which states that anytime there is a discrepancy in the price of the same good in two markets, natural economic forces (unless restricted) will eliminate that discrepancy and establish a single price. Suppose that the price in market 1 increases relative to the price in market 2. Individuals will now buy in the market with the lower price and not in the market with the higher price. This increase in the demand in market 2 and decrease in demand in market 1 will cause the two prices to come together. This principle applies to international markets as well: natural market forces will result in a single world price for the same good.

Suppose that purchasing power parity does not hold. For example, suppose that the wholesale price of an MP3 player in Canada is $100, and in Japan it is 10,000 yen, and that the exchange rate is currently 125 yen per dollar. The dollar price of the player in Japan is $80 (10,000 yen/125 yen per dollar). People expect the demand for the player in Canada to decrease (= a decrease in the demand for Canadian dollars), and the demand for the player in Japan to increase (= supply of dollars rising), which would lead to the exchange rate depreciating toward 100 yen per dollar (the purchasing power parity level). Their expectations will lead to a decrease in the demand for the Canadian dollar and an increase in the supply of the Canadian dollar, so that the exchange rate will depreciate even before the demand for the player adjusts!

The law of one price also holds for the price of assets such as bonds. Recalling from Chapter 25 that bond prices are inversely related to interest rates, we can see that interest rate parity is a version of the law of one price. For example, consider a situation where, taking into account the expected depreciation of the Canadian dollar, the Canadian interest rate was higher than the U.S. rate (which implies the price of bonds is lower in Canada). Buyers would demand Canadian bonds, raising their price and lowering Canadian interest rates. In addition, they would be selling U.S. bonds, lowering their price and raising U.S. interest rates. These actions occur until the interest rate differential between the two countries has shrunk to a level where it just reflects the expected depreciation of the Canadian dollar—interest rate parity holds.

SELF-TEST

True/False and Explain

Currencies and Exchange Rates

1 If the exchange rate between the Canadian dollar and the Japanese yen changes from 130 yen per dollar to 140 yen per dollar, the Canadian dollar has appreciated.

2 If the Canadian dollar can buy $0.75 U.S., the U.S. dollar can buy $1.25 Canadian.

3 In recent years, the Canadian dollar has tended to fluctuate versus European currencies, but it has been steady versus the U.S. dollar.

The Foreign Exchange Market

4 The demand for Canadian dollars by foreigners is automatically matched by Canadian demand for foreign currency.

5 A decrease in the exchange rate will increase the quantity demanded for Canadian dollars because exports become cheaper for foreigners.

6 An increase in the exchange rate will decrease the quantity supplied of Canadian dollars because expected profits increase from buying foreign currency and holding it until it increases in value.

7 At market equilibrium in the foreign exchange market, although all cross exchange rates with the Canadian dollar have adjusted, some cross rates between other currencies may not have adjusted to equilibrium.

Changes in Demand and Supply: Exchange Rate Fluctuations

8 An increase in Canadian interest rates increases demand for the Canadian dollar.

9 The demand and supply of Canadian dollars tend to move independently of each other.

10 Countries with currencies that are expected to appreciate will have higher interest rates than countries with currencies that are expected to depreciate.

11 If the yen price of the dollar is 100 yen per dollar and the price of a traded good is $10 in Canada, purchasing power parity implies that the price in Japan will be 1,000 yen.

12 If the foreign exchange value of the Canadian dollar is expected to increase, the supply of Canadian dollars increases.

Exchange Rate Policy

13 If the Bank of Canada sets a target exchange rate, and the demand for the Canadian dollar increases, the Bank of Canada will sell the Canadian dollar.

14 Under a currency union, foreign exchange rate risk disappears between the members of the union.

15 Under a flexible exchange rate, Bank of Canada policy will not affect the exchange rate.

Multiple-Choice

Currencies and Exchange Rates

1 Suppose that the dollar-yen foreign exchange rate changes from 140 yen per dollar to 130 yen per dollar. Then the yen has
- **a** depreciated against the dollar, and the dollar has appreciated against the yen.
- **b** depreciated against the dollar, and the dollar has depreciated against the yen.
- **c** appreciated against the dollar, and the dollar has appreciated against the yen.
- **d** appreciated against the dollar, and the dollar has depreciated against the yen.
- **e** neither appreciated nor depreciated, but the dollar has depreciated against the yen.

2 Suppose the exchange rate between the Canadian dollar and the British pound is 0.5 pounds per dollar. If a radio sells for 38 pounds in Britain, what is the dollar price of the radio?
- **a** $19
- **b** $26
- **c** $38
- **d** $57
- **e** $76

3 The market in which the currency of one country is exchanged for the currency of another is called the
- **a** money market.
- **b** capital market.
- **c** foreign exchange market.
- **d** forward exchange market.
- **e** international trading market.

4 Consider Table 26.1. Between 2004 and 2005, the Canadian dollar has __________ versus the euro and __________ versus the yen.
- **a** appreciated; depreciated
- **b** appreciated; appreciated
- **c** depreciated; depreciated
- **d** depreciated; appreciated
- **e** not changed; not changed

TABLE 26.1

Currency	2004 Exchange Rate	2005 Exchange Rate
EU euro	2 euros/dollar	3 euros/dollar
Japanese yen	120 yen/dollar	90 yen/dollar

5 Consider Table 26.1. Between 2004 and 2005, the yen
- **a** must have depreciated in value versus the euro.
- **b** must have appreciated in value versus the euro.
- **c** may or may not have appreciated in value versus the euro.
- **d** will have appreciated in value versus the euro if the euro has a high weight in the Canadian trade index.
- **e** will have appreciated in value versus the euro if the euro has a lower weight in the Canadian trade index.

The Foreign Exchange Market

6 If the demand for Canadian dollars increases, this is matched by
- **a** an increase in the demand for foreign exchange.
- **b** an increase in the supply of foreign exchange.
- **c** an increase in the supply of Canadian dollars.
- **d** a decrease in the demand for foreign exchange.
- **e** a decrease in the supply of foreign exchange.

7 The quantity of Canadian dollars demanded depends on all of the following *except*
- **a** the exchange rate.
- **b** the interest rate in Canada.
- **c** interest rates in the rest of the world.
- **d** the Canadian demand for imports.
- **e** the expected future exchange rate.

8 A decrease in the exchange rate increases the quantity demanded of Canadian dollars because
- **a** exports become more expensive for foreigners.
- **b** imports become more expensive for Canadians.
- **c** expected profits from buying Canadian dollars increase.
- **d** expected profits from buying foreign currency decrease.
- **e** cross exchange rates adjust quickly.

9 A Canadian living on the U.S. border reacts to a decrease in the exchange rate by shopping less in the United States. This is an example of
- **a** the imports effect.
- **b** the exports effect.
- **c** the expected profit effect.
- **d** purchasing power parity.
- **e** the expected exchange rate effect.

10 Which of the following best describes the expected profit effect?
- **a** A lower exchange rate leads to an importer using the forward market to lower exchange rate risk.
- **b** A lower exchange rate leads to buying foreign currency to hold it until it appreciates.
- **c** A higher exchange rate leads to buying foreign currency to hold it until it appreciates.
- **d** A higher exchange rate leads to buying Canadian dollars to hold them until they appreciate.
- **e** A higher exchange rate leads to an exporter using the forward market to lower exchange rate risk.

11 An increase in the exchange rate increases the quantity supplied of Canadian dollars because
- **a** imports become cheaper for Canadians, increasing the demand for imports and therefore the demand for foreign currency which equals an increase in the supply of Canadian dollars.
- **b** imports become more expensive for Canadians, increasing the demand for imports and therefore the demand for foreign currency which equals an increase in the quantity supplied of Canadian dollars.
- **c** exports become cheaper for foreigners, increasing the demand for exports and therefore the demand for foreign currency which equals an increase in the quantity supplied of Canadian dollars.
- **d** expected profits increase from buying Canadian dollars and holding them until the Canadian dollar appreciates in value, which increases the quantity supplied of Canadian dollars.
- **e** expected profits increase from selling foreign currency and holding it until it appreciates in value, which increases the quantity supplied of Canadian dollars.

12 If the exchange rate is too high in the foreign exchange market,
- **a** there is a surplus and the exchange rate will increase.
- **b** there is a surplus and the exchange rate will decrease.
- **c** exports are cheap, and the demand curve will shift right.
- **d** there is a shortage and the exchange rate will decrease.
- **e** there is a shortage and the exchange rate will increase.

Changes in Demand and Supply: Exchange Rate Fluctuations

13 Which of the following quotations best describes purchasing power parity?
- **a** "The recent high Canadian interest rate has increased the demand for the Canadian dollar."
- **b** "The market feeling is that the Canadian dollar is overvalued and will likely depreciate."
- **c** "The price of bananas is the same in Canada and the United States, adjusting for the exchange rate."
- **d** "The expected depreciation of the Canadian dollar is currently lowering demand for it."
- **e** None of the above.

14 If you think that the exchange rate will depreciate, you can expect to make money by
- **a** only buying Canadian dollars.
- **b** only buying U.S. dollars.
- **c** only selling Canadian dollars.
- **d** only selling U.S. dollars.
- **e** both buying U.S. dollars and selling Canadian dollars.

15 When would the exchange rate decrease in value the most?
- **a** When the supply and demand of dollars both increase.
- **b** When the supply of dollars increases, and the demand decreases.
- **c** When the supply of dollars decreases, and the demand increases.
- **d** When the supply and demand of dollars both decrease.
- **e** When there is intervention by the Bank of Canada.

16 Which of the following shifts the supply curve of Canadian dollars rightward?
- **a** An increase occurs in the demand for foreign goods by Canadian citizens.
- **b** A decrease occurs in the demand for Canadian goods by foreigners.
- **c** The dollar is expected to appreciate next year.
- **d** U.S. interest rates decrease.
- **e** None of the above.

17 Which of the following shifts the demand curve for Canadian dollars rightward?
- **a** An increase occurs in the demand for foreign goods by Canadian citizens.
- **b** A decrease occurs in the demand for Canadian goods by foreigners.
- **c** The dollar is expected to appreciate.
- **d** The dollar is expected to depreciate.
- **e** U.S. interest rates increase.

18 If the interest rate in Canada is greater than the interest rate in Japan, interest rate parity implies that
- **a** the inflation rate is higher in Japan.
- **b** Japanese financial assets are poor investments.
- **c** the yen is expected to depreciate against the dollar.
- **d** the yen is expected to appreciate against the dollar.
- **e** Canadian financial assets are poor investments.

19 Consider Figure 26.1 Which graph best shows the impact of an increase in demand for Canadian exports?
- **a** Graph (a)
- **b** Graph (b)
- **c** Graph (c)
- **d** Graph (d)
- **e** Graph (e)

FIGURE **26.1**

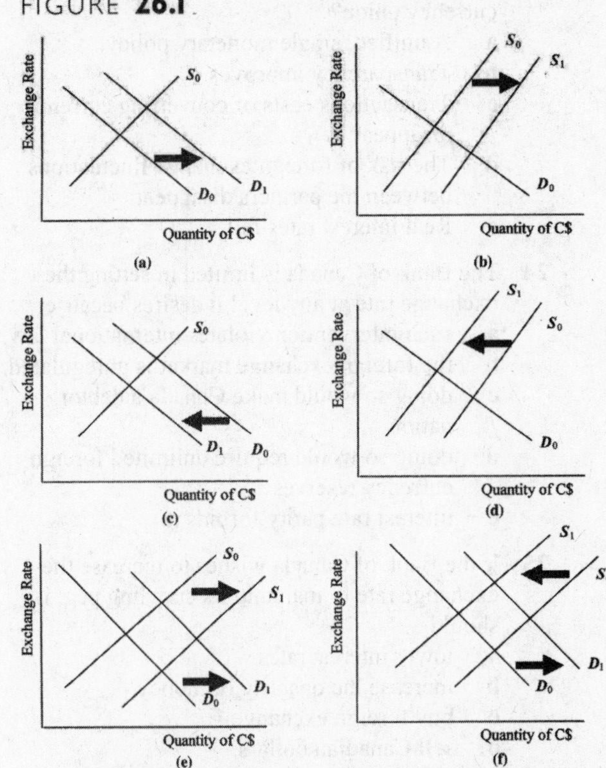

20 Consider Figure 26.1 Which graph best shows the impact of an increase in the Canadian interest rate differential?
- **a** Graph (a)
- **b** Graph (c)
- **c** Graph (d)
- **d** Graph (e)
- **e** Graph (f)

21 Consider Figure 26.1 Which graph best shows the impact of a decrease in Canadian demand for imports?
- **a** Graph (a)
- **b** Graph (b)
- **c** Graph (c)
- **d** Graph (d)
- **e** Graph (f)

Exchange Rate Policy

22 Consider Figure 26.1 Which graph best shows the actions of a central bank preventing the exchange rate from rising above the target value?
- **a** Graph (a)
- **b** Graph (b)
- **c** Graph (d)
- **d** Graph (e)
- **e** Graph (f)

23 Which of the following is *not* a benefit of a currency union?
- **a** A unified, single monetary policy.
- **b** Transparency improves.
- **c** Transactions costs of converting currency disappear.
- **d** The risk of foreign exchange fluctuations between the partners disappear.
- **e** Real interest rates fall.

24 The Bank of Canada is limited in setting the exchange rate at any level it desires because
- **a** such intervention violates international law.
- **b** the foreign exchange market is unregulated.
- **c** doing so would make Canada a debtor nation.
- **d** doing so would require unlimited foreign currency reserves.
- **e** interest rate parity forbids it.

25 If the Bank of Canada wishes to increase the exchange rate to maintain its crawling peg, it should
- **a** lower interest rates.
- **b** increase the quantity of money.
- **c** buy foreign exchange.
- **d** sell Canadian dollars.
- **e** buy Canadian dollars.

Short Answer Problems

1 Suppose that there is an increase in demand for Canadian exports. Illustrate and explain with a graph of the foreign exchange market what this change will do when there is a
- **a** flexible exchange rate.
- **b** fixed exchange rate.

2 What determines the value of the exchange rate, in a market with no government intervention?

3 What is purchasing power parity?

ⓒⓣ **4** Consider the following headline from the December 12, 1997 issue of *The Globe and Mail*: "Dollar Hits New 11-1/2 Year Low: Interest Rate Hike Expected After Recurrence of Asian Flu Forces Bank of Canada to Intervene." Clearly the Canadian dollar's exchange rate was decreasing in value during December 1997. Explain briefly but carefully why an increase in interest rates by the Bank of Canada would help to reverse this decrease.

ⓒⓣ **5** Explain how an expected increase in the exchange rate can be a self-fulfilling prophecy.

6 Table 26.2 shows some cross exchange rates for the Canadian dollar.

TABLE 26.2 CROSS EXCHANGE RATES

	USD	JPY*	CAD
USD	—	0.78	?
JPY*	?	—	?
CAD	1.06	0.83	—

Note: USD = U.S. dollar, JPY* = 100 Japanese yen, CAD = Canadian dollar.

- **a** Fill in the missing values in the table, showing all calculations.
- **b** Check that the cross exchange rates line up, by seeing if you could make money by starting with $100 Canadian, buying some USD, using your USD to buy some Japanese yen, and then use your yen to buy Canadian dollars. (Ignore minor rounding errors of 1% or less.)

7 Suppose that one month later, the Canadian values in the final row now read:

	USD	JPY*	CAD
CAD	1.20	0.69	—

- **a** Against which currency or currencies has the Canadian dollar depreciated?
- **b** List at least two factors that might have caused this appreciation.
- **c** Against which currency or currencies has the Canadian dollar appreciated?
- **d** List at least two factors that could have caused this depreciation.

8 Suppose that the exchange rate between the Canadian dollar and the euro is 2 euros per dollar.
- **a** What is the exchange rate in terms of dollars per euro?
- **b** What is the price in dollars of a camera selling for 250 euros?
- **c** What is the price in euros of a computer selling for 1,000 dollars?

9 You are trying to decide whether to buy some laptops for your business in either Canada or the United States. Looking at identical machines on the Dell Canada and the Dell U.S. Web sites, you find that they sell for US$2,000 in the United States and C$3,000 in Canada.

a Where would you buy the laptop if the exchange rate between the Canadian dollar and the U.S. dollar was US$0.80 per C$?

b If there is a profit opportunity, where would you resell it if you wanted to make a profit? (Ignore any taxes, tariffs, transportation costs, and differences in quality.)

c Does purchasing power parity hold?

ⓒⓣ **d** If many Canadian *and* American businesses acted like you, and if the exchange rate was flexible, what would happen to the value of the exchange rate? What would be the new equilibrium exchange rate that would make purchasing power parity hold for laptops, if the U.S. dollar price and the Canadian dollar price stayed constant?

10 Go to the Government Documents section of your library, or to the *Bank of Canada Review*, or to the Statistics Canada Web site (**www.statcan.ca**). Find data for the years 1985–95 on the value of the exchange rate in terms of U.S. cents, and data on Canadian and U.S. interest rates (use the prime interest rate banks charge to their best businesses). Construct a table of the Canadian interest rate differential versus the exchange rate, and discuss what kind of relationship you find.

ANSWERS

True/False and Explain

1 T Dollar is more valuable—takes more yen to buy one dollar. (612–613)

2 F Inverting $0.75 USD/CAD yields $1.33 = 1/0.75. (613)

3 F See Text Figure 26.4. (614)

4 F Automatically matched by the *supply* of foreign currency. (615)

5 T If $CAD is cheaper, it takes less foreign currency to buy each $CAD, making our exports cheaper, increasing demand for exports which increases quantity demanded of $CAD. (615–616)

6 F The expected profits effect is correct, but the extra buying of foreign currency leads to *increased* selling of Canadian dollars. (617)

7 F All cross rates will be adjusted by profit-seeking buying and selling behaviour. (618)

8 T This increases interest rate differential, making Canadian assets more attractive to foreigners. (619)

9 F Both affected by expected future exchange rate and interest rates, and so move together. (619–622)

ⓒⓣ **10 F** If expected to appreciate, this expected appreciation implies increased earnings in foreign currency terms, which increases demand for their bonds, which decreases interest rates until interest rate parity holds. (619–622)

11 T Under purchasing power parity, the yen price identical in each country. $10 × 100 yen/$ = 1,000 yen. (622)

12 F Expected increase in foreign exchange value of dollar implies a profit opportunity from holding dollars, which increases demand for dollars. (619–622)

13 T Shifts supply curve of Canadian dollars rightward, offsetting shift in demand. (623–624)

14 T Buying and selling between members now uses the same currency. (624–625)

15 F Will not affect it intentionally, but might affect it unintentionally, since changes in monetary policy affects interest rates, which affect the demand and supply of Canadian dollars. (623)

Multiple-Choice

1 d It takes less yen to buy dollar, so the dollar depreciated. Via inverse relationship, yen has appreciated. (612–613)

2 e $76 = £38 × ($2 per £). (612–613)

3 c Definition. (612)

4 a It takes more marks to buy $1 (increase in value), and less yen (decrease in value). (612–613)

ⓒⓣ **5 b** 2004: 1/60 euro/yen = (2 euros/$)/(120yen/$). 2005: 1/30 euro/yen = (3 euros/$)/(90 yen/$). Takes more euros in 2005 to buy 1 yen, so yen has appreciated. (614)

6 b Buyers of Canadian $ will supply foreign exchange to buy it. (615)

7 d This factor affects the supply of Canadian $. (615–617)

8 c Expected profits effect—low Canadian $ is likely to appreciate. (615–616)

9 a Definition. (615–616)

10 c High Canadian $ value = low foreign currency value, which is then more likely to appreciate and make a profit. (615–618)

11 a Imports effect. (617)

12 b If exchange rate high, quantity supplied will be high by law of supply and quantity demanded low by law of demand, leading to a surplus (quantity supplied > quantity demanded) and therefore downward pressure on the price (exchange rate). (618)

13 c Two currencies have same purchasing power. (622)

14 e You will wish to buy foreign currency, since it will increase in value, which requires you to sell Canadian dollars. (619–621)

15 b Draw a graph. (620–621)

16 a Increased demand for foreign currency increases supply of Canadian dollars. (620)

17 c **a** has no impact on demand, **b**, **d**, and **e** shift it leftward. (619)

18 d Therefore Canadian dollar expected to depreciate, offsetting the interest rate differential. (622)

19 a Greater demand for exports means greater demand for Canadian $ to buy the exports. (619–621)

20 e Higher interest rate differential makes Canadian assets more desirable, leading to an increase in the demand for these assets (and therefore an increase in the demand for the Canadian $) and a decrease in the demand for foreign assets (and therefore a decrease in the demand for foreign currency = a decrease in the supply of Canadian currency). (619–621)

21 c Lower Canadian demand for imports means lower Canadian demand for foreign currency = decrease in supply of Canadian $. (619–621)

22 d Central bank will be working to raise the supply of Canadian $ by selling Canadian dollars (buying foreign exchange) to match an increase in demand. (623)

23 a This is an outcome of union, but is a potential cost, as now countries cannot have different policies even when that is appropriate. (624–625)

24 d Such intervention requires buying/selling Canadian dollars, which changes foreign currency reserves, which cannot occur forever. (623–624)

25 e This increases demand for Canadian dollars. **a** decreases demand, **b**–**d** increase supply. (623–624)

Short Answer Problems

1 a Under a flexible exchange rate, the government does not intervene. Therefore, the exchange rate will adjust to find the new equilibrium. An increase in demand for Canadian exports leads to an increase in the demand for Canadian dollars in order to buy those exports, shown in Figure 26.2 on the next page as a rightward shift in the demand curve. The result is a new equilibrium with a higher exchange rate (ER_1) and a higher quantity of Canadian dollars exchanged ($C\$_1$) each day in the foreign exchange market.

FIGURE **26.2**

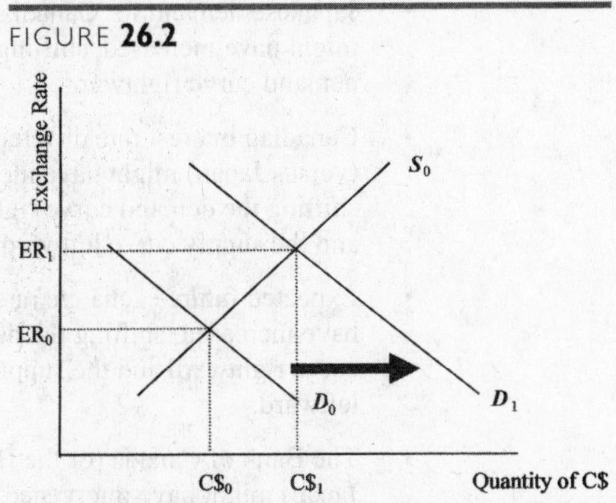

b Under a fixed exchange rate, the government intervenes to keep the exchange rate fixed at the target (original) value. Therefore, the exchange rate will *not* adjust to find the new equilibrium. As above, an increase in demand for Canadian exports leads to an increase in demand for Canadian dollars in order to buy those exports, shown in Figure 26.3 here as a rightward shift right in the demand curve. However, now the Bank of Canada supplies Canadian dollars to match this increase (buying foreign currency), so there is also a rightward shift in the supply curve. The result is a new equilibrium with the same exchange rate (ER_0) and an even higher quantity of Canadian dollars exchanged ($C\$_2$) each day in the foreign exchange market.

FIGURE **26.3**

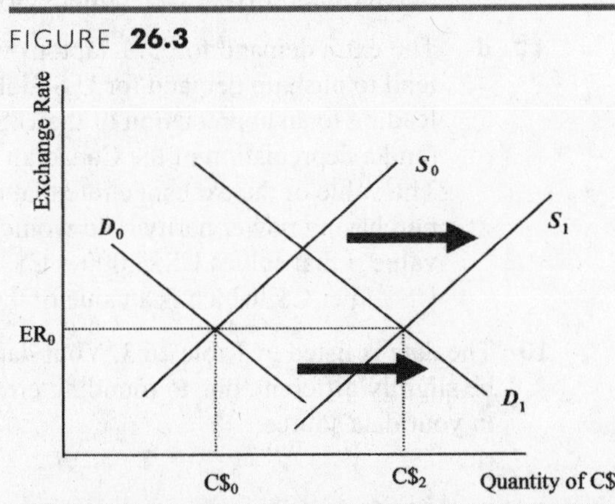

2 The value of the exchange rate is determined by supply and demand. The supply of the Canadian dollar is affected by three things—changes in the Canadian interest rate differential, changes in the expected future exchange rate, and the Canadian demand for imports. The demand for the Canadian dollar is also affected by the first two factors, as well as by the world demand for Canadian exports.

3 Purchasing power parity follows from arbitrage and the law of one price. It means that the value of money is the same in all countries. For example, if the exchange rate between the dollar and the yen is 120 yen per dollar, purchasing power parity says that a good that sells for 120 yen in Japan will sell for 1 dollar in Canada. Thus, the exchange rate is such that money (dollars or yen) has the same purchasing power in both countries.

4 An increase in Canadian interest rates increases the Canadian interest rate differential, which increases the desirability of Canadian assets relative to foreign assets. This increase in turn increases demand for Canadian dollars by foreigners, and decreases demand for foreign exchange by Canadians, which decreases the supply of the Canadian dollar. These shifts in supply and demand increase the value of the exchange rate.

5 If the exchange rate is expected to increase, there will be an increase in the quantity demanded for Canadian dollars to try and make a profit from the increase. In addition, there will be a decrease in the quantity supplied of Canadian dollars, because the expected increase implies a decrease in the value of foreign currency and therefore a decrease in the demand for foreign currency, which is matched by a decrease in the quantity supplied of Canadian dollars. The impact of these two changes is a shift leftward in the supply curve and a shift rightward in the demand curve for Canadian dollars, which both put upward pressure on the Canadian exchange rate!

6 **a** Table 26.2 Solution here shows the appropriate values. Values are calculated by inverting the existing values.

TABLE **26.2** SOLUTION

	USD	JPY*	CAD
USD	—	0.78	0.94
JPY*	1.28	—	1.21
CAD	1.06	0.83	—

b Recall that the columns for each currency tell us what they buy. $100 Canadian will buy US$94. Going to the USD column, we can see that US$94 will buy 120 (= 94 × 1.28) hundreds of yen. Going to the JPY* column, we can see that 120 hundreds of yen can buy $100 (= 120 × 0.83) Canadian. Therefore, the cross rates do line up.

7 a One U.S. dollar now buys more Canadian dollars (1.20 > 1.06), so that the U.S. dollar has appreciated against the Canadian dollar, which means the Canadian dollar has depreciated against the U.S. dollar.

b There are five possible reasons for the depreciation, depending on what factors might shift the demand or supply curve of the Canadian dollar:

- Canadian demand for U.S. imports might have increased, shifting the supply curve rightward.
- U.S. demand for Canadian exports might have decreased, shifting the demand curve leftward.
- Canadian interest rate differential (versus the United States) might have decreased, shifting the demand curve leftward and the supply curve rightward.
- Expected future exchange rate might have decreased, shifting the demand curve leftward and the supply curve rightward.
- The Bank of Canada might have intervened in the market, shifting the supply curve rightward by buying U.S. dollars.

c 100 Japanese yen now buy less Canadian dollars (0.69 < 0.83), so the yen has depreciated, or the Canadian dollar has appreciated versus the yen.

d There are five possible reasons for the appreciation, depending on what factors might shift the demand or supply curve of the Canadian dollar:

- Canadian demand for Japanese imports might have decreased, shifting the supply curve leftward.
- Japanese demand for Canadian exports might have increased, shifting the demand curve rightward.
- Canadian interest rate differential (versus Japan) might have increased, shifting the demand curve rightward and the supply curve leftward.
- Expected future exchange rate might have increased, shifting the demand curve rightward and the supply curve leftward.
- The Bank of Canada (or the Bank of Japan) might have intervened in the market, shifting the supply curve leftward by selling yen.

8 a If 1 dollar can be purchased for 2 euros, the price of a euro is 1/2 dollar per euro.

b At an exchange rate of 2 euros per dollar, it takes 125 dollars to obtain the 250 euros needed to buy the camera.

c At an exchange rate of 2 euros per dollar, it takes 2,000 euros to obtain the 1,000 dollars needed to buy the computer.

9 a The Canadian laptop costs US$2,400 = C$3,000 × US$0.80 per C$. Therefore, it is cheaper from the U.S. Web site.

b It is profitable to buy it in the United States for US$2,000 and sell it in Canada for US$2,400.

c No, the two currencies do not have the same purchasing power—U.S. dollars buy more.

ⓒⓣ **d** The extra demand for U.S. laptops would tend to push up demand for U.S. dollars, leading to an appreciation of the U.S. dollar (and a depreciation of the Canadian dollar). The value of the exchange rate that makes purchasing power parity hold would be the value A that solves US$2,000 = C$3,000 × US$$A$ per C$, which is a value of 0.667.

10 The data is listed in Table 26.3. Your data may be slightly different, due to rounding errors, etc. in your data source.

TABLE **26.3**

Year	Differential	US$/C$
1985	0.70	0.732
1986	2.27	0.720
1987	1.31	0.754
1988	1.43	0.813
1989	2.45	0.845
1990	4.06	0.856
1991	1.55	0.873
1992	1.23	0.827
1993	−0.07	0.775
1994	−0.38	0.732
1995	−0.17	0.729

Source: Bank of Canada Review, various issues.

We can see that there is a rough positive relationship between the differential and the value of the exchange rate. As the differential rose through the middle of the time period, so did the value of the exchange rate, driven by an increase in the demand for Canadian dollars and a decrease in the supply of Canadian dollars. As the differential fell towards the end, so did the exchange rate. The relationship is not exact, but it does meet the rough predictions of our theories.

Chapter 27
Inflation

KEY CONCEPTS

Inflation: Demand-Pull and Cost-Push

Inflation is the ongoing increase in the price level (P) with money losing value.

- Inflation rate = annual percentage change in price level = $\frac{P_1 - P_0}{P_0} \times 100\%$

Demand-pull inflation arises from increasing aggregate demand due to increases in quantity of money or government expenditures or exports.

- In short run, result is increased P (inflation), increased Y, decreased unemployment to below natural rate.
- Unemployment less than the natural rate creates labour shortage, which leads to increased wages and costs. *SAS* shifts leftward, price level increases even more, but real GDP back to original level.
- If *AD* shifts rightward again, and wages increase again, a *demand-pull inflation spiral* may result.
- Persistent inflation requires persistent increases in quantity of money.

Cost-push inflation arises from decreasing aggregate supply, due to increase in costs (increase in money wage rates and money prices of raw materials).

- *SAS* shifts leftward, firms decrease production, creating stagflation (increased price level, decreased real GDP).
- If government or Bank of Canada shifts *AD* rightward in response, price level increases again, so that input owners raise input prices again, and a *cost-push inflation spiral* may result.
- If no government or Bank response—economy remains with high unemployment.

The Quantity Theory of Money

Quantity theory of money predicts increase in quantity of money leads to equal percentage increase in price level.

- Quantity theory starts with definition of **velocity of circulation** ($V = PY/M$), which leads to the equation of exchange ($MV = PY$).
  - Assumes velocity and potential GDP are unaffected by Δ quantity of money.
  - Then, $\% \Delta P = \% \Delta M$.
- Historical evidence suggests money growth rate correlated with the inflation rate, but greater than the inflation rate.

Effects of Inflation

Incorrect inflation forecasts are costly in labour markets.

- If inflation > anticipated, then money wages set too low and employers gain, workers lose income, but firm has trouble keeping workers as a result.
- If inflation < anticipated, then money wages set too high and employers lose, workers gain income, but firm lays off workers as a result.

Incorrect forecasts in capital markets lead to incorrect borrowing/lending and income redistribution.

- If inflation > anticipated, then interest rates set too low, and borrowers gain at expense of lenders, but both wished to have made different decisions.
- If inflation < anticipated, then interest rates set too high, lenders gain at expense of borrowers, but both wished to have made different decisions.

People forecast inflation in different ways, including hiring specialists, who make best possible forecast on the basis of all available relevant information (a **rational expectation**).

- If increase in *AD* correctly anticipated, then money wages adjust to keep up with anticipated inflation, Δ price level only, no Δ real GDP or employment.
- If increase in *AD* more than expected, then increase in money wage only reflects expected part, and result is new above-full-employment equilibrium to right of potential GDP. Eventual increase in money wages shifts *SAS* leftward again.
- If increase in *AD* less than expected, then increase in money wage to reflect expected change results in a new below-full-employment equilibrium to left of potential GDP.

Anticipated inflation decreases potential GDP and lowers economic growth due to higher transactions costs, tax effects, and increased uncertainty.

Inflation and Unemployment: The Phillips Curve

Phillips curve shows relationship between inflation and unemployment.

- **Short-run Phillips curve** (*SRPC*) shows relationship between inflation and unemployment for a given expected inflation rate and natural rate of unemployment. It is negatively sloped.
- In short run, if actual inflation > expected, then movement up and leftward along *SRPC*.
- **Long-run Phillips curve** (*LRPC*) shows relationship between inflation and unemployment when actual inflation = expected. It is vertical at the natural rate of unemployment.
- Decrease in expected inflation rate shifts *SRPC* downward.
- Increase in natural rate of unemployment shifts both *LRPC* and *SRPC* rightward.

Interest Rates and Inflation

Changes in nominal rate of interest are due largely to changes in expected inflation.

- Real interest rate determined by global investment demand and saving supply plus national risk differences.
- Nominal interest rate determined by money demand and quantity of money.
- An increase in expected inflation leads to an increase in nominal interest rate by equivalent amount, keeping real rate of interest constant.

HELPFUL HINTS

1 An important concept introduced in this chapter is that of a *rational expectation*—the best possible forecast on the basis of all available relevant information. Text Figure 27.9 applies this concept to forecasting the price level. We know the *actual* price level occurs in the short run at the intersection of the *AD* curve and the *SAS* curve, and in the long run at the intersection of the *AD* curve and the *LAS* curve. In Figure 27.9, when *AD* is expected to increase to AD_1, the best *forecast* of the new price level (the forecast most likely to be correct) is at the intersection of AD_1 and *LAS*, yielding a wage demand that in turn leads to SAS_1.

Note that the rational expectation of the price level will be at the intersection of the *expected* aggregate demand curve and the *expected short-run* aggregate supply curve in the short run, and the *expected long-run* aggregate supply curve in the long run. The *actual* equilibrium, which determines the *actual* price level, is at the intersection of the *actual* aggregate demand curve and the *actual short-run* aggregate supply curve.

2 An important equation in this chapter is the equation of exchange:

$$\text{Quantity of money} \times \text{Velocity of circulation} = \text{Price level} \times \text{Real GDP}$$

This equation simply says that the quantity of money times the average number of times each dollar is spent (equalling total expenditure) is equal to the dollar value of the goods and services on which it was spent. The equation is always true by definition—it is an identity. If we further assume that the velocity of circulation and potential GDP are independent of the quantity of money, we get the quantity theory of money. These assumptions imply that when the quantity of money increases by 10 percent, the price level must increase by 10 percent in order to maintain equality between the two sides of the equation.

SELF-TEST

True/False and Explain

Inflation: Demand-Pull and Cost-Push

1 If the price level at the beginning of 2000 is 120 and the price level at the beginning of 2001 is 130, the rate of inflation is 8.3 percent.

2 Increases in government expenditures alone can create persistent inflation.

3 An increase in exports cannot create demand-pull inflation.

4 Inflation resulting from expansionary monetary policy is an example of cost-push inflation.

5 Stagflation occurs when real GDP decreases and the price level increases.

The Quantity Theory of Money

6 If the quantity of money is $50 billion and nominal GDP is $200 billion, the velocity of circulation is 1/4.

Effects of Inflation

7 When inflation is unanticipated there are no negative effects on the economy.

8 If people expect aggregate demand to increase but it does not, the price level will increase and real GDP will decrease.

9 If an increase in aggregate demand is correctly anticipated, inflation will not occur.

10 If there is an unexpected increase in the rate of inflation, employers will gain at the expense of workers.

11 A rational expectation is a forecast that is always correct.

Inflation and Unemployment: The Phillips Curve

12 The short-run Phillips curve shows that if there is an increase in the inflation rate, unemployment will decrease.

13 The long-run Phillips curve shows a tradeoff between inflation and unemployment.

14 If there is an increase in the expected rate of inflation, then the long-run Phillips curve shifts rightward.

Interest Rates and Inflation

15 An increase in expected inflation leads to an equivalent increase in the nominal interest rate.

Multiple-Choice

Inflation: Demand-Pull and Cost-Push

1 The current year's price level is 180, and the rate of inflation over the past year has been 20 percent. What was last year's price level?
- a 100
- b 144
- c 150
- d 160
- e 216

2 Demand-pull inflation occurs when
- a aggregate demand increases.
- b aggregate supply decreases.
- c input costs increase.
- d people incorrectly forecast inflation.
- e unemployment is above the natural rate.

3 Which of the following would cause the aggregate demand curve to keep shifting rightward year after year?
- a a one-time tax cut
- b a one-time increase in government expenditures on goods and services
- c inflation
- d continuous excess wage demands
- e a positive rate of money growth

4 An increase in the price level due to an increase in the price of oil
- a will create stagflation in the short run and *will* trigger a cost-push inflation spiral.
- b will create stagflation in the short run and *may* trigger a cost-push inflation spiral.
- c will raise output above potential GDP.
- d must lead to an increase in the wage rate.
- e must lead to a decrease in the wage rate.

5 Figure 27.1 illustrates an economy initially in equilibrium at point *a*. What would cause the short-run aggregate supply curve to shift from SAS_0 to SAS_1?
- a an increase in the price of oil
- b an increase in the price level
- c an increase in the marginal product of labour
- d an increase in the demand for money
- e a decrease in wages

FIGURE 27.1

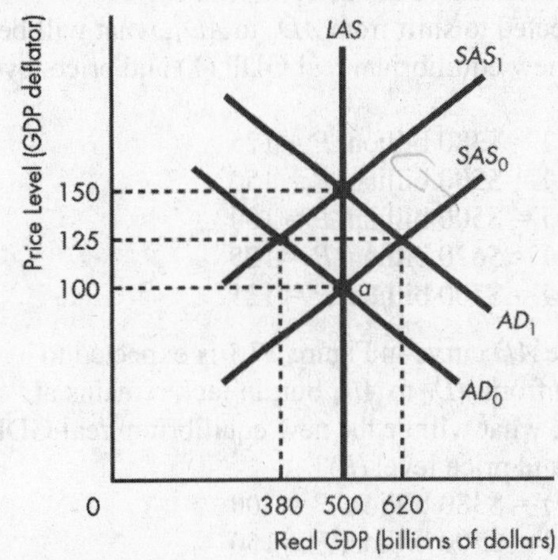

The Quantity Theory of Money

6 The quantity theory of money begins with the equation of exchange, $MV = PY$, and then adds the assumptions that
- a velocity varies inversely with the rate of interest, and the price level is independent of the quantity of money.
- b velocity and the price level are independent of the quantity of money.
- c potential GDP and the quantity of money are independent of the price level.
- d potential GDP and the price level are independent of the quantity of money.
- e velocity and potential GDP are independent of the quantity of money.

7 According to the quantity theory of money,
- a V/M is constant.
- b Y/M is constant.
- c Y/P is constant.
- d M/P is constant.
- e M/V is constant.

8 According to the quantity theory of money, an increase in the quantity of money will increase the price level
- a but have no effect on real GDP or the velocity of circulation.
- b as well as increasing both real GDP and the velocity of circulation.
- c as well as increasing real GDP but decreasing the velocity of circulation.
- d as well as decreasing real GDP but increasing the velocity of circulation.
- e but have no effect on real GDP while decreasing velocity of circulation.

Effects of Inflation

9 If the *AD* curve in Figure 27.1 is correctly expected to shift from AD_0 to AD_1, what will be the new equilibrium real GDP (*Y*) and price level (*P*)?
   a Y = $380 billion, P = 125
   b Y = $500 billion, P = 150
   c Y = $500 billion, P = 100
   d Y = $620 billion, P = 125
   e Y = $500 billion, P = 125

10 If the *AD* curve in Figure 27.1 is expected to shift from AD_0 to AD_1 but, in fact, remains at AD_0, what will be the new equilibrium real GDP (*Y*) and price level (*P*)?
   a Y = $380 billion, P = 100
   b Y = $500 billion, P = 150
   c Y = $500 billion, P = 100
   d Y = $620 billion, P = 125
   e Y = $380 billion, P = 125

11 If the *AD* curve in Figure 27.1 is expected to remain at AD_0 but, in fact, shifts to AD_1, what will be the new equilibrium real GDP (*Y*) and price level (*P*)?
   a Y = $380 billion, P = 125
   b Y = $500 billion, P = 150
   c Y = $500 billion, P = 100
   d Y = $620 billion, P = 125
   e Y = $500 billion, P = 125

12 Which of the following business quotes illustrates costs associated with an anticipated inflation?
   a "The bank is losing money on its loans, given the current rate of interest."
   b "Wage increases were low last year, but I am having trouble keeping workers."
   c "I find I have to send invoices out to customers twice a month now, because of the higher inflation."
   d "The low inflation rate means my borrowing costs are too high."
   e None of the above.

13 If the rate of inflation is lower than anticipated,
   a lenders gain at the expense of borrowers, and workers gain at the expense of employers.
   b borrowers gain at the expense of lenders, and workers gain at the expense of employers.
   c lenders gain at the expense of borrowers, and employers gain at the expense of workers.
   d borrowers gain at the expense of lenders, and employers gain at the expense of workers.
   e lenders gain at the expense of borrowers, and whether employers or workers gain is uncertain.

14 In an economy with the price level greater than expected and output above the natural rate, which of the following is a possible explanation, *ceteris paribus*?
   a Potential real GDP has increased by more than expected.
   b Potential real GDP has increased by less than expected.
   c Aggregate demand has decreased by more than expected.
   d Aggregate demand has increased by less than expected.
   e Aggregate demand has increased by more than expected.

15 A fully anticipated increase in the rate of inflation
   a is not costly because contracts can be adjusted.
   b benefits both workers and employers.
   c is costly because it increases the value of money.
   d is costly because it encourages an increase in the frequency of transactions.
   e is costly because it redistributes from lender to borrower.

16 Which of the following is *not* true of a rational expectation forecast?
   a It uses all available information.
   b It can be wrong.
   c It is always correct.
   d It is the best possible forecast.
   e Sometimes economic agents purchase their forecasts from specialists.

17 The price level is expected to decrease because of an expected decrease in aggregate demand. If aggregate demand remains unchanged, the actual price level
a stays the same and real GDP stays the same.
b decreases and real GDP decreases.
c increases and real GDP increases.
d increases and real GDP decreases.
e decreases and real GDP increases.

Inflation and Unemployment: The Phillips Curve

18 The short-run Phillips curve shows the relationship between
a the price level and real GDP in the short run.
b the price level and unemployment in the short run.
c unemployment and real GDP in the short run.
d inflation and unemployment, when inflation expectations can change.
e inflation and unemployment, when inflation expectations do not change.

19 Figure 27.2 illustrates an economy's Phillips curves. What is the natural rate of unemployment?
a 9%
b 6%
c 4%
d depends on the actual inflation rate
e cannot be determined without more information

FIGURE 27.2

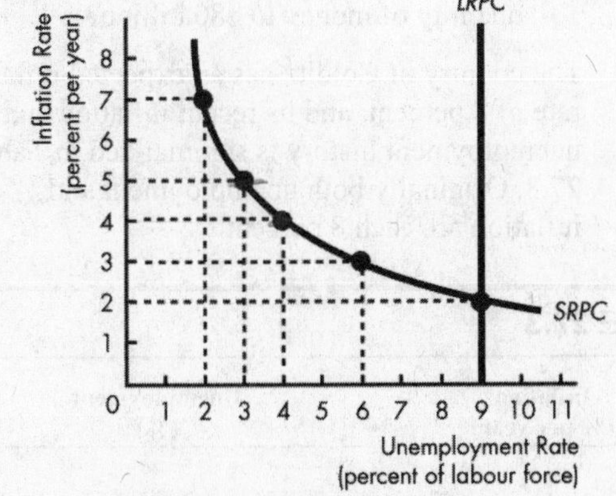

20 Figure 27.2 illustrates an economy's Phillips curves. What is the expected inflation rate?
a 9%
b 4%
c 2%
d depends on the actual inflation rate
e cannot be determined without more information

21 Figure 27.2 illustrates an economy's Phillips curves. If the current inflation rate is 4 percent, what is the current unemployment rate?
a 9%
b 6%
c 4%
d 3%
e cannot be determined without more information

22 If the inflation rate is lower than the expected inflation rate,
a unemployment will be above the natural rate.
b the natural rate of unemployment will increase.
c the expected inflation rate will increase.
d unemployment will be below the natural rate.
e the economy must off the *SRPC*.

23 If there is a fully anticipated increase in the inflation rate,
a unemployment will be below the natural rate.
b unemployment will be above the natural rate.
c the natural rate of unemployment will increase.
d the economy must be off the *LRPC*.
e the economy must be on the *LRPC*.

Interest Rates and Inflation

24 Suppose the initial nominal rate of interest is 8 percent and the expected rate of inflation is 5 percent. If the expected rate of inflation increases to 8 percent, what is the new nominal rate of interest?
a 3%
b 8%
c 11%
d 13%
e 16%

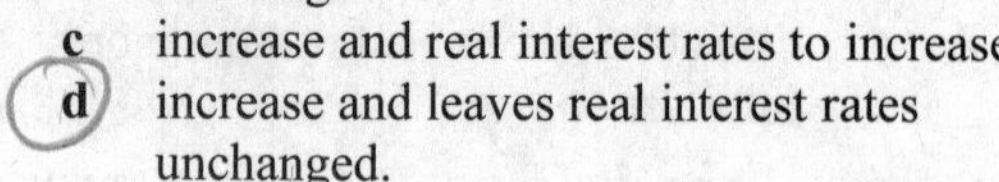

25 A correctly anticipated increase in the rate of growth of the quantity of money causes nominal interest rates to
   a decrease and real interest rates to decrease.
   b decrease and leaves real interest rates unchanged.
   c increase and real interest rates to increase.
   d increase and leaves real interest rates unchanged.
   e increase and real interest rates to decrease.

Short Answer Problems

1 What happens to the price level and real GDP if the government increases expenditures on goods and services and that increase is not anticipated (the price level is not expected to change)?

2 Explain how the events in Short Answer Problem **1** might lead to a demand-pull inflation spiral.

3 What is the relationship between the expected rate of inflation and nominal interest rates?

4 Explain carefully the difference between the short-run Phillips curve and the long-run Phillips curve.

(ct) 5 Sometimes politicians or other commentators say: "Unemployment is a more serious economic and social problem than inflation. Increasing inflation by a small amount in order to lower unemployment is therefore worthwhile." Briefly evaluate this statement.

6 Why does inflation start? Why does it persist?

7 Table 27.1 gives the initial actual aggregate demand and short-run aggregate supply schedules for an economy in which the expected price level is 80, and potential real GDP is 500.
   a What is actual real GDP and the actual price level?

TABLE 27.1 AGGREGATE DEMAND AND SUPPLY

Price Level	Real GDP Demanded	Real GDP Supplied
60	600	400
80	500	500
100	400	600
120	300	700
140	200	700

   b In year 1 the economy is in the equilibrium characterized in a. It is expected that in year 2, aggregate demand will be as given in Table 27.2. (Assume that the long-run aggregate supply curve is not expected to shift, and does not shift.) What is the vertical amount of the expected shift in the aggregate demand curve when real GDP is $500 billion?

TABLE 27.2 AGGREGATE DEMAND AND SUPPLY

Price Level	Real GDP Demanded	Real GDP Supplied
60	800	
80	700	
100	600	
120	500	
140	400	

(ct) c What is the (long-run) rational expectation of the price level for year 2?

(ct) d The expected shift in aggregate demand will cause the short-run aggregate supply (SAS) curve to shift. What will be the new SAS curve? For each price level, give the new values of real GDP supplied in the last column of Table 27.2.

8 According to the quantity theory of money, what is the effect of an increase in the quantity of money? What assumptions of the theory are crucial for this effect to occur? Why?

9 We observe an economy in which the price level is 1.5, real GDP is $240 billion, and the quantity of money is $60 billion.
   a What is the velocity of circulation?
   b According to the quantity theory of money, what is the result of an increase in the quantity of money to $80 billion?

10 The country of Colditz has an expected inflation rate of 8 percent, and its recent inflation and unemployment history is summarized in Table 27.3. Originally both unemployment and inflation are each 8 percent.

TABLE 27.3

Inflation (% per year)	Unemployment (%)
12	4
10	6
8	8
6	10
4	12

   a What is Colditz's natural rate of unemployment?

b Draw a graph of Colditz's short-run and long-run Phillips curves.

c If inflation unexpectedly increases to 12 percent per year, explain what happens to unemployment, and show it on your graph.

d Return to the original situation. If the expected inflation rate increases to 10 percent, and the actual inflation rate increases to 10 percent, explain and show on your graph what happens, *ceteris paribus*, to inflation and unemployment.

ANSWERS

True/False and Explain

1 T Inflation rate = $[(P_1 - P_0)/P_0] \times 100 = [(130 - 120)/120] \times 100 = 8.3$. (632)

2 F Persistent inflation requires persistent increases in quantity of money. (634–635)

3 F Increase in exports shift *AD* rightward, which can create demand-pull inflation. (634–635)

4 F Cost-push inflation is due to increase in input costs. (633–637)

5 T Definition. (635–637)

6 F $V = PY/M = 200/50 = 4$. (638)

7 F It makes payments from long-term contracts unpredictable, hurting one side or other. (640–643)

ⓒⓣ **8 T** If expected increase in aggregate demand, there is an increase in wage demands, which leads to leftward shift *SAS* curve, but no Δ *AD* curve, resulting in stagflation. (640–643)

9 F *AD* shifts rightward, *SAS* shifts leftward due to higher wage demands, so price level increases. (640–643)

ⓒⓣ **10 T** Wage increases, on the basis of expected inflation, are too low, resulting in lower real wages. (640–641)

11 F Correct on *average*. (641)

12 T Movement up and leftward along the *SRPC*. (644–646)

13 F It is vertical at the natural rate of unemployment. (646)

14 F Movement upward along the *LRPC*. (644–647)

15 T Lenders demand compensation for expected inflation, borrowers are willing to pay it. (648–649)

Multiple-Choice

ⓒⓣ **1 c** Inflation rate = $[(P_1 - P_0)/P_0] \times 100$, or $20 = [(180 - P_0)/P_0] \times 100$—solve this for P_0. (632)

2 a Definition. (633)

3 e **a** and **b** have one-time effects, **c** is caused by Δ*AD,* and **d** is a supply-side effect. (634–635)

4 b Increase in price of oil leads to leftward shift *SAS* curve, creating cost-push inflation (stagflation), which *may* trigger cost-push inflation spiral if government raises aggregate demand. (635–637)

5 a Increase in price of crucial input leads to increase in costs of production, and leftward shift *SAS*. (635–637)

6 e See text discussion. (638–639)

ⓒⓣ **7 d** Because theory assumes *Y/V* (= *M/P*) is constant. (638–639)

8 a Due to assumption that neither GDP nor velocity affected by Δ quantity of money. (638–639)

9 b Expected *P* found from intersection of expected $AD = AD_1$, and actual new *SAS* is set here, and new equilibrium is where actual *AD* and new *SAS* cross. (641–642)

10 e Expected *P* found from intersection of *LAS* and expected $AD = AD_1$, and actual new *SAS* is set here, and new equilibrium is where actual *AD* and new *SAS* cross. (641–642)

11 d Expected *P* found from intersection of *LAS* and expected $AD = AD_0$, and actual new *SAS* is set here, and new equilibrium is where actual *AD* and new *SAS* cross. (641–642)

12 c Example of higher transactions costs, the others are unanticipated inflation costs. (640–643)

13 a Because interest rates and wage rates too high given actual inflation rate. (640–643)

ct 14 e Draw a graph. (641–642)

15 d Higher inflation decreases value of money, so people decrease money holdings, which leads to increase in transactions. (640–643)

16 c Correct on *average*. (641)

17 e Decrease in expected price level shifts rightward *SAS*, so new equilibrium to the right of *LAS* along original *AD* curve. (641–642)

18 e Definition. (644–645)

19 a *LRPC* is at natural rate. (646)

20 c Expected inflation rate is where *SRPC* crosses *LRPC*. (646)

21 c Found by reading off the *SRPC*. (644–645)

22 a Draw a Phillips curve. (644–647)

23 e Economy just moves up the *LRPC*. (644–647)

24 c Initially, real rate = 8 – 5 = 3%. New nominal rate = real rate + expected inflation = 3 + 8 = 11%. (648–649)

25 d Increase in growth rate of quantity of money increases inflation rate, which increases nominal rate by same amount (since anticipated). No change in real rate, which is determined on world capital markets. (648–649)

Short Answer Problems

1 An increase in government expenditures on goods and services shifts the aggregate demand curve rightward. If the price level is not expected to change, the short-run aggregate supply curve remains unchanged, and the increase in aggregate demand causes the price level to increase and real GDP to increase.

2 The higher price level leads to demands for higher wages, which push up the costs of production and shift the *SAS* curve leftward, leading to a further increase in the price level and a decrease in real GDP. A demand-pull inflation spiral could result *if* the government once again raises the level of their purchases or if the government continues to run a deficit (financed by printing money). *AD* will then continue to shift rightward, triggering leftward shifts in *SAS*, leading to the demand-pull inflation spiral.

3 When the rate of inflation is expected to increase, the nominal interest rate will also increase to compensate for the increased rate at which the purchasing power of money is eroding. Lenders and borrowers are interested in the quantity of goods and services that a unit of money will buy. Lenders will insist on the higher interest rate, to compensate for the loss of purchasing power of money, and borrowers will agree because they realize that the dollars they repay will buy fewer goods and services.

4 The short-run Phillips curve is constructed assuming that the expected inflation rate is constant, and is therefore downward-sloping. As a result, if there is an increase in the inflation rate (and therefore a decrease in real wages), there will be a decrease in unemployment to a rate below the natural rate. The long-run Phillips curve is constructed assuming that the expected inflation rate adjusts fully to reflect changes in the actual inflation rate, and is therefore vertical at the natural rate of unemployment. If there is an increase in the actual inflation rate, there is an equivalent increase in the expected inflation rate (so that the real wage rate stays constant), and the rate of unemployment stays constant at the natural rate.

ct 5 Partially this statement is a value judgment, based on the tradeoff of a higher cost to society from the higher inflation versus the gain to society from a lower inflation rate. In this case, we would need to evaluate the costs of inflation vis-à-vis the costs of unemployment. However, there is also an objective (positive) problem with this statement. In the short run, such a tradeoff does exist, represented by the downward-sloping short-run Phillips curve. In the long run, there is no such tradeoff. As a result, a higher inflation rate will lead to a lower unemployment rate in the short run, but eventually inflation expectations will increase, shifting upward the short-run Phillips curve, and unemployment returns to the natural rate. Therefore in the long run, increasing inflation will have no impact on the unemployment rate, but will increase the costs to society that come from the higher inflation.

6 Inflation is an increase in the price level, and starts with either a shift rightward in the *AD* curve due to increases in the quantity of money, government spending, or exports (demand-pull inflation), or with a shift leftward in the *SAS* curve due to increases in wages or raw materials prices (cost-push inflation). However, the increase in the price level in either case can only persist if an inflation spiral results from the initial shock. A demand-pull or cost-push inflation spiral starts when increases in aggregate demand and shifts leftward in *SAS* chase each other up the long-run aggregate supply curve.

7 **a** Actual real GDP and the actual price level are determined by the intersection of the aggregate demand curve and the short-run aggregate supply curve. Real GDP is $500 billion and the price level is 80, because at a price level of 80, the quantity of real GDP demanded equals the quantity of real GDP supplied ($500 billion).

b The price level associated with $500 billion of real GDP demanded for the original aggregate demand curve (Table 27.1) is 80. The price level associated with $500 billion of real GDP demanded for the new expected aggregate demand curve (Table 27.2) is 120. Therefore the aggregate demand curve is expected to shift upward by 40.

ⓒⓣ **c** The rational expectation of the price level is at the intersection of the expected aggregate demand curve (Table 27.2) and the expected long-run aggregate supply curve. Long-run aggregate supply is equal to $500 billion and is not expected to change. Since the price level associated with $500 billion of real GDP demanded is 120, the rational expectation of the price level is 120.

ⓒⓣ **d** The quantities of real GDP supplied for the new *SAS* curve are shown in completed Table 27.2 Solution. The original expected price level is 80. From part **b** we know that the new expected price level is 120, which implies that the *SAS* curve shifts up by 40. Thus at each quantity of real GDP supplied, the price level on the new *SAS* curve is 40 points higher than on the original *SAS* curve (Table 27.1).

For example, real GDP supplied of $500 billion now requires a price level of 120 rather than 80. Similarly, real GDP supplied of $400 billion now requires a price level of 100 rather than 60. (*Note*: The values in parentheses in this table are inferred by extrapolation rather than calculated from Table 27.1.)

TABLE 27.2 SOLUTION

Price Level	Real GDP Demanded	Real GDP Supplied
60	800	(200)
80	700	(300)
100	600	400
120	500	500
140	400	600

8 According to the quantity theory of money, an increase in the quantity of money causes an equal percentage increase in the price level. The required assumptions are that velocity and potential GDP are independent of changes in the quantity of money, so that changes in the quantity of money affects only the price level.

9 **a** The velocity of circulation is defined by

$$\text{Velocity of circulation} = \frac{\text{Price level} \times \text{Real GDP}}{\text{Quantity of money}}$$

With the values for the price level, real GDP, and the quantity of money given in this problem, we have

$$\text{Velocity of circulation} = \frac{1.5 \times 240}{60} = 6$$

b The quantity theory of money predicts that an increase in the quantity of money causes an equal percentage increase in the price level. An increase in money from $60 billion to $80 billion is a one-third (33%) increase. Thus the quantity theory of money predicts that the price level will increase by a third (33%). Since the initial price level is 1.5, the predicted price level will be 2.0. (This value can also be confirmed by using the equation of exchange.)

10 **a** The natural rate of unemployment is the rate of unemployment when the actual rate of inflation equals the expected rate of inflation—in this case, the natural rate of unemployment is 8 percent.

b See Figure 27.3. The long-run Phillips curve is vertical at the natural rate of unemployment. The current short-run curve is $SRPC_0$ (ignore the other short-run curve for the moment).

FIGURE 27.3

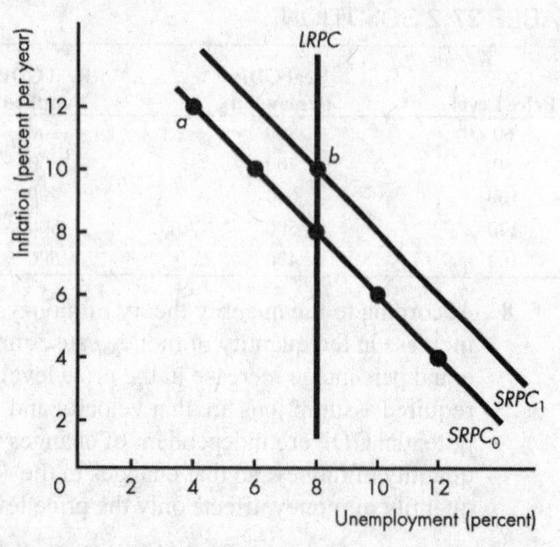

c The relevant short-run Phillips curve is $SRPC_0$, the curve for an expected inflation rate of 8 percent. From the curve (or Table 27.3), with inflation equal to 12 percent, unemployment is 4 percent at the point *a*.

d An increase in the expected inflation rate shifts the short-run Phillips curve to a new curve ($SRPC_1$), with the new curve crossing the long-run Phillips curve at the new expected inflation rate of 10 percent. (The actual shape of the curve is not clear without further information, so we are assuming the new curve is parallel to the old curve.) If the actual inflation rate is 10 percent, the unemployment rate will be 8 percent, at the natural rate, at the point *b*.

Chapter 28 Monetary Policy

KEY CONCEPTS

Monetary Policy Objective and Framework

The Bank of Canada Act sets out the objectives of monetary policy.

- ♦ The Bank controls the quantity of money and interest rates to avoid inflation and prevent excessive swings in GDP growth and unemployment.
- ♦ Current inflation control target range is 1 to 3 percent a year, with a target of 2 percent trend inflation.
  - The measure of inflation is the CPI, but the Bank also focuses on **core inflation** (CPI excluding the eight most volatile prices and indirect taxes).
  - Since range set in mid-1990s, actual inflation rate has been within target range, with minor deviations.
- ♦ Benefits of a target range are clear understanding by financial markets and as anchor for inflation expectations.
  - Critics argue that the Bank should pay more attention to unemployment rate and real GDP growth.
- ♦ The Governing Council of the Bank of Canada is responsible for conduct of monetary policy, with briefings by Bank economists.
- ♦ Governor of the Bank of Canada consults with Minister of Finance.

The Conduct of Monetary Policy

The Bank of Canada can control only one policy instrument: quantity of money (monetary base) or exchange rate or short-term interest rate.

- ♦ The Bank targets the short-term interest rate, specifically the **overnight loans rate** (interest rate on overnight loans members of LVTS make to each other).

The process used to *set* the chosen target can be either

- ♦ **Instrument rule**—sets the policy instrument at level based on current state of the economy.
- ♦ **Targeting rule**—sets the policy instrument so forecast policy level equals the target level. Bank of Canada uses targeting rule, announcing its target eight times a year.

Two tools used to *achieve* the chosen target.

- ♦ **Operating band** is the target overnight rate plus or minus 0.25 percentage points.
  - Top of operating band = the **bank rate** (overnight rate + 0.25%), the interest rate Bank of Canada charges big banks on loans. Since a bank can always borrow at bank rate, overnight rate never goes higher than this.
  - Bottom of the band = the **settlement balances rate**, the interest rate the Bank of Canada pays for reserves banks hold at Bank of Canada. Since a bank can always earn settlement balances rate, overnight rate never goes lower than this.
  - Bank of Canada can always make overnight loans rate fall within target range.
- ♦ **Open market operations** (purchase or sale of government securities by the Bank) move overnight rate to the target rate.
  - If Bank of Canada buys government bonds, this increases banking system reserves (= increased supply of overnight funds), increasing loans, lowering the overnight rate.
  - If Bank of Canada sells government bonds, this decreases banking system reserves (= decreased supply of overnight funds), decreasing loans, raising the overnight rate.

Monetary Policy Transmission

Changing the overnight rate affects aggregate demand (*AD*), real GDP growth and inflation through several channels.

- ♦ With lower overnight rate, other interest rates fall.
  - With lower interest rates, exchange rate falls, increasing net exports and *AD*.
  - With lower interest rates, consumption and investment increase, increasing *AD*.
  - Increasing *AD* increases real GDP growth and inflation, although takes up to two years for full effects.
- ♦ Higher overnight rate has opposite effects, decreasing *AD*, real GDP growth, and inflation.
- ♦ Historical evidence shows changes in overnight rate create different effects on long-term and short-term interest rates.
  - Because banks can easily choose between overnight loans and Treasury bills as short-term assets, they are close substitutes and the two rates move closely together.
  - The 10-year government bond rate and long-term corporate bond rate are close substitutes (although corporate rate slightly higher on average), so these two rate move closely together.
  - Short-term and long-term bond rates usually move together, but are not close substitutes, and sometimes move in different directions.
- ♦ The exchange rate responds to the interest rate differential (the gap between Canadian and U.S. rates), but the relationship is weak since many other key factors in the foreign exchange market.

Expenditure plans are affected by the real interest rate.

- ♦ **Nominal interest rate** is percentage return on an asset in terms of money.
- ♦ **Real interest rate** is percentage return in terms of what money will buy = nominal rate – inflation rate.
- ♦ Nominal interest rate is opportunity cost of holding money, real rate is opportunity cost of spending.
- ♦ The lower real interest rate, the lower the opportunity cost of spending, the greater autonomous consumption expenditure and investment.
- ♦ The lower real interest rate, the lower Canadian dollar's exchange rate, the greater net exports.
- ♦ The lower the overnight interest rate, the lower the nominal interest rate (and therefore the real interest rate), the higher **interest-sensitive expenditure** (autonomous consumption, investment, net exports).

The final link in the transmission chain is a change in *AD* changing real GDP and the price level.

- ♦ With real GDP < potential GDP, lowering overnight rate increases *AD*, which increases real GDP and price level, leading to a faster convergence to potential GDP.
- ♦ If real GDP > potential GDP (inflationary pressure), increasing overnight rate decreases *AD*, lowering pressure.
- ♦ Monetary policy is sometimes wrong due to time lags before policy takes effect.
- ♦ Historical evidence shows that when Bank of Canada changes overnight rates, real GDP growth changes, but with a lag.

Alternative Monetary Policy Strategies

The Bank of Canada uses inflation rate targeting rule, but has four possible alternative strategies.

- ♦ **Taylor rule** is an overnight rate instrument rule that sets the target rate in response to the current inflation rate and the current estimate of the output gap. If inflation is above the target, or real GDP is above potential GDP, Taylor rule raises overnight rate.
- ♦ **McCallum rule** is a monetary base instrument rule based on quantity theory of money. Set the monetary base to grow at rate equal to target inflation rate plus long-term real GDP growth plus medium-term velocity growth rate.
- ♦ Exchange rate targeting rule (could be a fixed exchange rate or a crawling peg), loses control over the inflation rate. The problem is the **real exchange rate** (relative price of the GDP baskets of goods and services in Canada and the United States) often changes unpredictably and is hard to offset.
- ♦ Friedman's ***k*-percent rule** is a money targeting rule that sets the quantity of money to grow at *k* percent per year = the growth rate of potential GDP. Requires a stable money demand function.

HELPFUL HINTS

1 Let's use a numerical example to review how the Bank of Canada can get the overnight rate to be in the middle of the target range. Suppose that the Bank wishes the overnight rate to be 3.5 percent, which means the operating band will be 3.25 to 3.75 percent.

First, let us review how the Bank can guarantee that the overnight rate will be within the 0.5 percent target range. There are two key factors for keeping the rate in the range. One is that the Bank of Canada is willing to lend as much money as members of the LVTS want to borrow at the bank rate (which is set at the upper end of the target, 3.75%). If the overnight rate was 4 percent, no member of the LVTS would borrow at this rate as they could borrow at the (lower) bank rate. Therefore the overnight rate is less than or equal to the bank rate. The second factor is that the Bank of Canada is willing to allow the members of the LVTS to hold as many deposits at the Bank of Canada as they want, and to earn the settlement balances rate of 3.25 percent. If the overnight rate was 3 percent, no bank would lend at this rate as they could earn 3.25 percent. Therefore, the overnight rate is greater than or equal to the settlements balances rate. In sum:

Settlement balances rate ≤ overnight rate ≤ bank rate

3.25% ≤ overnight rate ≤ 3.75%

As long as the Bank of Canada is willing to meet all borrowing/lending requirements implied by the rates it sets, it can force the *actual* overnight rate to be in this range. However, if the actual rate gets stuck at one end, it would be difficult for the Bank to continuously accept deposits or loan out money. Therefore, in this case it must use open market operations to affect the amount of reserves and the overnight rate.

2 Next, let's review how open market operations work. They affect the overnight rate via their impact on banking system reserves. Remember that one liability of the Bank of Canada is banks' deposits at the Bank of Canada (which are part of the banks' reserves). In addition, the largest class of assets of the Bank of Canada is its holdings of government securities. Finally, recall that if total assets increase, due to the conventions of double-entry bookkeeping, total liabilities must increase by the same amount.

An open market purchase by the Bank of Canada of government securities is an increase in its assets paid for by an increase in its liabilities, principally an increase in the deposits of banks at the Bank of Canada. This increase in deposits at the Bank of Canada is an increase in the banks' reserves, leaving them with excess reserves they will lend out, initially in the overnight market, pushing down the overnight rate.

3 Be careful to avoid making a very common error when working through open market operations. When the Bank of Canada buys or sells securities, private bank reserves at the Bank of Canada change. Many students automatically put the changed bank reserves at the Bank of Canada under assets in the Bank's balance sheet, because they are an asset on the *private bank balance sheet*. However, this is an error—the reserves are a deposit at the Bank of Canada, and therefore a *liability* to the Bank of Canada.

SELF-TEST

True/False and Explain

Monetary Policy Objective and Framework

1 The monetary policy objective of the Bank of Canada is to avoid inflation and prevent excessive swings in the exchange rate.

2 The Bank of Canada's current inflation target is a range of 1 to 3 percent per year for core inflation.

3 The benefits of a target range include creating an anchor for inflation expectations.

The Conduct of Monetary Policy

4 Increasing the bank rate will increase the amount of lending by the banking system.

5 Bank deposits at the Bank of Canada are an asset of the Bank of Canada and a liability of the banking system.

6 If the Bank of Canada sells government securities in the open market, bank reserves decrease.

7 If the Bank of Canada wants to decrease interest rates, it should buy government securities in the open market.

Monetary Policy Transmission

8 A decrease in the overnight rate shifts the *AD* curve rightward.

9 An increase in the overnight rate decreases the exchange rate.

10 A decrease in the overnight rate reduces inflationary pressures.

11 The opportunity cost of holding money is the nominal interest rate.

12 The overnight rate and the 10-year government bond rate move very closely together.

13 A lower interest rate creates more consumption spending via induced consumption.

Alternative Monetary Policy Strategies

14 To follow Friedman's *k*-percent rule, the Bank of Canada would set the growth rate of money equal to the target inflation rate plus long-term real GDP growth plus the medium term velocity growth rate.

15 Under the Taylor rule, if real GDP is greater than potential GDP, the Bank of Canada should raise the overnight rate.

Multiple-Choice

Monetary Policy Objective and Framework

1 Why does the Bank of Canada pay close attention to the core inflation rate in addition to the overall CPI inflation rate?

- **a** The core rate is more volatile and therefore a better predictor of trend inflation.
- **b** The core rate includes taxes, while the overall CPI rate does not.
- **c** The core rate has a lower average value and therefore makes the Bank look better.
- **d** The core rate is less volatile and a better predictor of future CPI inflation.
- **e** The core rate excludes eight volatile prices and is therefore more likely to stay within the target band.

2 One criticism of the Bank of Canada's focus on an inflation control target is that

- **a** if inflation falls below the target range a recession will result.
- **b** if inflation edges above the target range, the Bank will decrease aggregate demand and create a recession.
- **c** the Bank pays too much attention to unemployment and real GDP growth and not enough to inflation control.
- **d** it makes setting expectations of inflation difficult.
- **e** the Bank rarely achieves its target.

3 Who is responsible for setting monetary policy in Canada?
- a The government of Canada dictates monetary policy.
- b The Governor of the Bank of Canada is solely responsible.
- c The Bank of Canada's economists are primarily responsible.
- d The Governing Council of the Bank of Canada is solely responsible.
- e The Governing Council of the Bank of Canada is responsible, after consultation with the government of Canada.

The Conduct of Monetary Policy

4 If the Bank of Canada aims to lower the overnight rate, it will
- a lower the bank rate and settlement balances rate, as well as buy government securities.
- b lower the bank rate, increase the settlement balances rate, as well as buy government securities.
- c lower the bank rate and settlement balances rate, as well as sell government securities.
- d raise the bank rate and settlement balances rate, as well as buy government securities.
- e raise the bank rate and settlement balances rate, as well as sell government securities.

5 The Bank of Canada's current decision-making rule
- a uses the overnight loans rate target to affect the current state of the economy.
- b uses open market operations to affect the current state of the economy.
- c uses the overnight loans rate target to hit the inflation rate target.
- d uses open market operations to try and affect the exchange rate.
- e uses the growth rate of the monetary base to affect lending.

6 The bank rate is the interest rate
- a banks charge their very best loan customers.
- b banks pay on term deposits.
- c the Bank of Canada pays on reserves held by banks.
- d the Bank of Canada charges when it lends reserves to banks.
- e received for holding Government of Canada Treasury bills.

7 Which balance sheet in Table 28.1 shows the initial impact on the banking sector of an open market purchase by the Bank of Canada of $100 million worth of government securities from the banking sector?
- a (a)
- b (b)
- c (c)
- d (d)
- e none of the above

TABLE 28.1 BANKING SYSTEM BALANCE SHEET (MILLIONS)

(a)

Assets		Liabilities
Reserves	+100	
Securities	–100	

(b)

Assets		Liabilities
Reserves	–100	
Securities	+100	

(c)

Assets		Liabilities
Reserves	+100	Deposits+100

(d)

Assets	Liabilities	
	Deposits	+100
	Securities	–100

8 In an expansionary open market operation, the Bank of Canada
- a sells government bonds, decreasing bank reserves, decreasing lending, decreasing the overnight rate.
- b sells government bonds, decreasing bank reserves, decreasing lending, increasing the overnight rate.
- c sells government bonds, decreasing bank reserves, increasing lending, increasing the overnight rate.
- d buys government bonds, increasing bank reserves, increasing lending, decreasing the overnight rate.
- e buys government bonds, increasing bank reserves, increasing lending, increasing the overnight rate.

9 The current overnight loans rate is 3 percent, with the Bank of Canada's operating band set at 2.75 to 3.25 percent. If the Bank of Canada lowers their operating band to 2.25 to 2.75 percent, which of the following is one of the reasons the overnight rate will fall to within this new range?
 a Since the banking system can now borrow from the Bank of Canada at 2.75 percent, no bank would borrow on the overnight loan market at 3 percent.
 b Since the banking system can now borrow from the Bank of Canada at 2.25 percent, no bank would borrow on the overnight loan market at 3 percent.
 c Since the banking system can now earn 2.75 percent from the Bank of Canada, no bank would lend on the overnight loan market at 3 percent.
 d Since the banking system can now earn 2.25 percent from the Bank of Canada, no bank would lend on the overnight loan market at 3 percent.
 e There is a legal requirement that the overnight rate must be within the Bank of Canada's operating band.

10 The current overnight loans rate is 3 percent, with the Bank of Canada's operating band set at 2.75 to 3.25 percent. If the Bank of Canada lowers their operating band to 2.25 to 2.75 percent, what type of open market operation might they have to carry out to get the overnight rate to the middle of the target?
 a Buying foreign exchange in the foreign exchange market
 b Buying Canadian dollars in the foreign exchange market
 c Selling foreign exchange in the foreign exchange market
 d Buying government securities in the open market
 e Selling government securities in the open market

Monetary Policy Transmission

11 Why is the exchange rate a key monetary variable?
 a It is one of the four main policy rules.
 b It is a key policy objective.
 c It is a barometer of monetary policy.
 d It shows how much the monetary base must be multiplied in order to measure the resulting increase in the quantity of money.
 e It is part of the channel by which a change in the overnight rate affects aggregate demand.

12 The headline "The Bank of Canada Has Cut the Bank Rate" suggests that the Bank of Canada is trying to
 a lower inflationary pressures.
 b increase the overnight loans rate.
 c stimulate aggregate demand.
 d raise the value of the Canadian dollar.
 e help banks make profits.

13 In a situation of unemployment, a decrease in the overnight rate will lead to a(n)
 a increase in real GDP and the price level.
 b increase in real GDP, but a decrease in the price level.
 c increase in real GDP, but no change in the price level.
 d increase in the price level, but no change in real GDP.
 e decrease in the price level and real GDP.

14 Consider Figure 28.1. Which graph represents an anti-inflationary monetary policy?
 a (a)
 b (b)
 c (c)
 d (d)
 e none of the above

FIGURE 28.1

(a)

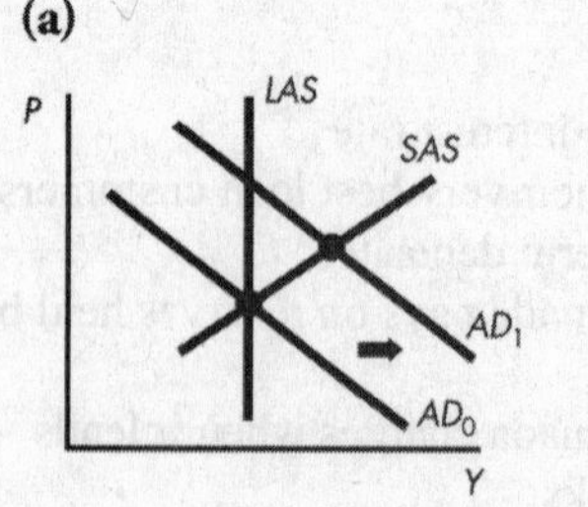

(b)

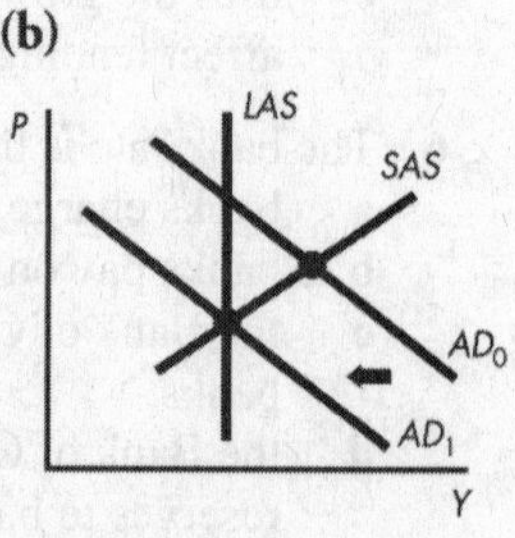

(c)

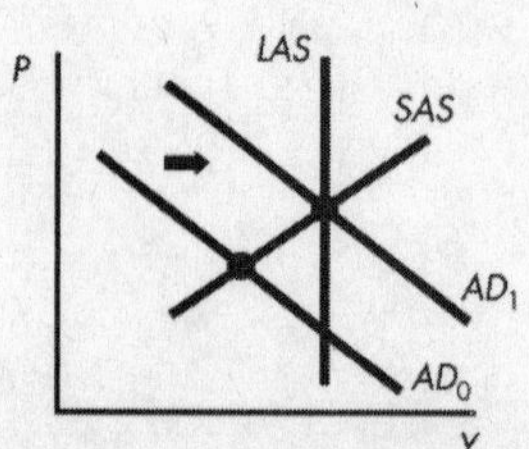

(d)

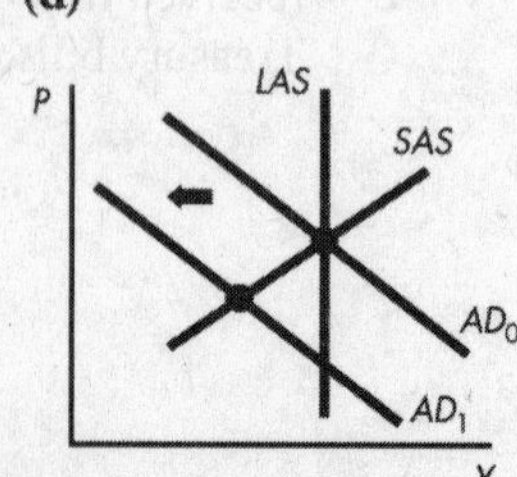

15 Consider Figure 28.1. Which graph represents an attempt to lower unemployment with monetary policy?
- **a** (a)
- **b** (b)
- **c** (c)
- **d** (d)
- **e** none of the above

16 An expansionary monetary policy will
- **a** increase interest rates and decrease the exchange rate.
- **b** have no impact on interest rates, but increase the exchange rate.
- **c** have no impact on interest rates nor on the exchange rate.
- **d** decrease interest rates and increase the exchange rate.
- **e** decrease interest rates and the exchange rate.

17 Which of the following statements about historical evidence on monetary policy is *true*?
- **a** The overnight interest rate move inversely with short-term interest rates.
- **b** The overnight interest rate is not related to short-term interest rates.
- **c** When the Bank of Canada lowers the overnight rate, real GDP rises immediately.
- **d** When the gap between Canadian and U.S. interest rates increases, the exchange rate tends to decrease.
- **e** When the gap between Canadian and U.S. interest rates increases, the exchange rate tends to increase.

18 Which of the following statements *correctly* describes an anti-inflationary monetary policy?
- **a** "The Bank of Canada's recent purchases of government securities is stimulating the housing sector."
- **b** "The Bank of Canada's recent moves to lower interest rates are behind the recent decreases in the value of the Canadian dollar."
- **c** "The Bank of Canada's recent moves to increase the overnight loans rate are leading to less lending and less consumer spending."
- **d** "The Bank of Canada's recent sales of government securities are stimulating the housing sector."
- **e** "The Bank of Canada's recent moves to decrease the value of the Canadian dollar are leading to more spending in the economy."

19 If the inflation rate increases by 3 percent and the nominal interest rate increases by 2 percent, the
- **a** real interest rate increases.
- **b** opportunity cost of holding money increases.
- **c** opportunity cost of holding money decreases.
- **d** opportunity cost of spending increases.
- **e** autonomous consumption expenditure decreases.

20 An increase in the real interest rate will
- **a** decrease autonomous consumption expenditure.
- **b** increase investment.
- **c** decrease the exchange rate.
- **d** increase net exports.
- **e** decrease the nominal interest rate.

21 An increase in the overnight interest rate will
- **a** decrease the real interest rate, the inflation rate held constant.
- **b** decrease nominal interest rates.
- **c** decrease aggregate demand.
- **d** increase aggregate demand.
- **e** not change the nominal interest rate.

22 A higher Canadian interest rate will
- **a** increase the demand for Canadian dollars because more people move money into Canada to take advantage of the higher interest rate.
- **b** decrease the demand for Canadian dollars because more people move money out of Canada to take advantage of the higher interest rate.
- **c** increase the demand for Canadian dollars because more people move money out of Canada to take advantage of the higher interest rate.
- **d** decrease the demand for Canadian dollars because more people move money into Canada to take advantage of the higher interest rate.
- **e** not affect the demand for Canadian dollars.

23 Changing the overnight rate affects aggregate demand through several channels. Which of the following is *not* one of those channels?
- **a** Higher real interest rates lower net exports.
- **b** Higher real interest rates raise consumption expenditure.
- **c** Higher real interest rates lower investment spending.
- **d** Lower real interest rates raise consumption expenditure.
- **e** Lower real interest rates raise investment spending.

Alternative Monetary Policy Strategies

24 Suppose the Bank of Canada's current monetary policy strategy has the monetary base growing at a target rate. This strategy is an example of
- a a Taylor rule.
- b a McCallum rule.
- c an inflation targeting rule.
- d an exchange rate target rule.
- e monetary target rule.

25 In order for Friedman's *k*-percent rule to work, it requires
- a stable long-term real GDP growth.
- b a good estimate of the output gap.
- c the real exchange rate to be predictable.
- d a stable money demand function.
- e good knowledge of the velocity growth rate.

Short Answer Problems

1 Suppose that the Bank of Canada is following an exchange rate target of a fixed exchange rate. Currently there is downward market pressure on the exchange rate.
- a Explain how the Bank of Canada could use monetary policy to offset this downward pressure.
- b Explain how each component of interest-sensitive expenditure is affected by this policy.

2 How does an open market purchase of government securities lead to a decrease in the overnight rate? What are the ripple effects of this policy on the different components of aggregate expenditure?

3 Consider the following balance sheets for the Bank of Canada and the Bank of Speedy Creek:

TABLE 28.2

Bank of Speedy Creek

Assets		**Liabilities**	
Reserves	60	Deposits	1,000
Securities	100		
Loans	840		
	1,000		

Bank of Canada

Assets		**Liabilities**	
Government securities	9,000	Bank of Canada notes	10,000
Loans to banks	500	Chartered banks' deposits	1,000
Other net assets	2,000	Government deposits	500
	11,500		11,500

- a Suppose that the Bank of Canada buys all $100 of securities from the Bank of Speedy Creek. Show what happens to the balance sheets of the Bank of Speedy Creek and the Bank of Canada as a result of this action, explaining as you go. What does this action do to the reserves in the banking system?
- b If this action is carried out at a broader level among all the banks of the banking system, explain what will likely happen next in the overnight loans market.

4 Explain what the open market operation in Short Answer Problem 3 does to short-term and long-term interest rates, aggregate demand, real GDP, and the price level. Be sure to explain the channels by which the monetary policy affects aggregate demand.

5 Suppose there is an increase in the overnight rate and therefore in other interest rates. Using a graph of the aggregate demand–aggregate supply model, show what happens to the price level and the level of real GDP in the short run and in the long run.

6 Consider the following data, from the imaginary country of Sarconia:

Current inflation rate	3% per year
Current overnight rate	4% per year
Current growth rate of real GDP	3% per year
Estimated (long-term) growth rate of potential GDP	3% per year
Current unemployment rate	5%
Estimate of natural unemployment rate	7%
Current growth rate of monetary base	12% per year

a Is Sarconia suffering from an inflationary gap, is it suffering from a recessionary gap, or is it right at potential GDP? How do you know?

b If the Bank of Sarconia has an inflationary target of 2 to 4 percent per year, what would be the appropriate policy strategy?

c If the Bank of Sarconia follows a Taylor rule with an inflationary target of 2 to 4 percent per year, what would be the appropriate policy strategy?

d If the Bank of Sarconia follows a McCallum rule with an inflationary target of 2 to 4 percent per year, what additional information would you need to be able to figure out the appropriate policy strategy?

e If the Bank of Sarconia follows a Friedman *k*-percent rule, what would be the appropriate policy strategy?

ct 7 In Short Answer Problem 6, you should have found different appropriate policy conclusions for each of the rules in parts **b**, **c**, and **e**. Explain what differences in the crucial factors underlying each rule leads to the different policy conclusions.

ct 8 "If banking system reserves are increasing, this is a sign that loans and deposits will soon expand." Evaluate this statement.

9 Consider the following "quotation" from the *Regional Post*:

Interest Rates Crash After Bank of Canada Action

by J. S. Smith

The Bank of Canada cut interest rates dramatically yesterday. … [T]he bank cut its target for overnight rates to 3.25% from 4.00%. The major banks quickly followed suit, cutting the cost of borrowing for their best customers (the prime rate) to 5.50% from 6.25%. This change was following by reductions in other rate, including mortgage rates.

Explain the link from the overnight rate target to the prime rate that the major banks charge their best customers.

10 If the Bank of Canada wishes to reduce inflationary pressure, explain briefly what steps they will have to carry out in the overnight loans market.

ANSWERS

True/False and Explain

1 F Avoid inflation and prevent excessive swings in real GDP growth and unemployment. (656)

2 F 1 to 3 percent for overall inflation. (656–657)

3 T See text discussion. (657)

4 F Higher bank rate increases cost of borrowing reserves, so banks wish to hold more reserves, so they *decrease* loans. (658–661)

5 F Asset of banking system (part of reserves) and liability of Bank of Canada (deposit at Bank). (661)

6 T If securities are sold, people buy them with deposits that are transferred to Bank of Canada, leading to decrease in reserves. (661)

7 T Buying government bonds increases reserves, which leads to an increase in the supply of overnight funds. Banks respond by loaning out more, lowering the overnight rate. (661)

8 T Lower overnight rate pushes down short-term and long-term interest rates, which increases interest-sensitive expenditure and shifts *AD* curve rightward. (663)

9 F Higher overnight rate pushes up interest rates, which raises the Canadian interest rate differential, which raises the demand for the Canadian dollar and therefore the exchange rate. (665)

10 F Lower overnight rate pushes down short-term and long-term interest rates, which increases interest-sensitive expenditure and shifts *AD* curve rightward, pushing up price level. (663–669)

11 T The opportunity cost of money is the real interest rate on other assets (the nominal interest rate minus the inflation rate) – the real interest rate on money (minus the inflation rate) = the nominal interest rate. (666)

12 F They move together, but not that closely. See Text Figure 28.7. (663–664)

13 F Via autonomous consumption. (665–667)

14 F Should set it equal to the growth rate of potential GDP. (670–671)

15 T See formula. (670)

Multiple-Choice

1 d See text discussion. (656)

2 b Anti-inflationary policy leads to decreased *AD*, which can lead to recession and unemployment. (656)

3 e See text discussion. (658)

4 a Lowering the two rates will force the overnight rate down in between these two rates (see Helpful Hint 1), and buying securities will increase banking system reserves, leading to more overnight loans, which pushes the rate down. (660–662)

5 c Overnight loan rate is the policy instrument aimed at the policy objective of the inflation rate. (658–660)

6 d Definition. (660)

7 a Bank of Canada credits banking sector's reserves at central bank and in return gets securities from banking sector. (661)

8 d Buying bonds increases reserves to pay for them, which creates excess reserves, leading to increase in funds available for lending in the overnight loans market, which pushes down the overnight rate. (661–662)

9 a The upper end of the band is the bank rate, the rate the Bank of Canada charges for borrowing from it. No profit-seeking bank will pay more than this rate to borrow, forcing down the actual overnight rate to less than or equal to this rate. (660–662)

10 d They will need to buy securities in order to raise banking system reserves in order to increase funds for lending in the overnight market in order to push down the overnight rate. (660–662)

11 e Δ overnight rate leads to Δr, which Δ demand for Canadian dollar and exchange rate, which ΔNX and *AD*. (665)

12 c Lowering the bank rate lowers costs of borrowing to replenish reserves, so banking system will maintain lower reserves, and lend out more money, lowering interest rates and stimulating interest-sensitive expenditure and *AD*. (663–669)

13 a Decrease in overnight rate shifts *AD* rightward, increasing real GDP and price level if initial equilibrium is left of full employment (draw a graph). (668–669)

14 b Output is above natural rate (inflationary gap), and policy is attempting to reduce *AD* to reduce the gap. (668–669)

15 c Output is below the natural rate (recessionary gap) and policy is attempting to increase *AD* to reduce the gap. (668–669)

16 e Decrease in overnight rate decreases interest rates, which decreases demand for Canadian dollar and therefore exchange rate. (663–665)

17 e See text discussion. (663–669)

18 c All other changes lead to lower interest rates and higher aggregate expenditure, shifting *AD* rightward. (663–669)

19 b Nominal interest rate increases, opportunity cost of money increases. Real interest rate decreases since increase in inflation rate > increase in nominal interest rate, so opportunity cost of spending decreases and spending increases. (665–667)

20 a Higher cost of borrowing decreases borrowing and spending. (665–667)

21 c Higher overnight rate increases other interest rates and therefore decreased consumption, investment and net exports. (665–667)

22 a People trying to earn more on their money buy Canadian assets and must buy Canadian dollars to buy the Canadian assets. (665)

23 b Higher real interest rates lower borrowing and spending. (663–669)

24 b Definition. (670–671)

25 d See text discussion. (671)

Short Answer Problems

1 a If the Bank of Canada pushes up the overnight loans rate, this would increase other interest rates in the economy. Increasing interest rates will increase the interest rate gap between Canada and other countries, increasing demand for the Canadian dollar. This increase in turn increases the exchange rate, offsetting the initial downward pressure.

b The higher exchange rate will lower net exports. The higher interest rates will push up the real interest rate, and therefore lower autonomous consumption and investment.

2 An open market purchase of government securities by the Bank of Canada increases the reserves of the banking system by increasing one of its components—banks' deposits at the Bank of Canada. When the securities are purchased from banks, the Bank of Canada pays for the securities by crediting the bank's deposit at the Bank of Canada, which directly increases their reserves. The banks will now have more reserves, and will try to lend more on the overnight market (and will need to borrow less), which puts downward pressure on overnight rates.

The lower overnight rates creates substitution effects, pushing down other interest rates, which increases consumption and investment spending. The lower interest rates also lower demand for the Canadian dollar, which lowers the value of the exchange rate, and increases net exports.

3 a The impact of the purchase on the balance sheets is shown in Table 28.3 below.

TABLE 28.3

(a) Changes in Balance Sheets

Bank of Speedy Creek

Assets		Liabilities	
Reserves	+100	Deposits	0
Securities	–100		
Loans	0		
	0		

Bank of Canada

Assets		Liabilities	
Government securities	+100	Bank of Canada notes	0
Loans to banks	0	Ch. banks' deposits	+100
Other net assets	0	Government deposits	0
	+100		+100

(b) Positions After the Open Market Operation

Bank of Speedy Creek

Assets		Liabilities	
Reserves	160	Deposits	1,000
Securities	0		
Loans	840		
	1,000		

Bank of Canada

Assets		Liabilities	
Government securities	9,100	Bank of Canada notes	10,000
Loans to banks	500	Ch. banks' deposits	1,100
Other net assets	2,000	Government deposits	500
	11,600		11,600

The Bank of Canada increases its securities by 100, and pays for it by increasing the Bank of Speedy Creek's deposits at the Bank of Canada by 100, which is an increase in this bank's reserves by 100 (matching the decrease in security holdings). The balance sheets in Table 28.3 show the changes, and then the new positions.

The increase in banks' deposits of 100 also increases the reserves of the banking system by 100.

b The Bank of Speedy Creek now likely has excess reserves of 100, since deposits are unchanged by the operation. If this operation is at a broader level, other banks will also have excess reserves. They will try to lend out these excess reserves in the overnight loans market (and will need to borrow less), and this will put downward pressure on the overnight rate.

4 The lower overnight rate pushes down short-term interest rates, and to some degree long-term interest rates. Lower interest rates increase consumer spending (e.g., more borrowing, less saving) and investment spending. In addition, lower interest rates lower the exchange rate, leading to more net exports. Therefore, the aggregate demand curve shifts rightward, increasing real GDP and the price level in the short run, as shown in Text Figure 28.10.

5 The consequences of an increase in the overnight rates are illustrated in Figure 28.2. The economy is initially in long-run equilibrium at point *a*, the intersection of AD_0 and SAS_0 (and *LAS*). The price level is P_0 and GDP is at potential, Y^*. An increase in the overnight rate lowers interest-sensitive expenditure and shifts the *AD* curve leftward, from AD_0 to AD_1. The new short-run equilibrium is at point *b*. The price level decreases to P_1 and real GDP decreases to Y_1. In the long run, however, input prices also decrease, which shifts *SAS* rightward, from SAS_0 to SAS_1. A new long-run equilibrium occurs at point *c*. In the long run, the price level decreases further to P_2, while real GDP returns to potential, Y^*.

FIGURE 28.2

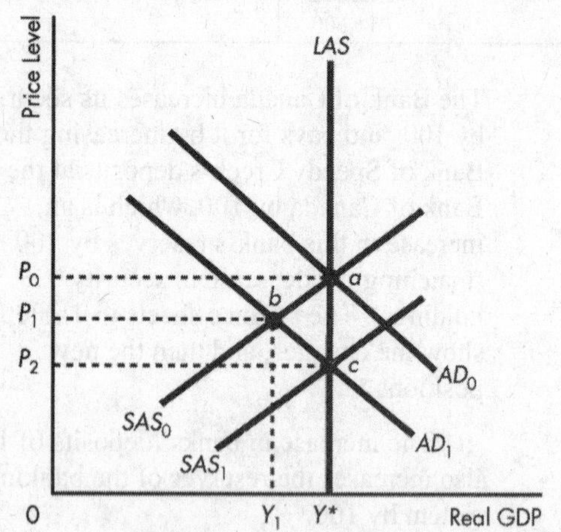

6 a Since unemployment is below the natural rate, real GDP is above potential GDP and there is an inflationary gap.

b Since inflation is exactly in the middle of the inflationary target range, the appropriate policy would be to do nothing different.

c A Taylor rule follows the following formula:

$$R = R^* + \pi + 0.5(\pi - \pi^*) + 0.5G$$

R is the overnight rate, R^* is the neutral real overnight rate (2% according to Taylor), π is the inflation rate, π^* is the target rate, and *G* is an estimate of the output gap. Substituting in the information from question, and assuming a value of π^* equal to the middle of the target range, we see:

$$R = 2 + 3 + 0.5(3 - 3) + 0.5G, \text{ or}$$

$$R = 5 + 0.5G$$

We do not know what *G* is, but if there is an inflationary gap, $G > 0$. Therefore, the overnight rate should be higher than 5 percent. Since it is currently 4 percent, it needs to be raised.

d The McCallum rule sets the growth rate of the monetary base equal to the target inflation rate (3%) plus the long-term real GDP growth rate (3%) plus the medium-term velocity growth rate. We would need to know the medium-term velocity growth rate in order to set the appropriate growth rate of the monetary base.

e The Friedman *k*-percent rule sets the growth rate of the quantity of money equal to the growth rate of potential GDP, which is 3 percent per year. Since the current growth rate of the monetary base is 12 percent per year, Sarconia would have to lower this growth rate dramatically by raising the overnight rate.

ⓒⓣ 7 The simple inflationary rule of part **b** only focuses on the inflation target, which was currently being met, and not on any future problems. Both the Taylor rule (which also looks at the output gap as a source of future inflationary pressures) and the Friedman *k*-percent rule (which looks at the growth rate of the money supply as a source of future inflationary pressures) try and forecast future pressures and offset them before they occur. As stated earlier, we do not have the correct information for the McCallum rule, but its use of medium-term velocity in its formula would also lead to a different result.

ct 8 Banking system reserves might be increasing for two reasons, which will have opposite future effects on loans and deposits. It might be as a result of an open-market operation, wherein the Bank of Canada is buying securities and pumping up the reserves of the banking system. This creates *excess* reserves, which will be lent out, creating deposits expansion.

A second reason might be because the Bank of Canada has raised the overnight loan rate, making it more expensive for banks to be short of reserves. Then, banks will raise their *desired* reserves in order to avoid being short. In this case, they will be shrinking their loans (and therefore deposits) in order to increase their desired reserves.

9 The overnight rate is the rate banks in the banking system charge each other when there are shortages in reserves at the end of the day. If this rate climbs dramatically, banks will find themselves wanting to hold more reserves. To do this, they will call in loans to their other customers and raise loan rates, since these are substitutes for overnight loans.

10 To reduce inflationary pressure, the Bank of Canada needs to reduce aggregate demand. To do this, the Bank must reduce interest-sensitive expenditure, and to do this, they need to raise interest rates. To raise the overnight rate, the Bank would raise its target range for the overnight rate. In addition, they would probably carry out an open market operation. To raise the overnight rate, they would need to reduce banking system reserves by carrying out an open market sale of government securities. If they sell securities to the banking system, these securities will be paid for out of reserves, reducing the amount of reserves.

Chapter 29 Fiscal and Monetary Interactions

KEY CONCEPTS

Macroeconomic Equilibrium

Earlier chapters explored *SAS* = *AD* equilibrium and *MD* = *MS* equilibrium separately. This chapter explores how real GDP and interest rate are simultaneously determined.

- Short-run equilibrium (in the goods and services market) determines real GDP and the price level where *SAS* = *AD*.
  - *AD* depends on *r*.
  - Higher *r* creates lower interest-sensitive expenditure (*IE* = *C* + *I* + *NX*), and lower *AD*, lower *Y* and *P*.
- Money market equilibrium (in the money market) determines *r* where *MD* = *MS*.
  - *r* depends on *AD*.
  - Higher *AD* creates higher *Y* (and higher *MD*) and higher *P* (lower *MS*), and therefore higher *r*.
- There is only one value of *Y*, one value of *P* and one value of *r* that give simultaneous or joint money market equilibrium and goods and services market equilibrium.

Fiscal Policy in the Short Run

Expansionary fiscal policy increases AD through increased government expenditures, increased transfer payments, or decreased taxes.

- First-round effects: increased government expenditure creates multiplier effects and increases quantity of real GDP demanded.
- Second-round effects: increased real GDP demanded increases real GDP and price level.
  - Increase in *Y* shifts *MD* rightward, increasing *r* and decreasing interest-sensitive expenditure, shifting *AD* curve leftward somewhat.
  - Increase in *P* shifts *MS* leftward, increasing *r* and decreasing interest-sensitive expenditure and quantity of real GDP demanded (movement along *AD* curve).
- Tendency for expansionary fiscal policy to increase *r* and decrease investment (*I*—the most important part of interest-sensitive expenditure) is called **crowding out**.
- Expansionary fiscal policy may increase *I* (**crowding in**) by increasing expected profits.
- Increase in *r* may cause **international crowding out** by increasing exchange rate, decreasing *NX*.

Monetary Policy in the Short Run

Expansionary monetary policy increases *AD* through increased quantity of real money.

- First-round effects: increased quantity of real money decreases *r*, increasing interest-sensitive expenditure, shifting *AD* curve rightward.
- Second-round effects: identical to second-round fiscal policy effects.
- Overall decrease in *r* decreases demand for the Canadian dollar, decreasing the exchange rate, increasing net exports.

Relative Effectiveness of Policies

- Fiscal policy more powerful if
  - Money demand *responsive* to interest rates (ΔMD leads to small Δr).
  - Interest-sensitive expenditure *unresponsive* to interest rates (given Δr leads to small Δ expenditure).

- Monetary policy more powerful if
  - Money demand *unresponsive* to interest rates (ΔMS leads to large Δr).
  - Interest-sensitive expenditure *responsive* to interest rates (given Δr leads to large Δ expenditure).
- **Keynesians** in the 1950s believed economy was inherently unstable; fiscal policy more effective due to little crowding out.
- **Monetarists** in the 1950s believed economy was inherently stable; monetary policy more effective due to lots of crowding out.
- Empirical evidence showed both policies were effective.

Policy Actions at Full Employment

Starting at full employment, expansionary fiscal policy shifts *AD* rightward, and creates above-full-employment equilibrium (inflationary gap).

- Labour shortage puts upward pressure on money wages.
- Higher money wages create third-round effects—shifting *SAS* leftward.
- As *SAS* shifts leftward, *Y* decreases and *P* increases as economy moves to long-run equilibrium.
- Result is complete crowding out—interest-sensitive expenditure decreases by amount *G* increases.

Starting at full employment, expansionary monetary policy shifts *AD* rightward, and creates above-full-employment equilibrium (inflationary gap). Third-round effects identical to fiscal policy third-round effects.

- These effects create the **long-run neutrality proposition**—in the long run, a change in the quantity of money changes the price level only, and leaves all real variables unchanged.

Policy Coordination and Conflict

Government and Bank of Canada can work together to achieve common goals (**policy coordination**), or pursue conflicting goals (**policy conflict**).

- Monetary and fiscal policy both alter *AD*, but have opposite effects on interest and exchange rates in the second round.
  - Expansionary fiscal policy increases *r* and increases exchange rate, decreasing *I* and *NX*.
  - Expansionary monetary policy decreases *r* and decreases exchange rate, increasing *I* and *NX*.
  - Coordination allows an increase in *AD* with desired Δr by correctly mixing monetary and fiscal policy.
- Bank of Canada targeting the interest rate can cause problems with fiscal policy.
  - If the Bank of Canada keeps *r* constant, fiscal policy can have bigger than intended effects.
  - Difficult to adjust *r* correctly in response to fiscal policy—errors can create inflationary or recessionary gaps.

HELPFUL HINTS

1 Chapters 23 and 24 examined the goods and services markets in isolation using the *AD–SAS* model and assuming that the interest rate was given. When the interest rate changed, aggregate demand changed, resulting in a new equilibrium level of real GDP.

Similarly, Chapters 25 and 28 examined the money market in isolation by using the money supply and money demand model and assuming that the level of real GDP and the price level were given. When the level of real GDP changed, the demand for real money changed, and when the price level changed, the real money supply changed, resulting in a new equilibrium. The equilibrium values of real GDP and the price level were determined assuming a value for the interest rate, and the equilibrium interest rate was determined assuming a value for real GDP and for the price level.

This chapter puts the two models of these markets together and simultaneously determines equilibrium real GDP, the price level, and the equilibrium interest rate. Examining the simultaneous equilibrium reveals important *second-round* effects of fiscal and monetary policy that did not appear in the partial analysis of earlier chapters. One example of these second-round effects is crowding out. Because of crowding out, the fiscal policy multipliers in the full model are smaller than the multipliers examined in the partial model of Chapter 24.

2 The major focus of this chapter is on channels of monetary or fiscal policy—how an initial change in monetary or fiscal policy is transmitted through the economy to its eventual effect on aggregate demand. The graphical analysis in the text is valuable in studying these channels.

The economy initially starts out in equilibrium, then a change in either monetary or fiscal policy throws a market out of equilibrium. As this market changes and moves toward a new equilibrium, changes are triggered in other markets. Eventually a new, simultaneous equilibrium is achieved in all markets.

It is helpful to augment the graphical analysis with simple "arrow diagrams" that show the *sequence* of changes as the economy adjusts to an initial policy change. For example, the interest rate transmission channel of monetary policy is represented by the following arrow diagram:

(i) First round:

↑ *M* → ↑ *MS*

↑ *MS* → ↓ *r* (link 1)

↓ *r* → ↑ *IE* (link 2)

↑ *IE* → ↑ *AD*

↑ *AD* → ↑ real GDP, ↑ *P*

Second round:

↑ real GDP → ↑ *MD*

↑ *P* → ↓ *MS*

↓ *MS* , ↑ *MD* → ↑ *r*

↑ *r* → ↓ *IE*

↓ *IE* → ↓ *AD*

↓ *AD* → ↓ real GDP, ↓ *P*

This diagram indicates that an expansionary monetary policy (an open market purchase of government securities by the Bank of Canada) will cause the quantity of money to increase (↑ *M*), increasing the quantity of real money (↑ *MS*). This increase in turn will result in a decrease in the interest rate (↓ *r*) that will increase expenditure (↑ *IE*), which is a part of aggregate demand (↑ *AD*). This increase will cause real GDP and the price level to begin increasing (↑ real GDP, ↑ *P*), the end of the first-round effects.

However, the increase in real GDP and the price level cause second-round effects—the higher real GDP leads to a rightward shift in the demand for real money (↑ *MD*), the higher price level shifts the real money supply curve leftward (↓ *MS*). The increase in the demand for real money and the decrease in the quantity of real money will cause the interest rate to increase (↑ *r*), causing expenditure (↓ *IE*) and aggregate expenditure (↓ *AD*) to decrease, which will decrease real GDP and the price level (↓ real GDP, ↓ *P*). This crowding-out effect offsets somewhat the initial changes, but the economy still eventually converges to a new equilibrium. (Ignore link 1 and link 2 in the arrow diagram for the moment.)

An arrow diagram can be a convenient way of summarizing the more detailed graphical analysis. Arrow diagrams can also reveal effects that can weaken or strengthen a policy's impact on aggregate demand.

3 The transmission channel of fiscal policy (e.g., an increase in government expenditures on goods and services), is represented by the following arrow diagram:

(ii) First round:

↑ *G* → ↑ *AD*

↑ *AD* → ↑ real GDP, ↑ *P*

Second round:

↑ real GDP → ↑ *MD*

↑ *P* → ↓ *MS*

↓ *MS*, ↑ *MD* → ↑ *r* (link 1)

↑ *r* → ↓ *IE* (link 2)

↓ *IE* → ↓ *AD*

↓ *AD* → ↓ real GDP, ↓ *P*

The amount of government expenditures on goods and services is represented by *G*. Otherwise the notation is the same as used above. (Once again, ignore link 1 and link 2.)

4 The strength of the effect of a change in the quantity of money on aggregate demand depends on the responsiveness of the demand for real money to changes in the interest rate, and the responsiveness of interest-sensitive expenditure to changes in the interest rate.

The arrow diagram given by (i) illustrates how these factors affect the strength of monetary policy. The link between the increase in the quantity of real money and the subsequent decrease in the interest rate is indicated as link 1.

If the demand for real money is very sensitive to interest rate changes (the *MD* curve is very flat or interest-elastic), this link is quite weak—a given increase in the quantity of real money will have only a small effect on the interest rate. This small effect in turn means a relatively small effect on expenditure. Link 2 captures the effect of a change in the interest rate on interest-sensitive expenditure. If expenditure is very sensitive to interest rate changes (the interest-sensitive expenditure curve is very flat or interest-elastic), this link is quite strong—a given decrease in the interest rate will have a very large effect on interest-sensitive expenditure, most importantly on investment (*I*).

We can also examine the factors that determine the strength of the effect of fiscal policy on aggregate demand. Links 1 and 2 of (ii) are the relevant links; indeed they are the same as links 1 and 2 for monetary policy. If the demand for real money is very sensitive to interest rate changes (the *MD* curve is very flat), link 1 is quite weak, the amount of crowding out is small, and fiscal policy is strong. Similarly, if interest-sensitive expenditure is very sensitive to interest rate changes (the interest-sensitive expenditure curve is very flat), link 2 is quite strong, the amount of crowding out is large, and fiscal policy is weak.

Links 1 and 2 are critical in the transmission process and the focus of the Keynesian-monetarist controversy. Think about the extreme Keynesian and monetarist positions in terms of these links. The existence of a liquidity trap (horizontal *MD* curve assumed by an extreme Keynesian) makes monetary policy ineffective because it completely breaks link 1—an increase in the quantity of real money will have no effect on the interest rate. It also makes fiscal policy very strong, because there is no crowding out (an increase in real GDP has no impact on interest rates and interest-sensitive expenditure).

The existence of a vertical interest-sensitive expenditure curve (assumed by an extreme Keynesian) makes monetary policy ineffective because it completely breaks link 2. Similarly, the existence of a horizontal interest-sensitive expenditure curve or a vertical *MD* curve (assumed by an extreme monetarist) implies complete crowding out and therefore ineffective fiscal policy.

Note that the same effects that create a strong fiscal policy create a weak monetary policy, and vice versa.

5 The effects of changes in monetary policy or fiscal policy on the exchange rate are very important in economies like Canada with large foreign sectors. Changes in interest rates change the demand for the Canadian dollar in the same direction. This change, in turn, causes an appreciation in the Canadian dollar if the interest rate increases, and a depreciation if the interest rate decreases. However, fiscal and monetary policy differ crucially on this effect, having opposite effects on interest rates.

Expansionary fiscal policy *increases* interest rates, *increasing* the exchange rate, *decreasing* net exports, thus *offsetting* the expansionary policy. However, expansionary monetary policy *decreases* interest rates, *decreasing* the exchange rate, *decreasing* net exports, thus *augmenting* the expansionary policy.

SELF-TEST

True/False and Explain

Macroeconomic Equilibrium

1 An increase in the interest rate causes the interest-sensitive expenditure curve to shift leftward.

2 An increase in the demand for money causes the interest rate to rise.

3 An increase in real GDP shifts the demand curve for real money leftward.

Fiscal Policy in the Short Run

4 Crowding in is always more powerful than crowding out.

5 If aggregate demand increases because of increased government expenditures on goods and services, interest rates decrease and investment increases.

6 An increase in government expenditures lowers the exchange rate.

Monetary Policy in the Short Run

7 If aggregate demand increases because of an increase in the quantity of real money, interest rates decrease and investment increases.

8 An increase in the quantity of money causes the interest rate to increase.

9 An increase in the quantity of money causes the exchange rate to increase.

Relative Effectiveness of Policies

10 Other things equal, a change in the quantity of money will have a larger effect on aggregate planned expenditure the more responsive expenditure is to the interest rate.

11 Crowding out will be greater if the interest-sensitive expenditure curve is very steep.

12 Keynesians consider the economy to be relatively unstable.

Policy Actions at Full Employment

13 In the *AS–AD* model at full employment, in the long run an expansionary monetary policy leads only to an increase in price, not an increase in real GDP.

14 Crowding out is 100 percent if the economy starts out in a long-run equilibrium.

Policy Coordination and Conflict

15 Coordination of monetary and fiscal policy means that an expansionary policy can be implemented without any crowding out.

Multiple-Choice

Macroeconomic Equilibrium

1 Which of the following best describes how aggregate demand affects the interest rate?

a An increase in aggregate demand increases the price level, increasing money demand and increasing the interest rate.

b An increase in aggregate demand decreases the price level, increasing the supply of real money and increasing the interest rate.

c A decrease in aggregate demand decreases the price level, increasing money demand and increasing the interest rate.

d An increase in aggregate demand increases real GDP, increasing money demand and increasing the interest rate.

e An increase in aggregate demand increases real GDP, increasing the supply of real money and increasing the interest rate.

2 Which of the following best describes how the interest rate affects aggregate demand?
a A lower interest rate increases the quantity of investment demanded, increasing aggregate demand.
b A higher interest rate increases the quantity of investment demanded, increasing aggregate demand.
c A higher interest rate decreases the quantity of investment demanded, increasing aggregate demand.
d A higher interest rate increases consumption, increasing aggregate demand.
e A higher interest rate increases net exports, increasing aggregate demand.

3 Consider Figure 29.1. Why is the situation depicted *not* a consistent equilibrium?
a The level of aggregate demand is inconsistent with the interest rate.
b The money market and the *AS–AD* graph are not individually in equilibrium.
c The *AS–AD* equilibrium occurs at a different level of real GDP than the level of real GDP assumed for the demand curve for real money.
d The level of expenditure in part (b) is inconsistent with the level of expenditure in part (c).
e Aggregate demand is greater than aggregate supply.

4 Suppose Figure 29.1 depicts the actual current position of an economy. When this economy moves to equilibrium, real GDP will be
a less than $800 billion and the interest rate will be higher than 4%.
b less than $800 billion and the interest rate will be lower than 4%.
c more than $800 billion and the interest rate will be higher than 4%.
d more than $800 billion and the interest rate will be lower than 4%.
e none of the above.

5 A change in interest rates (price level held constant) affects aggregate demand through which one of the following changes?
a a shift of the interest-sensitive expenditure curve and movement along the aggregate demand curve
b a shift of both the demand for real money curve and the interest-sensitive expenditure curve
c a shift of both the interest-sensitive expenditure curve and the aggregate demand curve
d a movement along both the interest-sensitive expenditure curve and the aggregate demand curve
e a movement along the interest-sensitive expenditure curve and a shift of the aggregate demand curve

FIGURE **29.1**

(a)

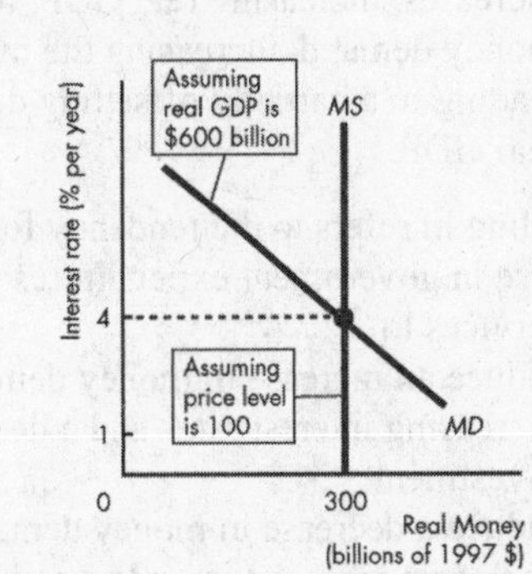

(b)

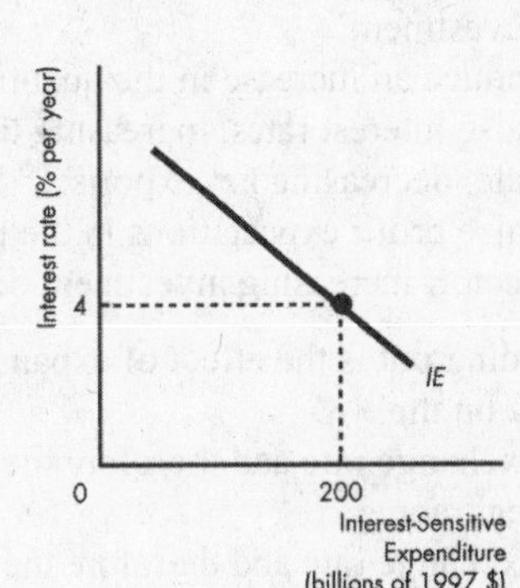

(c)

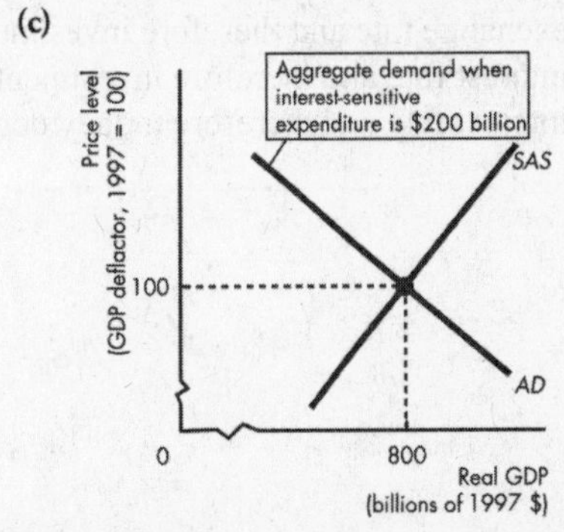

Fiscal Policy in the Short Run

6 Which of the following sequences best describes an expansionary fiscal policy? Government expenditures increase, therefore aggregate demand
  a increases, increasing real GDP, increasing money demand, decreasing the interest rate, further increasing real GDP.
  b increases, increasing the price level, increasing quantity of real money, decreasing the interest rate, further increasing real GDP.
  c decreases, increasing real GDP, increasing money demand, decreasing the interest rate, further increasing real GDP.
  d increases, decreasing the price level, increasing money demand, decreasing the interest rate, leading to a partially offsetting increase in real GDP.
  e increases, increasing real GDP, increasing money demand, increasing the interest rate, leading to a partially offsetting decrease in real GDP.

7 Crowding in refers to the tendency for an increase in government expenditures on goods and services to
  a induce an increase in money demand, increasing interest rates and a decrease in investment.
  b induce a decrease in money demand, decreasing interest rates and an increase in investment.
  c induce an increase in the quantity of money.
  d raise interest rates, increasing the exchange rate, decreasing net exports.
  e raise profit expectations in the private sector, increasing investment demand.

8 Crowding out is the effect of expansionary fiscal policy on the
  a exchange rate and therefore the quantity of real money.
  b exchange rate and therefore the level of imports.
  c exchange rate and therefore investment.
  d interest rate and therefore investment.
  e interest rate and therefore money demand.

9 The total impact of a *contractionary* fiscal policy is to decrease real GDP,
  a reduce the interest rate, and reduce investment.
  b reduce the interest rate, and increase investment.
  c increase the interest rate, and reduce investment.
  d increase the interest rate, and increase investment.
  e none of the above.

10 Overall, a tax cut will
  a increase aggregate demand by causing consumption to increase.
  b increase aggregate demand by causing the interest rate to decrease.
  c decrease aggregate demand by causing consumption to decrease.
  d decrease aggregate demand by causing the interest rate to increase.
  e decrease aggregate demand by causing investment to decrease.

11 Which of the following effects could offset fiscal policy?
  a The crowding-in effect
  b The exchange rate effect
  c The import effect
  d The consumption effect
  e The bond rate effect

Monetary Policy in the Short Run

12 Which of the following describes the start of a *second-round* effect of an expansionary monetary policy?
  a Interest rates decrease, Canadian dollar appreciates, prices of exports decrease, and prices of imports increase.
  b Interest rates increase, Canadian dollar depreciates, prices of exports increase, and prices of imports decrease.
  c Interest rates decrease, Canadian dollar appreciates, prices of exports increase, and prices of imports decrease.
  d Interest rates increase, Canadian dollar depreciates, prices of exports decrease, and prices of imports increase.
  e Interest rates decrease, investment increases, aggregate expenditure increases, real GDP increases, and demand for real money increases.

13 The stimulative effects of fiscal and monetary policy on aggregate demand are reduced when the resulting increase in the price level increases interest rates, which in turn decrease

- **a** just investment, but not net exports nor consumption.
- **b** just net exports, but not investment nor consumption.
- **c** just consumption, but not investment nor net exports.
- **d** both consumption and investment, but not net exports.
- **e** all three of consumption, investment, and net exports.

14 Consider the *AS–AD* model with unemployment. After an expansionary monetary policy has increased aggregate demand, the overall effect on real GDP is

- **a** a decrease because of the increase in the price level.
- **b** an increase even more than the initial aggregate demand effect because of the increase in the price level.
- **c** zero due to the increase in the price level.
- **d** zero due to the decrease in the price level.
- **e** an increase but less than the initial aggregate demand effect because of the increase in the price level.

15 The total impact of a contractionary monetary policy is to decrease real GDP,

- **a** reduce the interest rate, and reduce investment.
- **b** reduce the interest rate, and increase investment.
- **c** increase the interest rate, and reduce investment.
- **d** increase the interest rate, and increase investment.
- **e** none of the above.

16 An increase in the quantity of real money will eventually lead to an increase in real GDP, which will shift the demand curve for real money

- **a** leftward, causing the interest rate to decrease.
- **b** leftward, causing the interest rate to increase.
- **c** rightward, causing the interest rate to decrease.
- **d** rightward, causing the interest rate to increase.
- **e** rightward, causing the quantity of real money to increase.

Relative Effectiveness of Policies

17 Monetary policy will have the *smallest* effect on aggregate demand when the responsiveness of the demand for real money to the interest rate is

- **a** large and the responsiveness of expenditure to the interest rate is large.
- **b** large and the responsiveness of expenditure to the interest rate is small.
- **c** small and the responsiveness of aggregate supply to the interest rate is large.
- **d** small and the responsiveness of expenditure to the interest rate is small.
- **e** small and the responsiveness of expenditure to the interest rate is large.

18 Consider an economy where the demand for real money is very responsive to changes in the interest rate. The problem with monetary policy in this economy is that

- **a** there will be a high level of crowding out.
- **b** monetary policy will create changes in the exchange rate that offset the monetary policy.
- **c** a change in the interest rate creates only a small change in expenditure.
- **d** a change in the quantity of real money creates too large a change in the interest rate.
- **e** a change in the quantity of real money creates only a small change in the interest rate.

19 Statistical evidence from a variety of historical and national experiences suggests that

- **a** fiscal policy affects aggregate demand and monetary policy does not.
- **b** monetary policy affects aggregate demand and fiscal policy does not.
- **c** both fiscal policy and monetary policy affect aggregate demand.
- **d** neither fiscal policy nor monetary policy affect aggregate demand.
- **e** fiscal policy affected aggregate demand only during the Great Depression of the 1930s.

20 A Keynesian believes the economy is inherently

- **a** unstable, and fiscal policy is more important than monetary policy.
- **b** unstable, and monetary policy is more important than fiscal policy.
- **c** stable, and fiscal policy is more important than monetary policy.
- **d** stable, and monetary policy is more important than fiscal policy.
- **e** stable, and crowding out is strong.

Policy Actions at Full Employment

21 If the aggregate supply curve was vertical, expansionary fiscal policy would cause all of the following *except*
- **a** an increase in investment.
- **b** a decrease in the quantity of real money.
- **c** an increase in interest rates.
- **d** an increase in the price level.
- **e** a decrease in investment.

22 Which of the following is the long-run neutrality proposition?
- **a** Changes in the quantity of money change the price level only, not real variables.
- **b** Changes in the quantity of money change real variables only, not the price level.
- **c** In the long run, fiscal policy is 100% crowded out.
- **d** In the long run, investment is completely unresponsive to changes in the interest rate, so monetary policy does not work.
- **e** In the long run, money demand is completely unresponsive to changes in the interest rate, so fiscal policy does not work.

23 If there is an expansionary fiscal policy at full employment, which of the following effects does *not* occur in the long run?
- **a** crowding out
- **b** higher price level
- **c** international crowding out
- **d** labour shortages increase the wage rate
- **e** increases in money demand permanently increase the interest rate

Policy Coordination and Conflict

24 Coordinating fiscal and monetary policy is better for the economy because it
- **a** allows cheap financing of the deficit.
- **b** allows the desired change in interest rates by appropriately mixing monetary and fiscal policy.
- **c** has the opposite effects on the interest rate and the exchange rate.
- **d** can stop inflation.
- **e** none of the above.

25 Aggregate demand can be increased by either expansionary monetary policy or expansionary fiscal policy. Which of the following is a correct comparison?
- **a** The interest rate will increase under the monetary policy and decrease under the fiscal policy.
- **b** The interest rate will decrease under the monetary policy and increase under the fiscal policy.
- **c** The interest rate will increase under both.
- **d** The interest rate will decrease under both.
- **e** What happens to the interest rate depends on the size of the original policy effect.

Short Answer Problems

1 Trace the main steps following an increase in the quantity of real money.

2 Why does an increase in the quantity of real money have a smaller effect on aggregate demand if the demand for real money is very responsive to changes in the interest rate?

3 Explain how an increase in the quantity of real money increases aggregate demand through a change in the exchange rate.

4 How does crowding out take place?

ⓔ 5 Consider an economy that has real GDP less than potential, and needs an expansionary policy. Evaluate an expansionary fiscal policy versus an expansionary monetary policy, on the basis of the following four considerations:
- **a** the empirical evidence on the relative effectiveness of each policy
- **b** the impacts of each on expenditure
- **c** the impacts of each on potential GDP
- **d** the impacts of each on the deficit

6 Figure 29.2 depicts an economy. Note that MD_0 corresponds to real GDP = $400 billion, MD_1 corresponds to real GDP = $500 billion, and MD_2 corresponds to real GDP = $600 billion. MS_0 corresponds to a price level of 110, and AD_0 corresponds to an expenditure level of 100.

a What are the equilibrium values for real GDP, the interest rate, and expenditure?

b Is this equilibrium a consistent equilibrium? Why or why not?

FIGURE **29.2**

(a)

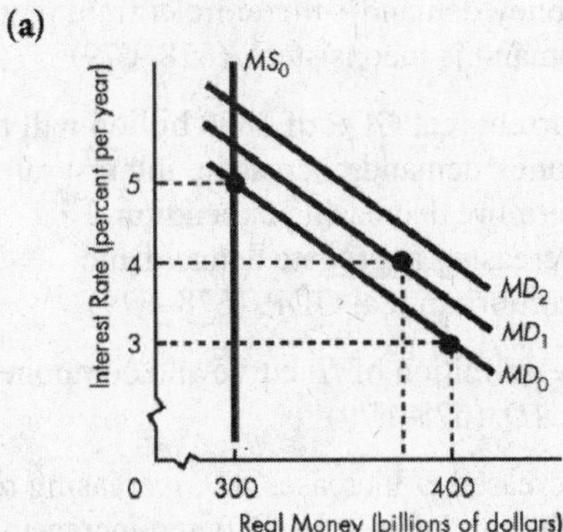

(b)

Interest Rate (percent per year)

5

4

3

IE

0

100 150 200

Interest-Sensitive Expenditure (billions of dollars)

(c)

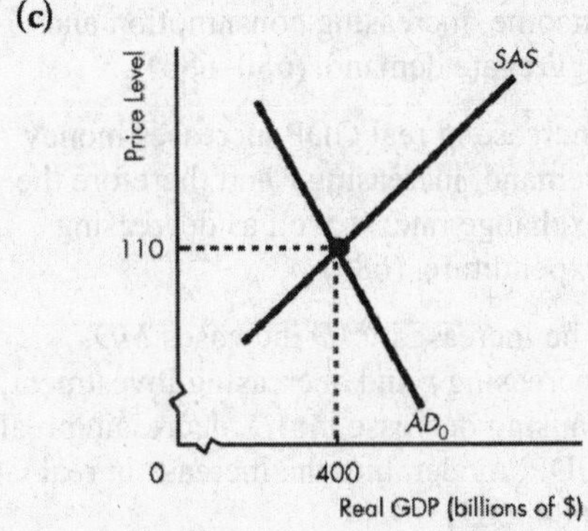

7 Consider again the economy depicted by Figure 29.2. Suppose that the Bank of Canada increases the quantity of real money from $300 billion to $400 billion.

a What is the initial effect on the interest rate? Illustrate this effect on Figure 29.2.

b What effect will this change in the interest rate have on expenditure?

c As a result of this change in expenditure, what happens to the quantity of real GDP demanded if the multiplier is 2? Illustrate this change on Figure 29.2.

d As best you can (not worrying too much about exact numbers), show on Figure 29.2 what the final equilibrium is after this change, explaining what has happened to the interest rate, expenditure, real GDP, and the price level as a result of the increase in the quantity of real money.

8 Suppose that as a result of the increase in real GDP in Short Answer Problem 7, firms' expectations of future profits increase.

a What happens to expenditure as a result?

b What will be the first- and second-round results of this increase in firms' profit expectations? Specifically, what happens to *AD*, *IE*, *MD*, *r*, real GDP, and the price level? (A written explanation is sufficient.)

9 Suppose the economy in Short Answer Problem 7 was initially at full employment. Describe what would happen in the *AD–SAS* equilibrium in the long run after the increase in the quantity of real money.

10 When Canada had a large debt in the early 1990s, some analysts called for the Bank of Canada to erase the debt by printing money and buying up all the outstanding government bonds. Explain why the Bank of Canada strongly resisted this policy suggestion.

ANSWERS

True/False and Explain

1 F Increase in r leads to movement up along *IE* curve. (678)

2 T Draw a graph. (678)

3 F More real GDP means more spending, increasing desired inventory holdings, shift *rightward* in demand curve. (678)

4 F Depends on relative strength of each effect, which is unknown. (683)

5 F Increase in *G* increases real GDP and *P*, increasing *MD* and decreasing *MS*, creating an increase in r and therefore a decrease in *I*. (680–683)

6 F Increase in government expenditures increases real GDP, increasing money demand, increasing r, increasing demand for Canadian dollar, increasing the exchange rate. (683)

7 T Increase in *MS* decreases r, increasing *I*, which shifts *AD* rightward. (684–685)

8 F Increase in *MS* creates an excess supply of money, decreasing interest rates. (684–687)

9 F Increase in *MS* decreases r, decreasing demand for Canadian assets, decreasing demand for Canadian dollar and therefore decreasing the exchange rate. (687)

10 T ΔMS works by Δr creating ΔIE and therefore ΔAD, so if impact of r on *IE* is larger, impact of ΔMS on *AD* is larger. (688)

11 F Steep *IE* curve is not responsive to an increase in r. Crowding out happens due to expansionary fiscal policy creating an increase in r, and the smaller the impact of the increase in r, the smaller the crowding out. (687)

12 T See text discussion. (688–689)

ⓒ **13 T** In the long run, the economy returns to a full-employment equilibrium. (690–691)

14 T The increase in government expenditures shifts *AD* curve rightward, but net effect is zero for real GDP. (690)

15 T By picking the appropriate mixture of fiscal policy (which tends to increase r) and monetary policy (which tends to decrease r), the authorities can have no change in r, and therefore no crowding out. (692–693)

Multiple-Choice

1 d Increases in aggregate demand increase real GDP which increase spending and money demand and therefore the interest rate. (678)

2 a See text description. (678)

ⓒ **3 c** The higher equilibrium real GDP will shift money demand—therefore current money demand is inconsistent. (678–679)

ⓒ **4 a** Current real GDP of $800 billion will raise money demand, increasing interest rate, and therefore decreasing expenditure, decreasing aggregate demand and equilibrium real GDP. (678–679)

5 e By definition of *IE* curve and components of *AD*. (678–679)

6 e Increased *G* increases *AD*, increasing real GDP (and therefore *MD*) and increasing P (and therefore decreasing quantity of real money). Both increase r, and decrease quantity interest-sensitive expenditure, decreasing *AD* and real GDP. (680–683)

7 e Definition. (683)

8 d Definition. (683)

9 b Decrease in real GDP and *P* decreases money demand and increases *MS*, decreasing interest rate and therefore increasing investment expenditure. (680–683)

10 a Decrease in taxes increases disposable income, increasing consumption and aggregate demand. (680–683)

11 b Increase in real GDP increases money demand, increasing r and therefore the exchange rate, as well as decreasing expenditure. (683)

12 e The increase in *AD* increases *MD*, increasing r and decreasing investment, causing decrease in *AD*, decreasing real GDP, moderating the increase in real GDP. (684–687)

13 e Increase in price level creates an increase in r, increasing cost of borrowing, lowering C and I; increase in r increases demand for Canadian dollar, increasing exchange rate and decreasing NX. (684–687)

14 e Shift rightward in AD curve increases price level leads, increasing r and decreasing quantity demanded of real GDP. (684–687)

15 c Decrease in real GDP and P decreases money demand and increases MS, decreasing interest rate (somewhat offsetting original increase), increasing expenditure but not enough to overcome initial decrease in expenditure. (684–687)

16 d Money demand depends positively on real GDP, so higher real GDP increases money demand and increases interest rate. (684–687)

17 b Sensitive MD implies a ΔMS leads to small Δr, and unresponsive IE implies Δr leads to small Δ investment. (688)

18 e Because with sensitive money demand, Δ interest rate needed to get money market in equilibrium after Δ quantity of real money is small. (688)

19 c See text discussion. (688–689)

20 a See text discussion. (688–689)

21 a Expansionary policy creates crowding out (decrease in I). (690–691)

22 a Definition. (691)

23 e Real GDP is unchanged, so money demand is unchanged. (690–691)

24 b Monetary and fiscal policy have opposite effects on interest rates—using both at same time in different strengths means can get Δr at desired level. (692)

25 b Under fiscal policy, crowding out increases interest rate. Under monetary policy, increase in quantity of real money decreases interest rate. (692)

Short Answer Problems

1 If there is an increase in the quantity of real money,

- The money supply curve will shift rightward and the interest rate will decrease.
- The lower interest rate will cause investment to increase.
- The increase in investment increases aggregate demand.
- The increase in aggregate demand increases real GDP and the price level.
- Increasing real GDP causes the demand curve for real money to shift rightward and the increasing price level causes the money supply curve to shift leftward, causing the interest rate to increase.
- The higher interest rate will cause interest-sensitive expenditure to decrease.
- The decrease in expenditure means that aggregate demand decreases somewhat, but the economy converges to a new equilibrium with higher real GDP.

2 If the demand for real money is very responsive to changes in the interest rate, the demand curve for real money is very flat. Thus when the quantity of money increases and the money supply curve shifts rightward, the resulting change in the equilibrium interest rate will be small. *Ceteris paribus*, a small interest rate change will lead to a small change in investment and a small change in aggregate demand.

3 An increase in the quantity of money shifts the money supply curve rightward and decrease the interest rate. The lower interest rate (relative to interest rates in other countries) will cause people to want to sell low-interest Canadian financial assets and buy relatively high-interest foreign financial assets. Therefore the demand for dollars decreases and the demand for foreign currencies increases, which results in a lower exchange rate relative to foreign currencies. This decrease in the exchange rate will cause net exports to increase, as foreigners can now buy Canadian goods for less (in terms of their currencies) and Canadians must pay more (in dollars) for foreign goods. The increase in net exports creates an increase in aggregate demand.

4 Crowding out is the tendency for expansionary fiscal policy to cause the interest rate to increase and thus investment to decline. Expansionary fiscal policy "crowds out" investment. An increase in government expenditure on goods and services increases real GDP and the price level, causing the demand curve for real money to shift rightward, and the money supply curve to shift leftward. Thus the equilibrium interest rate will increase.

© **5 a** The empirical evidence is that both policies work with a fair degree of strength, so you could pick either.

b An expansionary fiscal policy raises interest rates, and therefore will decrease investment, while an expansionary monetary policy decreases interest rates and will raise investment. On these grounds, you would tend to pick monetary policy.

c The fiscal policy decreases investment, which means in the long run less capital stock and less growth of potential GDP, while the monetary policy has the opposite effect. On these grounds, you would tend to pick monetary policy.

d Expansionary fiscal policy usually means some combination of more spending and lower taxes, which leads to a higher deficit. Expansionary monetary policy has no impact on the deficit, so you would tend to pick it.

6 a The equilibrium value for real GDP is at the intersection of the AD_0 and SAS curves—$400 billion. The equilibrium value for the interest rate is 5 percent, since the relevant MD curve is MD_0 when real GDP is $400 billion. At an interest rate of 5 percent, expenditure is $100 billion (part (b)).

b This equilibrium is a consistent equilibrium because equilibrium real GDP is $400 billion when the interest rate is 5 percent and the equilibrium interest rate is 5 percent when real GDP is $400 billion. In other words, it is a consistent equilibrium because the values of real GDP and the interest rate that give money market equilibrium and AS–AD equilibrium are the same.

7 a The initial effect of an increase in the quantity of real money from $300 billion to $400 billion is to decrease the interest rate from 5 percent to 3 percent. This shift is illustrated in part (a) of Figure 29.2 Solution as the shift from MS_0 to MS_1.

b The decrease in the interest rate from 5 percent to 3 percent will increase expenditure from $100 billion to $200 billion.

c If the multiplier is 2, the $100 billion increase in expenditure translates into a rightward shift of the AD curve by $200 billion (quantity of real GDP demanded rises by $200 billion), as shown.

d The increase in the quantity of real GDP demanded will raise real GDP and the price level. The rise in real GDP will shift the MD curve rightward, and the rise in the price level will shift the MS curve leftward, as shown in Figure 29.2 Solution. Your graph might have different numerical values, but the final value of the interest rate should be between 3 percent and 5 percent, etc. The result is a shift leftward in the AD curve to AD_2, and a movement along this new AD curve to the new equilibrium with real GDP = $500 billion and the price level = 120.

FIGURE **29.2** SOLUTION

(a)

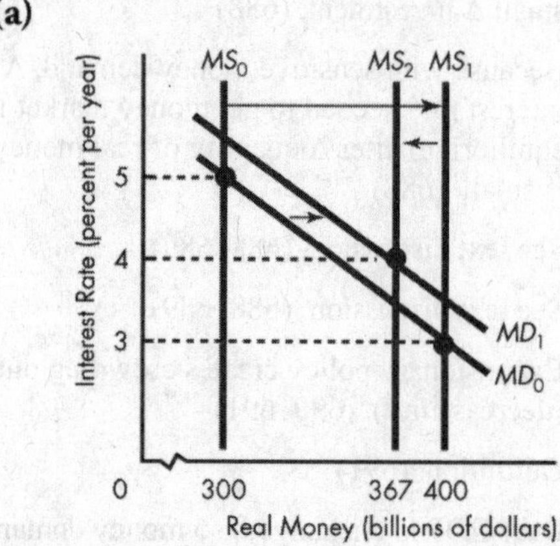

(b)

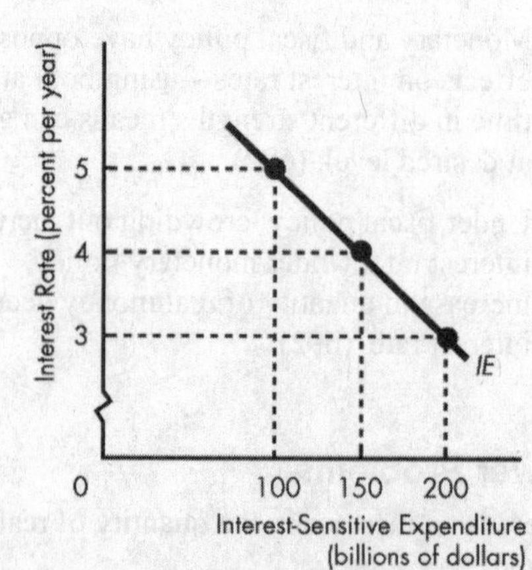

(c)

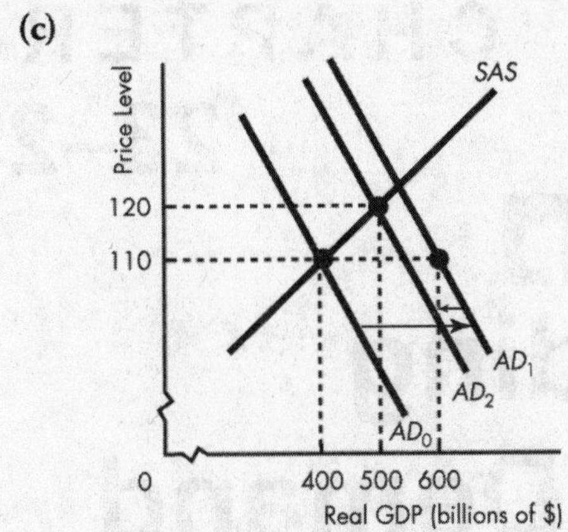

8 a The higher profit expectations leads firms to raise their investment demand, shifting the *IE* curve rightward.

b The higher investment demand increases the quantity of real GDP demanded—the *AD* curve shifts rightward. The shift in the curve leads to higher real GDP and a higher price level, which leads to the second-round effects—real money demand increases as a result of the higher real GDP and the quantity of real money decreases due to the higher price level, leading to higher interest rates, which in turn lead to lower expenditure, decreasing aggregate demand, and lower real GDP, which somewhat crowds out the first-round effects.

9 If the economy was initially at full employment, after the move to the new equilibrium at the intersection of AD_2 and *SAS*, the economy is in an above-full-employment equilibrium. As a result, there will be a shortage of labour, which will lead to an increase in the wage rate. This increase in the wage rate increases the costs of production, and aggregate supply decreases—the *SAS* starts shifting leftward, until the economy goes back to full employment at the original level of real GDP, with a higher price level.

10 If the Bank of Canada buys up the debt, this is equivalent to an enormous open-market purchase of government securities. The result will be a large rise in the quantity of money, which will lower interest rates, increase interest-sensitive expenditure, and shift the *AD* curve rightward, creating strong inflationary pressure. Since the Bank considers resisting inflation its primary objective, it would strongly resist such a proposal.

CHAPTERS 23–29

Part 8 Wrap Up

Understanding Aggregate Demand and Inflation

PROBLEM

The Canadian economy is originally in a full-employment equilibrium. Suppose that the U.S. economy *unexpectedly* goes into recession.

a Holding constant the price level, carefully explain (and show on a graph) what these changes do to aggregate expenditure and aggregate demand. Explain what happens to each component of aggregate expenditure and real GDP.

b Next, show on your graph and explain what happens to aggregate expenditure and aggregate demand in the short run when the price level adjusts.

c The Bank of Canada decides to redress the economy's problems by carrying out an expansionary monetary policy. Give an example of the changes to the overnight rate target and the type of open market operation the Bank of Canada would carry out. Show what happens to the balance sheets of the Bank of Canada and the banking sector as a result of the initial impacts of the operation. What is the overall impact of expansionary monetary policy on bank reserves and the overnight rate?

d Explain what this policy will do to interest rates, investment, net exports, and aggregate demand, holding constant the price level.

e Next, with the price level adjusting, explain what this policy does to the *AS–AD* equilibrium in the short run.

f Does the quantity theory of money hold in this economy?

Midterm Examination

You should allocate 56 minutes for this examination (28 questions, 2 minutes per question). For each question, choose the best answer.

1 The consumption function shows the relationship between consumption expenditure and
- **a** the interest rate.
- **b** the price level.
- **c** disposable income.
- **d** saving.
- **e** nominal income.

2 A *contractionary* fiscal policy leads to
- **a** a rightward shift in the *AD* curve equal to the multiplier times the policy change.
- **b** a leftward shift in the *AD* curve equal to the multiplier times the policy change.
- **c** a leftward shift in the *SAS* curve.
- **d** an increase in *Y* equal to the multiplier times the policy change, in the short run.
- **e** an increase in *Y* equal to the multiplier times the policy change, in the long run.

3 A chartered bank can create money by
- **a** selling some of its investment securities.
- **b** increasing its reserves.
- **c** lending its excess reserves.
- **d** printing more cheques.
- **e** converting reserves into securities.

4 Which of the following quotations best describes the interest rate parity effect?
a "The recent high Canadian interest rate has increased the demand for the Canadian dollar."
b "The market feeling is that the Canadian dollar is overvalued and will likely appreciate."
c "The price of bananas is the same in Canada and the United States, adjusting for the exchange rate."
d "The expected appreciation of the Canadian dollar is currently lowering demand for it."
e None of the above.

ct 5 Which of the following quotations *correctly* describes the impact of monetary policy on the economy?
a "House sales are down a lot, due to the lower interest rates."
b "The lower interest rates created by the central bank are creating lower exports."
c "The tightening of monetary policy is helping sell goods abroad."
d "Businesses are investing more, now that interest rates have become higher."
e "The lower interest rates created by the central bank are creating more jobs."

6 International crowding out refers to the tendency for an increase in government expenditures on goods and services to induce a(n)
a decrease in interest rates, decreasing the exchange rate, increasing net exports.
b decrease in interest rates, leading to a withdrawal of foreign funds from Canada.
c increase in interest rates, decreasing the exchange rate, increasing net exports.
d increase in interest rates, increasing the exchange rate, increasing net exports.
e increase in interest rates, increasing the exchange rate, decreasing net exports.

7 If real GDP is less than aggregate planned expenditure,
a aggregate planned expenditure will increase.
b real GDP will decrease.
c the price level must decrease to restore equilibrium.
d imports must be too large.
e aggregate planned expenditure will decrease.

8 Which of the following is *not* a source of budgetary revenues?
a personal income taxes
b transfer payments
c corporate income taxes
d indirect taxes
e investment income

9 Consider the following data on the economy of Adanac:

Currency reserves of private banks	$ 5 billion
Currency in circulation	15 billion
Demand deposits of banks	40 billion
Demand deposits of other financial institutions	50 billion
Personal savings deposits at other financial institutions	125 billion
Nonpersonal notice deposits at banks	200 billion

In this economy, what is the value (in billions of dollars) of M1? of M2+?
a 105; 230
b 110; 235
c 55; 430
d 55; 230
e 60; 430

10 Which of the following would cause the dollar to depreciate against the yen?
a an increase in the Canadian monetary supply
b an increase in interest rates in Canada
c a decrease in interest rates in Japan
d an increase in the expected future exchange rate
e an increase in the current exchange rate

11 A rise in the natural rate of unemployment is shown as a
a rightward shift in the long-run Phillips curve only.
b leftward shift in the long-run Phillips curve only.
c rightward shift in the short-run Phillips curve only.
d leftward shift in both the short-run and long-run Phillips curves.
e rightward shift in both the short-run and long-run Phillips curves.

12 Suppose OPEC unexpectedly collapses, decreasing the price of oil. This is a positive aggregate supply shock. As a result, in the short run the price level will
a increase and real GDP will increase.
b increase and real GDP will decrease.
c decrease and real GDP will increase.
d decrease and real GDP will decrease.
e increase and real GDP will stay the same.

13 An open market purchase of government securities by the Bank of Canada will

a increase bank reserves and thus increase the overnight rate.

b decrease bank reserves and thus decrease the overnight rate.

c increase bank reserves and thus decrease the overnight rate.

d decrease bank reserves and thus increase the overnight rate.

e decrease bank reserves but increase the overnight rate if banks have excess reserves.

14 When is there complete crowding out of an expansionary fiscal policy?

a if the economy was originally in an under full-employment equilibrium

b if the economy was originally in a full-employment equilibrium

c when there is policy conflict with the Bank of Canada

d when there is policy coordination to ensure the resulting change in the interest rate is zero

e if there is a liquidity trap in the money market

15 Suppose that investment increases by $10 billion. Which of the following *reduces* the effect of this increase in autonomous expenditure on equilibrium real GDP?

a an increase in the marginal propensity to consume

b a decrease in the marginal propensity to import

c a decrease in the marginal tax rate

d a steeper *SAS* curve

e a flatter *SAS* curve

16 When induced taxes are added to an economy with only autonomous taxes,

a fiscal policy multipliers are made stronger.

b discretionary fiscal policy is eliminated.

c there will always be a structural deficit.

d there will always be a cyclical deficit.

e fluctuations in aggregate expenditure are reduced.

17 An increase in the exchange rate lowers the quantity demanded of Canadian dollars because

a exports become cheaper for foreigners, increasing demand for Canadian exports and therefore decreasing the quantity demanded of the Canadian dollar.

b imports become cheaper for Canadians, increasing demand for imports and therefore decreasing the quantity demanded of the Canadian dollar.

c imports become more expensive for Canadians, decreasing demand for imports and therefore decreasing the quantity demanded of the Canadian dollar.

d expected profits increase from selling foreign exchange and buying Canadian dollars, decreasing the quantity demanded of the Canadian dollar.

e expected profits decrease from buying Canadian dollars, decreasing the quantity demanded of the Canadian dollar.

18 According to the quantity theory of money, a decrease in the quantity of money will cause

a both the price level and real GDP to decrease.

b both the price level and real GDP to increase.

c the price level to decrease, but real GDP will stay constant.

d the price level to decrease and real GDP to increase.

e the price level to increase and real GDP to decrease.

19 An attempt to stimulate the economy by using the overnight rate target would

a lower the bank rate and the settlement balances rate, creating more excess reserves, creating more loans and lower interest rates on loans.

b raise the bank rate and the settlement balances rate, creating more excess reserves, creating more loans and lower interest rates on loans.

c raise the bank rate and the settlement balances rate, creating less excess reserves, creating less loans and higher interest rates on loans.

d lower the bank rate and the settlement balances rate, creating less excess reserves, creating less loans and higher interest rates on loans.

e lower the bank rate and the settlement balances rate, creating more excess reserves, creating more loans and higher interest rates on loans.

20 There will be no crowding out if
- **a** demand for real money is totally unresponsive to changes in the price level.
- **b** money supply is totally unresponsive to changes in the interest rate.
- **c** investment is very responsive to changes in the interest rate.
- **d** investment is totally unresponsive to changes in real GDP.
- **e** demand for real money is totally unresponsive to changes in real GDP.

21 Which of the following does *not* necessarily occur when the goods and services market and the money market are simultaneously and jointly in equilibrium.
- **a** The quantity of real money supplied equals the quantity of real money demanded.
- **b** The quantity of real GDP supplied equals the quantity of real GDP demanded.
- **c** The interest rate in the money market equilibrium matches the interest rate needed for aggregate demand to be correct.
- **d** The price level from the goods and services market equilibrium matches the price level needed for the real money supply to be correct.
- **e** Real GDP equals potential GDP.

22 Whenever the inflation rate is above the target, or there is a positive output gap, the Bank of Sarconia raises the overnight rate target. The Bank of Sarconia is following
- **a** an inflation targeting rule.
- **b** a McCallum rule.
- **c** a Taylor rule.
- **d** an exchange rate target rule.
- **e** a monetary target rule.

23 An increase in expected inflation raises the nominal interest rate because
- **a** borrowers require compensation for the inflation eroding the value of money.
- **b** lenders require compensation for the inflation eroding the value of money.
- **c** the inflation creates higher transactions costs.
- **d** the real rate of interest rises by an amount equal to the increase in expected inflation.
- **e** none of the above.

24 Suppose that the Bank of Canada is following a flexible exchange rate policy. What happens if the demand for Canadian dollars increases?
- **a** The Bank of Canada will buy Canadian dollars.
- **b** The Bank of Canada will sell Canadian dollars.
- **c** The Bank of Canada will buy foreign exchange.
- **d** The Bank of Canada will sell foreign exchange.
- **e** The Bank of Canada will do nothing.

25 The amount of real money people want to hold will increase if either real income increases or the
- **a** price level increases.
- **b** price level decreases.
- **c** interest rate increases.
- **d** interest rate decreases.
- **e** price of bonds decreases.

26 Suppose that the desired reserve ratio is 0.20 and the currency drain ratio is 0.30. What is the money multiplier?
- **a** 0.39
- **b** 2.0
- **c** 2.4
- **d** 2.6
- **e** 13

27 If the *MPC* is 0.6, and the slope of the *AE* function is 0.4, what is the autonomous tax multiplier?
- **a** −1.67
- **b** −1.50
- **c** −1.00
- **d** 1.00
- **e** impossible to calculate without further information

28 In a recent study, the University of Underfunded argued that it created four times as many jobs as people it hired directly. This argument illustrates the idea of
- **a** the marginal propensity to consume.
- **b** the multiplier.
- **c** government spending.
- **d** the tax multiplier.
- **e** universities wasting taxpayers' dollars.

ANSWERS

Problem

a The U.S. recession decreases their imports of Canadian goods, which means a decrease in our exports. This decrease in exports decreases aggregate planned expenditure, represented by a shift downward in the *AE* curve to AE_b in Figure P8.1. The decrease in aggregate expenditure increases inventories, which leads to firms lowering production, decreasing real GDP by a multiple of the initial decrease in aggregate expenditure—the new equilibrium is at *b*, compared with the original equilibrium at *a*. The shift down in aggregate expenditure is also shown as a shift leftward in aggregate demand in part (b) of the graph.

Consumption is lower because of the decrease in real GDP. Investment is unchanged. Government purchases are unchanged. Exports are lower because of the shock, and imports are also lower because of the decrease in real GDP.

FIGURE **P8.1**

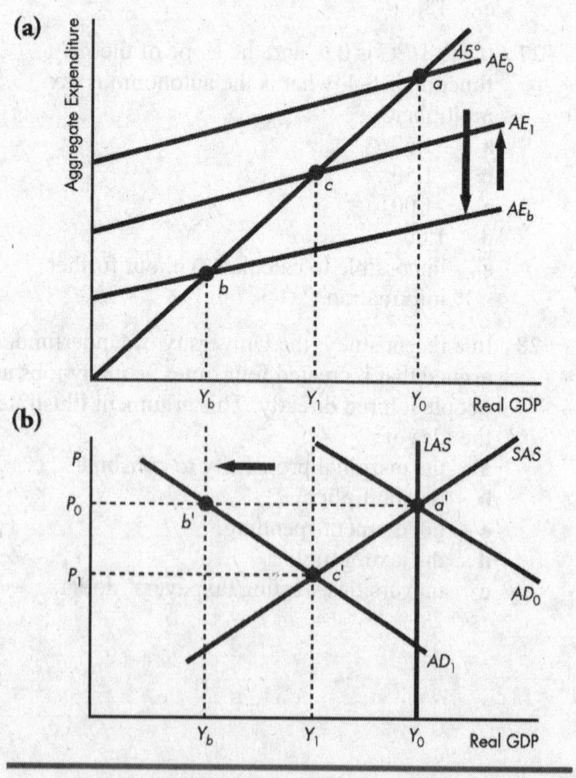

b After the shock, at the original price level aggregate demand is less than aggregate supply ($Y_b < Y_0$). This surplus leads to a decrease in the price level. *Since the decrease in AD was unexpected, so is the decrease in the price level—there is no shift in the SAS curve.* This decrease in the price level in turn leads to a decrease in the real quantity supplied in the short run (the movement from *a'* to *c'*), as well as an increase in the real money supply, which leads to a decrease in the interest rate, an increase in investment and aggregate expenditure (from AE_b to AE_1), and a movement along the aggregate demand curve from *b'* to *c'*.

c The Bank of Canada wants to lower interest rates, and will do so by lowering the overnight target range (lowering the bank rate and the settlements balance rate) and by purchasing government securities. The Bank of Canada buys these securities from private banks and pays for them by crediting the banks' deposits at the Bank of Canada (which are reserves). The result of such a purchase is shown in Table P8.1.

TABLE **P8.1**

Bank of Canada		Banking System	
Assets	**Liabilities**	**Assets**	**Liabilities**
Government securities (+)	Bank deposits (+)	Reserves (+)	
		Government securities (–)	

The lower overnight target rate and the open market operation lead to excess reserves in the banking system. The banks will try to increase their overnight lending and reduce their overnight borrowing, which pushes down overnight rates.

d The lower overnight rates create substitution effects and lower other interest rates in the economy. The lower interest rate leads to an increase in interest-sensitive expenditure and aggregate demand, as well as to a decrease in the demand for Canadian dollars and therefore a decrease in the value of the Canadian dollar and an increase in net exports and aggregate demand.

e The higher aggregate demand translates into a shift rightward in the aggregate demand curve, which increases the price level, triggering a movement along the short-run aggregate supply curve, increasing real GDP.

f No, it does not, because one of the crucial assumptions of the quantity theory does not hold—since the economy is in the short run, real GDP is not independent of changes in the quantity of money.

MIDTERM EXAMINATION

1 c Definition. (536–541)

2 b Multiplier calculation holds constant the price level. (576–579)

3 c Lending its reserves is done by crediting borrowers' deposits, creating more deposits = more money. (596–600)

4 a If two currencies do not have the same interest rate, market conditions will change the demand for assets and the dollar. (620–622)

ⓒⓣ **5 e** Decrease in r leads to increase in C (so **a** wrong), increase in I (so **d** wrong), increase in NX (so **b** and **c** wrong), and they all lead to increase in AD, which creates more jobs. (663–669)

6 e Definition. (683)

7 a Firms' sales > production decreases inventories, leading to increased production. New equilibrium has higher real GDP = higher AE. (541–545)

8 b Outlay. (564–565)

9 c M1 = currency in circulation + banks' demand deposits, M2+ = M1 + (personal savings and nonpersonal notice deposits at banks) + deposits at other financial institutions. (591–592)

10 a **a** decreases interest rates, which decrease demand for Canadian dollars. **b**–**d** are increase in demand, **e** move along, not a shift. (619–622)

11 e $LRPC$ is vertical at new higher natural rate, and $SRPC$ shifts with it since it crosses $LRPC$ at natural rate. (646)

12 c This will lead to a fall in the cost of production and a rightward shift in SAS. (635–637)

13 c Bank of Canada pays for securities by crediting banks' reserves, which creates excess reserves and more lending, lowering the overnight rate. (661)

14 b At full employment, leftward shift SAS offsets rightward shift AD. (690)

15 d This effect leads to more ΔP, less ΔY. All others make effect larger. (551–555)

16 e Induced taxes act as automatic stabilizer. Multipliers are weaker, can still do discretionary policy, and there may or may not be a cyclical/structural deficit depending on other factors. (574–576)

17 e Definition of expected profit effect. (615–616)

18 c In long run, real GDP is independent of Δ quantity of money. (638–639)

19 a Decrease in bank rate and settlement balances rate decreases cost of borrowing from central bank, creating decrease in desired reserves, creating excess reserves, creating increase in loans, etc. (658–662)

20 e Because then Δ real GDP due to fiscal policy has no impact on real money demand or on interest rates. (680–683)

21 e Equilibrium might be short-run unemployment or above-full-employment equilibrium. (678–679)

22 c See Taylor rule formula. Other formulas ignore output gap. (670–671)

23 b Borrowers are paying the money, so are happy if its value erodes, the higher transactions costs do not affect interest rates, and the real rate is set independently of inflation. (649)

24 e Under flexible exchange rate regime, the Bank ignores the exchange rate market. (623–624)

25 d Real money demand is not affected by Δ price level, decrease in price of bonds creates increase in interest rate, which lowers quantity of real money demanded. (601–603)

26 d Money multiplier = (1 + currency drain ratio)/(currency drain ratio + desired reserve ratio) = (1 + 0.3)/(0.2 + 0.3) = 2.6. (599–600)

27 c Autonomous tax multiplier = $-MPC$/(1 – slope of AE) = –0.6/(1 – 0.4) = –1.0. (572–573)

28 b University spending creates multiplier effects. (546–549

Chapter 30 The Economy at Full Employment

KEY CONCEPTS

Real GDP and Employment

The production possibilities frontier is the boundary between combinations of goods that can be produced and those that cannot.

- Such a relationship exists between real GDP and leisure—more real GDP requires less leisure and more time spent working.
- The **production function** (*PF*) shows the relationship between real GDP and quantity of labour employed, all other influences constant.
  - Increase in quantity of labour employed creates movement up along *PF*.

Labour productivity is real GDP per hour of labour, and increases with

- More physical capital.
- More **human capital** (people's knowledge and skills). Human capital can increase from **learning-by-doing** (on-the-job education from experience).
- Technological advances.

An increase in labour productivity shifts *PF* upward.

The Labour Market and Aggregate Supply

The labour market determines the quantity of labour hours employed and real GDP supplied.

- **Quantity of labour demanded** = number of labour hours hired by all firms.
- **Demand for labour** (*LD*) = quantity of labour demanded at each real wage rate.
- **Real wage rate** = **money wage rate** (in current dollars)/price level.
- **Marginal product of labour** = Δ real GDP per hour of additional labour.
  - As labour hours increase, marginal product of labour decreases (law of diminishing marginal returns).
- Firms hire labour as long as marginal product of labour > real wage rate. *LD* curve is marginal product of labour curve.
- Increase in real wage, movement up *LD* curve.
- *LD* curve shifts rightward if physical capital increases or technology advances.

Quantity of labour supplied = number of hours labour services households plan to work.

- **Supply of labour** (*LS*)—quantity of labour supplied at each real wage rate.
- Increase in real wage rate increases quantity labour supplied because
  - Hours per person increase (if effect of increasing opportunity cost of leisure outweighs effect of desire for more leisure).
  - Labour force participation rate increases.

Real wage rate adjusts to create full-employment labour market equilibrium where *LD* = *LS*.

- Level of real GDP at full employment is potential GDP.
- Vertical **long-run aggregate supply curve** is relationship between quantity of real GDP supplied and price level when real GDP = potential GDP.
  - When *P* changes, money wage rate also changes to keep real wage rate at the level that makes *LD* = *LS*, so that employment is

unchanged and therefore *LAS* curve is vertical at potential GDP.

- ♦ Upward-sloping **short-run aggregate supply (*SAS*) curve** is relationship between quantity of real GDP supplied and price level, money wage and all other influences constant.
  - Along *SAS* (with constant money wage), if *P* increases, real wage falls, and quantity of labour demanded increases and real GDP increases.

Changes in Potential GDP

Real GDP increases if economy recovers from recession or potential GDP increases.

- ♦ Potential GDP increases if population or labour productivity increase.
- ♦ Increasing population increases labour supply.
  - As a result, real wage rate decreases, increasing hiring and potential GDP.
- ♦ Increase in labour productivity increases demand for labour.
  - As a result, real wage rate increases, quantity labour supplied increases, and potential GDP increases.

Unemployment at Full Employment

The unemployment rate at full employment is the natural rate of unemployment.

- ♦ Two broad reasons for unemployment—job search and job rationing.
- ♦ **Job search** is the activity of looking for an acceptable job.
  - Constant change in labour market implies there is always job search.
  - Normal job search generates the natural rate of unemployment.
  - If real wage rate > equilibrium, job search high.
  - Job search increases if proportion of working-age population increases, if unemployment compensation increases, or if technological change increases structural change.
- ♦ **Job rationing** is paying an above-equilibrium wage that creates a surplus of labour and frictional unemployment. Two reasons:
  - Firms pay **efficiency wages**—higher wages designed to maximize profits by increasing work effort, decreasing labour turnover rate (therefore lowering recruiting costs), and increasing quality of labour.
  - **Minimum wage** legally keeps wages above equilibrium value for some workers.
- ♦ Job rationing creates a surplus of labour that adds extra job search.

HELPFUL HINTS

1 This chapter deepens our understanding of aggregate supply: the relationship between the price level and the quantity of real GDP supplied. Chapter 22 introduced the basic *AS–AD* model, and showed some of its usefulness in exploring the economy. Chapters 23–29 examined aggregate demand in detail, while Chapters 30 and 31 examine aggregate supply in detail.

2 Our work at understanding aggregate supply is broken down into two related issues—the production function and the labour market.

The first issue is: How is the quantity of real GDP supplied determined in general? When the capital stock and the state of technology are given, the maximum amount of real GDP that can be produced depends on the quantity of labour employed. This relationship between employment and the quantity of real GDP supplied is captured by the production function.

To understand how the quantity of real GDP supplied is determined, we need to pursue the second issue: How is the level of employment determined? The answer is in the labour market. The demand for labour is determined by firms, and the supply of labour is determined by households. If money wages continuously adjust to clear the labour market, the level of employment will always be the equilibrium level with full employment. If, on the other hand, money wages are fixed in the short run, the level of employment can deviate from its equilibrium level.

Since our interest is in aggregate supply, we want to know how the quantity of real GDP supplied varies as the price level varies. This desire brings us to a third issue: How do changes in the price level affect employment and real GDP? It turns out that if money wages continuously adjust, the level of employment, and thus the quantity of real GDP supplied, is independent of the price level. Whatever the price level, the wage rate will adjust so that the unique equilibrium level of employment is achieved. This adjustment implies a long-run aggregate supply curve that is vertical at potential GDP.

On the other hand, if wages are constant, the level of employment, and thus the quantity of real GDP supplied, depends on the actual value of the price level relative to the expected value of the price level. If the price level turns out to be equal to its expected value, the equilibrium level of employment (full employment) results. If the price level is higher than expected, the level of employment turns out to be higher than the equilibrium value and thus real GDP supplied will be larger than potential GDP. If the price level is lower than expected, employment will be less than equilibrium and real GDP supplied will be less than potential GDP. This result implies a positively sloped short-run aggregate supply curve.

3 As Chapter 21 explained, there are four different *types* of unemployment—frictional, structural, seasonal, and cyclical. The first three of these make up the natural rate of unemployment.

Defining the types of unemployment does not *explain* them. This chapter provides two explanations of unemployment to help us see the origin of the three types of natural unemployment.

Frictional unemployment comes from job search (there is always job search in the economy because of changes in the fortunes of individual firms, people searching for good matches), and from job rationing, leading to a wage above the equilibrium wage, with queuing for jobs as a result. It is often the result of a downturn in one firm.

Structural unemployment comes from excessive job search in times of structural change due to technological change. It is due to a downturn in a specific industry or region.

Seasonal unemployment is due to job search in specific seasons when certain types of jobs do not exist.

SELF-TEST

True/False and Explain

Real GDP and Employment

1 The production possibilities frontier is the relationship between real GDP and the quantity of labour employed.

2 More human capital causes a movement along the production function.

3 The only way labour productivity can increase is if there is more physical capital.

The Labour Market and Aggregate Supply

4 If the real wage rate decreases, the opportunity cost effect implies that households will increase the time spent working.

5 The diminishing marginal product of labour implies that the demand for labour curve is negatively sloped.

6 As the real wage rate increases, the quantity of labour demanded decreases, other things remaining constant.

7 If the marginal product of each unit of labour increases, the demand for labour curve shifts rightward.

8 In the short run, an increase in the price level will increase the quantity of real GDP supplied.

Changes in Potential GDP

9 Increasing population decreases the real wage rate and potential GDP.

10 An increase in labour productivity decreases real wages and increases potential GDP.

11 Japan's population is shrinking and its labour productivity is increasing. The net effect will definitely be an increase in potential GDP.

Unemployment at Full Employment

12 Job rationing keeps real wages too high and creates cyclical unemployment.

13 Equilibrium in the labour market occurs when labour demand equals labour supply and unemployment is zero.

14 Full employment is when there is 0 job search unemployment.

15 With efficiency wages, firms pay lower than equilibrium wages to earn higher profits.

Multiple-Choice

Real GDP and Employment

1 The production function shows
- **a** how much real GDP changes as the capital stock changes, all else remaining the same.
- **b** how much real GDP changes as the price level changes, all else remaining the same.
- **c** how much labour demand changes as the real wage rate changes, all else remaining the same.
- **d** how much labour demand changes as the money wage rate changes, all else remaining the same.
- **e** none of the above.

2 Which of the following would shift the production function upward?
- **a** a decrease in the stock of capital
- **b** a decrease in the real wage rate
- **c** an increase in labour employed
- **d** an increase in the price level
- **e** a technological advance

3 An increase in an economy's stock of human capital causes
- **a** a shift outward in the leisure hours—real GDP *PPF* and a movement along the production function.
- **b** a movement along the leisure hours—real GDP *PPF* and a shift upward in the production function.
- **c** a shift outward in the leisure hours—real GDP *PPF* and a shift upward in the production function.
- **d** a movement along the leisure hours—real GDP *PPF* and a movement along the production function.
- **e** no change in the leisure hours—real GDP *PPF* and a movement along the production function.

4 An increase in the quantity of labour supplied (driven by a fall in leisure consumed) causes
- **a** a shift outward in the production possibilities frontier and a movement along the production function.
- **b** a movement along the production possibilities frontier and a shift upward in the production function.
- **c** a shift outward in the production possibilities frontier and a shift upward in the production function.
- **d** a movement along the production possibilities frontier and a movement along the production function.
- **e** no change in the production possibilities frontier and a movement along the production function.

5 Which of the following is an example of learning-by-doing?
- **a** The use of a laptop instead of pen and paper to keep class notes.
- **b** A student being better at note-taking at the end of the fourth year of university than in the first year of university.
- **c** A student with five economics classes doing better in a third-year business class than one with only one economics class.
- **d** A student installing a software upgrade on their computer.
- **e** Falling asleep on your economics text while studying.

The Labour Market and Aggregate Supply

6 Which of the following quotations describes a rightward shift in the labour demand curve?
- **a** "Recent higher wage rates have led to more leisure being consumed."
- **b** "The recent lower price level has induced people to work more hours."
- **c** "The recent higher real wage rate has induced people to work more hours."
- **d** "The recent investment in capital equipment has raised hiring by firms."
- **e** "Adding extra workers leads to lower productivity of each additional worker."

7 If tacos sell for $2 each at the Burning Belly Taco Stand, and the wage rate of a taco maker is $60 per day, the real wage rate faced by the Burning Belly manager is equivalent to
- **a** 2 tacos per day.
- **b** $60 per day.
- **c** 120 tacos per day.
- **d** $2 per day.
- **e** 30 tacos per day.

8 Initially, tacos sell for $2 each at the Burning Belly Taco Stand, and the wage rate of a taco maker is $60 per day. Suppose that the price of a taco increases to $2.50 after a *National Inquisitor* story linking tacos to baldness cures. The profit-maximizing Burning Belly manager will
- **a** employ more taco makers because the real wage rate has increased to $2.50 per day.
- **b** employ fewer taco makers because the real wage rate has increased to $2.50 per day.
- **c** employ the same number of taco makers because the wage rate is unchanged.
- **d** employ more taco makers because the real wage rate has decreased to 24 tacos per day.
- **e** start advertising "I'm the owner, but I'm a customer too."

9 The labour demand curve is
- **a** positively sloped and shifts with a change in the capital stock.
- **b** positively sloped and shifts with a change in the quantity of labour employed.
- **c** negatively sloped and shifts with a change in the capital stock.
- **d** negatively sloped and shifts with a change in the quantity of labour employed.
- **e** negatively sloped and shifts with a change in the real wage rate.

10 The demand for labour curve shows that, as the
- **a** price level increases, the quantity of labour demanded decreases.
- **b** real wage rate increases, the quantity of labour demanded increases.
- **c** money wage rate increases, the quantity of labour demanded decreases.
- **d** money wage rate increases, the quantity of labour demanded increases.
- **e** real wage rate increases, the quantity of labour demanded decreases.

11 In the short run, if the price level decreases, the real wage rate will be
- **a** lower than the equilibrium real wage rate, and employment will decrease.
- **b** lower than the equilibrium real wage rate, and employment will increase.
- **c** higher than the equilibrium real wage rate, and employment will decrease.
- **d** higher than the equilibrium real wage rate, and employment will increase.
- **e** equal to the equilibrium real wage rate, and employment will stay constant.

12 In the long run, if the price level decreases, the real wage rate will be
- **a** lower than the equilibrium real wage rate, and employment will decrease.
- **b** lower than the equilibrium real wage rate, and employment will increase.
- **c** higher than the equilibrium real wage rate, and employment will decrease.
- **d** higher than the equilibrium real wage rate, and employment will increase.
- **e** equal to the equilibrium real wage rate, and employment will stay constant.

13 If the money wage rate is $12 per hour and the GDP deflator is 150, what is the real wage rate per hour?
- **a** $18
- **b** $15
- **c** $12
- **d** $8
- **e** $6

14 A profit-maximizing firm will hire additional units of labour up to the point at which
- **a** workers are no longer willing to work.
- **b** the marginal product of labour is zero.
- **c** the marginal product of labour is a maximum.
- **d** the marginal product of labour is equal to the real wage.
- **e** the marginal product of labour is equal to the money wage.

15 Which of the following quotations describes the upward-sloping labour supply curve?
- **a** "Recent higher wage rates have led to more leisure being consumed."
- **b** "The recent lower price level has induced people to work fewer hours."
- **c** "The recent higher real wage rate has induced people to work more hours."
- **d** "The recent high investment in capital equipment has raised hiring by firms."
- **e** "Adding extra workers leads to lower productivity of each additional worker."

16 Which of the following variables is *not* held constant in deriving the short-run aggregate supply curve?
- **a** the level of wages
- **b** raw material prices
- **c** climate
- **d** price level
- **e** technology

Changes in Potential GDP

17 The demand for labour and the supply of labour are both increasing, but the demand for labour is increasing at a faster rate. Over time we expect to see the
- **a** real wage rate rising and employment decreasing.
- **b** real wage rate and employment increasing.
- **c** real wage rate decreasing and employment increasing.
- **d** real wage rate and employment decreasing.
- **e** long-run aggregate supply curve shifting leftward.

18 An increase in potential GDP is shown as
- **a** a shift outward in the production possibilities frontier and a movement along the production function.
- **b** a movement along the production possibilities frontier and a shift upward in the production function.
- **c** a shift outward in the production possibilities frontier and a shift upward in the production function.
- **d** a movement along the production possibilities frontier and a movement along the production function.
- **e** either a shift in the production possibilities frontier and the production function, or a movement along each curve, depending on the source of the change.

19 *Ceteris paribus*, an increase in labour productivity results in
- **a** a higher real wage rate and higher potential GDP per hour of work.
- **b** a lower real wage rate and higher potential GDP per hour of work.
- **c** a higher real wage rate and lower potential GDP per hour of work.
- **d** a lower real wage rate and lower potential GDP per hour of work.
- **e** a constant real wage rate in the long run.

20 *Ceteris paribus*, an increase in the population results in
- **a** a higher level of labour employed and higher potential GDP per hour of work.
- **b** a lower level of labour employed and higher potential GDP per hour of work.
- **c** a higher level of labour employed and lower potential GDP per hour of work.
- **d** a lower level of labour employed and lower potential GDP per hour of work.
- **e** a constant level of labour employed and constant potential GDP per hour of work.

Unemployment at Full Employment

21 Which of the following quotations best describes job search unemployment?
a "Wages are so good at the factory, they always have enough applicants to pick whomever they want for the job."
b "Professors with tenured jobs are refusing to take pay cuts to help hire new professors."
c "Wages have failed to fall in the current economic downtown, creating extra unemployment."
d "People are taking too long to find jobs, because employment insurance is so generous."
e All of the above.

22 Which of the following is *not* a possible explanation for unemployment?
a job search
b efficiency wages
c minimum wages
d job market turnover
e part-time searches

23 Job search unemployment increases if
a the proportion of working-age population decreases.
b unemployment compensation becomes less generous.
c technological change slows down.
d unemployment compensation becomes more generous.
e none of the above.

24 An efficiency wage refers to wages
a paid below the equilibrium wage rate in order to increase the firm's efficiency.
b set to generate the efficient level of employment.
c paid above the equilibrium wage rate in order to increase worker productivity.
d being too high because of minimum wage laws.
e off of the production possibilities frontier.

25 Which of the following government policies would *lower* the unemployment rate?
a increasing unemployment benefits
b raising the minimum wage
c closing down employment agencies
d reducing unemployment benefits
e decreasing aggregate demand

Short Answer Problems

1 Explain why the labour force participation rate increases as the real wage rate increases. Why does this factor help explain the positive slope of the labour supply curve?

2 What determines the demand for labour?

3 Table 30.1 gives information about the production function for the country of Orania, where L = units of labour per day (measured in the millions) and Y = units of output per day (real GDP, millions of constant dollars per day).

TABLE 30.1 PRODUCTION FUNCTION

L	Y	MP_L
0	0	
1	8	
2	15	
3	21	
4	26	
5	30	
6	33	

a There are 6 units of labour available for leisure or labour supply in Orania. Graph Orania's production possibilities frontier.
b Complete the last column of Table 30.1 by computing the marginal product of labour (MP_L). Remember to place the marginal product halfway between the two rows.
c How much labour will be demanded if the money wage rate is $6 and the GDP deflator is 150?
d Draw a graph of the demand for labour.

4 Table 30.2 gives the supply of labour schedule for Orania.

TABLE 30.2 SUPPLY OF LABOUR

Real Wage Rate	Quantity of Labour Supplied
8	7.5
7	6.5
6	5.5
5	4.5
4	3.5
3	2.5

a On the graph from Short Answer Problem **3d**, draw the supply of labour curve.
b What is the equilibrium real wage rate?

c What is the equilibrium level of employment?

d What is the level of output at this level of employment?

ct **5** **a** If the natural rate of unemployment in Orania is 10 percent, calculate the labour force and the units of labour unemployed in equilibrium.

b Since labour demand equals labour supply in Orania, how can there be any unemployment?

6 Now suppose that a technological advance gives Orania a new production function summarized in Table 30.3.

TABLE **30.3** NEW PRODUCTION FUNCTION

L	Y	MP_L
0	0	
1	10	
2	19	
3	27	
4	34	
5	40	
6	45	

a On your *PPF* graph from Short Answer Problem **3a**, graph Orania's new *PPF*.

b Complete the last column of Table 30.3 by computing the marginal product of labour. Remember to place the marginal product halfway between the two rows.

c On the graph from Short Answer Problems **3c** and **4a**, draw the new demand for labour curve.

d In the long run, what will be the new equilibrium real wage rate, level of employment, and level of output? (The supply of labour curve is unchanged.)

7 In Short Answer Problem **6**, what happened to potential GDP and the *SAS* and *LAS* curves? Have they shifted?

ct **8** "The theory of job rationing tells us firms keep real wages too high and therefore create extra unemployment. Real wages should be forced downward to create more employment." Discuss this statement in the light of efficiency wages.

ct **9** Consider the following statement. "A major source of unemployment is job search due to employment insurance. It would be better for the economy if we eliminated employment insurance." What would eliminating employment insurance do to job search and unemployment levels? Is it clearly better for the economy if we eliminate employment insurance? Explain briefly.

10 Is the natural rate of unemployment constant? Briefly explain what factors can change the natural rate of unemployment.

ANSWERS

True/False and Explain

1 F Definition given is for production function. (706)

2 F Causes shift in *PF*. (708)

3 F Technological advances or increases in human capital raise labour productivity too. (707–708)

4 F Decrease in real wage rate leads to decrease in opportunity cost of leisure, which leads to increase in leisure. (711–712)

5 T If hire more labour, diminishing marginal returns imply decrease in marginal product. Firms will hire more labour only if real wage rate decreases. (709–711)

6 T Definition of labour demand curve. (709–711)

7 T Increase in marginal product leads to increase in output per worker and therefore increase in number desired at a constant real wage rate. (709–711)

8 T Upward-sloping *SAS* curve. (713–714)

9 F Increasing population increases labour supply, and decreases real wage, but more labour is hired so potential GDP increases. (714–715)

10 F It will shift *LD* curve rightward, and increase real wage rate. (716–717)

11 F Shrinking population will lower potential GDP, increasing labour productivity will increase it, net effect is ambiguous. (715–717)

12 F It creates frictional unemployment, since it is independent of the cycle. (720–721)

13 F Even in equilibrium there is natural unemployment. (719–720)

14 F There is always some job search and job rationing unemployment. (719)

15 F Pay higher than equilibrium wages. (720–721)

Multiple-Choice

1 e Definition: how much real GDP changes as the labour hired changes. (706)

2 e Technological advance increases productivity of labour. (707–708)

3 c The change increases labour productivity, which shifts both curves. (706–708)

4 d Decreasing leisure creates move along *PPF* (more real GDP, less leisure), and the increase in labour supply creates move along *PF*. (706–708)

5 b The student has learned by repetition. (707–708)

6 d More physical capital leads to higher productivity and more labour demand. **a**, **b**, and **c** are *LS* effect, **e** movement along curve. (709–711)

7 e Real wage rate = money wage rate/price of good = \$60/\$2 = 30. (709–711)

8 d Real wage = \$60/\$2.50 = 24 < 30 leads to hire more labour since cheaper. (709–711)

9 c Negatively sloped due to diminishing marginal product. **d** and **e** imply movements along the curve. (709–711)

10 e Demand for labour depends inversely on real wage rate. (709–711)

11 c Lower price level leads to higher real wage (since money wage constant), so labour demanded decreases. (713–714)

12 e Money wage adjusts to any price level changes, so real wage constant, and therefore no change in labour hired. (713–714)

13 d Real wage = (money wage/price level) × 100. (709–711)

14 d Here profits maximized. (709–711)

15 c Higher wages, higher quantity of labour supplied. **a**, **b** are opposite relationships, **d** and **e** refer to labour demand. (711–712)

16 d Price level is on the vertical axis. (713–714)

17 b Draw a graph. (717–718)

ⓒⓣ **18 e** If labour productivity is the original change, there is a shift in the curves. If the change is due to a change in labour force participation rates, there is a movement along the curves. If it is due to a population change, there is a shift in the *PPF* and a movement along the *PF*. (714–717)

19 a Productivity increase increases labour demand, which raises real wage rate. Potential GDP per hour of work = productivity, so it must have increased. (716–717)

20 c Labour supply shifts right, real wage falls, more people are hired, but due to diminishing marginal productivity potential GDP per hour of work falls. (715–716)

21 d **a** and **b** are job rationing unemployment, **c** is cyclical unemployment. (719–721)

22 e These workers are employed while searching. (719–721)

23 d Individuals can afford to spend more time in job search. (719–720)

24 c Definition. (720–721)

25 d This change will reduce length of job search. (719–720)

Short Answer Problems

1 Individuals compare the value of working (the real wage) to the value of activities outside the labour force (e.g., education, taking care of children). If the real wage rate is too low, an individual will not even enter the labour force. As the real wage rate increases, it will exceed the value of alternative activities of an increasingly larger group of people; thus the labour force increases relative to the size of the working age population; the labour force participation rate increases.

As this rate increases, more individuals offer to supply labour; thus, the quantity of labour supplied increases. Because the original impetus was an increasing real wage rate, the real wage rate and the quantity of labour supplied are positively related.

2 The demand for labour is set where the real wage rate equals the marginal product of labour. The marginal product of labour is affected by the physical and human capital stock, and the technology. Therefore in the short run the demand for labour is affected by the real wage rate, physical and human capital stock, and level of technology.

3 **a** The *PPF* graph is labelled PPF_0 in Figure 30.1 below.

FIGURE **30.1** ORANIA'S *PPF*

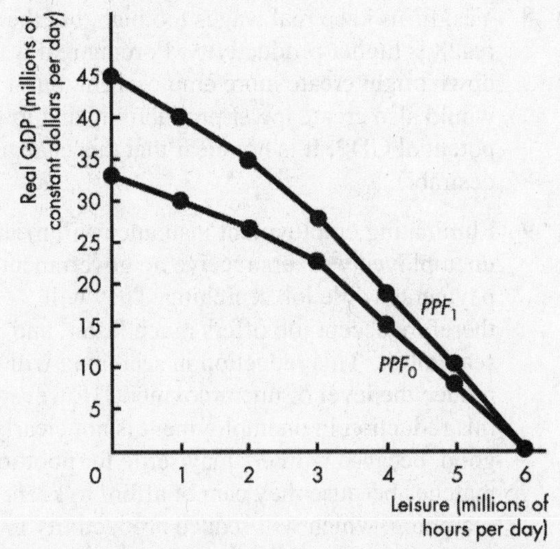

b Completed Table 30.1 is shown here as Table 30.1 Solution. The marginal product of labour is the additional output produced by an additional unit of labour.

TABLE **30.1** SOLUTION

L	*Y*	MP_L
0	0	
		8
1	8	
		7
2	15	
		6
3	21	
		5
4	26	
		4
5	30	
		3
6	33	

c The real wage rate is computed as follows: Real wage rate = (money wage rate × 100)/GDP deflator.

In this case, the money wage rate is $6 per unit and the GDP deflator is 150. Therefore the real wage is $4. Since a profit-maximizing firm will hire labour until the marginal product of labour is equal to the real wage rate, we can see that the quantity of labour demanded at a real wage rate of $4 is 4.5 units.

d The graph of the demand curve for labour (labelled LD_0) is given in Figure 30.2. The demand curve for labour is the same as the marginal product of labour curve (see Table 30.1 Solution).

FIGURE **30.2**

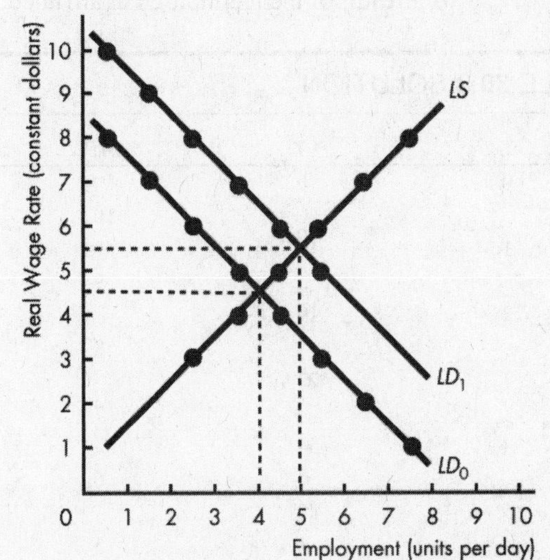

4 **a** Figure 30.2 illustrates the supply curve of labour (labelled *LS*) on the same graph with the LD_0 curve from Short Answer Problem **3**.

b The equilibrium real wage rate is $4.50 since the quantity of labour demanded and supplied are both equal to 4 units per day. This result can be seen from the graph or the tables.

c The equilibrium level of employment is 4 units.

d From the production function in Table 30.1, we can see that 4 units of labour will yield 26 units of output per day.

5 a If the unemployment rate is 10 percent,

- 0.10 = (labour force – employed)/labour force, or
- Labour force × 0.10 = labour force – 4, or
- Labour force × 0.9 = 4, or
- Labour force = 4/0.9 = 4.44

Therefore, there are 0.44 units unemployed.

b Even at full employment, there is always some job search and job rationing unemployment, equal to the natural rate of unemployment.

6 a The new production possibilities graph is graphed in Figure 30.1 as PPF_1.

b Completed Table 30.3 is shown here as Table 30.3 Solution. Note that the marginal product of each unit of labour has increased as a result of the technological advance.

TABLE **30.3** SOLUTION

L	*Y*	MP_L
0	0	
		10
1	10	
		9
2	19	
		8
3	27	
		7
4	34	
		6
5	40	
		5
6	45	

c Figure 30.2 gives the graph. Notice that the new labour demand curve, LD_1 (which comes from the new MP_L relationship), lies rightward of LD_0.

d It can be seen from Figure 30.2 or Tables 30.2 and 30.3 that the quantity of labour demanded equals the quantity of labour supplied at a real wage rate of $5.50. The level of employment is now 5 units of labour per day, which implies an output of 40 units per day (from Table 30.3).

7 Since labour productivity has increased, we have seen the resulting increase in potential GDP. This increase in potential GDP shifts the *LAS* curve rightward from 26 to 40, and the *SAS* curve moves with it.

8 Yes, firms keep real wages too high, but the result is higher productivity. Forcing real wages down might create more employment, but it would also create lower productivity and lower potential GDP. It is not clear that this change is desirable.

9 Eliminating employment insurance will mean unemployed workers receive no government payments while job searching. They will therefore accept job offers much faster, and search less. This reduction in searching will reduce the level of unemployment. However, this reduction in unemployment is not clearly good, because workers may settle for poor job matches because they cannot afford to keep searching, which will reduce productivity in the economy.

10 The natural rate of unemployment is determined by the amount of job search and job rationing. Job search is affected by the proportion of working-age population, by unemployment compensation, and by technological change. Job rationing is affected by the use of efficiency wages and the level of the minimum wage. Changes in any of these underlying factors will change the level of the natural rate of unemployment.

Chapter 30 Appendix: Deriving the Long-Run and Short-Run Aggregate Supply Curves

KEY CONCEPTS

The Aggregate Supply Curves

Aggregate supply plays a key role in determining real GDP in both the short run and the long run.

- ♦ *LAS* curve shows links between labour market, production function, and real GDP when money wage rate fully adjusts.
- ♦ *SAS* curve shows links between labour market, production function, and real GDP when money wage rate is sticky.

Deriving the Long-Run Aggregate Supply Curve

LAS curve is vertical at potential GDP.

- ♦ When price level increases, real wage rate falls and there is excess demand for labour.
  - Money wage rate then increases until the real wage rate returns to the level that makes *LD* = *LS*.
  - Result: full employment and real GDP produced = potential GDP.
- ♦ When price level falls, money wage rate also falls, *LD* = *LS*, and employment and real GDP produced are unchanged.
- ♦ *LAS* shifts rightward if
  - Population grows, so that *LS* shifts rightward, real wage rate decreases.
  - Labour productivity increases, so that *LD* shifts rightward, real wage rate increases.

Short-Run Aggregate Supply

SAS curve shows relationship between quantity of real GDP supplied and price level, holding money wage, etc. constant.

- ♦ In the short run, employment is set by firms' hiring, given the real wage—*LD* may not equal *LS*.
- ♦ In the short run, increase in *P* decreases real wage rate, so that labour demand increases and so does employment, leading to increase in real GDP produced.
- ♦ Overall result: price level increases, quantity of real GDP supplied increases in the short run—the *SAS* is upward-sloping.
- ♦ If *LAS* shifts, so does *SAS*.
- ♦ If the money wage increases,
  - *LAS* is unaffected.
  - Real wage rate increases, quantity of labour demanded decreases, employment and production decrease, *SAS* shifts leftward.
- ♦ A shift in *AD* creates a price change and a movement along *SAS*.

SELF-TEST

True/False and Explain

Deriving the Long-Run Aggregate Supply Curve

1 A decrease in the price level decreases employment in the long run.

2 After an increase in the price level, the real wage rate will be lower in the long run.

3 The *LAS* shifts rightward if labour productivity increases.

Short-Run Aggregate Supply

4 A decrease in the price level decreases employment in the short run.

5 An economy is initially in macroeconomic equilibrium and then expected future profits decrease. Real GDP will fall in the short run.

6 After an increase in the price level, the real wage rate will be lower in the short run.

7 An increase in the money wage rate will shift both the *SAS* curve and the *LAS* curve leftward.

Multiple-Choice

Deriving the Long-Run Aggregate Supply Curve

1 Which of the following quotations describes a movement along a long-run aggregate supply curve?
- **a** "The recent higher price levels have lowered production in the country."
- **b** "The recent higher price levels have raised production in the country."
- **c** "The recent higher price levels have led to compensating increases in wages, with no changes in labour hired or production."
- **d** "The recent lower price levels have led to lower production in the country."
- **e** None of the above.

2 The aggregate supply curve is vertical at full-employment real GDP if
- **a** the real wage rate adjusts continually so as to leave the labour market always in equilibrium.
- **b** the money wage rate is fixed but the real wage rate changes due to changes in the price level.
- **c** employment is determined by the quantity of labour demanded.
- **d** employment is determined by the quantity of labour supplied.
- **e** employment is determined by the money usage.

3 The *LAS* curve always shifts rightward if
- **a** the money wage rate increases.
- **b** the money wage rate decreases.
- **c** the real wage rate increases.
- **d** the real wage rate decreases.
- **e** the population increases.

4 Figure A30.1 depicts the labour market. The price level, measured by the GDP deflator, is 150. What is the money wage rate in equilibrium?
- **a** $8
- **b** $12
- **c** $15
- **d** $18
- **e** $24

FIGURE A30.1

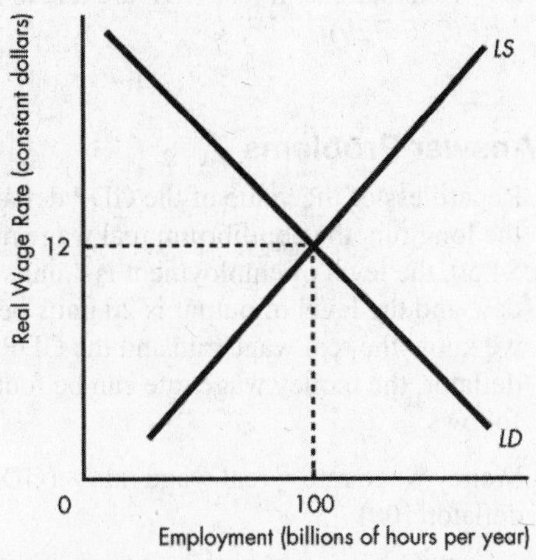

Short-Run Aggregate Supply

5 Refer to Figure A30.1 and assume that when the money wage was set, the GDP deflator was expected to remain constant at 150. If the GDP deflator actually turns out to be 200 in the short run, the real wage rate will be

- **a** $9, and employment will be less than 100 billion hours per year.
- **b** $9, and employment will be more than 100 billion hours per year.
- **c** $24, and employment will be less than 100 billion hours per year.
- **d** $24, and employment will be more than 100 billion hours per year.
- **e** $6, and employment will be more than 100 billion hours per year.

6 Which of the following quotations describes a shift rightward in a short-run aggregate supply curve?

- **a** "The recent higher price levels have lowered production in the country."
- **b** "The recent higher price levels have raised production in the country."
- **c** "The recent higher price levels have led to compensating increases in wages, with no changes in labour hired or production."
- **d** "The recent lower price levels have led to lower production in the country."
- **e** None of the above.

7 In the short run, employment is determined by the

- **a** quantity of labour demanded at the actual real wage rate.
- **b** quantity of labour supplied at the actual real wage rate.
- **c** intersection of the demand for labour and supply of labour curves.
- **d** intersection of the aggregate demand and aggregate supply curves.
- **e** price level.

8 In the long run, an increase in real GDP implies that

- **a** potential GDP has increased.
- **b** aggregate demand has increased.
- **c** the economy has moved up its short-run aggregate supply curve.
- **d** the price level has increased.
- **e** real wages have fallen.

Short Answer Problems

1 Consider the labour market for Orania derived earlier in Chapter 30, at the end of Short Answer Problem **4**. Suppose Orania is operating on its long-run aggregate supply curve.

- **a** If the GDP deflator is 100, what is the equilibrium money wage rate, the level of employment, and the level of output?
- **b** If the GDP deflator is 80, what is the equilibrium money wage rate, the level of employment, and the level of output?
- **c** If the GDP deflator is 120, what is the equilibrium money wage rate, the level of employment, and the level of output?
- **d** Draw Orania's long-run aggregate supply curve.

2 Now suppose Orania has a fixed money wage, set at $4.50. Assuming Orania is in the short run, answer the following questions.

- **a** If the actual value of the GDP deflator is 100, what is the real wage rate, the level of employment, and the level of output?
- **b** If the actual value of the GDP deflator is 82, what is the real wage rate, the level of employment, and the level of output?
- **c** If the actual value of the GDP deflator is 128, what is the real wage rate, the level of employment, and the level of output?
- **d** On the graph from Short Answer Problem **1d**, indicate three points on the short-run aggregate supply curve for Orania. Draw part of that curve by connecting the points.

3 Suppose the price level increases unexpectedly. In the short run, what will happen to the money wage rate, the real wage rate, employment, and real GDP?

ANSWERS

True/False and Explain

1 **F** In the long run, real wage rate stays constant and so does employment. (724–726)

2 **F** In the long run, money wage adjusts equivalently, and real wage rate stays constant. (724–726)

3 **T** *PF* shifts upward, movement along it too, increase in potential GDP. (724–726)

4 **T** In the short run, the decrease in price level leads to an increase in the real wage rate and a decrease in employment. (726–729)

5 **T** Fall in expected future profits shifts *AD* curve leftward, movement along *SAS* curve leads to new short-run equilibrium at lower real GDP. (726–729)

6 **T** In short run, money wage is constant. (726–729)

7 **F** Changes in money wage rate shift *SAS* only, not *LAS*. (726–729)

Multiple-Choice

1 **c** No Δ employment leads to no Δ production—vertical *LAS*. (724–726)

2 **a** Vertical *AS* implies *LAS* implies real wage adjusts. (724–726)

3 **e** Δ money wage change *SAS* only, Δ in real wage rate may be part of another change that shift the *LAS*, but cannot tell for sure. (724–726)

4 **d** Real wage set where *LD* = *LS* at $12, Money wage = real wage × price level/100. (724–726)

5 **b** Actual real wage = (money wage/price level) × 100, and lower real wage leads to more labour demanded. (726–729)

6 **e** **a** is nonsense, **b**, **c**, and **d** are movements along curves. (726–729)

7 **a** Firms select labour hired given actual real wage rate. (726–729)

8 **a** Fluctuations in real GDP are due to Δ*LAS*. (726–729)

Short Answer Problems

1 Regardless of the value of the GDP deflator, in the long run, the equilibrium real wage rate is $4.50, the level of employment is 4 units per day, and the level of output is 26 units per day. If we know the real wage rate and the GDP deflator, the money wage rate can be found as follows:

Money wage rate = real wage rate × (GDP deflator/100)

a If the GDP deflator is 100, a real wage rate of $4.50 suggests a money wage rate of $4.50.

b If the GDP deflator is 80, a real wage rate of $4.50 suggests a money wage rate of $3.60.

c If the GDP deflator is 120, a real wage rate of $4.50 suggests a money wage rate of $5.40.

d The long-run aggregate supply curve (labelled *LAS*) is given in Figure A30.2. Parts **a**, **b**, and **c** indicate that at every price level output is 26 units per day.

FIGURE **A30.2** SOLUTION

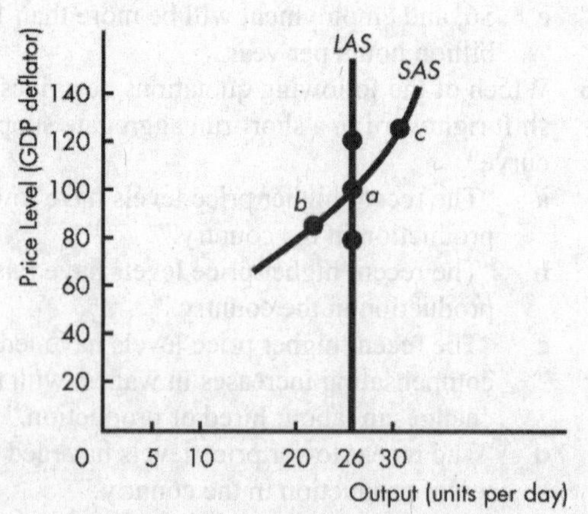

2 a If the actual value of the GDP deflator is 100, since the money wage rate is fixed at \$4.50, the real wage rate is \$4.50. This real wage rate implies that employment is 4 units and output is 26 units.

b If the actual value of the GDP deflator is 82, since the money wage rate is fixed at \$4.50, the real wage rate is \$5.50 (4.5/82 × 100 = 5.5). Employment is determined by the demand for labour which, at a real wage of \$5.50, is 3 units. This employment level means that (from Table 30.1) output is 21 units.

c If the actual value of the GDP deflator is 128, since the money wage rate is fixed at \$4.50, the real wage rate is \$3.50. Employment is determined by the demand for labour and is 5 units. From Table 30.1, this employment level implies an output of 30 units.

d Figure A30.2 indicates three points on the short-run aggregate supply curve in the sticky-wage economy: point *a* corresponds to output = 26, GDP deflator = 100; point *b* corresponds to output = 21, GDP deflator = 82; point *c* corresponds to output = 30, GDP deflator = 128. The points are connected to give a portion of the short-run aggregate supply curve (labelled *SAS*).

3 In the short run, an increase in the price level will, at the constant money wage rate, reduce the real wage rate. Because the money wage rate does not adjust in the short run, this lower real wage rate will remain and, since the level of employment is determined by the demand for labour, the level of employment will increase. The quantity of real GDP supplied will increase via the aggregate production function.

Chapter 31 Economic Growth

KEY CONCEPTS

Long-Term Growth Trends

Canada's growth rate was low in the 1950s, higher in the 1960s, slower in the 1970s and 1980s, and faster in the late 1990s.

- Internationally, between 1960 and 1990, Canada caught up to the United States, but Japan and other Asian countries have been catching up to both countries.
- Since 1990 Canada has fallen behind somewhat.

The Causes of Economic Growth: A First Look

Growth requires the essential precondition of an appropriate *incentive* system.

- Three institutions are crucial to an incentive system: markets, property rights, and monetary exchange.

This source of growth eventually runs its course—for further growth to continue we need

- Saving and investment in new capital, which increases capital per worker.
- Investment in human capital (including by learning and repetitively doing tasks).
- Discovery of new technologies.

Growth Accounting

Growth accounting calculates how much of economic growth is due to growth of labour and capital or to technological change.

- Real GDP supplied (Y) depends on quantity of labour (N), quantity of capital (K), and state of technology (T)—summarized in **aggregate production function** $Y = F(N, K, T)$.
- **Labour productivity** is real GDP per hour of labour (Y/N).

Productivity growth comes from growth in capital per hour of labour and technological change (which includes human capital).

- **Productivity curve** (PC) is relationship between real GDP per hour of labour and capital per hour of labour, holding constant technology.
  - Increase in capital per hour of labour creates movement up along PC.
  - Technological change creates upward shift of PC.
  - Increase in one input, other inputs held constant, increases output at a diminishing rate—**law of diminishing returns**.
- **One-third rule** says, on average, one percent increase in capital per hour of labour (with no change in technology) leads to 1/3 of 1 percent increase in output per hour of labour.
- The one-third rule can be used to calculate contribution of capital growth to real GDP growth, and to study reasons for changes in productivity growth:
  - 1961–73—high productivity growth due to high technological change and strong capital accumulation.
  - 1973–96—lower productivity growth due to slowdown in technological change and lower capital accumulation.
  - 1996–2001—speedup in technological change.
  - 2002–2004—no productivity growth at all.

Main suggestions for increasing economic growth rates:

- Stimulate saving by tax incentives.
- Subsidize research and development.
- Target high-technology industries.

- ♦ Encourage international trade.
- ♦ Improve education quality.

Growth Theories

Classical growth theory argues real GDP growth is temporary, because it leads to population explosions.

- ♦ Advances in technology increase real GDP per hour of labour.
- ♦ Since real GDP per hour > **subsistence real GDP per hour** (minimum needed to maintain life), population grows, which lowers capital per hour of labour, and therefore output per hour of labour back to subsistence.

Neoclassical growth theory says real GDP per person grows due to technological change inducing growth in capital per person.

- ♦ Assumes population growth rate is roughly independent of economic growth.
- ♦ The driving force of economic growth is technological change, and its interaction with capital accumulation.
- ♦ Ongoing *exogenous* technological advances increases the rate of return on capital, increasing saving and investment, increasing capital per person, creating real GDP growth.
- ♦ As capital per hour of labour increases, the rate of return on capital decreases to the target rate, and capital accumulation and growth end.
- ♦ Neoclassical growth theory predicts growth rates and income levels per person in different countries should converge, but this convergence doesn't happen empirically.

New growth theory attempts to overcome this shortcoming by explaining technological changes as a profit-maximizing choice.

- ♦ New discoveries are sought for (temporary) profits, but once made, discoveries are copied and benefits dispersed through economy, *without* diminishing returns.
- ♦ Knowledge is a special kind of capital not subject to diminishing returns.
- ♦ Inventions increase rate of return to knowledge capital until > target saving rate, resulting in increased capital per person and real GDP growth.
- ♦ Rate of return > target rate, which increases saving and capital per person and real GDP growth with *no automatic slowdown* because rate of return to capital does not diminish.

HELPFUL HINTS

1 Economic growth is a powerful force in raising living standards. Countries become rich by achieving high rates of growth in per person GDP and maintaining them over a long period of time. The role of compounding of income can create startling effects. We can see this effect by examining the post-1973 productivity growth slowdown. Growth between 1947 and 1973 was 3.2 percent per year, but after 1973 only 1.7 percent per year. This slowdown means that between 1973 and 2005, real GDP per person rose by about 73 percent (= $[(1.018)^{32} - 1] \times 100$). However, if economic growth had continued at the pre-1973 rate of 3.2 percent, real GDP per person would have increased by about 173 percent (= $[(1.032)^{32} - 1] \times 100$). Even the worst recession over this time period only lowered real GDP per person by about 5 percent (the point made by Robert Lucas in the discussion of the Lucas Wedge in Chapter 19). Avoiding the productivity growth slowdown would clearly have had a big payoff!

2 The key to understanding the different theories of growth is understanding the role of "the law of diminishing returns" in each theory. This law states that adding more of one input, other inputs held constant, eventually leads to a situation of diminishing returns to adding extra inputs.

In neoclassical theory, the discovery of a new technology increases the rate of return on capital above the target rate for savers, which increases saving and investment, increasing the amount of capital used. However, the increase in capital eventually leads to diminishing returns. As an example, we might think of the introduction of new and more powerful computers. As the number of computers increases, holding constant the number of workers, the extra output of the *n*th computer will not be as high as the productivity of the first computer. Eventually, the productivity of the extra capital must decrease (so that the rate of return decreases), and economic growth automatically slows down.

New growth theory has a different idea of technology and capital, with no diminishing returns, and no slowdown in economic growth. New growth theory examines "knowledge capital," a concept of technology that is not embodied so much in capital, but in ideas. These ideas might include new management techniques, or new processes of production (such as the assembly line) that can be copied from business to business without encountering diminishing returns. As an example, consider the introduction of new and better software (such as the first word processing package). As more copies of the software are introduced into different businesses around the country, we do not run into diminishing returns, at least not until the entire country has access to the new knowledge. Even then, new software will be continually developed and introduced without diminishing returns (so that the rate of return does *not* decrease), and economic growth need not automatically slow down.

SELF-TEST

True/False and Explain

Long-Term Growth Trends

1 Canada's growth speedup in the 1990s was quite unusual in Canadian history.

2 Asian countries are catching up with Canada's real GDP per person.

The Causes of Economic Growth: A First Look

3 Specialization is the crucial source of current growth.

4 Higher levels of human capital, with the same level of physical capital per person, will not raise per person income.

5 The three preconditions for economic growth are markets, property rights, and the discovery of new technologies.

Growth Accounting

6 When a country adopts a better technology, its productivity curve shifts upward.

7 Rapid changes in technology create growth without need for new capital.

8 High economic growth has typically been accompanied by high saving rates.

9 The slowdown in productivity growth after 1973 was due to a slowdown in the growth of capital per hour of labour, with a constant rate of technological change.

10 The most dramatic economic growth success stories have almost always involved rapid expansion of international trade.

11 The productivity curve shows the relationship between real GDP and labour inputs.

Growth Theories

12 Neoclassical growth theory argues economic growth eventually slows down because the rate of return on capital diminishes as the amount of capital increases.

13 Classical growth theory argues economic growth leads to a smaller population growth rate.

14 Neoclassical growth theory requires ongoing technological change to get ongoing economic growth.

15 In new growth theory, diminishing returns do not occur for knowledge capital.

Multiple-Choice

Long-Term Growth Trends

1 Canada's economic growth rates were highest in which of the following decades?
- **a** the 1930s
- **b** the 1960s
- **c** the 1970s
- **d** the 1980s
- **e** the 1990s

2 Compared to the growth in other countries, between 1960 and 1990 Canada
- **a** fell behind most other countries.
- **b** dramatically caught up to and passed other countries.
- **c** worsened dramatically versus the United States, but did better versus other countries.
- **d** did as well or better than most countries except certain Asian countries.
- **e** none of the above.

3 Which of the following statements about Canada's long-term growth trends is *false*?
- **a** Economic growth has tended to be steady, except for the business cycle.
- **b** Economic growth shows periods of slow and high growth.
- **c** Economic growth was faster in the 1990s compared to the 1980s.
- **d** Economic growth has been generally faster in Japan than in Canada.
- **e** African countries have fallen further behind Canada in recent years.

The Causes of Economic Growth: A First Look

4 Which of the following is *not* a source of economic growth?
- **a** increasing stock market prices
- **b** better educated workers
- **c** growing stock of capital equipment
- **d** an appropriate incentive system
- **e** advances in technology

5 Markets are an essential precondition to growth because
- **a** they suffer from diminishing returns.
- **b** they allow countries to benefit from high saving rates.
- **c** prices send signals that create incentives.
- **d** people have an assurance that their income and savings will not be confiscated.
- **e** they discourage consumer spending.

6 The basic sources of economic growth include all of the following *except*
- **a** saving and investment in new capital.
- **b** investment in human capital.
- **c** discoveries of new techniques.
- **d** discoveries of new management processes.
- **e** discouraging market systems.

7 A good incentive system
- **a** leads to specialization and exchange, with higher GDP per person.
- **b** is all that is needed to have continuous growth.
- **c** solves the problem of diminishing returns.
- **d** has no role for government.
- **e** can have the rate of return on capital above the target rate of savers for an extended period of time.

Growth Accounting

8 Suppose that productivity increased 20 percent last year. Capital per hour of labour increased by 12 percent as well. The increase in capital was responsible for
- **a** all of the productivity increase.
- **b** 80% of the productivity increase.
- **c** 60% of the productivity increase.
- **d** 40% of the productivity increase.
- **e** 20% of the productivity increase.

9 Suppose that productivity increased 20 percent last year. Capital per hour of labour increased by 12 percent as well. An increase in technology was responsible for
a all of the productivity increase.
b 80% of the productivity increase.
c 60% of the productivity increase.
d 40% of the productivity increase.
e 20% of the productivity increase.

10 Which of the following was a cause of Canada's post-1973 growth slowdown?
a higher population pressures
b lower saving
c diminishing returns
d slowdowns in technological change
e too-rapid increases in technological change

11 If there were significant technological advances last year, and the capital stock per hour of labour grew by 9 percent,
a the rate of return on capital must have decreased.
b economic growth would have been less than 3%.
c economic growth would have been more than 3%.
d economic growth would have been about 3%.
e the target rate of savers must have fallen.

12 Which of the following is a suggestion for increasing Canadian economic growth rates?
a Stimulate saving by taxing consumption.
b Reduce the time period for patents to increase replication.
c Put less public research funds into universities.
d Protect our industries from foreign competition.
e Tax education.

13 One of the reasons technological change slowed down after 1973 was the
a energy-inefficiency of new capital stock.
b lack of new capital stock.
c one-third rule.
d law of diminishing returns.
e introduction of new environmental protection laws and regulations.

14 It is argued that governments must subsidize research and development
a because there is too little private saving.
b it is too expensive for small firms.
c there are external benefits to research and development that firms ignore.
d in order to take advantage of the gains from specialization and exchange.
e in order to overcome diminishing returns.

15 The aggregate production function shows the relationship between
a real GDP supplied and the quantity of labour, the quantity of capital, and the state of technology.
b real GDP per hour of labour and capital per hour of labour, technology level constant.
c real GDP per hour of labour, and knowledge capital per hour of labour, technology level constant.
d real GDP supplied and the quantity of labour and the quantity of capital.
e real GDP per hour of labour and capital per hour of labour.

Growth Theories

16 The law of diminishing returns
a holds only for knowledge capital.
b states that if capital increases by 1%, real GDP increases by about 1/3 of a percent.
c states that if capital increases by 1%, real GDP increases by about 3%.
d holds for both physical and knowledge capital.
e does not hold for knowledge capital.

17 In neoclassical growth theory, if the rate of return on capital exceeds the target rate of savers, then
a the rate of return on capital will eventually decline.
b capital per hour of labour will decrease.
c real GDP per hour of labour will decrease.
d the rate of return on capital will never decline.
e population growth will explode.

18 In new growth theory, if the rate of return on capital exceeds the target rate of savers, then
a the rate of return on capital will eventually decline.
b capital per hour of labour will decrease.
c real GDP per hour of labour will decrease.
d the rate of return on capital will never decline.
e population growth will explode.

19 Which theory of economic growth argues that growth always slows down unless there are new technological inventions?

a classical theory
b neoclassical theory
c new growth theory
d old growth theory
e none of the theories

20 Which theory of economic growth concludes that technological advances are influenced by the profit motive?

a classical theory
b neoclassical theory
c new growth theory
d old growth theory
e none of the theories

21 Incentives are important in the new growth theory because they

a imply there are no diminishing returns.
b lead to higher rates of saving.
c imply that economic growth does not lead to population growth.
d create specialization and exchange.
e lead to profit-seeking searches for new discoveries.

22 In the classical growth theory, economic growth eventually stops after a technological advance because of

a diminishing returns.
b knowledge capital being easily replicated.
c the rate of return on capital decreasing back down to the target rate of savers.
d real GDP per person becoming too high.
e high population growth resulting from increasing real GDP per person.

23 The important difference between knowledge capital and physical capital is that knowledge capital

a can be replicated without diminishing returns.
b cannot be held in your hand.
c leads to an automatic slowdown in growth.
d cannot be replicated without diminishing returns.
e none of the above.

24 The rate of return on capital does not decline in new growth theory because

a the productivity of capital diminishes as more capital is employed per hour of labour.
b technological advances occur frequently due to profit-seeking activities.
c discoveries can be replicated without diminishing their marginal productivity.
d the target rate of savers is constant.
e population growth in response to high real GDP per person keeps the rate of return on capital high.

25 The key difference between neoclassical growth theory and new growth theory is that

a capital is not subject to diminishing returns under new growth theory.
b capital is subject to diminishing returns under new growth theory.
c increases in technology increase population which drives workers' incomes back down to the subsistence level in neoclassical theory.
d technological advances are exogenous in new growth theory.
e the one-third rule only holds in new growth theory.

Short Answer Problems

1 Why is an appropriate incentive system a precondition to growth?

2 Why does this source of growth eventually run its course?

3 Explain what happens in classical growth theory when advances in technology increase real GDP per person.

4 Some economists speculate that the Asian miracle economies have achieved such fast growth at least partially due to their adeptness at replicating new technology from other countries. Explain how and why this replicating is such a good source of growth.

5 Paul Krugman and others have argued that in fact the Asian miracle economies' extra-high economic growth is mostly due to the mobilization of capital and labour resources that were previously underutilized, and that therefore North American worries that these countries will catch up to and surpass Canada and the United States are unfounded. Assuming his argument is true, explain why this argument implies that these worries are unfounded.

6 Use the concept of a productivity curve to explain why an increase in the amount of capital per hour of labour will lead to economic growth.

ⓔ 7 You are given the data in Table 31.1 on the economy of Erehwon where the one-third rule holds, and the labour supply and population is unchanging over these three years. Do the calculations needed to show the contributions of changes in capital per hour of labour (as a fraction of the total change) and technological change to productivity growth, and fill in the rest of the table.

TABLE 31.1

Year	1998	1999	2000
Capital per hour of labour ($)	125	150	200
Productivity ($)	35	40	44.4
Contribution of capital	—	?	?
Contribution of technological change	—	?	?

8 On a graph, sketch the productivity curves from Short Answer Problem 7 for the three years, showing the production points for each of the three years.

9 Consider the following productivity curve:

TABLE 31.2

Capital per Hour of Labour	Real GDP per Hour of Labour
100	60
120	64
156	70

The economy is originally producing 60 units of real GDP per hour of labour in year 1.

a Does this productivity curve roughly meet the one-third rule?

b Graph this productivity curve, and the current point of production. Suppose that there is a technological advance that increases real GDP per hour of labour by 20 percent, holding constant the capital per hour of labour. Show the impact of this change in a new table and on your graph.

c In year 2, real GDP per hour of labour is now 84 units. Show this point on your graph. How much (if any) of the increase in real GDP was due to the technological advance, and how much (if any) was due to an increase in the capital per hour of labour?

ⓔ 10 Some commentators have argued that Japan has had a higher growth rate than countries such as Canada or the United States because the Japanese care more about the future and less about present consumption, reflected in a lower target interest rate for savers. Explain within the context of growth theory whether this argument seems sound.

ANSWERS

True/False and Explain

1 F Growth was higher in the 1960s. (734)

2 T See text discussion. (735–736)

3 F It is the initial source of growth, but once specialization is high, growth slows down. (737–738)

4 F Human capital growth is part of advances in technology. (738)

5 F Third precondition should be monetary exchange. (737–738)

6 T Technological advance increases productivity, capital per hour of labour unchanged. (740)

7 F Rapid technological change is embodied in new human and physical capital. (741)

8 T See discussion of East Asian economies. (742)

9 F Due to slowdown in both—see text discussion. (741)

10 T See text discussion. (741)

11 F Relationship between real GDP per hour of labour and capital per hour of labour, technology level constant. (740)

12 T Due to the law of diminishing returns. (745–747)

13 F Economic growth increases real GDP per hour, which increases population growth. (743–744)

14 T A technological advance increases rate of return on capital, which is now > target rate, which increases savings and investment, and therefore capital per hour of labour, which leads to more economic growth, but rate of return on capital decreases due to diminishing returns, which means growth eventually stops, unless there is more technological change. (745–747)

15 T Because knowledge capital can be duplicated at essentially zero marginal cost. (747–749)

Multiple-Choice

1 b See text discussion. (734)

2 d See text discussion. (735)

3 a Growth rates have fluctuated. (734–737)

4 a Prices have no impact on productivity, others increase it. (737–738)

5 c Incentives to specialize, trade, save, and invest. (737–738)

6 e See text discussion. (737–738)

7 a It eventually no longer contributes to growth, does not solve diminishing returns, government is needed to allocate property rights, and has little to do with rate of return on capital. (737–738)

ⓔ **8 e** By one-third rule, capital increase of 12 percent leads to real GDP per hour of labour increase in 4 percent, or 20 percent of productivity increase. (740–741)

ⓔ **9 b** From **8**, 80 percent is left over for technology to explain. (740–741)

10 d See text discussion. (741)

11 c One-third rule says capital growth leads to real GDP per hour of labour of about 3 percent, but technological growth will add to this amount. (740–741)

12 a **b** would lower return to and number of inventions, **c** would lower research and number of inventions, and trade and education should be encouraged. (742)

13 e See text discussion. (742)

14 c See text discussion. (742)

15 a Definition. (740)

16 e Holds for ordinary capital, but not for knowledgeable capital. (740–749)

17 a If rate of return on capital > target rate, saving increases supply of capital, increasing capital per hour of labour (and more real GDP per hour of labour), decreasing rate of return on capital due to law of diminishing returns. (745–747)

ⓔ **18 d** If rate of return on capital > target rate, saving increases supply of capital, increasing capital per hour of labour (and in real GDP per hour of labour), but no change in rate of return on capital since the law of diminishing returns doesn't hold for knowledge capital. (747–749)

19 b Due to diminishing returns to capital. (743–749)

20 c This is a core assumption of the theory. (747–749)

21 e This assumption makes technological change endogenous, and continuous. (747–749)

22 e This growth leads to decrease in real GDP per hour of labour. (743–744)

23 a Due to its nature—see text discussion. (747–749)

24 c Therefore as increase in capital stock, rate of return on capital does not diminish. (747–749)

25 a Due to the different nature of knowledge capital. (747–749)

Short Answer Problems

1 Incentive systems create economic growth by increasing specialization, saving, investment and exchange. They include

- Markets to send signals and enable people to specialize, exchange, save, and invest (all of which increase growth).
- Property rights to ensure income and savings are not confiscated and hence encourage people to work and save.
- Monetary exchange to facilitate transactions and encourage trade.

2 This source creates growth by increasing specialization. Eventually the level of specialization is so high, there is little left to be gained from further specialization.

3 Technology advances increase in the demand for labour, and real GDP per hour of labour. As real GDP per hour goes up, the rate of population growth increases, increasing the supply of labour, decreasing real GDP per hour back down to the subsistence wage rate, so workers are no better off than at the beginning.

4 Knowledge capital can be replicated without running into diminishing returns, so that the rate of return on capital increases after the replication, which in turn brings more saving and investment, and therefore capital per hour of labour can increase without limit, implying that growth can increase without limit.

5 If the growth is due to increasing the amounts of capital and labour, then eventually these countries will run into diminishing returns to each of these inputs, which means that the increases in productivity will slow down, meaning that economic growth will also slow down.

6 The productivity curve illustrates how output per hour increases as the stock of capital per hour increases, given the state of technology. If the amount of capital per hour of labour increases, the productivity of workers is increasing, which means that output per hour of labour is increasing—that is, there is faster economic growth. This effect is illustrated graphically by movements up along the graph of the productivity curve.

7 Table 31.1 is reproduced below as Table 31.1 Solution, with the calculations in place.

TABLE 31.1 SOLUTION

Year	1998	1999	2000
Capital per hour of labour ($)	125	150	200
Productivity ($)	35	40	44.4
Contribution of capital	—	46.6%	100%
Contribution of technological change	—	53.4%	0

The percentage change in capital from 1998 to 1999 was 20 percent ((25/125) × 100), implying a resulting percentage change in productivity of 6.67 percent. The total change in productivity was 14.3 percent ((5/35) × 100), leaving 7.63 percent due to technological change. Capital's contribution was (6.67/14.3) × 100 = 46.6 percent, and technology's contribution was 53.4 percent.

The percentage change in capital from 1999 to 2000 was 33 percent ((50/150) × 100), implying a resulting percentage change in productivity of 11 percent. The total change in productivity was 11 percent ((4.4/40) × 100), leaving no contribution due to technological change. Capital's contribution was 100 percent.

8 The graphs are shown in Figure 31.1. Note that from Table 31.1 the three yearly points must be where shown, and given our result about technological change in 1999 and 2000, the shift in 1999 and no shift in 2000 must be so.

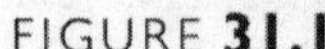
FIGURE 31.1

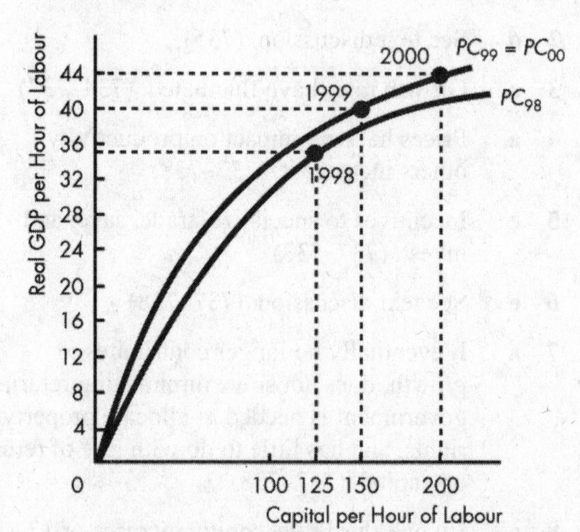

9 **a** Between 100 and 120, the percentage change in capital per hour is (20/100) × 100 = 20%, while the percentage change in real GDP per hour is (4/60) × 100 = 6.67%. One-third of 20 percent is 6.67 percent. Between 120 and 156, the percentage change in capital per hour is (36/120) × 100 = 30%, while the percentage change in real GDP per hour is (6/64) × 100 = 9.4%. One-third of 30 percent is 10 percent, a little bit higher than 9.4 percent. The one-third rule roughly holds.

b Figure 31.2 shows the original productivity curve as PC_0, with the three points from the table graphed on it, with the current production point marked as year 1. A 20 percent increase in productivity would lead to a shift upward in the productivity curve to PC_1, shown in Table 31.3, and graphed as PC_1, with the new production point marked as *a*.

TABLE 31.3

Capital per Hour of Labour	Real GDP per Hour of Labour
100	72
120	76.8
156	84

FIGURE 31.2

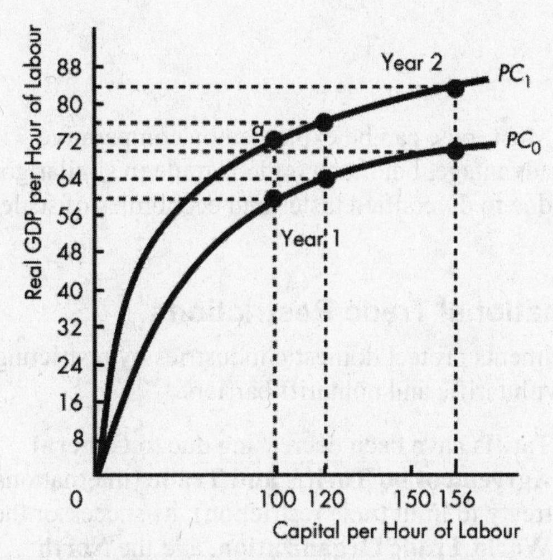

c The point is labelled as year 2 on the graph. We can see that the increase in real GDP per hour of labour from 60 to 84 units is broken down into two components. The technological change is shown as the movement from the point year 1 to the point *a*, a total change of 12 units or 50 percent (= (12/24) × 100) of the total change. The increase in capital per hour must be from 100 to 156 units to get production up to 84 units, and is shown as the movement from the point *a* to the point year 2. This change is a total of 12 units or 50 percent (= (12/24) × 100) of the total change.

ⓔ **10** The lower the target interest rate for savers, the more willing a person or country is to forgo current consumption and save for the future. Since Japan has a lower target rate, in any given situation Japan's saving rate will be higher. This higher saving in turn means the increase in the supply of capital in Japan is higher in any situation. Therefore, in general, Japan will have a higher capital stock per person than Canada, and it will generally be increasing each year at a higher rate, which in turn leads to a higher growth rate of real GDP per person in Japan than in Canada. Thus this argument seems hold true.

Chapter 32 Trading with the World

KEY CONCEPTS

Patterns and Trends in International Trade

Imports are goods and services we buy from other countries, **exports** are what we sell to other countries.

- ♦ Canada's major exports and imports are motor vehicles and capital goods, our major trading partner is the United States.
- ♦ Trade includes trade in services, such as tourism.
- ♦ **Net exports** = value of exports – value of imports.

The Gains from International Trade

Countries can produce anywhere on or inside production possibilities frontier (*PPF*).

- ♦ Slope of *PPF* = Δ *y*-axis variable/Δ *x*-axis variable = opportunity cost of one more *x*-axis variable.
- ♦ A country has comparative advantage in production of good for which it has lowest opportunity cost.

A country gains from trading by buying goods from countries with lower opportunity costs and selling the goods for which it has lower opportunity cost.

- ♦ **Terms of trade** = quantity needed to export to buy 1 unit of imports.
- ♦ Countries pay for their imports with their exports—value of exports = value of imports.
- ♦ Countries react to new terms of trade by producing more exported good and less imported good.
- ♦ *Both* countries gain by specializing—both can therefore *consume outside* their *PPF*.
- ♦ Most trade can be explained by comparative advantage, but much trade is trade in similar goods, due to diversified tastes and economies of scale.

International Trade Restrictions

Governments protect domestic industries by restricting trade with tariffs and nontariff barriers.

- ♦ Tariffs have been decreasing due to **General Agreement on Tariffs and Trade** (international treaty to limit trade restriction), its successor the **World Trade Organization**, and the **North American Free Trade Agreement.**

Tariffs are taxes on imported goods.

- ♦ Tariffs increase import price, decreasing imports, increasing domestic production.
- ♦ Net losses to importing country because new price > original import price.
- ♦ Tariffs lower imports in home country and exports to foreign country.

Nontariff barriers restrict supply of imports, which increases domestic price and domestic production.

- ♦ **Quotas** set import quantity restriction, with quota licences distributed by home country.
- ♦ **Voluntary export restraints** (VERs) set export quantity restrictions, with foreign distributors having export licences.

The Case Against Protection

Trade restrictions are used despite losses of gains from trade for three somewhat credible reasons—to protect **infant industries**, prevent foreign companies from **dumping** their products on world markets at prices less than cost, and to save jobs in import-competing industries.

A country may restrict trade for the following less credible reasons:

- ♦ To protect strategic industries for national security.
- ♦ To compete with cheap foreign labour.
- ♦ To bring diversity and stability.
- ♦ To penalize lax environmental standards.
- ♦ To protect a national culture.
- ♦ To prevent rich countries from exploiting developing countries.

The biggest problem with protection is that it invites retaliation from other countries.

- ♦ There are two reasons for trade restrictions:
    - Tariff revenue is an attractive tax base for governments in developing countries.
    - To protect groups/industries that suffer disproportionately under freer trade.
- ♦ In Canada, employment insurance and interprovincial transfers provide some compensation for losses due to free trade.

The Balance of International Payments

The balance of payments accounts measure Canada's international transactions.

- ♦ Current account—net exports + net interest payments + net transfers.
- ♦ Capital account—foreign investment in Canada – Canadian investment abroad.
- ♦ Official settlements account—net changes in Canada's official international reserves (government's holdings of foreign currency). If official reserves increase, official settlement balance is negative.
- ♦ Current account balance + capital account balance + official settlements balance = 0.
- ♦ To pay a current account deficit we must borrow from abroad or decrease official reserves.

International finance categories of countries:

- ♦ Flow categories:
    - Net borrower—borrowing more from rest of world than lending in current year (capital account surplus).
    - Net lender—lending more to rest of world than borrowing in current year (capital account deficit).
    - Being a net borrower not a problem if it is to finance investment that generates higher income to pay debts, as has been recent case in Canada.
- ♦ Stock categories:
    - Debtor nation—has borrowed more than lent to rest of world over its history.
    - Creditor nation—has lent more than borrowed to rest of world over its history.

Current account balance is primarily determined by net exports ($NX = X - M$).

- ♦ Via circular flow, net exports ($X - M$) = private sector balance ($S - I$) + government sector balance ($NT - G$).
- ♦ Government budget deficit and current account deficit move together (twin deficits).

The North American Free Trade Agreement

Despite protectionism pressures, Canada has a free trade agreement with the United States and Mexico.

- ♦ This agreement involves
    - Reducing common tariffs to zero in phases.
    - Reducing nontariff barriers.
    - Freer trade in energy and services.
    - Future negotiations on subsidies.
    - A dispute-settling mechanism.
- ♦ Total effects of the agreement are unknown at the moment, but they do include large increases in the total volume of trade, with significant changes in some sectors.

HELPFUL HINTS

1 This chapter applies the fundamental concepts of opportunity cost and comparative advantage from Chapter 2 to the problem of trade between nations. The basic principles are the same for trade between individuals in the same country and between individuals in different countries.

Many people involved in debates about trade seem confused by the concept of comparative advantage, partially because they implicitly consider *absolute advantage* as the sole reason for trade. A country has an absolute advantage if it can produce all goods using less inputs than another country. However, such a country can still gain from trade. Consider California and Saskatchewan. California has a better climate and, with widespread irrigation, has an absolute advantage in the production of all agricultural products. Indeed, California frequently has more than one harvest a year! This absolute advantage would seem to imply that California has no need to trade with Saskatchewan. Saskatchewan, however, has a *comparative advantage* in the production of wheat. Therefore California will specialize in fruits and trade them for wheat. California could easily grow its own wheat, but the opportunity cost would be too high—the lost fruit crops. By specializing and trading, both California and Saskatchewan can gain.

2 One of the crucial results of this chapter is that both countries can gain from trade. This gain occurs because the post-trade price is between the two countries' pre-trade opportunity costs. We can see this gain illustrated in Text Figure 32.3, in which the equilibrium price of a car is 3 tonnes of grain, between the pre-trade opportunity costs of 1 tonne and 9 tonnes.

Students are often puzzled by where to put the price when working through these types of examples. How did the authors come up with the value of 3? In a sense, it is an arbitrary value, one they just plucked out of a hat. Given the logic of voluntary trade, it must be between the two pre-trade values of 1 and 9. However, by redrawing the export supply and the import demand curves with different slopes, the authors might have arrived at a value of 6 tonnes. This result would have been equally logical, and equally valid.

In the real world, the strength of the demand for specific products by the consumers of each country will determine the slopes of the export supply and import demand curves, and determine just where the equilibrium price is set. In your examples, either you will be able to pick where you want the price to be (given that it must be between the two pre-trade opportunity costs) or you will be given some specific information telling you where the price is.

3 An important economic effect of trade restrictions is that a tariff and a quota have the same effects. A voluntary export restraint (VER) is also a quota, but it is one imposed by the exporting country rather than by the importing country.

All trade restrictions raise the domestic price of the imported goods and reduce the volume and value of imports. They also reduce the value of exports by the same amount as the reduction in the value of imports. The increase in price that results from each trade restriction produces a gap between the domestic price of the imported good and the foreign supply price of the good.

The difference between the alternative trade restrictions lies in which party captures this excess. In the case of a tariff, the government receives the tariff revenue. In the case of a quota imposed by the importing country, domestic importers who have been awarded a licence to import capture this excess through increased profit. When a VER is imposed, the excess is captured by foreign exporters who have been awarded licences to export by their government.

4 The major point of this chapter is that there are considerable gains from free trade. Why then do countries have such a strong tendency to impose trade restrictions? The key is that while free trade creates overall benefits to the economy as a whole, there are both winners and losers. The winners gain more in total than the losers lose, but the losers tend to be concentrated in a few industries.

Given this concentration, free trade will be resisted by some acting on the basis of rational self-interest. Even though only a small minority benefit while the overwhelming majority will be hurt, it is not surprising to see trade restrictions implemented. The cost of a given trade restriction to *each* of the majority will be individually quite small, while the benefit to *each* of the few will be individually large. Thus the minority will have a significant incentive to see that restriction takes place, while the majority will have little incentive to expend time and energy in resisting trade restriction.

5 To understand the source of pressures for trade restrictions, let us summarize those who win and lose from trade restrictions.

Under the three forms of restrictions (tariffs, quotas, and VERs) *consumers* lose, because the price of the imported good increases. *Domestic producers* of the imported good and their factors of production gain from all three, because the price of the imported good increases. *Foreign producers* and their factors of production lose under all three schemes, because their export sales decrease. Under quotas and VERs, the *holders of import licences* gain from buying low and selling high (they may be foreign or domestic). *Government* gains tariff revenue under tariffs and, potentially, votes under other schemes.

Given this list, it is hardly surprising that the main supporters of trade restrictions are domestic producers and their factors of production.

SELF-TEST

True/False and Explain

Patterns and Trends in International Trade

1 When a Canadian citizen stays in a hotel in France, Canada is exporting a service.

The Gains from International Trade

2 If a country can produce all goods cheaper than other countries, it will not benefit from trade.

3 Trading according to comparative advantage allows all trading countries to consume outside their *PPF*.

4 If Atlantis must give up 3 widgets to produce 1 watch and Beltran must give up 4 widgets to produce 1 watch, Atlantis has a comparative advantage in the production of watches.

International Trade Restrictions

5 When governments impose tariffs, they are increasing their country's gain from trade.

6 A tariff on a good will raise its price and reduce the quantity traded.

7 A quota will cause the price of the imported good to decrease.

The Case Against Protection

8 Japan is dumping steel if it sells steel in Japan at a lower price than it sells it in Canada.

9 Since Mexican labour is paid so much less than Canadian labour, entering into a free trade agreement with Mexico guarantees Canada will lose jobs to Mexico.

10 Elected governments are slow to reduce trade restrictions because there would be more losers than gainers.

The Balance of International Payments

11 There can be no such thing as a balance of payments surplus/deficit, because by definition a *balance* of payments must always *balance*.

12 A larger government sector deficit always leads to a higher current account deficit.

13 If a nation is a net borrower from the rest of the world, it must be a debtor nation.

14 If Canada borrows more from the rest of the world than it lends to the rest of the world, Canada has a capital account surplus.

The North American Free Trade Agreement

15 The impact of the North American Free Trade Agreement has been significant changes in some sectors, but no overall change in the total volume of trade.

Multiple-Choice

Patterns and Trends in International Trade

1 Which of the following is a Canadian service export?

a A Canadian buys dinner while travelling in Switzerland.
b A Swiss buys dinner while travelling in Canada.
c A Canadian buys a clock made in Switzerland.
d A Swiss buys a computer made in Canada.
e A Canadian buys a Canadian computer in Switzerland.

The Gains from International Trade

2 In Atlantis, 1 unit of capital and 1 unit of labour are required to produce 1 watch, and 2 units of capital and 2 units of labour are required to produce 1 widget. What is the opportunity cost of producing one watch?

a the price of 1 unit of capital plus the price of 1 unit of labour
b 1 unit of capital and 1 unit of labour
c 2 units of capital and 2 units of labour
d 1/2 widget
e 2 widgets

3 Refer to Figure 32.1. The opportunity cost of 1 beer in Partyland is ______, and the opportunity cost of 1 beer in Cowabunga is ______.

a dependent on where on the *PPF* we measure it; dependent on where on the *PPF* we measure it
b 100 pizzas; 25 pizzas
c 3 pizzas; 1 pizza
d 1 pizza; 1 pizza
e 1 pizza; 1/3 pizza

FIGURE **32.1** PARTYLAND AND COWABUNGA—*PPF* FOR BEER AND PIZZA

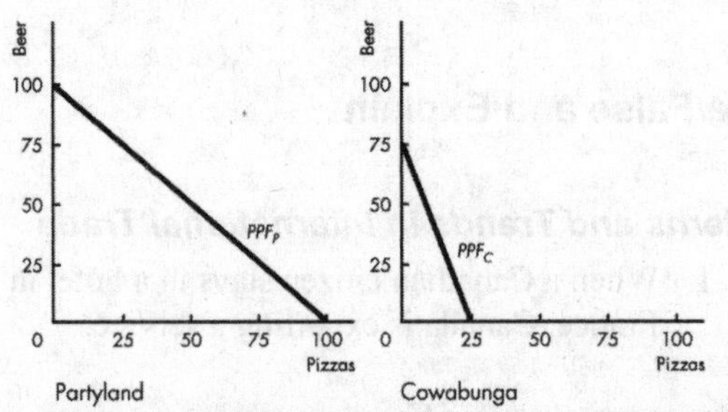

4 Refer to Figure 32.1. The opportunity cost of 1 pizza in Partyland is ______, and the opportunity cost of 1 pizza in Cowabunga is ______.

a dependent on where on the *PPF* we measure it; dependent on where on the *PPF* we measure it
b 100 beers; 25 beers
c 3 beers; 1 beer
d 1 beer; 1 beer
e 1 beer; 3 beers

5 Refer to Figure 32.1. If trade occurs between Partyland and Cowabunga,

a there will be a lot of drunk turtles.
b Partyland will supply both pizza and beer, because it has a comparative advantage in both.
c Cowabunga will supply both pizza and beer, because it has a comparative advantage in both.
d Partyland will supply pizza, and Cowabunga will supply beer.
e Partyland will supply beer, and Cowabunga will supply pizza.

6 Refer to Figure 32.1. If trade occurs between Partyland and Cowabunga, the terms of trade will be
- **a** 1 beer for 1 pizza.
- **b** 1 beer for 1/3 pizza.
- **c** 1 beer for 3 pizzas.
- **d** somewhere between 1 beer for 1 pizza and 1 beer for 3 pizzas.
- **e** somewhere between 1 beer for 1 pizza and 1 beer for 1/3 pizza.

7 Compared to no trade, how does international trade change the consumption possibilities of each country?
- **a** It allows each country to consume more of the goods it exports, but less of the goods it imports.
- **b** It allows each country to consume more of the goods it imports, but less of the goods it exports.
- **c** It allows each country to consume more of the goods it exports and imports.
- **d** It allows each country to consume less of the goods it exports and imports.
- **e** It allows each country to consume more of either the good it exports or the good it imports, but not both.

International Trade Restrictions

8 Consider Table 32.1. Under free trade, the international price of donut holes would be $______ per hundred donut holes, and ______ million holes would be exchanged.
- **a** 0.75; 6
- **b** 1.00; 3
- **c** 1.25; 4
- **d** 1.25; 5
- **e** 1.50; 4

TABLE 32.1 INTERNATIONAL TRADE IN DONUT HOLES

International Price (dollars per 100 holes)	Glazeland's Export Supply of Holes (millions)	Snorfleland's Import Demand for Holes (millions)
0.50	1	10
0.75	2	8
1.00	3	6
1.25	4	4
1.50	5	2
1.75	6	0

9 Consider Table 32.1. Snorfleland's donut hole producers convince their government that there is a need to protect the domestic industry from Glazeland's cheap imports. (They argue that holes are a crucial food group.) In response, Snorfleland's government sets an import quota of 3 million donut holes. The resulting price of a donut hole in Snorfleland will be $______ per hundred holes, and domestic production of donut holes will ______.
- **a** 0.75; decrease
- **b** 0.75; increase
- **c** 1.25; remain unchanged
- **d** 1.38; increase
- **e** 1.38; remain unchanged

10 A tariff on watches which are imported by Atlantis will cause the
- **a** demand curve for watches in Atlantis to shift leftward.
- **b** demand curve for watches in Atlantis to shift rightward.
- **c** supply curve of watches in Atlantis to shift leftward.
- **d** supply curve of watches in Atlantis to shift rightward.
- **e** demand and the supply curve of watches in Atlantis to shift leftward.

11 When a *quota* is imposed, the gap between the domestic price and the export price is captured by
- **a** consumers in the importing country.
- **b** the domestic producers of the good.
- **c** the government of the importing country.
- **d** foreign exporters.
- **e** the domestic importers of the good.

12 When a *voluntary export restraint* agreement is reached, the gap between the domestic import price and the export price is captured by
- **a** consumers in the importing country.
- **b** the domestic producers of the good.
- **c** the government of the importing country.
- **d** foreign exporters.
- **e** the domestic importers of the good.

13 When a *tariff* is imposed, the gap between the domestic price and the export price is captured by
- **a** consumers in the importing country.
- **b** the domestic producers of the good.
- **c** the government of the importing country.
- **d** foreign exporters.
- **e** the domestic importers of the good.

The Case Against Protection

14 Which of the following is *not* an argument for protectionism?
- **a** to protect strategic industries
- **b** to save jobs in import-competing industries
- **c** to gain a comparative advantage
- **d** to allow infant industries to grow
- **e** to prevent rich nations from exploiting poor nations

15 The biggest problem with protection is that
- **a** it invites retaliation from trading partners.
- **b** losers are not compensated.
- **c** it worsens environmental standards.
- **d** it can worsen national security.
- **e** it lowers wages.

16 Why is international trade restricted?
- **a** because government revenue is costly to collect via tariffs
- **b** in order to get higher consumption possibilities
- **c** to realize the gains from trade
- **d** due to rent-seeking
- **e** because free trade creates economic losses on average

The Balance of International Payments

17 $NX =$
- **a** $C + I + G$
- **b** $(S + I) - (NT + G)$
- **c** $(G - NT) + (I - S)$
- **d** $(S - I) + (G - NT)$
- **e** none of the above

18 Suppose Canada initially has all balance of payments accounts in balance (no surplus or deficit). Then Canadian firms increase their imports from Japan, financing that increase by borrowing from Japan. There will now be a current account
- **a** surplus and a capital account surplus.
- **b** surplus and a capital account deficit.
- **c** deficit and a capital account surplus.
- **d** deficit and a capital account deficit.
- **e** deficit and a capital account balance.

19 The country of Mengia came into existence at the beginning of year 1. Given the information in Table 32.2, in year 4 Mengia is a
- **a** net lender and a creditor nation.
- **b** net lender and a debtor nation.
- **c** net borrower and a creditor nation.
- **d** net borrower and a debtor nation.
- **e** net lender and neither a creditor nor a debtor nation.

TABLE 32.2

Year	Borrowed from Rest of World (billions of dollars)	Lent to Rest of World (billions of dollars)
1	60	20
2	60	40
3	60	60
4	60	80

20 Assuming that Mengia's official settlement account is always in balance, in which year or years in Table 32.2 did Mengia have a current account surplus?
- **a** year 1
- **b** year 2
- **c** years 1, 2, and 3
- **d** years 1 and 2
- **e** year 4 only

21 If Mengia's official settlement balance was in deficit every year, for which year or years in Table 32.2 can you say for sure there was a current account surplus?
- **a** year 1
- **b** year 2
- **c** years 2 and 3
- **d** years 1 and 2
- **e** years 3 and 4

22 Suppose that a country's government expenditures are \$400 billion, net taxes are \$300 billion, saving is \$300 billion, and investment is \$250 billion. This country has a government budget
- **a** surplus and a private sector surplus.
- **b** surplus and a private sector deficit.
- **c** deficit and a private sector surplus.
- **d** deficit and a private sector deficit.
- **e** surplus and a private sector balance.

23 The distinction between a debtor or creditor nation and a net borrower or net lender nation depends on
- **a** the distinction between the level of saving in the economy and the saving rate.
- **b** the distinction between the level of saving in the economy and the rate of borrowing.
- **c** the distinction between the stock of net borrowing and the flow of net borrowing.
- **d** the distinction between exports and imports.
- **e** nothing really; they are the same.

24 If the current account is in deficit, and the capital account is also in deficit, the change in official reserves is
- **a** negative.
- **b** positive.
- **c** probably close to zero, but might be either negative or positive.
- **d** zero.
- **e** not affected.

The North American Free Trade Agreement

25 Examining the implementation of the North American Free Trade Agreement has revealed
- **a** Canada has been severely damaged by the agreement.
- **b** Canada has been helped enormously by the agreement.
- **c** free trade does not work.
- **d** all losers from free trade will be compensated.
- **e** large increases in trade, benefiting consumers, but costing some jobs.

Short Answer Problems

1 Why can *both* parties involved in trade gain?

2 Suppose Atlantis imposes a tariff on its imports of watches from Beltran. How does the tariff affect the domestic price of watches, the export price, the quantity imported, the quantity of watches produced domestically, and Atlantis's exports to Beltran?

3 It is often argued by union leaders that tariffs are needed to protect domestic jobs. In light of your answers to Short Answer Problem 2, evaluate this argument.

4 The international transactions of a country for a given year are reported in Table 32.3.

TABLE 32.3

Transaction	Amount (billions of dollars)
Exports of goods and services	100
Imports of goods and services	130
Transfers to the rest of the world	20
Loans to the rest of the world	60
Loans from the rest of the world	?
Increases in official reserves	10
Net interest payments	0

- **a** What is the amount of loans from the rest of the world?
- **b** What is the current account balance?
- **c** What is the capital account balance?
- **d** What is the official settlements balance?

5 Consider a simple world in which there are two countries, Atlantis and Beltran, each producing food and cloth. The *PPF* for each country is given in Table 32.4.
- **a** Assuming a constant opportunity cost in each country, complete the table.
- **b** What is the opportunity cost of food in Atlantis? of cloth?
- **c** What is the opportunity cost of food in Beltran? of cloth?
- **d** Draw the *PPF*s on separate graphs.

TABLE 32.4 ATLANTIS AND BELTRAN—*PPF* FOR FOOD AND CLOTH

Atlantis		Beltran	
Food (units)	Cloth (units)	Food (units)	Cloth (units)
0	500	0	800
200	400	100	600
400		200	
600		300	
800		400	
1,000		—	—

6 Suppose that Atlantis and Beltran engage in trade.
- **a** In which good will each country specialize?
- **b** If 1 unit of food trades for 1 unit of cloth, what will happen to the production of each good in each country?
- **c** If 1 unit of food trades for 1 unit of cloth, draw the consumption possibilities frontiers for each country on the corresponding graph from Short Answer Problem **5**.
- **d** Before trade, if Atlantis consumed 600 units of food, the most cloth it could consume was 200 units. After trade, how many units of cloth can be consumed if 600 units of food are consumed?

7 Continue the analysis of Atlantis and Beltran trading at the rate of 1 unit of food for 1 unit of cloth.

a If Atlantis consumes 600 units of food and 400 units of cloth, how much food and cloth will be consumed by Beltran?

b Given the consumption quantities and the production quantities from Short Answer Problem **6b**, how much food and cloth will Atlantis and Beltran import and export?

8 Figure 32.2 gives the import demand curve for shirts for Atlantis, labelled *D*, and the export supply curve of shirts for Beltran, labelled *S*.

a What is the price of a shirt under free trade?

b How many shirts will be imported by Atlantis?

FIGURE **32.2**

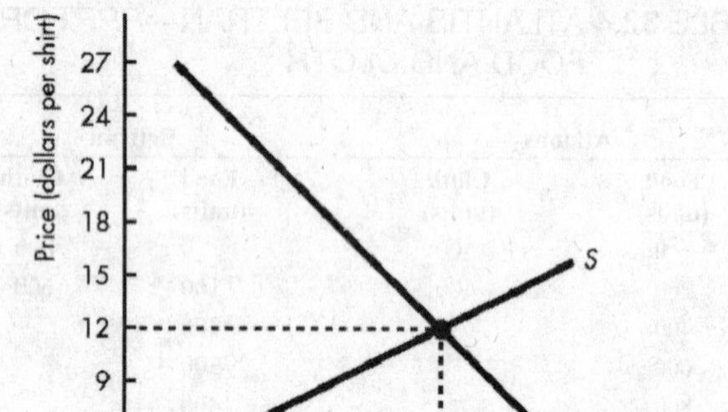

9 Suppose the shirt makers in Atlantis of Short Answer Problem **8** are concerned about foreign competition and, as a result, the government of Atlantis imposes a tariff of $9 per shirt.

a Using Figure 32.2, show what will happen to the price of a shirt in Atlantis.

b What is the price the exporter will actually receive?

c How many shirts will be imported by Atlantis?

d What is the revenue from the tariff? Who captures it?

10 Suppose that instead of a tariff, Atlantis imposes a quota of 4 million shirts per year.

a With the aid of a new graph, show what will be the new price of a shirt in Atlantis.

b What price will the exporter actually receive?

c How many shirts will be imported by Atlantis?

d What is the difference between the total amount paid by consumers and the total amount received by exporters—the "excess profit"? Who captures it?

ANSWERS

True/False and Explain

1 F Canada is importing (using) a service. (756)

2 F If comparative advantage exists, gains from trade exist. (757–762)

3 T Countries will specialize and trade to consume outside *PPF*. (757–761)

4 T Atlantis has a lower opportunity cost (3 widgets < 4 widgets) = lost widgets per unit of gained watches. (758–759)

5 F Trade restrictions reduce gains from trade. (764–766)

6 T Tariff shifts export supply curve leftward, which increases price and decreases quantity traded. (763–766)

7 F Quota decreases supply, which increases price. (766)

8 F Dumping would be selling in Canada at lower price than in Japan. (768)

9 F We must also examine the productivity of workers in each country, and Canadian workers are more productive. (768)

10 F They will be slow because losers' losses are individually much greater than winners' gains. (770–771)

ⓔ **11 F** Overall flow of money in/out of country = sum of the three balances of payment must balance. Individual balances may be in deficit/surplus/balance. (772–774)

ⓒ **12 F** Twin deficits tend to move together, but depends on reaction of private sector surplus/deficit. (775–776)

13 F May or may not be true. Net borrower implies *current* net borrowing > 0. Debtor nation implies sum of *all* net borrowing > 0. (774)

14 T Definition—note which way the money is flowing. (772–774)

15 F There has been a large increase in the total volume of trade. (776–777)

Multiple-Choice

1 b **a** and **c** are imports, **d** and **e** are exports of a *good.* (756)

2 d Opportunity cost measures in foregone goods, not inputs. (757–758)

3 e Opportunity cost of 1 more beer = lost pizza. For Partyland, going from 0 beer to 25 beers costs 25 pizzas (one for one). Do same calculation for Cowabunga. (757–758)

4 e Same type of calculation as in **3**. (757–758)

5 d Each specializes where they have comparative advantage (lowest opportunity cost). (757–759)

ⓒ **6 e** Terms of trade between the opportunity costs in each country at the pre-trade equilibrium. (757–759)

7 c Consumption possibilities frontier is outside *PPF*. (759–761)

8 c Equilibrium is where export supply = import demand. (764–766)

9 d Equilibrium is where quota = import demand increases price. Higher domestic price increases domestic production. (766)

10 c Tariff increases domestic price = export price + tariff, or a shift leftward in supply curve. (764–765)

11 e Under quota, domestic government allocates the licence to import. (766)

12 d Because they have right to export. (766)

13 c They collect tariff revenue = import price – export price. (764–765)

14 c See text discussion. (767–770)

15 a See text discussion. (767–770)

16 d See text discussion. (770–771)

17 e $(S—I) + (NT - G)$ from equality of injections and leakages in circular flow. (775–776)

ⓒ **18 c** Imports > exports implies current account deficit. Borrowing > lending implies capital account surplus. (Think about which direction money is flowing.) (772–774)

19 b Current lending > borrowing implies net lender. Sum of past borrowing > sum of lending implies debtor nation. (772–774)

20 e Official settlements balance = 0 implies current account surplus = capital account deficit, which occurs only when lending > borrowing. (772–774)

ⓒ **21 e** Since current account + capital account + official settlements account = 0, when official settlements is a deficit, to be sure current is a surplus, it must be the case that capital is 0 or a deficit. (772–774)

22 c Government sector deficit = $NT - G = 300 - 400 = -100$. Private sector surplus = $S - I = 300 - 250 = +50$. (775–776)

23 c Net lender implies stock of investments rising. Debtor nation implies negative flow of interest payments on investments. (774)

24 a Official settlements balance = –(Capital account + Current account) = Surplus, which implies change in official reserves < 0. (772–774)

25 e See text discussion. (772–773)

Short Answer Problems

1 For two potential trading partners to be willing to trade, they must have different comparative advantages; that is, different opportunity costs. Then they will trade and both parties will gain. If the parties do not trade, each will face its own opportunity costs. A price at which trade takes place must be somewhere between the opportunity costs of the two traders. This result means that the party with the lower opportunity cost of the good in question will gain because it will sell at a price above its opportunity cost. Similarly, the party with the higher opportunity cost will gain because it will buy at a price below its opportunity cost.

2 A tariff on an imported good will *raise its price to domestic consumers* as the export supply curve shifts leftward. The export price is determined by the original export supply curve. As the domestic price of the good increases, the quantity of the good demanded decreases, and thus the relevant point on the original export supply curve is at a lower quantity and a *lower export price*. This lower quantity means that the quantity imported decreases. The increase in the domestic price will also lead to an *increase in the quantity of the good supplied domestically*.

When Atlantis imposes a tariff on its imports of watches, not only does the volume of imports shrink, but also the volume of exports of widgets to Beltran will shrink by the same amount. Thus a balance of trade is maintained. The export price of watches received by Beltran and the quantity exported decreases when a tariff is imposed. This decrease in the price and the quantity exported means that the income of Beltran has decreased. This result implies that the quantity of widgets (Atlantis' export) demanded by Beltran will decrease and thus Atlantis' exports decline.

3 This argument has some truth to it. As Short Answer Problem **2** shows, the tariff will lead an increase in domestic production of the protected good, which will lead to an increase in jobs in that industry. However, as Short Answer Problem **2** also shows, the same tariff will reduce foreign income, and reduce foreign purchases of our goods, reducing our exports and our export production, reducing jobs in the export industry. The net effect on jobs is unclear, but it is definitely not large.

4 **a** Current account balance + Capital account balance + Official settlements balance = 0, or (100 – 130 – 20) + (Loans from rest of world – 60) + (–10) = 0, so Loans from rest of world = 120.

b The current account balance is a $50 billion deficit: exports minus imports minus transfers to the rest of the world plus net interest payments to the rest of the world.

c The capital account balance is a surplus of $60 billion: loans from the rest of the world minus loans to the rest of the world.

d Because official reserves increased, the official settlements balance is –10.

5 **a** Completed Table 32.4 is shown here as Table 32.4 Solution. The values in the table are calculated using the opportunity cost of each good in each country. See **b** and **c** below.

TABLE **32.4** SOLUTION

Atlantis		Beltran	
Food (units)	**Cloth (units)**	**Food (units)**	**Cloth (units)**
0	500	0	800
200	400	100	600
400	300	200	400
600	200	300	200
800	100	400	0
1,000	0	—	—

b To increase the output (consumption) of food by 200 units, cloth production (consumption) decreases by 100 units in Atlantis. Thus the opportunity cost of a unit of food is 1/2 unit of cloth. This opportunity cost is constant as are all others in this problem, for simplicity. Similarly, the opportunity cost of cloth in Atlantis is 2 units of food.

c In Beltran a 100-unit increase in the production (consumption) of food requires a reduction in the output (consumption) of cloth of 200 units. Thus the opportunity cost of food is 2 units of cloth. Similarly the opportunity cost of cloth in Beltran is 1/2 units of food.

d Figure 32.3, parts (a) and (b) illustrate the production possibilities frontiers for Atlantis and Beltran, respectively labelled PPF_A and PPF_B. The rest of the diagram is discussed in the solutions to Short Answer Problems **6** and **7**.

FIGURE **32.3**

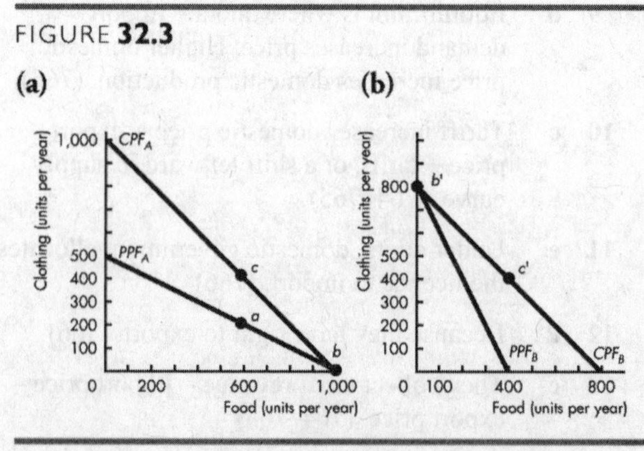

6 a We see from the solution to Short Answer Problems **5b** and **c** that Atlantis has a lower opportunity cost (1/2 unit of cloth) in the production of food. Therefore Atlantis will specialize in the production of food. Beltran, with the lower opportunity cost for cloth (1/2 unit of food), will specialize in cloth.

b Each country will want to produce every unit of the good in which they specialize as long as the amount they receive in trade exceeds their opportunity cost. For Atlantis, the opportunity cost of a unit of food is 1/2 unit of cloth, but it can obtain 1 unit of cloth in trade. Because the opportunity cost is constant, Atlantis will totally specialize by producing all of the food it can: 1,000 units per year, point *b* in Figure 32.3(a). Similarly, in Beltran, the opportunity cost of a unit of cloth is 1/2 unit of food but a unit of cloth will trade for 1 unit of food. Since the opportunity cost is constant, Beltran will totally specialize in the production of cloth and will produce 800 units per year, point *b*' in Figure 32.3(b).

c The consumption possibilities frontiers for Atlantis and Beltran, labelled CPF_A and CPF_B, are illustrated in Figure 32.3, parts (a) and (b) respectively. These frontiers are straight lines that indicate all the combinations of food and cloth that can be consumed with trade. The position and slope of the consumption possibilities frontier for an economy depend on the terms of trade between the goods (one for one in this example) and the production point of the economy.

The consumption possibilities frontier for Atlantis (CPF_A), for example, is obtained by starting at point *b* on PPF_A, the production point, and examining possible trades. For example, if Atlantis traded 400 units of the food it produces for 400 units of cloth, it would be able to consume 600 units of food (1,000 units produced minus 400 units traded) and 400 units of cloth, which is represented by point *c*.

d If Atlantis consumes 600 units of food, trade allows consumption of cloth to be 400 units, 200 units more than possible without trade. The maximum amount of cloth that can be consumed without trade is given by the production possibilities frontier. If food consumption is 600 units, this outcome is indicated by point *a* on PPF_A. The maximum amount of cloth consumption for any level of food consumption with trade is given by the consumption possibilities frontier. If food consumption is 600 units, this outcome is indicated by point *c* on CPF_A.

7 a Since Atlantis produces 1,000 units of food per year (point *b* on PPFA), to consume 600 units of food and 400 units of cloth (point *c* on CPFA) it must trade 400 units of food for 400 units of cloth. This outcome means that Beltran has traded 400 units of cloth for 400 units of food. Since Beltran produces 800 units of cloth, this result suggests that Beltran must consume 400 units of food and 400 units of cloth (point *c*' on CPF_B).

b Atlantis exports 400 units of food per year and imports 400 units of cloth. Beltran exports 400 units of cloth per year and imports 400 units of food.

8 a The price of a shirt under free trade will occur at the intersection of Atlantis' import demand curve for shirts and Beltran's export supply curve for shirts. This result occurs at a price of $12 per shirt.

b Atlantis will import 6 million shirts per year.

9 a The effect of the $9 per shirt tariff is to shift the export supply curve (*S*) leftward. This outcome is shown as a shift from *S* to *S*' in Figure 32.2 Solution. The price is now determined by the intersection of the *D* curve, which is unaffected by the tariff, and the *S*' curve. The new price of a shirt is $18.

FIGURE **32.2** SOLUTION

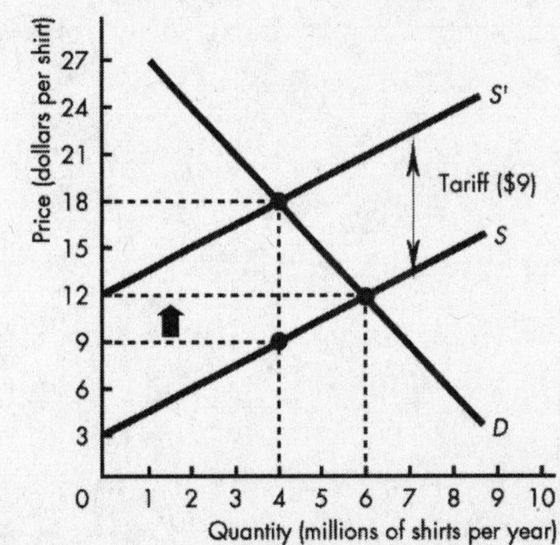

b Of this $18, $9 is the tariff, so the exporter only receives the remaining $9.

c Atlantis will now import only 4 million shirts per year.

d The tariff revenue is $9 (the tariff per shirt) × 4 million (the number of shirts imported), which is $36 million. This money is received by the government of Atlantis.

10 a The quota restricts the quantity that can be imported to 4 million shirts per year regardless of the price; it is represented by a vertical line in Figure 32.4 (which corresponds to Figure 32.2). The market for shirts will thus clear at a price of $18 per shirt.

FIGURE **32.4**

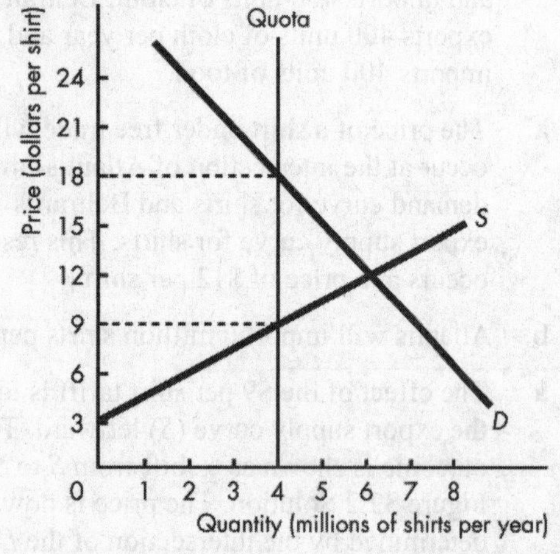

b This $18 price is received by the people who are given the right to import shirts under the quota. The amount received by the exporter is $9, given by the height of the *S* curve at a quantity of 4 million shirts per year.

c Atlantis will import 4 million shirts per year, the quota limit.

d The "excess profit" is $9 per shirt (the $18 received by the importer minus the $9 received by the exporter) × 4 million shirts, which is $36 million. This profit is captured by the importers who have been rewarded by the government of Atlantis because they have been given the right to import under the quota. This licence is essentially a right to make an "excess profit."

CHAPTERS 30–32

Part 9 Wrap Up

Aggregate Supply, Economic Growth, and International Trade

PROBLEM

Autarkia has just signed a free-trade agreement with the country of Liberalonia, its major trading partner (currently 60 percent of each country's trade is with the other country). Under the new agreement, tariffs between the two countries will fall from an average level of 40 percent to an average level of around 0 percent. In addition, all nontariff barriers are to be removed.

a After the FTA is signed, what will happen to Autarkia's exports and imports? What will likely happen to the current account balance?

b Which sectors of Autarkia's economy will gain from the agreement? Which sectors will likely lose from the agreement?

c What is the likely effect on unemployment in Autarkia in the short term? What is the likely effect on unemployment in the longer term?

d Will this agreement likely have an effect on economic growth? If so, explain briefly how it will have an effect.

MIDTERM EXAMINATION

You should allocate 24 minutes for this examination (12 questions, 2 minutes per question). For each question, choose the one *best* answer.

1 Given that the use of all other factor inputs are held constant, a diminishing marginal product of labour might best be described as when the total number of hours worked in the economy

a increases and total output increases.
b increases and total output increases at a decreasing rate.
c increases and total output decreases.
d decreases and total output increases.
e increases and total output increases at an increasing rate.

2 Atlantis imports watches from Beltran and exports widgets to Beltran. Why would Atlantis prefer arranging a voluntary export restraint rather than a quota on watches?

a to avoid hurting Beltran's imports
b to prevent Beltran from retaliating by restricting Atlantis' exports
c to keep the domestic price of watches low
d to increase government revenue
e to help domestic producers

3 The key difference between neoclassical growth theory and classical growth theory is that
- **a** capital is not subject to diminishing returns under classical growth theory.
- **b** capital is subject to diminishing returns under classical growth theory.
- **c** increases in technology lead to increases in population that drive workers' incomes back down to the subsistence level in classical theory.
- **d** technological advances are exogenous in classical growth theory.
- **e** the one-third rule only holds in the neoclassical growth theory.

4 Which of the following quotations describes a shift rightward in an *LAS* curve?
- **a** "The recent higher price levels have lowered production in the country."
- **b** "The recent higher price levels have raised production in the country."
- **c** "The recent higher price levels have led to compensating rises in wages, so that there have been no changes in labour hired or production."
- **d** "The recent lower price levels have led to lower production in the country."
- **e** None of the above.

5 Suppose that productivity has increased by 15 percent over last year. Capital per hour of labour increased by 9 percent as well. The increase in capital was responsible for
- **a** all of the increase in productivity.
- **b** 80% of the increase in productivity.
- **c** 60% of the increase in productivity.
- **d** 33% of the increase in productivity.
- **e** 20% of the increase in productivity.

6 Suppose that productivity has increased by 15 percent over last year. Capital per hour of labour increased by 9 percent as well. An increase in technology was responsible for
- **a** all of the increase in productivity.
- **b** 80% of the increase in productivity.
- **c** 40% of the increase in productivity.
- **d** 33% of the increase in productivity.
- **e** 20% of the increase in productivity.

7 Which one of the following quotations describes a movement along the labour demand curve?
- **a** "Recent higher wage rates have led to more leisure being consumed."
- **b** "The recent lower price level has induced people to work more hours."
- **c** "The recent higher real wage rate has induced people to work more hours."
- **d** "The recent high investment in capital equipment has raised hiring by firms."
- **e** None of the above.

8 Suppose Musicland and Videoland produce two goods—CDs and videos. Musicland has a comparative advantage in the production of CDs if
- **a** fewer CDs must be given up to produce one unit of videos than in Videoland.
- **b** less labour is required to produce one unit of CDs than in Videoland.
- **c** less capital is required to produce one unit of CDs than in Videoland.
- **d** less labour and capital are required to produce one unit of CDs than in Videoland.
- **e** fewer videos must be given up to produce one unit of CDs than in Videoland.

9 Which theory of economic growth concludes that in the long run, people do not benefit from growth?
- **a** classical theory
- **b** neoclassical theory
- **c** new growth theory
- **d** old growth theories
- **e** none of the theories

10 Which of the following quotations describes job rationing unemployment?
- **a** "Wages are so good at the factory, they always have enough applicants to pick whomever they want for the job."
- **b** "Professors with tenured jobs are taking pay cuts to help hire new professors."
- **c** "Wages have failed to fall in the current economic downturn, creating extra unemployment."
- **d** "People are taking too long to find jobs, because employment insurance is so generous."
- **e** None of the above.

11 Acadia and Breton are currently engaged in free trade. Acadia imports cheese from Breton and exports sheep to Breton. If Acadia imposes a tariff on cheese, Acadia's cheese-producing industry will

a expand, and its sheep-producing industry will contract.
b expand, and its sheep-producing industry will expand.
c contract, and its sheep-producing industry will contract.
d contract, and its sheep-producing industry will expand.
e expand, and its sheep-producing industry will be unchanged.

12 Canada has a trade deficit when the

a value of Canadian exports of goods and services exceeds the value of Canadian imports of goods and services.
b value of Canadian exports of goods and services is exceeded by the value of Canadian imports of goods and services.
c value of Canadian exports of goods exceeds the value of Canadian imports of goods.
d value of Canadian exports of goods is exceeded by the value of Canadian imports of goods.
e current account balance is less than zero.

ANSWERS

Problem

a The decline in tariffs will make Autarkia's exports to Liberalonia cheaper for Liberalonians. As a result, exports will increase (probably strongly since the decline in tariffs is strong). Similarly, Autarkia's imports from Liberalonia will now become significantly cheaper, and so there will be a strong increase in imports. The impact of the agreement on the current account balance is unclear, since the relative strength of the two effects is unclear. However, it is likely that the two effects will be roughly equal, so the net impact on the current account balance is likely near zero.

b The export sectors of Autarkia's economy will gain from the agreement, since their sales will rise dramatically, and their price net of taxes should increase. The import-competing sectors will likely lose from the agreement, as the lower tariffs will lower the price of import goods in Autarkia, resulting in a loss for those sectors in sales to imports and therefore a loss in revenues from lower sales and a lower price.

c Part **b** explained how the export sector will be expanding, and the import-competing sector shrinking. This means more employment in the export sector and less in the import-competing sector. The net effect is likely roughly neutral in the longer term, once workers have retrained and relocated. However, in the short term Autarkia will have structural unemployment as workers are laid off in the import-competing sector, and it takes time for them to retrain and relocate. In the short term, unemployment will rise.

d Chapter 31 notes that "free international trade stimulates growth by extracting the gains from specialization and exchange" (text page 742). Entering into the agreement should increase economic growth.

MIDTERM EXAMINATION

1 b Definition. (709–711)

2 b Under a VER, exporting country gains excess revenue, which means it is less likely to retaliate, since hurt less. (766)

3 c In neoclassical theory, population growth is not driven by economic growth. In both theories, capital is subject to diminishing returns, technology is exogenous, and the one-third rule holds. (743–749)

4 e **a** is nonsense, **b**, **c**, and **d** are movements along curves. (724–726)

5 e By one-third rule, capital increase of 9 percent leads to increase in real GDP per hour of work of 3 percent, or 20 percent of increase in productivity. (739–742)

6 b Capital's effect was one-third of 9 percent or 3 percent, leaving 12 percent or 80 of the total increase due to technology. (739–742)

7 e **a**, **b**, **c** are *LS* effect, **d** shift in *LD* curve. (709–711)

8 e Definition. (757–758)

9 a In long run, technological advances increase demand for labour and real GDP per capita, so population increases which lowers real GDP per capita back to the original level. (743–749)

10 a This describes efficiency wages, a form of job rationing. (720–721)

11 a Tariff increases domestic price of cheese, decreasing imports, increasing domestic production. Decreased imports = decreased exports in Breton, decreasing its income, decreasing its imports = decrease in Acadia's exports, decreasing Acadia's sheep production. (764–766)

12 b Definition of balance of trade. (772–773)